BONDED THROUGH TRAGEDY
UNITED IN HOPE

The Catholic Church and East Timor's Struggle for Independence
A Memoir

Hilton Deakin
with Jim and Therese D'Orsa

Published in Australia by
Garratt Publishing
32 Glenvale Crescent
Mulgrave, Vic. 3170
www.garrattpublishing.com.au

1300 650 878
sales@garrattpublishing.com.au
www.garrattpublishing.com.au

© 2017 Jim D'Orsa and Therese D'Orsa

Cover image: © John Casamento used with permission
Cover design: Alexander Ulrich-Field
Typesetting: Mike Kuszla, J&M Typesetting
Indexing: Christopher Brennan
Photograph preparation: Br Ben Boonen cfc
Print Coordinated by Advent Print Management

All rights reserved. Except as provided by the Australian copyright law, no part of this book may be reproduced in any manner without prior permission in writing from the publisher. Every effort has been made to trace the original source of copyright material contained in this book. The publisher would be pleased to hear from copyright holders to rectify any errors or omissions.

9781925073324 (pb)

Cataloguing-in-Publication information for is available from the National Library of Australia
www.nla.gov.au

Aboriginal and Torres Strait Islanders: Please note images contained in this book may be of deceased *Indigenous* people.

This book honours those who suffered, and is dedicated to the memory of those who died, in the cause of East Timor's freedom.

CONTENTS

Glossary		ix
Foreword		xii
Introduction		1
1	Our Stories Determine Who We are	6
2	Meeting the Timorese for the First Time	15

PART ONE
THREE STORIES

1 Hilton's Story

3	A Boy from the Bush	27
4	Making a New Beginning: School Years	34
5	More New Beginnings: Seminary Years	42
6	Learning the Ropes: Assistant Priest	49
7	Priest and Anthropologist	56
8	Kalumburu	63
9	Finding my Voice	69

2 The East Timor Story

10	East Timor's Portuguese Legacy	77
11	De Facto Independence	86
12	Tragedy of Re-colonisation	97

3 The Church Story

13	The Indonesian Church's Orphan Child	111
14	East Timor: The Church and Human Rights	120
15	Australia and the Catholic Church in East Timor	128
16	The Roar of Silence: Australian Bishops' Response to the Developing Crisis	136

PART TWO
CONVERGENCE

17	Visiting Santa Cruz with Carlos Belo	151
18	Timorese Perspectives 1992	161
19	A Voice in the Wilderness	171
20	A Wider Mission: A Bigger Challenge	183
21	East Timor and Rwanda: Culture at its Best and Worst	194
22	1996 Becomes a Very Good Year	207
23	The Battle for Minds	220
24	An Odd Little Chapter	231
25	Prelude to a Nightmare 1998–Early 1999	238
26	Hilton's Rock	252
27	Fateful Fortnight in September	258
28	The Caritas Story	271
29	Salvation, Liberation and Other Dilemmas	284
30	End of the Beginning	297
	Bibliography	310
	Index	312

GLOSSARY

ABRI	Angkatan B*ersenjata Republik Indonesia* (Armed Forces of the Republic of Indonesia) – army, navy, and air force, and until April 1999 including police. When these were separated from the armed forces, the name of the Armed Forces was changed to TNI (see below)
ACBC	Australian Catholic Bishops' Conference
ACFID	Australian Council for International Development
ACFOA	Australian Council for Overseas Aid
ACM	Aboriginal Catholic Ministry
ACR	Australian Catholic Relief - later became Caritas
ACSJC	Australian Catholic Social Justice Council
AEC	Australian Episcopal Conference
Aitarak	Meaning 'thorn' - a feared militia operating around Dili
APCET	Asia-Pacific Coalition for East Timor
APEC	Asia-Pacific Economic Co-operation
APODETI	*Associacao Popular Democratica* (Timorese Popular Democratic Association)
ASDT	*Associacao Social Democratica Timorense* (Timorese Social Democratic Association)
CA	Caritas Australia
CAFOD	Catholic Agency for Overseas Development
CARE Australia	Humanitarian development agency with a special focus on women and girls
CAVR	*Comissão de Acolhimento, Verdade e Reconciliação de Timor Leste* (Truth and Reconciliation Commission)
CCJP	Catholic Commission for Justice and Peace
CET	Caritas East Timor
CI	Caritas Internationalis
CIIR	Catholic Institute for International Relations
CISET	Christians in Solidarity with East Timor
CIVIPOL	Civilian police
CNN	Cable News Network
CNRM	*Conselho Nacional da Resistência Maubere* (National Council of the Maubere Resistance)
CNRT	National Council of Timorese Resistance
Criados	Young men and boys who assisted Australian soldiers in East Timor during World War II.
CRS	Catholic Relief Services
CSIS	Centre for Strategic and International Studies

Estado Novo	Literally new state – the authoritarian regime inaugurated in Portugal by Salazar in 1932
ETADEP	East Timor Agricultural Development Program
ETAN	East Timor Action Network
ETHRC	East Timor Human Rights Centre
ETRA	East Timor Refugee Association
EU	European Union
FALINTAL	*Forcas Armadas de Libertcao Nacional De Timor* (National Armed forces for the Liberation of East Timor)
FRELIMO	*Frente de Libertacao de Mozambique* (Mozambique Liberation Front)
FRETILIN	*Frente Revolucionaria do Timor-Leste Independente* (Revolutionary Front of Independent East Timor)
IDPs	Internally displaced persons
IMF	International Monetary Fund
INGO	International Non-government Organisation
Integrasi	Goal and policy of East Timor's integration into Indonesia
INTEL	Indonesian Intelligence
INTERFET	International Force for East Timor
KKN	*Korupsi, kolusi, nepotisme* (corruption, collusion, nepotism)
Liurai	Chief or ruler of a part of East Timor
Lulik	Sacred animist house
Maubere	common people which FRETILIN sought to represent
MFA	*Movimento das Forcas Armada* (Armed Forces Movement) which overthrew the right-wing Portuguese government in 1974
MMET	Mary MacKillop East Timor
MMI	Mary MacKillop International Inc.
NATSICC	National Aboriginal and Torres Strait Islander Catholic Council
NCC	National Civic Council
NCJP	National Commission for Justice and Peace
NCRM	National Catholic Rural Movement
NGO	Non-government Organisation
Oan Kiak	Tetum for poor child
Operasi Komodo	Operation Komodo (giant lizard) - Campaign to integrate East Timor into Indonesia by a range of means
Orde Baru	New Order in Indonesia
Pancasila	Five Principles of the Indonesian state
PIDE	*Policia Internacional e de Defensa do Estado* (International and State Defence Police- the secret police under Salazar regime in Portugal

Posto	Administrative base in colonial times
RPF	Rwandan Patriotic Front
Suco	Municipality
Tebe tebe	Traditional dance of East Timor
TNI	*Tentara Nasional Indonesia* (Indonesian National Armed Forces) after 2000
Trocaire	(meaning 'compassion') is the official overseas development agency of the Catholic Church in Ireland
UDT	*Uniao Democratica Timorense* (Timorese Democratic Union)
UNAMET	United Nations Mission in East Timor
UNAMIR	United Nations Assistance Mission for Rwanda
UNICEF	The United Nations Children's Fund
UNMISET	United Nations Mission of Support in East Timor
UNTAET	United Nations Transitional Administration in East Timor
WFP	World Food Program
YCS	Young Christian Students
YCW	Young Christian Workers

FOREWORD

When Timor-Leste became the first new nation of the 21st century on 20th May 2002, Bishop Hilton was an honoured guest at our independence celebrations. It was a celebration that I had dreamed of for many decades, and one that in my darkest moments I thought would never happen.

It was at those times that the extraordinary resilience and strength of the Timorese people, and the courage and commitment of our many international friends, kept hope alive – friends like Bishop Hilton who chose to take up our cause, at the risk of upsetting the hierarchy of the Catholic Church and the Indonesian and Australian governments.

In 1992, he was one of very few Australians to travel to Dili. He met Bishop Belo and many other religious groups and returned to Australia to share our story. Bishop Hilton gave us a voice in Australia, at a time when our struggle was largely forgotten or ignored, and around the world in various forums within the Catholic Church and the wider community.

Bishop Hilton has been a great friend of the Timorese people and I am personally very grateful that he has been a friend, mentor and counselor to me.

I am also grateful that he is continuing to take up our cause, recently acknowledging that Timor-Leste's journey to independence is not over, as while we have secured our land borders, we have not yet achieved full sovereignty over our sea borders.

This book tells an important part of our history – the history of the church in our struggle. But it also tells the story of an incredible man, a man whose life embodies the best of Catholicism; an intelligent spirituality, a commitment to social justice and a genuine love of people.

Obrigado barak, Bishop Hilton.

His Excellency Xanana Gusmão
First President of the Republic of East Timor
Prime Minister of East Timor (August 2007-February 2015)
Currently Minister of Planning and Strategic Investment

INTRODUCTION

When in 2011 the Director of the Yarra Institute for Religion and Social Policy, Fr Bruce Duncan CSsR, asked us if we would be interested in working with Bishop Hilton Deakin on the story of his involvement in East Timor's fight for independence, we were at first a little hesitant. We knew something of the Bishop, Therese from her work as a director of the Catholic Education Commission of Victoria, and Jim through a family connection[1]. Bruce arranged a meeting with Hilton to discuss the project and as they say: 'The rest is history'. Across the next four years we met regularly with Hilton to get his story down on paper. This task was interrupted several times either by one or other of us being heavily committed to other projects, involved overseas, or otherwise unavailable.

There was a huge amount of material to work through. In the first instance as contributing authors we had only a rudimentary knowledge of East Timor, its history and its people. What knowledge we had was formed in the 1990s and since forgotten. Since 1992 Hilton had accumulated a massive collection of primary source material drawn from Church and public sources. Well over 1000 documents had to be sorted and classified. During the fight for independence John Miller established the East Timor and Indonesia Action Network (ETAN) in the United States. It subsequently morphed into an internet-based clearing-house for information on events in East Timor and Indonesia. Its archives, containing a unique collection of contemporaneous documents, also had to be worked through systematically. From 1992 to 2002 Hilton visited East Timor at least annually. He also undertook visits to other countries as a human rights activist speaking about the situation in East Timor. On these journeys Hilton kept travel diaries, often written in a cryptic style or in Latin, so that if they were confiscated, information in them could not be used to compromise people mentioned by name. These had to be deciphered. It took almost a year to get all this material into some sort of order, to work out a *modus vivendi* with Hilton, and to develop a scaffold within which his story could be told.

We soon discovered there is no shortage of accounts of events in East Timor written by journalists and academics. East Timor provides an important case study for political scientists and historians not least because it is the first instance of the United Nations setting up a new nation state virtually from scratch. How it went about the task has been of immense interest.

Most of these accounts focus on secular developments in East Timor. Hilton's story is told from a different perspective. His role is that of a participant observer from within

---

[1] Hilton had played an instrumental role in helping his aged aunt find a place in the Little Sisters Nursing Home Northcote at a time of acute need and the family had always been most grateful.

the Catholic Church which played a decisive role in shaping events in the lead up to the Indonesian invasion, during the occupation, and the subsequent United Nations intervention. Hilton was well placed to occupy this role both as an Australian bishop and as a professional anthropologist (something we were unaware of when we undertook this project).

Hilton was appointed bishop after he began his work of advocacy on behalf of the East Timorese and certainly not because of it. His appointment may have been a decision Rome subsequently regretted given his quite critical stance to official policy on East Timor. This often isolated him among his episcopal colleagues in Australia and earned him rebukes from one Apostolic Nuncio here. Undeterred by either his lack of seniority among the Australian Catholic bishops, or criticism from other Catholic quarters he soldiered on, not only on behalf of the East Timorese cause, but also on behalf of East Timorese refugees in Australia who found themselves pawns in a political game played by a national government caught between the demands of common humanity and those of appeasing the Indonesian government. His connection with local Timorese refugees gave Hilton's advocacy work a very human face often absent at the official Church level.

Hilton's appointment as bishop gave him a public standing that he used to good effect in Australia, in East Timor and overseas – so much so that a journalist from *The Age* newspaper, Alan Attwood, in a feature article famously dubbed him the 'ubiquitous bishop'![2] The Australian government would later recognise his work on behalf of the refugees and human rights by awarding him Member of the Order of Australia.

During 2012 we established a pattern that began by systematically working through Hilton's travel diaries and then interviewing him about the material they covered. We did this against the background of events happening at the time. These interviews were taped and later transcribed thus providing the basis for producing draft chapters. The drafts were then fleshed out using the resource materials available to us and then fed back to Hilton for clarification and comment.

We soon realised that it was impossible to tell the story of Hilton's involvement in East Timor without some detailed knowledge of his personal journey prior to his providential meeting with the Timorese in Melbourne in October 1991. His orientation to social justice had been fostered in his own family and through his longstanding involvement and friendship with Australia's Aboriginal people. Without the orientation which had been developing since childhood, Hilton may not have responded so decisively to the Timorese cry for justice as he did.

We also saw very early that it would be necessary to gain some experience of East Timor as Hilton had experienced it. The initial plan was for Jim to accompany Hilton on his annual visit to East Timor in 2012 and attend celebrations marking the first decade of independence. However, events transpired to make this impossible. Jose Ramos Horta, then the retiring President, wished to honour Hilton's work on behalf of the East Timorese cause by awarding him the Medal of East Timor, the country's highest civilian award. As well, Hilton was to be presented with the da Costa Lopes Medal, the country's highest religious award.

It was not until 2013 that Jim travelled to East Timor with Hilton and was able to

---

2   Alan Atwood 'Ubiquitous bishop' *The Age*, 6 May, 2000.

retrace with him many of the journeys made with Bishop Belo and to meet many of the people who appear in the story that follows. However, the most useful aspect of this visit was witnessing Hilton's interaction with ordinary East Timorese, whether meeting them in his formal capacity as bishop, or engaging with them in the supermarket, cafe etc to discuss where they thought their country was heading ten years after independence. In this context it was easy to see why people in East Timor dubbed him 'Bispo Maubere' – the bishop of the ordinary people. The East Timorese seemed to relish his lack of formality. It was clear that in meeting people Hilton brings his own style that includes a very Australian sense of humor.

Perhaps the biggest challenge in telling Hilton's story has been to catch this style and the 'voice' that goes with it. Hilton's resonant voice is certainly a wonderful asset that amplifies and adds intensity to his very personal style of interacting with people. Listening to hours of taped interviews has helped pick up its nuances and we leave it up to those who know Hilton well to say whether or not we have captured him in the text that follows. If we did not, then it was not for want of trying.

While the Catholic Church figures in many accounts of events in East Timor the story has not been told, certainly in English, from an insider's perspective. Hilton's story is possibly a first in this regard. Patrick Smythe's dissertation on the Church and East Timor is perhaps the only account that deals with the matter in any depth. In the academic and journalistic treatments of East Timor 'the Church' is generally conflated with 'Church leaders'. However the Catholic Church is a very complex body with many parts that function at a number of levels in any society. Hilton's story links the wider Church in Australia – involved Catholics and designated Church leaders - to that in East Timor and indeed to the global Church story. This convergence of stories highlights the complexity of Church operations and the simplification and distortions that are introduced when 'Church' is truncated simply to 'what Church leaders do'.

While many people in the modern world, including many Catholics, see religion as a private matter with no place in the public square, that is not Hilton's perspective and much of his story centres on how far the Church ought to become involved in the public square and in political issues, particularly when these impinge on human rights and matters of justice. Hilton held somewhat different ideas on these matters from some of his fellow Australian bishops with respect to both substance and style. He did not consider Vatican policy on East Timor, a policy that advocated integration with Indonesia, to be moral because of the cost in human lives and the destruction of local culture that this had entailed since 1975. He argued that the approach of the Australian Bishops' Committee for Justice Development and Peace of working only through official (Vatican and Indonesian) channels was flawed because it was not credible to the East Timorese, and only added to the pressure on their beleaguered bishops.

While the Australian and Indonesian bishops all recognised Catholic social teaching as providing the framework within which complex issues of justice need to be resolved, their inability to resolve how this teaching applies when competing Church interests are at stake highlights a lacuna in this teaching. Operating on the limits of Catholic social teaching Bishop Belo found himself in an ecclesiastical no man's land, forced to resolve complex matters on the ground in the face of blatant indifference and even hostility from Vatican diplomats bent on protecting the Church's interests and status in Indonesia, irrespective of the savage impact on human lives in East Timor. This is the really tragic dimension of the story that follows. In his fight for justice in East Timor Hilton proved to be one of Bishop Belo's principal allies, one who visited him each year through thick and thin, who shared in the celebration of his Nobel Peace Prize and the triumph of independence.

In 1993 Hilton was appointed Deputy Chair of Australian Catholic Relief, the local Catholic Church's official disaster relief and development agency. He subsequently became Chair of Caritas Australia in May 1997[3], and later president of Caritas Oceania (1999-2007). This appointment also carried with it the role of being one of the vice-presidents of Caritas Internationalis, co-ordinating body for the over 160 national Catholic agencies making up the Caritas group. Caritas Internationalis liaises with the United Nations in addressing global development issues and emergency relief. Hilton's experience of operating at this global level is a unique part of both his story and that of East Timor. Caritas Internationalis appointed Caritas Australia as its lead agency in dealing with the humanitarian crisis unfolding in East Timor after 1999. That this happened on Hilton's watch as chair was perhaps providential for the East Timorese and for the Church in Australia as Caritas Australia's intervention went a long way to enhancing its credibility in this country, something that has been of long-term benefit around the world subsequently.

In retrospect the stance Hilton took on East Timor has proved to be correct and that of certain of his colleagues, however well-intentioned, flawed. This is a matter for regret and something from which lessons can be derived. It takes courage to stand outside the crowd, even a crowd of bishops. Where does a person get that sort of courage? Does it just happen, or is it the by-product of a long process? As we explored Hilton's story we discovered that there was indeed a 'long process', and that this constitutes a fascinating tale.

We attempt to tell Hilton's story in two parts. In Part 1 entitled 'Three Stories' we have three narratives that unfold more or less separately. Firstly, there is 'Hilton's story' - the 'long process' referred to above that ended with his becoming the Vicar General in the Melbourne archdiocese under Archbishop Sir Frank Little. It was in this position that he first engaged with East Timorese seeking the Church's help. Secondly, there is the 'East Timor Story' a narrative that Hilton had to put together for himself in 1992 to understand the situation in East Timor. Thirdly, there is the story of the Catholic Church's involvement at many levels – the East Timorese church, the Indonesian church, the Australian church, other Catholic communities in solidarity with the East Timorese, and the Vatican all feature as players in this account.

The Church story we tell here is significant at a number of levels: as a nuanced acknowledgement of the role Church leaders at various levels played in the fight for independence; the complexity of politics within the Catholic Church in dealing with contentious issues affecting Church interests; the personal costs of Church leadership; the role faith played in helping the East Timorese negotiate the meaninglessness of life under Indonesian rule; the courage of those who stood up to defend the human rights of the East Timorese; the role cultural assumptions play in the perpetrating of injustice and oppression; the triumph of humanity over madness; and the difficult task of reconciliation once the madness has passed.

---

3   A position Bishop Deakin held till May 2003.

Introduction

There is much to be learned from Hilton's story of solidarity with the little ones of this world and his openness to learn from other peoples and cultures. In recent years he has developed knowledge of and friendship with Vietnamese people and their church that is contributing so much to the Australian Catholic community at this time. As a priest and anthropologist, even in retirement Hilton retains his life-long interest in indigenous peoples. This is expressed through his involvement in Aboriginal ministry in Australia and his support for the peoples of West Papua in their ongoing struggle for self-determination.

At the time of writing this is ongoing and Hilton continues to provide support for those engaged in the struggle for justice, that messy virtue that is love in action amidst the human condition wherever oppression exists and human aspiration is stifled. He continues to be very active fighting for a just settlement to the dispute between East Timor and Australia in regard to the oil and gas reserves in the Timor Sea. In his eighties, Hilton can also still be found on his annual sojourn to East Timor visiting remote villages in his capacity as Chair of the Oan Kiak Foundation, encouraging parents to enrol their children in schools so that they get an education that otherwise might not happen. When the 'bispo' visits a village in East Timor it is still a big event, one that can make good things happen.

Jim and Therese D'Orsa
May 23, 2015
Beatification day of one of Hilton's great heroes Blessed Oscar Romero

CHAPTER 1
OUR STORIES DETERMINE WHO WE ARE

In September 1994, after the civil war had ended in Rwanda, I visited that country as part of a team from Caritas Internationalis (CI), the Catholic aid and development organisation. The international community had stopped the genocide but revenge killings were still common. Our group had the task of assessing where money raised by Caritas in Australia should best be spent. Our mission involved consultation with the local Church authorities, government agencies and other NGOs already in the field. It also involved travelling around the country to visit refugee camps to gain some sense of what the situation was like on the ground now that a shaky peace was in place. This carried considerable risk as armed groups still manned unofficial roadblocks. We travelled with an interpreter and driver who could speak the local language, Kinyarwanda. When the van was stopped at one of these roadblocks we could only guess at what might happen next.

When you find yourself looking down the barrel of an AK47 rifle from the 'wrong' end, you experience a terrible sense of powerlessness. This is amplified when the eyes of the person holding the gun have the dead expression of a killer. I had seen that stare before on Indonesian soldiers in East Timor, and also in the eyes of their locally recruited militia. We had been warned by friends in Rwanda's capital Kigali that there was some danger associated with our journey. As a precaution, we had removed all our rings and watches. It was not uncommon in Rwanda at the time for people to have fingers and arms hacked off by machete-wielding gangs to get at these valuable objects.

Rwanda is a nominally Catholic country and, while the military had been brutalised by the events of the previous two years, they still drew the line at killing priests (and more so bishops). They understood this would bring them nothing but trouble, particularly if the bishop in question was a senior official of Caritas Internationalis[1], an aid group trying to help the people recover – or so the conversation between the soldier in charge of the road-block and our interpreter seemed to be going. At least I hoped so!

As they talked I was very conscious of two things. The first was the very large cheque 'in my pocket' as it were, and the second was that the whole scene was surreal! After all, I was a Catholic bishop from Melbourne Australia. How did I end up in this situation? The mind works in strange ways when confronted with the experience of total powerlessness.

---

1 Caritas Internationalis is the major Catholic aid and development group. It is a confederation of national agencies situated, at the time of writing, in 165 countries. Caritas Internationalis is based in Rome for where it provides some co-ordination commensurate with the independence of the local agencies.

However, this question remained with me long after the immediate crisis was resolved and we had continued on our journey.

I was in Rwanda because Caritas Australia (CA) had run a very successful appeal for Rwanda. Catholics, but not only Catholics, had responded very generously. I had volunteered to go as part of an international team because, as the Bishop in charge of CA, I felt it was my responsibility to do so. We simply wanted to help: to supply food, shelter and medicine to those in refugee camps. But we also needed to find out how this could happen. There was little information available in Australia. Australian troops had arrived in Rwanda by the time our party assembled in Kigali. They were part of the United Nations (UN) mission, and their task was to get the hospital in Kigali into some sort of order so it could function again. The country was still in a dreadful mess. The task of Caritas was to help. That is what the Church at its best does – it helps the marginalised live with both hope and dignity. This was central to the mission of its founder. This was why I was in Rwanda, and it was why I have become involved with the peoples of East Timor, Sri Lanka and West Papua. It is a form of engagement with people on the margins. Some of my colleagues in the local priesthood have, at various times, found it difficult to understand my support for these marginalised groups.

★

I suspect that our lives have a particular trajectory that, if we are reflective, we discern slowly and often obliquely, and then only in retrospect. We all have what I would call 'moments of destiny' in our lives. In these brief times we sense that our life's journey, often experienced as chaotic, has a direction. When we look back we can, if we are lucky, discern how life's disparate elements form part of a meaningful whole. The experience is momentary, for soon daily life closes in on us again, and we find ourselves back on the familiar track, with only a memory to encourage and guide us. However, we store such memories and they help us see new significance in what we do, and thus regenerate hope within us.

While this is certainly true of individuals, as my later study of anthropology would reveal, it is also true of all sorts of human groupings. These use different methods for retaining their collective memories. Among these, 'moments of destiny' play a central role because they determine how a people make sense of things.

Individuals very often interpret personal 'moments of destiny' by connecting them to the wider narratives of the group to which they belong, and with whom they identify. The personal story takes on added significance in the context of the communal story, and in the process may actually add to it. In a sense we define ourselves by our story and the stories of which we are a part. 'Moments of destiny' therefore help define both who we are and what we will become.

As an Australian Catholic priest I am caught up in a number of stories, and make sense of my personal 'moments of destiny' within those stories. My story is shaped by them and, in turn, I have endeavoured, sometimes consciously often unconsciously, to shape these larger stories as well. As a priest one has a significant capacity to do this, but this capacity was enhanced in 1993 when I became an auxiliary bishop in Melbourne. As a bishop you are invited into the Catholic story in new ways, some of which are exciting, others perplexing, and all inherently ambiguous. This is a theme I shall explore in the pages that follow.

★

Until 1991 my story was essentially an Australian Catholic story. My interests centered on Australia and its peoples, both indigenous and non-indigenous. The Hilton Deakin story encompassed my passions as both a churchman and an anthropologist. However what I did not know in October 1991 was that, despite the 'moments of destiny' that had so far set the trajectory of my life, things were about to change, and change decisively. My story was about to be caught up with that of the East Timorese, and life would never be the same again. At the time I was fifty-nine, rather late in life for a major change!

As I became involved with the East Timorese and their struggle for self-determination, I was brought into contact with many Australians and people from other countries whose passion is for justice and human rights. These are people who fight for those forced by circumstances, often not of their own choosing, to live on the margins of their society. Such people are 'prophetic voices' in their communities. Many of those with whom I became involved were Catholic; many were not. Almost universally, such voices are an irritant to the ordered world of bureaucrats, ecclesiastics and politicians, a challenge to the 'wise' men and women of academia, and the beloved (or the belittled) of the media. These people collectively could mobilise over one hundred thousand of their fellow Australians to march in support of East Timor. These I discovered were 'my' people, and they graciously welcomed me into their midst. On occasion I was their spokesperson.

In 1999 the East Timorese cause became a people's movement in Australia with the people well ahead of their government in expressing solidarity with the East Timorese. In fact the protest movement developed out of disillusionment with the Australian Government's approach. This too is a strand in the East Timor story.

★

My first meetings with the Timorese were accidental. In the 1960s I was appointed administrator of St Augustine's church, then part of the cathedral parish, in central Melbourne. St Augustine's ran a hospitality centre associated with the Church's mission to seamen, many of whom were from Catholic countries. The Seamen's Mission is part of an international network providing a place of welcome for sailors arriving in ports far from their home. Given the social nature of the encounters, friendships develop with local people, and Cupid weaves his charms. As a consequence I had officiated at the occasional Timorese wedding, but could not claim to know much about the country at all.

In October 1991, when I was Vicar General[2] in Melbourne, a group of East Timorese refugees came to see me to arrange a commemorative Mass for those killed since the

---

2   The Vicar General of a diocese is a position provided for in canon law (canons 478 and 479). Its purpose is to assist the bishop in the governance of the diocese. In the absence of a bishop, the Vicar General normally assumes the administration and governance of the diocese.

1975 Indonesian invasion. Little did any of us realise at the time what lay ahead. Before we could meet again, over two hundred people, including school and university students, were gunned down in the Santa Cruz cemetery in Dili.³ This excruciatingly sad event was to prove a 'moment of destiny' in all our lives, bonding us together in friendship, but it was also to prove a turning point for East Timor.

I later learned that there had been earlier and even larger massacres in East Timor. What was unique about Santa Cruz was that the event was filmed. The film was smuggled out of the country and fed to the international media. Television coverage of the event stunned the world and began the long slow process of mobilising world opinion decisively against the Indonesians. The Santa Cruz tragedy gained more media attention than had the long hard struggle of the pro-independence FRETILIN fighters. It played a significant role in putting the violations of human rights in East Timor on the international agenda (as had the Sharpeville shootings in South Africa in 1960). Indonesia's claim to East Timor was fatally wounded by the Santa Cruz massacre. This is an important part of the East Timor story and one strand I want to explore.

The massacre changed the trajectory of my life. As a moment of destiny, Santa Cruz opened up a new chapter in my story, one that would project me out of Melbourne and onto a global stage in pursuit of human rights. It was also the reason I found myself looking down the barrel of a killer's gun and feeling very vulnerable on a lonely road outside Kigali.

★

There are many excellent accounts of East Timor's story, for instance in books by James Dunn, Jill Jolliffe, James C Taylor, Lansell Taudevin and Irena Cristalis,⁴ to name but a few. The interest driving these books is essentially humanitarian and political. Cristalis has an anthropological interest as well. My interest, however, while it has elements in common with theirs, differs in some significant respects. My critique of these accounts is that they are essentially Western in their cultural orientation, and seem to assume that the East Timorese experience can be explained by appeal to Western standards. This misinterprets East Timorese culture, and thus key elements in their story, particularly the role religion plays in Timorese culture. Culture itself is a key element in the story. It is an element that the Indonesians failed to understand, and many Indonesian soldiers lost their lives as a consequence of this misunderstanding, not to mention many thousands of East Timorese. Invaders always seem to underestimate the power of indigenous cultures, to their peril. This was one thing the U.S. got right in the Pacific war, even if subsequently they have forgotten the lessons learned there.⁵

My interest is in the way religion and politics came together in East Timor as the

---

3   I was given a list containing 273 names of persons killed. I believe there were many more.
4   Jill Jolliffe *East Timor: Nationalism and Colonialism* (Brisbane: University of Queensland Press, 1978); John Taylor *Indonesia's Forgotten War: The Hidden History of East Timor* (London: Zed Books, 1992); James Dunn *Timor: A People Betrayed* (Sydney: ABC Books, 1996); Lansell Taudevin *East Timor: Too Little Too Late* (Sydney: Duffy and Snellgrove, 1999); Irena Cristalis *Bitter Dawn: East Timor - a People's Story* (London: Zed Books, 2002).
5   See Edward T Hall's classic *The Silent Language* (New York: Anchor Press, 1973) for an account of the role anthropologists played in the Pacific in the aftermath of World War II.

struggle for independence unfolded. The catalyst event at Santa Cruz cemetry in 1991, for instance, was a religious ceremony also used as a vehicle for political protest against Indonesian repression. When the shooting started at Santa Cruz, many of the survivors immediately made their way to the bishop's compound seeking sanctuary. It was the bishop who negotiated with the military for them to leave. It was a Catholic priest who retrieved film of the event hidden in the Santa Cruz cemetery. It was another Catholic priest who arranged to have it smuggled to Darwin the next day. As this case illustrates, religion did not play a role at the borders of the struggle; it was integral to its eventual success. It often sustained people when all earthly hope had gone. This is a part of the story that needs to be acknowledged.[6]

★

The events in East Timor occurred at an important time in the Church's own story, and this runs as sub-text to the relationship between the local Catholic Church in East Timor and the local Catholic Church in Indonesia. It also plays as sub-text in the apparently poor treatment successive leaders of the Church in East Timor were given by Vatican diplomats whose role was compromised by a severe conflict of interest in that they sought to mollify the Indonesian Government at the expense of the East Timorese Church community whom it was their responsibility to support. This too is part of the story.

A decade after the Second Vatican Council (1962-5), the Catholic Church was still in a state of flux as leaders in Australia sought to understand and implement its decrees, many of which were quite radical at the time, particularly those dealing with Church and state. The Church's proper role in the public square was far from clear or settled at the time.

Until 1963 when Pope John XXIII published his encyclical *Pacem in Terris (Peace on Earth)*, virtually on his deathbed, the Catholic Church had never formally acknowledged in its social teaching the existence of 'human rights' as set out in the UN Charter. This changed dramatically at the Second Vatican Council where, in a major document dealing with the Church's role in the modern world,[7] the language of rights is used freely, and includes not only individual rights but also recognition of a people's right to their culture. Pope Paul VI took Catholic teaching further in his Apostolic Letter of 1971 (*Octogesima Adveniens*) in suggesting that two aspirations drive the thrust to recognise human rights: the aspirations for equality and for participation (#22). He goes on to say:

> Through the statement of the rights of man and the seeking for international agreements for the application of these rights, progress has been made towards inscribing these two aspirations in deeds and structures. Nevertheless various forms of discrimination continually reappear – ethnic, cultural, religious, political

---

6 Catholic priest Patrick A. Smythe examined the role of the Church in the independence struggle in his PhD thesis, subsequently published as '*The Heaviest Blow*' - *The Catholic Church and the East Timor Issue* (Munster: Lit Verlag, 2004). While the framework of his study is heavily theological, the book is an important resource in telling the story of the Church in East Timor's struggle for self-determination, not the least because of the many interviews he conducted with key participants.

7 Vatican Council II *Gaudium et Spes (Pastoral Constitution on the Church in the Modern World)* has 36 reference to rights.

and so on. In fact, human rights are still too often disregarded, if not scoffed at, or else they receive only formal recognition… (*Octogesima Adveniens* #23)

In a relatively short time, the Church went from rejecting human rights as a creature of the Enlightenment, to declaring itself a champion of human rights. Its stance would move even more firmly in this direction again under John Paul II, who became pope in 1978, three years after the Indonesian invasion of East Timor. The rapid development of Catholic social teaching caught many bishops flat-footed when it came to its application in their local contexts. This meant that, in the case of the Australian and Indonesian bishops, both groups were very slow to react to a crisis unfolding on their respective doorsteps. This too is part of the East Timorese story.

The story also has to embrace the contribution from the Church in East Timor itself. The local Church had been only recently separated from Macau and placed under the charge of an Apostolic Administrator, when it had to deal with the ambiguities of the Japanese invasion, and without Australian help its clergy and religious would have been wiped out.[8] With the end of the war, the Portuguese returned and the 'Australian connection' was severed. In East Timor Church leaders again took Church-state relationships as defined in Portugal as the norm. When the fascist Salazar regime was finally overthrown in 1974, the bishop in East Timor, Jose Ribeiro (1918-2002), misread 'the signs of the times'. He believed that the future of the colony lay with Indonesia whose propaganda he gullibly swallowed, only to become totally disillusioned when the Indonesians invaded.

Fortunately, and perhaps providentially, the Church was then headed successively by two leaders, Monsignor da Costa Lopes and Bishop Carlos Filipe Ximines Belo, outstanding for their raw courage in dealing with a dangerous situation. While Belo's work for peace deservedly led to international acknowledgement, da Costa Lopes was made out of the same stern stuff as Australia's Mary MacKillop. Rarely has an important Church leader been so shabbily and unjustly treated by his peers in the Church. Yet da Costa Lopes served his people and the Church devotedly despite this. He was a man of great faith.

The Church is more than its leaders, important though their role is. Timorese priests, often with very deficient training, worked under appalling conditions and levels of surveillance following the Indonesian invasion. As the number of Catholics doubled, then trebled, and continued to grow exponentially, their position became impossible, yet they continued to mobilise lay catechists to meet the spiritual needs of their people. All of this is part of the story I wish to acknowledge.

As events unfolded, the local Catholic Church played an important role at key junctures in East Timor's struggle. This has gone largely unacknowledged in the English-speaking world. It is part of the East Timor story that needs to be told in the interests of balance. It says something important about the Catholic Church, what it is, how it functions, and the way it engages in the public square.

The Catholic Church's claim to be 'a champion of human rights' in the 1980s rested on less-than-firm foundations. These strengthened substantially when John Paul II became a decisive figure in the overthrow of communism in Eastern Europe. They firmed up again when da Costa Lopes and Belo began the task of undermining the moral basis of the

---

8   Many Timorese clergy and religious were evacuated to Australia and remained there till hostilities ceased.

Indonesian policy about integration (*integrasi*) by their defence of the human rights of the East Timorese so badly abused in the name of *integrasi*. The power of the Indonesians in the end could not overcome this defence. All of this is essential to the interplay of stories I wish to address. The Catholic Church became more fully the Church of Jesus through its engagement with East Timor. The East Timorese on the other hand became more able to enjoy and express a fuller humanity through their engagement with the Church. The relationship was one of reciprocity.

*

My view of the Church's role in East Timor is one from the margins rather than the mainstream. The main current of international Church life did not flow through East Timor in the period we are discussing; it was regarded as an ecclesiastical backwater. Furthermore, in the eyes of many Indonesian clergy, especially the Javanese, Timor, whether East or West, was regarded as primitive, a place where the people had 'just come out of the trees', as one Indonesian cleric expressed it to me, and so did not share their much superior Javanese culture. These clergy came to East Timor in support of the *transmigrasi*, and only saw what they expected to see. This further fuelled Indonesia's worldwide propaganda aimed at concealing what was happening in East Timor in the name of *integrasi*. Theirs was an unwitting contribution to the suffering of the East Timorese. This is also part of the story I wish to tell.

I became involved with the East Timorese, more or less by accident. As I worked with their leaders, I soon found myself sharing the marginalised position of East Timor's two great Church leaders, Monsignor Martinho da Costa Lopes and Bishop Carlos Belo. While some of my colleague bishops were wondering 'What is Hills up to?', a number were dead set against my involvement, and seemed to resent my friendship with Belo. The situation reflected tensions within the Catholic Church here in Australia that I inadvertently dragged into the East Timorese story. Another part of my account! This account therefore inevitably carries with it a certain bias (as indeed do most accounts). My reputed left-wing orientation has its source in a concern for people, a legacy of my professional involvement as an anthropologist specialising in indigenous peoples. That is an important part of my personal story, and one of which I am very proud.

While da Costa Lopes and Belo were from different generations, they were united in a common concern. *They put the interests of their people first.* That is to say, their concern lay first and foremost in people. In Belo's case, not surprisingly given his Salesian background, his major concern was the welfare of young people. The demands of the institution, important as these were, ran in second place to the needs of people. Belo and I became good friends because we both recognised that *pastoral needs have to take precedence in a crisis*.

*

The Catholic Church played an important role in the David and Goliath struggle of the people of East Timor to exercise their right to self-determination. The struggle was to cost tens of thousands of lives, most of them Catholic, some as a direct result of violence, others from malnutrition and poor health care, but all the consequence of resistance to Indonesian rule.[9] The Indonesian 'adventure' in East Timor virtually annihilated two generations of young people.

However, the tragedy did not stop there. Once the referendum on self-determination was decided, with close to eighty percent of those living in East Timor voting in favor of independence,[10] the Indonesians wreaked their revenge on the East Timorese, transporting many thousands against their will to West Timor and other islands in the archipelago, so that those East Timorese who favored *integrasi* could depart in relative safety, plundering unhindered as they went.[11] The Indonesians used their militias to torch the country.

★

The Church's position in this saga was always complex and sometimes compromised, so the story of its involvement contains both light and shade. The Indonesian invasion and the policy of *Pancasila*[12] forced the East Timorese to choose a religious allegiance, and the majority chose to become Catholic. At the beginning of the crisis approximately one-third of East Timorese were nominally Catholic; by its end, over ninety-five percent were Catholic. Something extraordinary was going on. The story of the Church's role has to interpret this historic change.

There have been various efforts to explain why this mass conversion occurred. Xanana Gusmao suggested the 'conversions' were as much about nationalism as about religion; another suggestion is that the East Timorese became Catholic as a protest against the Javanese, who were Muslim; both these explanations have some merit. However, there is also the view put forward by Belo, that in the face of suffering on a scale that encompassed almost every family in the country, a people collectively attuned to mysticism by their native animism, made sense of their suffering in terms of the suffering, death and resurrection of Jesus, a central element in the Christian experience. The Church was led by native Timorese clergy who stayed with their people *and shared their suffering* so that, in the period 1975-1999, the East Timorese Catholic Church became *a church of the people* with leaders who put themselves at risk for the welfare of their people. I witnessed this development at first hand after 1992.

The Church was universally recognised as the *only body that could protect people* from arbitrary Indonesian violence. It did this at both the practical level through mediation, and engaging in a dialogue with the Indonesian commanders about the abuse of human rights.

---

9   The estimates of the numbers of deaths in East Timor vary enormously, not least because of the difficulty of establishing accurately the original numbers of the East Timorese population. A well regarded source is that of the CAVR Report (Report of the Commission for Reception, Truth and Reconciliation entitled *Chega! (No more Stop Enough!)*. It puts the number in excess of 100,000 between 1974 and 1999. http://www.cavr-timorleste.org/en/chegaReport.htm
    This report provides the lower level of estimates. Others would put the number much higher at around 200,000. See discussion in Chapter 2.
10 Despite political differences among them, in 1999 the vote in favour of independence of East Timorese living in Australia was almost 100%.
11 Maliana, the principal town in the western border region, was 'deconstructed' as *integrasi* supporters retreating to West Timor stripped everything moveable and of value, including the roofing and window frames of buildings. All that remained were the shells.
12 Pancasila meaning 'Five Principles' is the philosophical foundation of the Indonesian state. It was first articulated by Sukarno in 1945. See www.indonesianembassy.org.uk/human_right-2.htm

The response varied. It would be wrong to think that all Indonesian military commanders supported violence as the way to bring about *integrasi*. However those opposed to violence were always in the minority, since East Timor was from the outset a project of the military 'hawks' and their prestige (and wealth) depended on its success. One of the most notorious of these was a Catholic, as were some of his principal strategists. This too is part of the story.

The triumph of the Catholic Church in East Timor was that, against all the odds, it became a Church of the *maubere*, of 'the ordinary East Timorese', most of whom had become marginalised in their own country. The Church in East Timor under Belo's leadership became a people's movement and, as such, was able to do things that many institutions can no longer do, and that is command public respect. Whether the Church can retain this respect post-independence seems an open question at the present time.

My argument is that during the Indonesian occupation, *both* the Catholic Church and the resistance movements kept hope alive, but by totally different means.

★

What follows is my tale told in the context of many other more important tales, all of which encompass the great suffering that the East Timorese had to endure for a quarter of a century. To put this all in some perspective, if you had been fifteen at the time of the invasion in 1975, you most probably would not have survived, but if you did, then you would have been approaching forty when the vote for independence was taken!

There is a lesson here for every person: our stories define who we are and so are meaningful, precious, and worth sharing. Our personal stories take on heightened meaning from the bigger stories of which they are part. These bigger stories shape our culture and sense of who we are. Keeping these bigger stories alive is important not only for us as individuals, but also to who we are as a people. The Catholic Church's involvement in East Timor is one of these bigger stories.

CHAPTER 2
MEETING THE TIMORESE FOR THE FIRST TIME

As I sat in my office in the Cathedral administrative complex on the 20th October 1991, minding my own business, I had no idea that a series of events was about to unfold that would change my life, and also a number of other people's lives, forever. At the time I had very little interest in East Timor. While East Timor had been in the news off and on, I really did not know much about it, nor did I feel myself called upon to learn more.

I looked up when my long-serving secretary, Joan Manshon, who had migrated to Australia from South Africa, came into the office to advise me that there were seven people in the foyer who would like to speak to me. She wasn't sure of their language, but thought it might be Spanish. As it turned out Joan was not far off the mark. The language they were speaking was Portuguese, and six of the seven people were East Timorese. Joan and I returned to the foyer to greet them and invited them to come into my office. The seven, three men and four women, looked a little nervous, and I remember asking Joan to get us all a cup of tea. We moved into the office and found chairs for everyone, and while we were waiting for the tea to arrive I asked them about the purpose of their visit.

Their leader, Justino Guterres, told me that the 7th December marked the sixteenth anniversary of the Indonesian invasion of Dili. Many people had been killed and raped as the country had been taken over, and many more had died since. What they wanted was a memorial Mass which could be attended by the East Timorese refugees now living in Melbourne. As we discussed the matter, I soon discovered that all of those present had relatives who had been killed by the Indonesian army, or had died of starvation as a consequence of the army's actions.[1] We discussed the invasion and the subsequent violence for some time, and as their request seemed genuine, I assured them that I would see what could be done. I asked if they knew how to prepare a liturgy for such an event. They said that this was not a problem as they were used to doing so in their parishes. One of the group, Palmyra Pires, later told me that this was an exaggeration!

I did not know it at the time, but I was speaking to a formidable group of people. It included Emilia Pires, from 2007 to 2015 the Minister of Finance in East Timor, and her

---

1 The Indonesian Foreign Minister at this time, Adam Malik, acknowledged that between 50,000 and 80,000 people lost their lives at the time of the invasion. This was out of a total population estimated to be around 600,000 at the time. See John Taylor *Indonesia's Forgotten War: The Hidden History of East Timor* (London: Zed Books, 1991), 83. Taylor is quoting from *Antara*, 23 February, 1979. As indicated in Chapter 1, estimates of deaths directly or indirectly resulting from the Indonesian invasion vary enormously.

sister, Palmyra, head of the East Timor Development Association, Justino Guterres who later became East Timor's ambassador to the Vatican, Cancio Noronha, the son of an East Timorese *liurai* (tribal chief) and his wife Maria, and Salustiano Freitas, an East Timorese refugee and activist. The group also included one Australian, Louise Byrne, who would also become prominent in East Timor's struggle for self-determination, and a good friend.

After more discussion I said something to the effect of, 'All right. How about you go away and come back with what you have prepared in three weeks' time. That will be 15 November. We will then have plenty of time to organise the whole thing. Make sure you bring the texts and hymns you want, and know who is going to do what'. As we headed to the door I indicated that I would try to get permission for the Mass from the Dean of the Cathedral, and from the Archbishop. The group were excited by this prospect so I cautioned them that, even if the Dean approved, the Mass would not go ahead unless the Archbishop also approved. I also said that I did not think there would be any major problems. My assurance sent the little delegation away happy.

I did not know it at the time but the Timorese had asked Archbishop Little to celebrate a commemorative Mass in the Cathedral in 1986 and had been refused. The reason was that the Eucharist had been overtly and improperly politicised by groups elsewhere, and as a result, Australian bishops were justifiably wary.

★

St Patrick's cathedral is one of the glories of Melbourne. It is an impressive example of Gothic revival architecture. During the long reign of Archbishop Daniel Mannix, the cathedral became a focal point for Catholicism in Melbourne. It is a 'sacred space', and its use is carefully controlled. The cathedral can hold a large crowd, and is the site of all major Catholic liturgies, including public funerals.

Much of my life has centered on the cathedral. As a schoolboy I spent eight years singing in the cathedral choir. As a member of Archbishop Little's staff I lived together with other members in the historic presbytery, since pulled down, next to the cathedral. Later, as Vicar General, my office was in the administrative complex behind it.

After meeting with the Timorese, I informed Archbishop Little of the day's events and what the East Timorese had requested. 'What do you think?' he asked. 'I think we should give them free rein and, if you like I will take charge of things.' Frank replied, 'Good then, that's OK'. I spoke later that night to the Dean, Fred Chamberlain, and with his blessing the date of the Mass was provisionally set for Sunday afternoon, the 8th December.

When the East Timorese group returned as planned on the 15th November, their world had changed forever. What they knew from their contacts was that three days earlier Indonesian troops had opened fire on a large group of people attending a commemorative service for a Sebastian Gomez at the Santa Cruz cemetery. The young independence activist had been shot by Indonesian soldiers as he walked through the gate of the Catholic church at Motael, Dili, in the fall-out from a protest a fortnight or so earlier. He had sought refuge in the church with two others. A young man, he wanted desperately to get to his home nearby. So he waited till it was dark, and crept out. The waiting soldiers shot him as he came out. Every time I go there, I think of him, and his blood flowing at the gate. The event is now recognised as of such national importance that a huge bronze statue of the stricken man dying in the arms of a friend stands on the foreshore opposite the church.

It is customary in East Timor to commemorate a person a short time after their death by walking in procession to the cemetery and placing a cross on the new grave. On the morning of the 12th November there had been an early Mass at Motael church followed by a procession to the grave for prayers and the placing of the cross. Because the procession was occurring before school started, a number of secondary school students had joined the people in the procession which soon turned into an independence demonstration. The shooting had occurred while the ceremony was in progress at the cemetery, and people were milling around outside the cemetery wall. On the 15th November we knew that many young people, perhaps as many as two hundred, had been killed.

Initial news reports here of the 'Dili Massacre' were sketchy, but having met with the East Timorese group I was most interested in finding out more of what had happened. I rang the Australian Department of Foreign Affairs for information, but the people I spoke to were not interested. They suggested I direct my enquiries to the Indonesian or the Portuguese consulates. Timor was not Australia's concern. Foreign Affairs did not want to be quoted. I contacted Timorese I knew in Melbourne and they were talking about two hundred and fifty killed, but that figure was not reported at the time.

It emerged much later that two hundred and ninety-three people had been killed. Bodies were disposed of in three mass graves. Most of the bodies were never found.[2] Many died at the site. Those who had been wounded were subsequently murdered at the Dili hospital where they had been taken for treatment.

The sheer savagery of the Indonesian army on this occasion indicates the depth and irrationality of their frustration at their lack of success in pacifying the East Timorese after sixteen years of occupation. Unable to overcome a resistance they could not see but feel, they took their revenge on the group that they could see. The Santa Cruz massacre was to become an indelible blot on Indonesia's international reputation, one that no amount of subsequent propaganda could remove.

The Indonesian army had clearly not anticipated that the massacre would be filmed, nor that film of the incident would be successfully smuggled to Australia and to the international television media. Two foreign journalists from the U.S. were in Dili at the time of the massacre. They were there to cover a visit by a Portuguese parliamentary delegation and the UN Special Rapporteur for Human Rights. Accompanying the journalists was a British cameraman, Max Stahl, filming undercover for Yorkshire television. He filmed from inside the cemetery and hid the film among the stones on a grave from where it was later retrieved. It was a grave on which a student who had been shot was lying. Max Stahl told an Italian missionary priest Stephano Renato, the parish priest of Atsabae, where the film was hidden. The next day, Renato braved the Indonesian soldiers who were still removing evidence of the massacre, declaring that he had come to pray for the dead. He knelt at the grave and retrieved the film. He then gave it to the priest in charge of the Salesian College at Comoro, Fr Walter Van Wouwe, who arranged to have it flown out to Darwin the following day with some returning tourists. That film was the beginning of the end for the Indonesians.

---

2   The East Timor Human Rights Centre, which Jose Ramos Horta and I founded, later compiled a list of 293 people who 'disappeared' on 12th November.

After the massacre the Indonesian army got wind of the fact that there was film footage and tipped off the Australian government. When Stahl and his two colleagues arrived in Darwin, they were strip-searched in case they had the film hidden on them. By doing this, the Australian Government became an accessory in covering up a major crime.

Film of the massacre appeared on international TV in January 1992, an event that was to galvanise support for the East Timorese cause around the world, particularly among human rights activists. The international mobilisation that followed illustrates the power of the media, and of images, in shaping public opinion.[3] However, as I met again with the East Timorese on the 15th November, this development still lay very much in the future.

*

When everyone was seated in my office I asked the group if they had prepared the Mass, and they indicated that they had. I can clearly remember what I said next: 'Things have changed since last we met. Most of you fled from Dili harbor in boats during the troubles in 1975. Two days ago there was a terrible slaughter in Dili that is being called the Santa Cruz massacre. What we will now do is have a funeral Mass instead of a commemorative Mass, since all of you will have lost someone. Instead of having it on Sunday afternoon, we will move it to Saturday 7th December, the anniversary of the invasion, and hold it at in the evening at 7:00pm. Let all the Timorese community know'.

The members of my Timorese group were obviously still in shock from what they were hearing about events in Dili, so I added what I had been able to find out, and they seemed fascinated that I was beginning to get interested in their cause and developing quite a passion about it.

I told them that having been considering the situation in the two days since the massacre occurred, I had decided to say something about it in the Cathedral. It would be heavily political without being political! My plan was to give my homily from the floor of the cathedral, rather than from the pulpit, as an expression of solidarity.

What I wanted to do as the celebrant and representative of the Church was to make a symbolic gesture that said clearly to the Timorese, 'I am down here talking with you, being with you. The Catholic Church stands in solidarity with you'. By the time I eventually got to sit down at my typewriter that afternoon I was outraged by what I had heard about soldiers indiscriminately killing defenceless young people and school children, and so I really went to town. I was slowly but surely being drawn into the East Timorese struggle. Nor did I resist!

*

On the Saturday evening around a thousand Timorese gathered in the cathedral, and they were not alone. There were other groups who came, even though they were not Catholic, to show solidarity with the Timorese in this hour of crisis. These included representatives of the trade union movement, human rights groups from other Christian churches, and

---

3 Some of the original film of the commemorative Mass and subsequent events taken by Max Stahl can be seen at youtube.com/watch?v=8NYdGad-0bs. It is sobering to realise that most of the wounded captured on film were subsequently murdered.

representatives of NGOs such as the Australian Council for Overseas Aid (ACFOA).[4]

The Timorese were quite withdrawn as almost every day since the 12th November they had been getting news that someone else they knew had been killed or was now listed among the growing number of missing. For a people who regard members of the extended family as very close, losing a cousin is felt in much the same way as losing a son or daughter. So the situation for those present was truly tragic.

When we reached the homily I moved from the altar. As I stood among them in the solemnity of the Cathedral that evening with the fading western sun bursting though its great stained glass windows, I was conscious of my heart going out to these people in their distress. I spoke what I hoped would be words of hope and encouragement:

> *Friends from East Timor, I welcome you all here tonight. It is indeed a moving sight to see so many of you gathered here, caring enough about what has happened in East Timor, and hoping deeply for peace and justice in that land.*
>
> *This very day is seared into the collective memory of all East Timorese. On this day 16 years ago, the Indonesian Army invaded your country and you lost control of your homeland and your future. This Mass was arranged to commemorate that sad event, and to remind the world that your land has been overrun, but invaders have not been able to take away your heart and soul from you. Since then, tragedy struck again, this time on November 12th, at Santa Cruz cemetery when armed forces fired into a crowd of people gathered around the grave of a young man killed by similar forces several weeks before. Our reasons for being here then, are etched with the bitter sorrow of yet another atrocity, a massacre of unknown, but unacceptable proportions.*
>
> *May I make one point here, before I go any further. Unless one wants to talk in very general and vacuous platitudes, anything one may say about East Timor touches on the political. Anything I may say may be given some political meaning, or seen to have overtones of such a nature. So be it. I speak of Jesus, of his Gospel, on the rights of the human person, on basic, legitimate rights we all have to peace, self-determination, and control of one's development. I speak of moral and spiritual values and principles. Unless these are embedded in the daily life and experiences of people, I am only beating the air with a stick of nonsense.*
>
> *Firstly, then, we remember in sorrow the invasion of East Timor in 1975. I daresay every one of you here tonight from Timor has suffered loss, pain and death in your families from that event and the constant harassment you have endured since then. Last November's massacre was not an isolated incident, but just the latest – is it even that now? – in a chain of killings, imprisonments, and violations of human life and rights. We will probably never know the full extent or list of victims. As so often happens with those guilty of such offences, figures are issued, suppressed, changed, or deliberately mixed to confuse, and consequently blunt the edge of accusation. But the figure of c.200,000 violent deaths in 16 years of occupation is a common figure used. And that makes this matter we commemorate an affair of immense and appalling violations.*

---

4   In 1999 when East Timor was being raped by the militias, we were to hold another Mass in the cathedral praying in solidarity with the suffering East Timorese people. On this occasion three Anglican bishops joined the many supporters of the East Timorese.

Calls are now being made for urgent, and hopefully, accurate investigations into the November massacre. The Australian Bishops recently renewed their call for such a probe. Their brother Bishops in Indonesia have expressed grave concern about the alarming details gathered by their own representatives. I do suggest that the present Indonesian investigations are suspicious from the start. They are in-house, and their objectivity will always be questioned – and they have already admitted that witnesses are loathe to come forward and give evidence out of fear of reprisals. There is also already confusion about the alleged facts of the matter, what actually happened, and the causes, being fed to the media and the international public.

An investigation by an outside body with authority and weight and resources, say the United Nations, should be permitted to investigate the event of the massacre. There are alleged violent follow-ups to this as well. These also need close scrutiny. And there is the whole question of the persistent violations of human rights ever since 1975.

It is one thing to have Indonesians claim this to be an internal matter and therefore no-one else's business. We would claim otherwise. Violation of basic human rights on the scale of what is going on in East Timor is the business of all fair-minded people. In a world fast becoming the predicted global village, what happens in one country that relies for so much on other countries, becomes the business of those other countries, but especially in matters such as the ones we remember here tonight.

But the violations have not been just of life and limb, serious enough though they are. The East Timorese have been denied basic rights that all people may claim to their culture, their religion, their language and their folk-ways. This has taken place through an imposed series of programs of enforced Islamization. It so happens that much of East Timor is Catholic, and, I understand, wishes to remain so. The Catholic Church in that country has been there for 400 years. The Timorese have an inspiring leader in the Apostolic Administrator of Dili, Bishop Belo. Let us give him, as a vibrant and focal figure in the struggle of freedom and self-determination, our prayerful support. He has stated publicly that the East Timorese have never been consulted about their future – it has been imposed on them, not least of all now, at the end of a gun.

It is not for me here during this Mass to be suggesting what the Australian Government should, or should not, be doing. But many of us remember, with shame, how the East Timorese were treated officially by this country in 1975 – and how we have persistently been advised by public figures to go slow on East Timor. The appeasement factor, for that is what it is, is still there, governed, so it seems, by the size of the Indonesian population and the possible loss of trade to our nation. People's rights are worth far more than that, no matter how painful and costly it may be to admit it.

We should remember the burdens of war the East Timorese shouldered alongside Australian armed forces during the Second World War. As the Australian Bishops said: 'We have an unpaid debt to those largely unsung heroes'.

This nation has gone out of its way to remember, with passion and firm intent, the savage sufferings of Soweto and what that signified, the massacre in Tienanmen Square, and the atrocities of the Gulf War. Let us remember with equal passion and moral indignation these events closer to home. Let us remember the event at Santa Cruz cemetery. Let us remember the many other sufferings the East Timorese people have endured in the silence that we have imposed on them. Let us pray that this silence be broken. Let us pray that our leaders speak out with moral indignation in the cause of right.

May God grant the East Timorese self-determination, peace and justice at last.

With that we went on to celebrate the Mass and reconnect with the great hopes and sense of unity that, in times of absolute distress, only the Mass can conjure up for Catholics. This Mass on the 7th December 1991 marked a turning point, a moment of destiny if you like, when the East Timorese and I were bonded through tragedy, even as we were united in hope.

★

I was determined that the sense of outrage we all felt on this occasion be communicated to others. So the text of my homily was provided to the local press, who ignored it. It was also provided to Reuters and AAP, and subsequently my comments were reported in two overseas papers, one in London and one in New York. From there they went around the world reaching many East Timor support groups and human rights groups via the *East Timor Action Network,* a US-based support group that monitored the international press and disseminated reports and articles on East Timor to other support groups.[5]

The event also marked the beginning of my long engagement, which often turned into a battle, with the local media whom I castigated for letting the whole East Timor tragedy unfold under their very noses, and simply ignoring it. In those days the self-interest of both the press proprietors and the Australian government lay in cosying up to Indonesia, whatever the human cost to the East Timorese. The latter were dispensable, a people whose rights were ignored in favour of 'the bigger picture'.

In a sense the attitude of leaders in the Australian Catholic Church at the time was little different from that of the government. They too were acting in terms of a perception of 'Catholic self-interest' and 'the Catholic big picture'. The Australian Bishops took their cues from the new papal nuncio. He in turn followed Vatican policy as set out by the long-serving, Secretary of State, Cardinal Agostino Casaroli. The message from the Vatican seemed to be: 'Go easy on all this. We have to play this game carefully because whatever we say might affect the Church in Indonesia.' There was more to the matter than this. However since this 'more' was never clearly explained, the Vatican seemed to be 'sacrificing a little fish to catch a big one' as da Costa Lopes once put the matter quite succinctly.

I can remember arguing about this with Archbishop Frank Little and saying in exasperation: 'Frank, if it is a matter of justice and the infringement of human rights, where do these come in? How more important is the Church in Indonesia?' Frank had no answer to my questions.

From 1975 onwards the Australian bishops were caught in a Vatican-policy bind that made it hard for them to act collectively as we shall see in a later chapter.

★

---

5   The corresponding group in Australia was *Christians in Solidarity with East Timor* (CISET).

Before we go any further, it will prove helpful to outline at least briefly how the Catholic Church is organised, and so correct common misunderstandings endlessly repeated in the secular press.

The Church around the world is organised into dioceses each headed by a bishop who is directly accountable to the pope. This accountability is usually exercised through the Vatican bureaucracy. In Australia, most capital cities are designated as archdioceses and are headed by an archbishop accountable to Rome in the same manner as are other diocesan bishops.

Since Australia is organised into states, the dioceses within a state usually work together in dealing with Government. The Archbishop is called the Metropolitan in regard to the state and has certain rights and responsibilities. A common misunderstanding, however, holds that the Archbishop is in charge of the other Bishops. In fact, he is in charge only of his own diocese. When the press wants a comment on an issue, they usually go to the Archbishop's office thinking that he speaks for the other diocesan Bishops and that these are his lieutenants. This assumption is incorrect except in the case when the bishops have an agreement in regard to some issue.

What applies to archbishops at the state level also applies to the cardinal at the national level. The cardinal, who traditionally has been based in Sydney, is not 'the head of the Church in Australia' as the press commonly claims. Reporters and lawyers often regard the cardinal as a 'chairman of the board'. This is not the case. The cardinal is simply the archbishop of Sydney.

The designation 'cardinal' has more to do with the organisation of the global Church than the national Church. Cardinals are technically 'advisors' to the Pope and assist him in the management of the global institution by serving as members of the various 'congregations' that make up the Curia – the central administration in Rome. Cardinals are the group who elect a new pope, a role most are familiar with.

In running an archdiocese, which usually contains a large Catholic population, the archbishop is assisted by auxiliary bishops who are accountable to him for Church life in a region of the diocese. Auxiliary bishops form a second tier in the episcopate. Their accountability is more local than global. Melbourne has had four auxiliary bishops working in this way with the archbishop since the 1960s. These are all appointed by Rome.

Since the Second Vatican Council (1962-5), the Australian Catholic Bishops' Conference (ACBC) has become an important body in the governance of the Church. The ACBC has a permanent national secretariat and the president is a bishop elected by his colleagues for a three-year term. The cardinal does not chair the ACBC unless he is elected president.

The ACBC operates through a two-tier committee structure. The top tier consists of twelve bishops' commissions covering various aspects of Church life. Episcopal commissions are supported by advisory councils. Catholic agencies are accountable to these councils.[6]

For instance, the Bishops' Commission for Justice, Ecology and Development (BCJED) acts on the advice of two councils each headed by a bishop: the Australian Catholic Social Justice Council and the National Council of Caritas Australia. The commission carries oversight for the work of the Australian Catholic Social Justice Council, Caritas Australia and Catholic Earthcare. Advisory councils are generally networked with comparable bodies in other countries.

---

6   In 2013 there were twelve Bishops' Commissions and twenty Councils.

The ACBC meets twice a year, and is the main vehicle for co-ordinating the Church's work both nationally and internationally.

★

Finally, the Vatican's global influence is felt in local churches in two principal ways.[7] The first is through Roman congregations that issue directives and guidelines for bishops to follow on a range of matters. The papal nuncio provides a second mechanism. The papal nuncio is technically the Vatican's ambassador. The nuncio has three key roles. As a diplomat, he is based in Canberra and his role there is to maintain cordial relationships with the incumbent government. As 'the Vatican's man' in a country, the nuncio is a direct channel for Vatican policy on international matters. As the Pope's representative, his role is to support the local church and provide advice and support to his fellow bishops. As a Church diplomat, he also reports on the local Church, and for want of a better term engages in 'talent spotting' to identify potential bishops.

The process by which bishops are appointed is arcane, to say the least. If a vacancy occurs due to a retirement or death, the nuncio's office seeks nominations for a replacement. He does this by canvassing the opinions of priests and lay people heading major Catholic agencies in the diocese where the vacancy exists. Those responding are sworn to secrecy. The nuncio's office then collates this data and 'after due consideration' three names are sent to the Congregation for Bishops in Rome. The Congregation makes its recommendation to the Pope who ratifies it. The final decision is his.

Many Catholics see the nuncio as a direct channel to the Vatican, so any complaints they wish to make about bishops or Church agencies are directed to the nuncio. This tactic is widely employed by right-wing groups in Australia. Not surprisingly then, the nuncio can be seen, from a certain point of view, as running the Church's spy service! This perception works against his being seen as a support for local bishops, and can result in them distancing themselves from him. Nuncios are appointed for a six-year term and then moved to another diplomatic posting. The multiple, and sometimes conflicting, demands of the role make it a difficult one.

★

Within an archdiocese, the archbishop is free to appoint his own immediate staff. The vicar general in an archdiocese is effectively the archbishop's chief-of-staff. If the archbishop is away, or incapacitated through illness, then it is the vicar general who takes over the running of the archdiocese within limits set by the archbishop.

In 1985, after eight years as parish priest at Mount Eliza, I was appointed Vicar General in the Melbourne archdiocese, and it was in this capacity that I met with the Timorese. It was perhaps fortunate that this 'moment of destiny' occurred just prior to the Christmas-New Year period, which is 'the slow season' for the Vicar General's office. This enabled

---

7   In Catholic parlance the term 'local church' can have two meanings – a commonplace meaning as in 'the church down the road', and a technical meaning that refers to the community of parishes that make up a diocese under the leadership of its bishop. This term 'local church' is sometimes extended in a broader usage to include the community of dioceses that make up a national church.

me to return to one of the haunts of my youth, the Victorian State Library, and read up anything I could lay my hands on about East Timor and its history. At the time the range of materials available there was limited so I began to assemble a file on East Timor made up of articles from journals and press cuttings. Access to the internet was still some way off!

As I look back now I realise that my engagement with the Timorese was not something that came out of the blue. I had been heading towards that moment all my life, but I had just not realised that this was the case. I now wonder how many other people, looking back at their lives, come to discern the pattern that is there. That such a pattern exists might seem for some to be a matter of chance, but people of faith interpret things differently. For them, there is always something providential in the way lives unfold. It is not *just* a matter of chance, something else is at play, and how we choose to name this 'something else' is important.

PART I
THREE STORIES:
1. Hilton's Story

CHAPTER 3
A BOY FROM THE BUSH

The American novelist, Chaim Potok, begins one of his books with the line, 'All beginnings are hard'. It is an insight that the main character later shares with his Jewish students as he encourages them to persevere in their study of the Torah.

> *'Be patient. You are learning a new way of understanding the Bible. All beginnings are hard.' And sometimes I add what I have learned on my own: 'Especially a beginning you make by yourself. That's the hardest beginning of all.'*[1]

I feel a similar trepidation in trying to set down the pattern of events that led me to become an advocate for human rights, and the struggles going on in our region as ordinary people seek to live their lives with peace and dignity in the face of oppressive injustice. The pattern may have been set by the times in which I was born, for in 1932 Australia was in the grip of the Great Depression.

At the time, the national unemployment rate was thirty percent, a figure surpassed only by that in Germany. Banks had devalued the Australian pound by thirty percent. Governments had cut spending by twenty percent. The Scullin government had fallen, and Phar Lap[2] and Don Bradman[3] were the national heroes. The great horse had just died in suspicious circumstances in the United States, an event that prompted national mourning. I was born at a time when 'depression' described not only the economic situation, it also described the national mood.

The Deakins are unusual among Australian Catholics in that we are descended from an English Catholic family, whose origins were in Wiltshire. Ours was a different Catholic story from that of our Irish co-religionists. My great grandfather, John Francis Deakin, had emigrated to Australia from Birmingham and, after a short stay in Bendigo where he married his wife, Sarah Godier, another English migrant, settled in Tocumwal on the

---

1 Chaim Potok *In the Beginning* (Harmondsworth: Penguin, 1976), 1.
2 Phar Lap was a famous Australian race horse which, from unpromising beginnings, went on to become a symbol of a deep myth in Australian culture – 'the Aussie battler', who wins through against the odds. The exploits of Phar Lap were a focus of hope that things could be better, and Australia could get through the Depression of the 1930s. Phar Lap won America's richest horse race, the Agua Caliente Handicap, and died shortly after in America in mysterious circumstances, further enhancing its iconic status.
3 Sir Donald Bradman was a legendary cricketer, whose prowess as a batsman many believe has not been surpassed. His successes in cricket were a focus of hope in Australian society during the Great Depression and beyond.

Murray in NSW. In the decades prior to the Depression, John demonstrated considerable business flair becoming the proprietor of the local hotel, bakery and forge. He invested in property in the district. His son, Frederick, my grandfather, converted his part in this legacy into a small farming property near Finley, seventeen kilometres north of Tocumwal. Other members of the family also had farms in the district. There is an area between Finley and Tocumwal called Deakins' Corner to this day. When drought and the Depression hit, credit all but disappeared for small farmers, and small-scale farming became a precarious way to support a family.

★

My first decade was spent at Finley in the Riverina, one hundred and forty kilometres west of Albury. At the time Finley could lay no claim to fame. At most, it had about twelve hundred people. My parents, Ruby and Stan, were failed farmers. As drought and the Depression took hold, Dad followed the pattern familiar in hard times of moving from farmer to farmhand, then abandoning his holding and moving the family into town to find work. These changes in the family fortunes meant that I had a strong sense that something, quite outside my parents' control, was very wrong. I soon learned that we had been the fortunate ones, since my father was never out of work during the Depression.

Dad was not a tradesman of any sort, but he worked as a labourer building the Mulwala channel that would deliver water from the Murray to the region, and eventually transform agriculture there. Having been driven off the land by drought and a tight economy, the irony of the situation must have irked him at times, but he was never one to complain.

During the Depression wages were low and my parents did it tough. We were poor, but as kids we did not notice this much, since we seemed the same as most others. In a small town it becomes pretty obvious, even to young eyes, that there are the 'haves' and there are the 'have nots' in this world. In Finley during the Depression years, owning a car or having a fridge meant you were a 'have'. My parents, like most of the rest, had to make do with their pushbike and Coolgardie safe, so we were easily classified![4]

By listening to my mother and father talk, I learned that governments and banks protect wealthy people, and that a good Labor politician called Jack Lang was trying to sort out the local banks in NSW. My parents could make no sense of the lack of effort by the federal government to create work for those 'out of work'. The term 'unemployed' was not used by working people in those days.

As children we did not understand these issues very well, but we did sense the passion with which our parents and their friends discussed them. This helped us define what was important for working people, and an impression was made that has stuck with me throughout my life. From an early age my unintended political education included the lessons that 'working people need to get a fair go', and that 'it is the job of government

---

4   An invention attributed to Arthur Patrick McCormick and used initially at Coolgardie on the goldfields of Western Australia. The Coolgardie safe employed the principle of evaporative cooling whereby hessian which formed the walls of the safe was dried by heat transferred from the food inside the safe thus keeping the food cool. Water draining from above kept the hessian wet, and so the process was continuous. The safe was eventually produced commercially and used widely throughout Australia by families like ours until supplanted by the refrigerator.

to make sure this happens, despite the best efforts of the bosses and the banks to prevent it'. This was all part of my beginning. Not one I made myself, mind you, but the one into which I was born.

★

With this beginning came a sense that all was not well in the social order. This sense was reinforced by other experiences. In the 1930s Finley had between a hundred and a hundred and fifty houses. Whenever I went shopping with my mother, we had to pass the police station. Every Wednesday morning there would be a queue of men lined up outside the station, often six or seven, all waiting to get what my mother called 'susso' – food parcels. The locals called Wednesday 'susso' day. The sustenance referred to was a bit of money and food – bread, meat and sugar. These were the blokes from the town who could not find work. There were also a number of men, unemployed men from the cities, whom you would see humping their swags, their 'Matildas', as they drifted into the town looking for work, only to move on. My mother kept a pot of soup on the hob to give them something when they turned up. This was an early lesson in working-class solidarity. These 'swagmen' walked everywhere. We never had to do that, but seeing their desperation left a deep, deep mark on me, when I was only a kid.

People did not talk much about 'social justice' in those days. They just shared the view that what was happening to ordinary people was not right. The idea of a government spending money to stimulate the economy so as to address a severe recession lay beyond the imaginal horizon of Australian politicians who were in thrall to the Bank of England, which provided their principal source of economic advice. So Australia in the 1930s did not get a 'New Deal', as happened in the United States. Rather, ordinary people were offered the 'bad deal' - an austerity package as wages were cut and taxes increased. My parents' efforts simply to make ends meet left an indelible impression on me, as it did on most young people of my generation.

The Depression enabled both communism and socialism to gain a foothold in Australia. The fight against communism is an important chapter in the Australian Catholic story. This battle, and particularly the wounds it opened up within the Catholic community, shaped the role that Australian church leaders were to play in the story of East Timor in the 1980s and 1990s.

★

At the end of the town there was a big piece of crown land usually called 'the common'. It was the custom for shires to have an area close to the town where people could get fresh milk. If they wanted to, and had the money, people could buy a cow, put it on the common, and go down and milk it. My family did not think this 'Victorian English' practice was a good idea. This may have been because we did not have enough money to buy a cow! However, I used often to go down there just for fun. On one of these occasions I found a cremation in progress. An itinerant hawker, most probably Indian, had died in the town and this was his burial ceremony. I thought it very strange that people should be 'burned up' instead of buried. When I asked my Mum about it, she simply said, 'That is what they believe in their culture'. This was the first time I can ever recall hearing the word 'culture' mentioned.

Growing up in Finley, I encountered 'culture' in another context. As I walked to school each day I used to pass a little house on the side of the dirt road, further along our street. At the back of the house there was a cowshed. There was a First Peoples family living there. We Deakins might have thought of ourselves as poor, but these people were *really* poor. There must have been eight or nine people living in the cowshed. Every now and then they would fight among themselves. Over time, however, I got to know the kids who lived there and we became good friends. This was despite the warning from my mother that 'they are not nice people', to which I used to say: 'They're fine. They talk like everyone else'.

What struck me about my new friends was that, despite being really poor, they were different, they were really different. They had a pride in their family's extensive tribal relations with what they called 'the country of our ancestors', and with their history and culture. Most likely they were Wiradjuri people. All of these Aboriginal friends are dead now – the majority killed in car accidents. My friendship with the Aborigines in Finley made a big impression on me. It raised questions in my mind about why people are so different, which I had difficulty formulating at the time, and little hope of answering. One thing I did take away from my Aboriginal experience is that Finley and its surrounds are 'my country', and I still love to return there for the peace it offers. Friendship was the soil in which the idea of 'culture' was planted in my mind. It would take some years to germinate, but it was a beginning that I made myself.

★

There were two schools in Finley, the State school and the much smaller St. Joseph's Catholic school. The Catholic school had about three dozen students from Grade 1 to Grade 6, taught by two Mercy Sisters. To my young mind they were the only people who came to the town specifically to do good. On the weekend the Sisters would go visiting 'the poor' – which, according to my mother, meant the 'very poor'! Somehow the Sisters always had a little parcel of food with them. I found out only later that the Nuns we so poor themselves that they went without meals from time to time because there was no money. As school kids we had to pay sixpence a week 'school money', and sixpence multiplied by thirty-six kids would not have gone far.

Even as a kid I was always interested in learning. Maybe this was part of the Deakin legacy I inherited from my great-grandfather. When he came from England, he brought his library of books with him. I still have two of his books – one is an early edition of the plays of William Shakespeare, and the other is the speeches of Edmund Burke.

Thanks to my mother's encouragement and her great love of reading, I could read before I went to school. The first book I ever read was about George Washington cutting down the cherry tree - a political thriller if ever there was one. Because I could read, and possibly because I was a handful at home, always asking questions, I was able to start school at four and a half, which was unusual even in those days.

The Catholic Church and the school were taken-for-granted parts of our life in Finley. There was no resident priest in the town. We were part of the Jerilderie parish. My father, Stan, was a Catholic and proud of it. His father had been an English Catholic at a time when being Catholic in England was a serious social impediment. This may have been why they emigrated - new country, new opportunities. My mother was not Catholic. She had strong faith in God, which she needed.

In the Depression years the Church played an important role in people's lives because life was just so precarious, especially for young children. Rates of child mortality were quite high. Medical services such as we take for granted today were unavailable, or unaffordable even when they were available. What services there were in small NSW country towns were fairly basic. This was certainly true in Finley.

Partly as a consequence, our family was hit by tragedy three times while we were there. My eldest brother, the firstborn, lived for only a short time. My immediate elder brother died in 1933 on my first birthday. He was two and a half. He was the second child in the Deakin family to die. This left me as the eldest in the family. Another brother was born in Finley, but he too died when I was about four and a half. One can only imagine the pain these events caused our parents. Fortunately, my younger sister, Nanette, and I were of an age that we did not fully grasp what was happening. However, you sensed somehow that, if life was precarious, it was also valuable. The love we both received at home clearly showed this. Later when we moved to Melbourne, two more children, Robin and Valerie were born.

*

My mother's character was formed by tragedy. She had a strong faith in God, a legacy of her Jewish ancestry, and of her early Methodist upbringing. As a young woman she learned to depend on it. It was her father's ancestry which was Jewish. He belonged to a family who migrated to England from Portugal some time in the nineteenth century. Ruby was a direct descendant of the British economist, David Ricardo, one of the founding figures of modern capitalist theory. She grew up in Nagambie in central Victoria, a district famous for its lake and wineries. My mother's father died quite young leaving his wife, Elizabeth, with three young children to raise. Elizabeth later married John Mitchell who worked as a blacksmith at the Nagambie forge. The Mitchells had another son, Edward. On completing school, my mother moved to Melbourne and worked at the Caulfield hospital.

In 1924 she invited her friend, Jessie Duncan, to spend the Christmas-New Year break with the family in Nagambie. Two days after Christmas the family organised a picnic. The idea was to row from the moorings part-way across the lake and a short distance up the Goulburn River to a quiet picnic spot. The group included Ruby's mother, Elizabeth, and step-father, John Mitchell, Jessie Duncan, and one of my mother's friends from Nagambie, Emily Forrest. As well there were two excited nine-year-olds - Edward and Emily's brother, Charles. John Mitchell was a powerful man and had no trouble rowing the party to a well-protected spot for their picnic where the group spent a lazy summer afternoon. At about 6:00pm they packed up their picnic gear for the return journey, and set out for home.

In the course of the afternoon, a southerly wind had blown up. It did not affect rowing on the river, but created a swell on the lake. When the boat moved out from the protection of the riverbank, it was hit by the combination of wind and rough water. When it began to take on water, the people in the boat moved, causing it to overturn, and everyone was thrown into the water. Unfortunately only two of the seven on board, Ruby and John, could swim.

My mother, most likely on her father's instructions, set out for the shore two hundred metres away, and ran to get help. In the meantime John got his wife, Elizabeth, to shore. He then swam back out into the lake to find Edward, and in the process perished. To compound events, Elizabeth recovered, but then collapsed, as she watched the tragedy unfold before her eyes. In doing so she fell back into the shallow water at the lake's edge where she drowned. When Ruby arrived back with help there was only one other survivor, her friend Jessica who had the presence of mind to grab hold of the upturned boat as it passed her and was blown to shore by the strong wind. When my mother got up that morning she had a family; by nightfall she was an orphan.

The incident had two legacies that became important in my life. Whenever we drove back to Finley, my mother would never let me take the route through Nagambie. That was until one day I said to her, 'Let's go to the Nagambie cemetery and find the graves of the people I am named after'. My full name is Hilton Forrest Deakin. We did this, and after that her fear of Nagambie and its traumatic memories began to recede. For my mother this was a hard beginning. The 'Nagambie Tragedy', as it was called in the papers, was reported nationwide.

Unfortunately, tragedy is endemic in human life. We are constantly challenged to make sense of it and to respond to it. This almost always involves taking the initiative, that is, making a beginning, however modest. Without this step we risk becoming another of tragedy's victims. As a priest you are regularly called upon to help families negotiate tragedies in their lives. It is part of the territory. You have to help people make a first step. In such circumstances, trying to interpret what has happened, however well-intentioned, is rarely helpful. Doing something to help another is what makes the difference. Without this, trauma can stay around as the elephant in the room for years. I always had the example of my mother to convince me of this. Her experience taught me a valuable lesson in how human beings function in times of tragedy. The lesson was to come to me again and again as I was confronted by the appalling human suffering of the East Timorese, both those in East Timor and those in Australia, as their country made the long and slow journey to nationhood. There is a lot of wisdom in Potok's comment that 'all beginnings are hard'. What he could also have added, and what experience has taught me, is that we are also the product of the beginnings we make ourselves.

★

With the outbreak of World War II my father 'joined up'. Like so many other rural workers who had laboured on national projects during the Depression, military service offered not only an escape from grinding labor, but the prospect of adventure and a chance to 'see the world'. More importantly, it also meant a steady income for the family back at home.

Our family story intersects with that of the Second World War at a number of points. My father saw military service in the Middle East. He fought in what is present-day Israel, and later in New Guinea. His brother, Alfred, fought in Europe, was captured by the Germans, and spent the last years of the war in a prisoner-of-war camp. One of my younger cousins took part in the allied landing at Balikpapan (today a city in East Kalimantan), one of the last engagements of the war. He was killed there, beheaded by the Japanese in 1945. I was thirteen when this shocking news came through.

When my father enlisted, my mother decided that the time had come to leave Finley. In her view, after the war, there would be very few opportunities for him to come back to in Finley. All the new opportunities would come in the big cities. So we moved to Melbourne and stayed at first with relatives in Thornbury which is to the north of the city.

I can still recall the sense of wonder I felt in coming to Melbourne. I was eleven at the time, and I had never seen an electric tram or an electric train. Neither had I seen the sea or ever been to 'the pictures'. For me, Melbourne seemed a magic world. However, the country was at war and we were soon reminded of present realities if we forgot to put up the blackout shutters at night. 'We don't want the Japanese to bomb the place', the adults would say. Such was the fear. It was justified, although not in the way we thought. It came out only later that the Japanese had been bombing along the coast of Western and northern Australia, and there were submarines caught and sunk in Sydney harbour. In the area of Western Australia where I was later to do my doctoral research, Kalumburu, six Aborigines and a missionary were killed by the Japanese bombing.

In those days young people were brought up to think that 'the Japs' and 'the Germans' were dreadful people. This message was reinforced by movies in the mid-1940s that specialised in caricatures of both races. I went to see lots of movies at this time, often with my mother who really enjoyed going to the cinema.

CHAPTER 4
MAKING A NEW BEGINNING: SCHOOL YEARS

When we moved to Melbourne a new chapter in my life opened up. My mother enrolled me at Our Lady of Lourdes Primary School in Thornbury which was then run by the Good Samaritan Sisters. My teacher, Sister Agnes Canning, recognised that I could sing, and that I had what she called 'perfect pitch'. I did not understand what that meant at the time. Sister Agnes called my mother and suggested that I should audition for the cathedral choir. She helped arrange this, and I was accepted. Winning a place in the cathedral choir was a really important new beginning for me. It opened a door that led into the world of music, and I willingly ran through it.

The story of the Melbourne cathedral choir can be traced back to 1858. The choir pre-dates St Patrick's Cathedral. However, for most of its history it was functional and quite unambitious in its achievements. In 1939 this changed. In that year the Vienna Mozart Boys Choir and its Director were trapped in Melbourne by the outbreak of the Second World War. Archbishop Mannix made them welcome and helped the members, many of whom were teenagers, find billets with Catholic families. In return, the group became the backbone of a revitalised Cathedral choir. Mannix appointed its Director, Georg Gruber, as the new St. Patrick's Cathedral choirmaster.[1] Many of the visiting choir's members settled in Australia after the war. From 1939 onwards Mozart's religious music became the order of the day in the Cathedral, and lifted the quality of the liturgies celebrated there, as Archbishop Mannix had hoped it would.

In the 1940s a local priest, Dr Percy Jones, who had trained overseas and gained a doctorate in sacred music, became the choirmaster. He introduced the *a cappella* form of polyphony, and extended the choir's repertoire. Recordings ensured that its achievements were put firmly on the Australian cultural map. By the late 1940s the cathedral choir was world famous. This was no easy feat, not least because a sustainable means had to be found to replace boy sopranos once their voices 'broke' in their early teens. With the support of the Christian Brothers who ran the schools close to the cathedral, a scholarship program was created, so that by the time we moved to Thornbury, boy sopranos were recruited from the Catholic primary schools around central Melbourne. They were given a scholarship

---

[1] Gruber's personal history was complex and scandalous. In 1941 he was interned on the grounds of being a Nazi. Several years later, after the war, he was deported. He completed his musical career in South Africa. James Griffin *Daniel Mannix: Beyond the Myths* (Mulgrave: Garratt Publishing, 2012), 268-9.

covering their school fees for as long as they sang in the choir.

This was how I came to attend St Patrick's Primary School in North Fitzroy, which in those days went up to Year 8. My scholarship was then extended to include secondary schooling at Parade College, also run by the Christian Brothers. This was a great help to my parents at the time, as school fees were a big drain on the family's limited finances.

Percy Jones was brilliant at getting the best out of the choir. In part this was due to his knowledge and skill as a musician, but equally it was because he had a personality that was just larger than life. In addition to training the choir, Percy also became Deputy Director of the Melbourne Conservatorium and, in consequence, something of a fixture in Melbourne high society. Percy was what psychologists call a 'significant other' in my life. He introduced me to music and opened up for me the beauty of the Church's artistic heritage. I always got on well with him, and he really liked my mother, who in the early years accompanied me to the cathedral when we sang there. He seemed fascinated by what she knew, and listened carefully to what she had to say. Well educated himself, I think he was amazed at how knowledgeable my mother had become as a result of her reading.

★

Percy Jones put the St Patrick's cathedral choir on the Australian cultural map by dint of hard work.[2] Being a member of the choir was personally demanding, and you really had to love music to stick with it. We mostly sang *a cappella* and this requires great concentration, so the practice regime and time commitment were demanding. The choir sang in the cathedral at the main Sunday Mass in the morning, and then returned on Sunday evening to sing compline. This meant that I made the journey from Thornbury to the cathedral twice each Sunday.

Being a member of the choir had some useful spin-offs. For instance, by the end of my first year, I was able to read Latin and make sense of Gregorian chant notation. More importantly I found myself immersed in a world of music and I loved it. I persuaded my mother, despite our limited finances, to buy a family piano, and practised assiduously. I played for many years, even studying piano at the Melbourne Conservatorium. I gave it up only when the arthritis in my fingers made playing impossible.

The cathedral choir played an important role in Catholic worship, and added significantly to the grandeur of the religious ceremonies this embraces. The liturgy reached a peak at Easter when the choir sang at the cathedral for four days on end. The Easter liturgies were presided over by the tall, gaunt and aged figure of the Archbishop, Dr Daniel Mannix. He never seemed to smile, and would just sit there immobile during services, rather like one of the cathedral pillars. I used to wonder sometimes if he was even awake!

When my voice broke I was lucky, as I quickly emerged as a tenor, and so was able to keep singing. However, when I decided to become a priest I was forced to make a difficult

---

2   The Second Vatican Council (1962-65) reformed the Catholic liturgy, which up till then was celebrated in Latin. One consequence of the reforms was that the Mass was celebrated in English so that people could understand it. This spelled the death knell for the type of music that Dr Jones had pioneered. He had little time for the new liturgical music, and died an unhappy man, seeing his classical repertoire displaced by something he regarded as massively inferior. He saw his life's work with the Cathedral choir turn to dust.

choice. The voice training you need to become a good tenor runs contrary to the training you need to become a good preacher. As a priest I had to find my voice, literally!

★

After completing Grade 8 at St Patrick's, I transferred to Parade College where I had some remarkable Christian Brothers as my senior teachers. One of these stands out, Br Leo Nelson. Because of his stocky appearance and aggressive manner we used to call him 'Pug', but never when he was within earshot! Br Nelson had just returned to Australia. He had been asked by the Brothers to go to India and then to South Africa to help set up new secondary schools in those countries. I remember him as being very interested in Catholic social teaching and the questions this raised. Br Nelson was proud of his working-class background, having grown up in Collingwood. He was a teacher with the Education Department before he joined the Brothers, and was one of the few Brothers to have graduated from University. Every Monday he would bring the editorial piece from *The Age* into class and have us dissect it. He showed us how the arguments presented were structured, and how they often carried implicit assumptions and unacknowledged biases. Long before the post-moderns, Brother Nelson was into 'deconstruction'. It was a challenging skill, but a very useful one to acquire.

★

In the early 1950s people grew genuinely concerned about the sort of country Australia was becoming. Peace had finally arrived and life was settling down. Major changes had occurred but their impact had not really been assessed. World War II brought certain social divisions to an end. Women had discovered a new place in society. There was no going back. As a new generation of Catholics moved up the social scale in the post-war years they wanted a role in shaping society. The Brothers encouraged us to share this aspiration. So when one of them asked for volunteers to sell the *Catholic Worker* on Saturday afternoons, I put up my hand and so began my monthly pilgrimage to the steps of Flinders Street Station.

The *Catholic Worker* contained a rich diet of intellectually stimulating commentary on how Catholic social principles could be put into action. The paper sought to give faith a context. It was through the *Catholic Worker* I first learned about Bob Santamaria, then the most powerful Catholic layman in Australia. The paper was produced by a group of educated laymen who belonged to the Catholic Worker Movement established in the United States during the Depression. This movement tried to carve out a pathway that was both anti-communist and anti-capitalist. It was part of a wider movement in the Church at the time called Catholic Action.

★

'Catholic Action' was a term that Pope Pius XII used to encourage Catholics to become actively involved in contributing to the new world that was coming into being as Europe was reconstructed out of the ashes of war. In Australia it became a movement with many facets. One was the fight against communism. However in some Church quarters anything left-wing was tagged with the label of 'communist'. So Catholic Action ran the risk of being co-opted by right-wing political interests.

Another facet was concern about church-state relationships. Here some groups were mesmerised by the ideal of a Christian state (which some bishops saw as a good idea). However, the models of this in Spain and Portugal were not encouraging. So a fierce debate developed, and the *Catholic Worker* provided a forum for new ideas to emerge. For a teenager, following this debate as it unfolded was heady stuff. At the heart of the issue was a bigger question: What does it mean to be Catholic in the new social environment that is emerging?

In the 1950s the bishops were clearly divided on how to answer this question. In Sydney they took a *reactive* stance. There, 'Catholic Action' was concerned with *the quality of Catholic life in parishes*. So priests concentrated on building up the Catholic community, creating sporting and social outlets for Catholics that protected them from dangers known collectively as 'the world'. This model placed Catholic Action under the control of the clergy and represented a quite closed Catholic view of the world.

A different Catholic worldview emerged in Melbourne where Archbishop Mannix took a quite *proactive* stance interpreting Catholic Action as *the independent action of ordinary Catholics to change the circumstances in which they lived*. However even here, there were two schools of thought.

The first was that generally associated with the Young Christian Workers (YCW) movement. It understood Catholic Action as the action of individual Catholics to bring about change in all the situations in which they found themselves, using the methodology of 'see, judge and then act'. The second school was that of Bob Santamaria and his followers who interpreted Catholic Action in terms of change brought about by collective political action. Many Bishops were very nervous about this development. For many of them, Catholic Action was non-political. They were much happier with the Sydney and YCW models than with that of B.A. Santamaria.

So when Catholics began to think about the sort of Australia they wanted to live in once the war was over, there was a range of options with respect not only to the vision on offer, but also with respect to the best ways to achieve whatever vision was espoused. This applied to the Bishops as well as to the lay folk. The *Catholic Worker,* by canvassing all sides of this debate as it unfolded, provided me with a wonderful political education.

Mannix was the leader of a small group of bishops seeking to address issues of 'structural injustice' long before this term was introduced into the Catholic lexicon. In his view Catholics of all political persuasions had little option but to become involved in the political debate and in the political action required to shape Australian society according to social justice principles. He wanted Catholics out in the public square. However, he realised that to be effective there they had to be well-educated, so we were encouraged at school to matriculate and go on to university studies. This news was joy to our young ears. I used to find it hard to reconcile Mannix the social activist with the gaunt immobile figure I saw at high Mass every Sunday.

While I was selling the *Catholic Worker* on one end of the steps to Flinders Street station, my opposition was the man selling *The Rock*, a virulently anti-Catholic Presbyterian paper, at the other end. Over the years we came to swap yarns and papers, and learned to respect each other, even as we held each other to be on the wrong side!

★

I was not blessed with much athletic ability. Since this made me a tad unusual at a Christian Brothers' school, I set about creating some alternative outlets for my energy. In the 1950s schools did not have libraries as they do today. If you wanted to find something out you had to find a library.

At Parade we were blessed in that the Victorian State Library was a short tram ride from the College. During my five years at Parade, my friend Mick Hunt and I decamped from school to the library's wonderful Reading Room each Friday. There, under the lofty roof with its huge domed skylight, and surrounded by walls lined three storeys high with books, we sat and read, our books illuminated by the brass bankers' lamps on our desk. As the sun went down, the room would be lit by the eerie green light of the reading lamps shining in the enveloping gloom. In this cosy and silent world it was easy to concentrate. Here I developed a hobby that was to become a passion - reading.

The State Library was a fantastic resource. I think I read everything available about the indigenous groups in Australia, their histories and their cultures. I came to understand why the term 'Aborigine' is a European misnomer. It is a word that pushes together peoples who are different, and who can be properly understood only when their cultural singularities, particularly their cultural myths and values, are taken into account. In the 1950s few whites in Melbourne had encountered anyone of indigenous origin, and most of my fellow students would have thought that 'Aborigines' spoke 'Aborigine' in much the same way as Australians spoke English.

My reading at the time came to include most of the anthropology texts I would later be called on to read in my studies of anthropology at Monash University two decades later. I was also able to find and read, in English translation, books on politics that would definitely not have been approved at Parade College. These gave me an entirely new perspective on politics from the ones I read about in the *Catholic Worker*.

Mick and I would abandon the public library just in time to catch the last tram home. These were exciting times for us intellectually. We just hoped there would still be something to eat when we got home!

★

In my first year at Parade, a junior St Vincent de Paul group was formed to help poor people. I joined up. Our main project was visiting the kids in a public hospital up the road from the school. This was called The Eye and Ear Hospital. It cared for poor inner-city kids with eye conditions and hearing problems. Rich kids were treated at the nearby private hospitals.

The annual highlight in my three years with this group came at Christmas when I played Santa Claus for the kids. In their imagination Santa came down from the roof because this is where he parked his reindeer and sleigh. The challenge for us was to make this happen, and so sustain the Santa myth for these young kids.

The Melbourne Fire Brigade, which was based next to the hospital, came to our rescue. The firemen lifted me onto the hospital roof using the extension ladder on one of the firetrucks. People today would have a fit if you suggested doing this, but at the time it was all taken as par for the course if sick kids were involved. It was great to see their joyful faces as we played out our Christmas pantomime. The Parade group met the children's parents who were part of the occasion. We all knew that we were doing something very worthwhile. The precarious nature of this annual adventure enabled me to rule out fireman as a possible future career!

The other St Vincent De Paul activity was to visit the Little Sisters Nursing Home in Northcote. Once a fortnight two of us visited, taking with us a supply of cigarettes, lollies and newspapers funded by the College. We would give these out to the patients and have a yarn with them. We visited about six people each time, and then would catch the five o'clock tram home to West Preston. While we helped a lot of old people in this way, we also learned a lot about life just from listening to their stories. Some were quite remarkable people.

*

My father was something of a fixture at our local parish Church, St Raphael's in West Preston, and when he told our local parish priest, Fr Leo O'Rourke, about my St Vincent de Paul visits, he recruited me to help him. When I went to confession one Saturday morning he caught up with me afterwards and asked, 'Hilton, what are you doing this afternoon?' 'Nothing much.' 'Good, then will you give me a hand?' 'Sure, Father.'

On a Saturday, Leo would set out in his car about midday and do the rounds of the local butchers, bakers and greengrocers who were closing up shop for the weekend. They would give him food packed in boxes. This was food they could not keep over the weekend. We would take the boxes back to the presbytery and sort the food out into another set of boxes labelled for certain families. The rest of the afternoon was spent delivering these boxes.

Leo always knew who was ill, who had just died, whose father was in jail, and so on. As Parish Priest he had his finger on the pulse of the parish when it came to need. He never made known how he spent his Saturday afternoons. I found his example inspiring. His quiet action gave 'preaching the Gospel' a very practical orientation for me. I discovered later that he personally paid the school fees for four, and sometimes five students, so enabling them to continue their Catholic education when trouble struck the family. When he died, the priests he played cards with were bereft, not only because they had lost a dear friend, but also because he owed them so much money!

Fr O'Rourke introduced me to the *service dimension of priesthood,* something that, despite all my long association with the Cathedral, I had not given much thought to at all. The Cathedral was about *the cultic dimension of priesthood*. While the latter is very public, the former is quite private. These two sets of experiences helped me gain a deeper understanding of what 'being Catholic' means. This was quite different from the Irish emphasis of the time that understood 'being Catholic' mainly in devotional terms. As someone with no Irish heritage in his background, I always found the 'Irishness' of the Australian Church jarring, and in the 1950s, it left me cold.

My connection to the *Catholic Worker* group had another important consequence. While I was still at school, I was asked by the Catholic Evidence Guild to become one of their speakers. I am not quite sure how this happened, but it certainly was an important beginning that introduced me to the confused social space we now call 'the public square'. In pre-television days, the public square had a physical location in Melbourne called Yarra Bend. It was in Batman Avenue. It has disappeared now, incorporated into the Melbourne Tennis Centre.

Yarra Bend was a place for public speeches and debates that were often very lively, and so could be highly entertaining. A crowd would gather there on a Sunday afternoon, and both protagonists and antagonists for various causes would come prepared to speak to whatever crowd they could draw. Interjections and sharp repartee were often the order of the day. The Catholic Evidence Guild was a fixture at this venue. As a seventeen-year-old, I cut my teeth as an orator in this demanding environment.

My training with the Guild was as the third speaker of the night at the Guild's secondary stand on the corner of Elizabeth and Collins streets. Speaking on a soapbox to a public audience requires training. You have to learn to use short sentences, short words, and to keep it tight, no matter what the topic. If you made a success of speaking at this venue where your audience was usually sober, then you graduated to the Yarra Bend where you sank or swam on your wits and your preparation. Catholic Evidence Guild speakers really had to know their stuff and develop a thick skin. *Sheehan's Apologetics*[3] taught you how to deal with all the usual objections to Catholic Church teaching. We studied this at school, which was a help. A thick skin was needed because other speakers, as well as people in the audience, would run interference on you. We also attracted our fair share of abusive drunks as well. Yarra Bend was no place for the faint-hearted.

In school we read about Catholic positions and had our in-class arguments about them. Defending Catholic positions in a very public forum, and in the face of hostile attacks, was something else. My Yarra Bend experiences forced me to do some very serious thinking.

Long before the Labor Party Split in 1955, I began to see that there would be major dangers ahead if religion and politics were conflated. History tells us clearly enough how religion has co-opted politics to its cause. But the converse is also true, and I was not convinced that Santamaria's Movement was not using the Church to achieve political goals under the guise of 'fighting communism'. Was the eventual aim to take over the Labor Party and use this as a means to take over the Government? My dad, who was the gentlest of men, and a great Labor man, was suspicious of this and simply could not abide Santamaria. As I grew up I came to share his view.[4] Our beginnings shape who we are!

Criticising Santamaria in Melbourne did not make me many friends in those days. If

---

3   The popular name for a book entitled *Apologetics and Catholic Doctrine*. This famous text by Archbishop Michael Sheehan was published originally by M.H. Gill & Son, Dublin in 1918. It was used in many English-speaking Catholic high schools and colleges over many decades.
4   The Catholic Action controversy that unfolded in my teenage years is well covered in Gerard Henderson's *Mr Santamaria and the Bishops* (Sydney: Studies in the Christian Movement, 1982) and in Bruce Duncan's masterly *Crusade or Conspiracy? Catholics and the Anti-communist Struggle in Australia* (Sydney: UNSW Press, 2001).

you did not believe unreservedly in what Santamaria said, you were not seen as a 'real Catholic', so I was counted among the damned even as a seventeen-year-old!

★

A cultural anthropologist might say that I had a very particular, even unique, enculturation and, looking back, it would be hard to disagree. Was it all a matter of chance, or was something else at work?

My beginnings were certainly laced with 'moments of destiny': being born in a country town during the Depression; befriending Aboriginal people as a young person rather than later in life; growing up in a loving, albeit poor family; becoming part of the Cathedral choir; completing my secondary education in the euphoria of the post-war years; meeting with some of the extraordinary people leading the Catholic Action movement; being able to camp out in the State Library to my heart's content; and coming to appreciate Leo O'Rourke's quiet form of service to his community. These moments all made an important contribution to my beginning, and they all, each in its own way, shaped who I became. They enabled me to find my voice, both literally and figuratively and also shaped how I later responded to the Timorese.

Many of my beginnings were hard. Of course, some of them were the result of my own choices. In this sense one of the 'hardest' of them all was to join the seminary.

CHAPTER 5
MORE NEW BEGINNINGS: SEMINARY YEARS

The Christian Brothers who taught me wanted their students to become thinking Catholic men. I had thought at times about being a priest, but had rarely talked to anyone about it. My range of interests and levels of engagement in 'things Catholic' led the Brothers to more or less take for granted that on finishing school I would be entering the seminary. Parade College was famous for producing priests and brothers, four or five a year. This was amazing for a school with about eighty in the two top classes.

I did decide to study for the priesthood, and chose the diocesan seminary. Unlike the situation today, in 1951 the seminary at Werribee was full. There were over one hundred and thirty students ranging from the very brilliant to the academically ordinary. We were packed in. The number of seminarians reflected Catholic life at the time. There was a sense of optimism and hope abroad, so that working for the Church captured the imagination of young people in a way that has rarely happened since. In the late '50s and early '60s there was a spike in vocations, not only to the priesthood but also to the religious congregations. As well, many Catholic lay people volunteered to work in First Peoples' communities.[1] It was an extraordinary time.

★

Archbishop Mannix invited the Jesuits to staff the seminary, and they had been in place for a good while by the time I arrived. Clerical education in the 1950s was very formal. There was an extraordinary emphasis placed on rote learning and deductive reasoning. It was an education designed to produce parrots rather than thinking Catholic men. The contrast with what we had received from the Christian Brothers at Parade could not have been more marked. We were being trained to think within a box. Those that the professors regarded as 'brilliant' were the ones with the best memories. Thinking and social analysis were irrelevant to Jesuit seminary education in those days. Our professors lived within the cultural horizon of pre-war Catholicism.

After the excitement of my times at Parade and with the Catholic Evidence Guild, the seminary was the intellectual equivalent of a cold shower. The sad thing was that

---

[1] The phrase 'First Peoples' acknowledges Aborigines as the first inhabitants of this country. Elsewhere in the book the term 'Aborigines' is used. Where an adjective is required, 'Aboriginal' is the term used.

this intellectually murky and undemanding world suited so many of the students. Those considered 'brilliant' and 'the future of the Church' could rattle off thesis after thesis without necessarily understanding what these were about. For me, most of what we were taught had little to do either with proclaiming the Gospel or even with real life situations. I had been transported to another planet where the aborigines spoke in Latin. We had been projected into the clerical socialisation process.

★

At school we had been taught to think inductively, working up and out from the evidence. In the seminary you were taught to think deductively, working down from some existing opinion, so conclusions could be drawn without reference to any real life situations. To succeed in this Alice in Wonderland world, some of us had to unlearn most of what we had learned in the last years of school. Of course our professors did not see the matter this way. They existed in their own detached world.

I found the way the seminary approached moral theology difficult to cope with, and Canon Law a very scary country indeed. What I also found frustrating was that the professors seemed so convinced of the rectitude of their reasoning that there was no possibility of dialogue. Power was used to suppress argument, and this is always dangerous. The strictures that were placed on us intellectually came as a real shock to me. For instance, the books available to us in the seminary library were heavily controlled. It was not an open library; it was a very ecclesiastical library. If you wanted to keep current in your reading, then you had little option but to smuggle books in, which I did.

In First Year reading kept me sane. I had my 'Russian period', and in the course of the year I read about forty Russian novels. Some of these I found in the Werribee public library, others in bookshops. I set out on the long journey to Dostoevsky through Tolstoy. The works of these great authors could not be included in the seminary library because they were 'written by non-Catholics'. Such was the mentality at Werribee. The Old Testament could have been excluded using that criterion!

★

Another trial at Werribee was the spirituality imposed on us there. I had always been attracted to the Franciscan style of spirituality, and if I had ever been tempted to join an order, I might have been a Franciscan. As to the possibility of being a Jesuit, I would have had to say, as we did in the Latin Mass, *Domine non sum dignus* (Lord, I am not worthy)!

The Jesuits naturally had a very high regard for their own spirituality. Across the period of our training our Jesuit professors required us to read a series of books dealing with the life of Christ, all written by fellow Jesuits. Maybe this strategy was designed to convince us that Jesus was a Jesuit! It seemed to me a bad case of putting the cart before the horse. All we really learned from the exercise was how Jesuits at the time thought. After eight years of Jesuit spirituality, I was glad to escape it. I then had to face the challenge of developing a spirituality appropriate to a diocesan priest. Fortunately I did not have to start from scratch, because the good thing about Jesuit training was that it taught you how to pray and develop habits of prayer without which ministry lacks authenticity.

As often happens in a closed religious world, some of the best formation we received in the seminary occurred by accident, that is as the consequence of relationships built up among the students. Individuals took on informal leadership roles and strongly influenced their peers. In this respect Damien Heath, who was later to become something of a *bete noir* for Australian Catholic Bishops, was outstanding. He was a genuine intellectual, someone who could become physically excited about new ideas. Long before Vatican II he was talking liturgical reform and about what was happening in France. He could read French and used to get new books written in French that he would break open for us. Damien introduced us to the Catholic intellectual world emerging in France, particularly to what would later be called the 'new theology' movement. We heard nothing of this from our professors.

I was fortunate to arrive at the seminary as scripture study began to take on board new developments in scholarship. Pope Pius XII knew that the Catholic embargo on using historical and literary methods in the study of scripture was no longer sustainable. In 1943 he lifted the embargo and Catholic scholars were permitted to use the historical and exegetical methods pioneered by their Protestant counterparts. By the early 1950s the results were starting to filter through, and this opened up a new world for us as seminarians. The days of literal reading of the Bible had come to an end. We were among the first group of seminarians to be taught what the new methods were, and discover the new questions being posed by Catholic scripture scholars. This was as close as we got to the frontiers of learning in eight years of seminary training – an oasis in the desert.

Students seemed to recognise more quickly than many of our Jesuit professors that a life of Christ could not be put together using the Gospels as if they were historical texts. This realization sharpened our critique of Jesuit spirituality, at least the Werribee version of it.

★

The professor handling Catholic social teaching was Charles Mayne SJ. Before coming to the seminary he had been very active in the Catholic Action movement, particularly with the approach used by the YCW. He opened us to the YCW's social analysis approach using the See, Judge, Act methodology.

Santamaria also had his finger in the seminary pie. He gave an annual lecture to final year seminarians just before their ordination. The rest of us could attend if we wished, which some of us did. Santamaria always spoke about his vision for the future of the Church. However, thanks to Damien Heath some of us were already exploring an alternative vision, that of Cardinal Emmanuel Suhard, Archbishop of Paris. Suhard had just published two influential pastoral letters – *The Church Today: Growth or Decline* (1948), and *Priests among Men* (1949).

Suhard was grappling with many of the same questions the Australian Bishops had tried to address in their social justice statements – the role of the Church in the modern world and the relationship between the Church and politics as changing social and economic conditions marginalised an increasing number of people. Even today, his writing is inspiring. Based largely in the thinking of Catholic philosopher Jacques Maritain, his thinking added something new to the debates going on in Australia.

Suhard was interested in trialling new ways in which the Church could reach out to and engage with working people. For instance, he supported the Young Christian Worker movement and commissioned a study of the Church in France that was published in 1943 under the challenging title *France: A Mission Country?*[2] This had quite an impact worldwide as it challenged the notion that France was 'a Catholic country'. The study suggested that the Church there was called upon, as a matter of absolute urgency, to be more missionary and outward-looking in its efforts to evangelise. These were developments that really piqued our interest – I loved reading Suhard - but I was always haunted by the thought that these were European writers writing about a Church in another country. Before long, our generation would have to deal with the same issues in Australia.

The worker-priest movement saw priests getting jobs working in factories for wages, and sharing the lot of their fellow workers. The priests undertook this role to express the Church's solidarity with the workers, most of whom had given the Church away. It was a quite revolutionary pastoral strategy. We were fed only little titbits about it in our lectures. We found out quite by accident that when one of the worker priests said Mass in French in the factory for his fellow-workers, Pope Pius XII personally banned him from ever saying Mass again.

In Rome's view, pastoral strategies had to conform to the law. Latin was the language of the Mass in 1952 and that was the law. People seemed a secondary factor. I often wondered what happened to that priest because, only a decade and a half later, all priests were celebrating the Mass in the vernacular. He certainly wasn't wrong in his pastoral orientation, and subsequent events would make the Pope's action look draconian.

A major problem for the worker-priests was that they were better educated than other factory workers of the era and soon became involved in the labour movement as leaders and not simply as workers. Then they had to decide how far they could go in this leadership role before they compromised their position as priests. The whole experiment hinged on resolving that dilemma. They had to ask themselves questions we were all wrestling with at the time: What does it mean to be a priest? What are the limits of my calling as a priest?

As young men studying for the priesthood these seemed very relevant questions to us. The worker-priests' experiences put some serious questions to the Catholic tradition.[3]

★

The central task of seminary training is learning what it means to be a priest. This is not something that others can simply pump into you; it is something that you have to discover for yourself. The meaning you discover in the seminary is rarely final, as the meaning of priesthood continues to unfold as you face up to the challenges of active ministry.

As a member of the choir, I was well aware of the pecking order among the clergy. This was most evident when the big Masses were celebrated. The processions could include archbishops, bishops, monsignors, priests and so on, all of whom knew their place in the ordered ranks, always with Dr Mannix bringing up the rear. The idea that there was a

---

2 Henri Godin and Yves Daniel *La France: Pays de Mission?* (Paris: Editions de Cerf, 1943)
3 In the 1970s I was able to stay in one of the parishes in Paris where the worker priests were based, and discuss the movement in some detail with them. The worker priest movement was eventually abandoned.

cultic dimension to priesthood was implanted in my head from a very tender age. At the same time I knew there was much more to it than that. There was the example of Fr Leo in West Preston who took food to hungry people and put kids through school on his meagre stipend. The service dimension of priesthood has always attracted me.

I have had a deep love of the Mass and the liturgy since my childhood days. Jesus, the person in the Gospels, has a strong hold on my mind and heart. My devotion to Mary has always been qualified by the centrality of Jesus. This runs counter to some forms of European spirituality which I encountered growing up, but is an important aspect of English Catholic spirituality where it seems to me the head and heart come together a bit more solidly.

Spirituality is another important dimension of priesthood. Here, I believe, the seminary let us down. The professors were not training diocesan priests to make sense of their ministry within a spirituality that was appropriate to the way in which diocesan priests actually live. As seminarians many of us rejected the notion of becoming pseudo-Jesuits, and this created tensions. These boiled over when one of the professors discovered me reading a book called *The Diocesan Priest* by French priest Eugene Masure.[4] He was far from happy.

Masure was a diocesan priest who wanted to make sense of his life starting from his experience of actually being a diocesan priest, and not by reference to some other group's spiritual tradition. His essential argument was that a diocesan priest does not have to accept the disciplined way of praying which the Jesuits or the Benedictines use, nor does he have to understand poverty and obedience in the way these are formulated for a religious congregation. Diocesan priests need another type of spirituality, one that flows from participation in the ministry of the local bishop. It is a spirituality that needs to be built around dedication to people, openness to others, and a pastoral approach to ministry that acknowledges the complexity of issues that ordinary people face on a daily basis. It must also acknowledge that diocesan priests do not have all the answers. In fact, sometimes we do not even know half the questions! The diocesan priest always needs to keep this in mind when he preaches the Gospel. While Masure's message spoke to some of our deepest aspirations, it was stoutly rejected by those teaching us who lived in a world of the kind of certainty that we, as students, were not convinced was any longer real.

★

My eight years in the seminary were fruitful and formative, but not always in the way those running the institution intended. I emerged with a very clear understanding that the role of the priest is to *preach the Gospel*. In addition, the priest has a duty to *share the gifts of the Church* (the sacraments) with the people, and *to be of service* to them all, but most especially to the poor and to others who live on the margins. While a priest is integral to the functioning of a local Church, he also has to be linked to the global Church, to the peoples who comprise it, and to its mission.

How an individual priest interprets his responsibility to preach the Gospel is shaped in

---

4 Eugene Masure *The Parish Priest* (Notre Dame: Fides Publishers, 1955). This is the title of the English translation. The original French title was *Prêtres Diocésains*.

large part by the relative weight he gives to the cultic and service dimensions of his role. The balance here is shaped by his spirituality. If the cultic is taken to extremes, he becomes a 'sacristy priest' and his mission is truncated, serving only those who come to him. If the service dimension is taken to extremes, the priest becomes a social or political activist, and again his mission is truncated, and the Gospel can easily be co-opted to serve some other cause. There is always a balance point that has to be struck, and as well as spirituality, context determines where this needs to lie. As a priest moves through life, this balance point inevitably has to be re-negotiated. The priest often does this in the course of prayer. These were the important lessons I took away from eight years at Werribee.

★

During my seminary years, I kept up my interest in Australia's Aboriginal peoples and their quest for justice in their own land. I kept up my reading on Aboriginal affairs in the State Library right through my seminary years. In one holiday break I travelled to Bathurst Island where the Missionaries of the Sacred Heart (MSCs) were very kind to me, and I stayed with them for two and a half weeks.[5] Bishop O'Loughlin, himself an MSC priest, was the Bishop of Darwin at the time. I found his views on assisting Aborigines really quaint. I also visited communities in Queensland and as far north as the mission at Yarrabah. Another holiday, I used my wages as a part-time 'postie' to fly to Cairns and stayed with an indigenous family there. On that trip I was introduced to Neville Bonner, the first Aboriginal senator in the Australian parliament. At the time, and given my family background, it blew my mind to think that an indigenous person could be a Liberal senator!

Sometimes experiences stay with you for a lifetime. On a visit to Cooktown I was walking along a footpath which had a very wide gutter because of the torrential rains experienced in that part of Australia. Some Aborigines were coming the other way. There were about ten of them, adults and some children. About fifty yards in front of me they left the footpath and started walking in the gutter. I walked past wondering what was going on. I then turned around and saw them getting back onto the footpath behind me. Puzzled I walked back to them and the ensuing conversation went something like this:

'Excuse me. What did you do that for?'
'You white fella.'
'What do you mean by that?'
'You white fella on footpath. We don't walk on footpath.'
'Who told you that?'
'White fella.'
'Don't ever do that to me again. You've got as much right to walk on this footpath as I have. You're walking into town. Will you come and have a cup of tea?'
'No. We can't do that in the shops.'

---

5   The seminary functioned from March to December each year. Outside these months we were free. Many of us became temporary postal-workers or got other jobs before Christmas to fund a holiday after Christmas. This gave us extended time to catch up with our families, something that religious did not get. We also had time off during the week of the ordinations. We welcomed these breaks from the routine of seminary life.

The racial discrimination these people had to endure really smacked me between the eyes. I had seen this as a kid but we were able to talk about things then. We sat around that fire in the cowshed in Finley and laughed it off. But twenty years on so little had changed and this was no laughing matter.

My visits to Aboriginal communities were important pastoral experiences that really kept me going during my seminary days. They connected my present with my past, and for someone living in the strange landscape of a Catholic seminary in the 1950s, they were experiences that kept me grounded and were an important reality check.

★

My time in the seminary came to a stormy end in 1958 when I clashed with the Rector, Fr James McInerny SJ who had a very particular way of looking at things. By the end of my final year I became exasperated with his approach, and told him so. His words fired back at me in anger have lingered ever since: 'You will do no good! You'll end up in trouble, no doubt about it.' Of course, in a way he was right, but the sort of trouble he had in mind was not the sort I eventually got myself into. I have many people to thank for that, especially the East Timorese.

CHAPTER 6
LEARNING THE ROPES: ASSISTANT PRIEST

After the long preparation in the seminary at Werribee, I was ordained at St Patrick's cathedral by Archbishop Justin Simonds in 1958. In the 1950s a young priest served an apprenticeship as a curate under the supervision of an experienced parish priest. My first placement was at St Monica's parish in Moonee Ponds where Monsignor Vin Willis was parish priest. He had a reputation among the Melbourne clergy as something of an ecclesiastical rascal, so I did not know what to expect when I was appointed to his parish.

Life in the presbytery at St Monica's was very formal. Vin was highly conservative, and I received a stiff introduction to clerical culture, in the Irish style. Wearing your Roman collar was *de rigeur* and treated as if it had always been 'the way things are done around here', even though we knew from the seminary that the Roman collar was an invention of the eighteenth century. Secondly, the parish priest imposed a curfew which applied to his curates. I was not given a key to the front door, and if I was not in by 9:00pm the Monsignor simply locked the door. A parish priest's power over curates in those days was extraordinary.

It was hard to take a trick with 'Mons' Willis, particularly when it came to money. However, I did score one significant victory. For the first two years I was at Essendon I was not allowed to buy a car. This made moving around the parish difficult, particularly if you were called out at night to attend someone who was dying. I bought a motorbike to overcome this problem, but this had its own dangers. After I had fallen off it the third time, courtesy of inconsiderate motorists, I sold it. By this stage I had grown confident enough to tell the parish priest that in future I would not be taking any sick calls at night, and he would have to attend them instead, since he had a car and I didn't. For good measure I also added, 'If you do not want to do that then go to the Archbishop and get me moved, but also tell him that I do not have a car.'

The Parish Priest's reply was almost immediate. 'Go and get a car!' to which I replied, somewhat tongue in cheek, 'But I do not have enough money to buy one.' 'How much do you need?'

The next morning, having called his bluff, I was off to the auto dealers to get my first car. It made parish work so much easier.

★

I served a four-year apprenticeship at St Monica's. In my final year there I began doing some work in the media. In the early 1960s TV was still fairly new, and 24-hour programming did not exist. The TV channels all closed down for the night about 11:00pm. Channel 9 brought its daily programming to a close with a program called *Epilogue* – different denominations providing a short reflection on some life-issue being discussed at the time. I did this on behalf of the Catholic Church. My association with Channel 9 provided a useful introduction to how the TV medium works, and how to craft words when speaking to a mass audience, especially with no one actually present!

While some of my colleagues thought this must be exciting work, I found the reality was quite different. As a priest you work with 'live' congregations in the celebration of the Mass. You know instantly whether what you say or do is engaging people. Once you have experienced this, it is hard to re-orient yourself to talking to a camera or into a microphone with no way of gauging the impact of what you are saying. The people at home watching the Mass on their TV screens, for instance, are unaware of the actual reality you face as the celebrant talking to a camera (and often to a cameraman who is bored stiff by the lack of action in what he is filming). This was far from exciting. The work did give one a presence in the media, and with this came some useful contacts and an appreciation of how to work with media people, which would come in handy later on.

However, this work combined with what I was doing around the parish took its toll, and after three years I was happy to leave it to others. There is such a thing as getting 'crazy busy' and as a priest you have to learn when you have reached this stage and step back.

★

In 1962 I was appointed to a ministry at St Augustine's Church in central Melbourne, while being based at St. Patrick's Cathedral presbytery where I soon discovered Irish clericalism reigned supreme. The clerical caste system that I had viewed from a distance as a choirboy became something entirely different when experienced up close and personal. My problems started with my name. Deakin is not an Irish name. So I had to put up with gibes from senior clerics: 'Where did you get a name like that?' 'Why haven't you got a decent name?' And so it went on. As a young priest sitting at the bottom of the table, there was not much you could do but endure the ribbing. It did nothing for my dislike of things Irish. I was fortunate in having a young Fr Frank Little around to defend me.

After four years of hands-on ministry I was beginning to come to terms with the culture of the Melbourne clergy in the lead-up to the Second Vatican Council. Pope John XXIII called the Council in 1959, and this was followed by two and a half years of preparation. The Preparatory Commission canvassed bishops around the world to identify matters the Council should address. This was something quite new and generated a good deal of discussion among the clergy. In turn, this provided a very useful window into the clerical culture of the time.

In the early 1960s theological attitudes were still influenced by Jansenism. This was a school of Catholic thought that first developed in France in the seventeenth century and laid claims to the authority of no less a figure than St Augustine. It spread via Irish clergy who were trained in France and brought the ideas back home to Ireland. Some of these clergy came to Australia and brought Jansenist attitudes with them. Jansenism also had a major impact on Catholic spirituality and on the devotional life of the Church. As a spirituality, Jansenism takes a particularly dark view of human nature, seeing it as essentially depraved. This situation had to be overcome through ascetical practices such as doing penance, fasting etc. In Catholic practice Jansenism resulted in an exaggerated emphasis on sin. This led to an equally exaggerated devotion to the sacrament of confession.

As a young priest in the confessional I found myself listening to shopping lists of sins, most of which concerned very minor matters. Catholics seemed to construe the priest's role in confession as akin to that of someone running a spiritual dry-cleaning shop that specialised in the removal of minor stains from their consciences. Any notion that the purpose of the sacrament was to strengthen a person's relationship with a loving God seemed lost. The God of Jansenism was an implacable tyrant.

Jansenism's pessimistic view of human nature placed the priest in a position of power as agent of this implacable God which was reflected in other aspects of the clergy's dealings with ordinary Catholics. A Catholic cultural world emerged based on a false premise. Nowhere in the New Testament does Jesus ask anyone: 'How many sins have you committed?' Rather, his constant approach is *relational*. 'Are you sorry?' meaning 'Start over, God is waiting for you.' This was Jesus' approach.

As a young priest in the 1960s, you sensed that this was all wrong and that things had to change, and when the first session of the Council concluded in 1962 we knew change was in the air. Today it is hard to convey to members of our rather sombre Church community the extraordinary hope that was alive in the Church during this period.

★

Being the junior priest in 'a gathering of eagles' at the cathedral presbytery had its upside, particularly when your presence was more or less taken for granted. Then you were called on to do all sorts of interesting things.

Archbishop Simonds was a regular visitor at the cathedral and, when he was well, liked to go for a walk in the nearby park or down to the city centre. He needed company, so on many of these occasions I was invited to go with him. At the time Justin Simonds was the effective head of the Melbourne Archdiocese. Dr Mannix was still alive but in his late nineties.

Prior to the Vatican Council there was no such thing as a retirement age for bishops, although some did retire. Not so Archbishop Mannix. In 1942 Rome appointed Simonds, then archbishop of Hobart, as his successor and twenty years on he was still waiting!

Justin Simonds was a jovial character, fond of a yarn, and in the course of our walks I got to learn a lot about the art of running a diocese. Included in my education were guidelines on what needs to be celebrated and what is best forgotten. It was flattering as a young priest to discover I had the confidence of the Archbishop. This was true of the Archbishop's secretary. He was hospitalised for some time after accidentally falling down a set of stairs at a diplomatic reception. While he was in hospital I was assigned the task of going through his mail to see whether there was anything important that needed his attention. This experience provided me with another insight into the range of challenges, pastoral and otherwise, that Church leaders face in running a major diocese.

★

While living at the cathedral, my main ministry was at St Augustine's church located at the bottom of Bourke St. As well as being a Mass centre for those living in central Melbourne, a number of other Church activities were based there. In the 1960s working at St. Augustine's brought you face to face with Melbourne's homeless who spent the night nearby in the old tram tunnels below Bourke St. They came to the church looking for something to eat. Feeding the homeless was an important part of the work at St Augustine's.

While I was based there I developed an interest in the Eastern churches, particularly by getting to know Ukrainian Catholics. I went to Mass in the cathedral of St Peter and Paul a couple of times, and could not get over how different it all was. I made friends with people and got to know the Ukrainian Catholic bishop, Bishop Ivan Prasko, quite well. My experience with the Ukrainian Catholics opened up a very different form of ecclesiology for me. The Roman bureaucrats used to call Eastern churches 'Eastern rites'. It took Vatican II before they were properly recognised as 'churches' in their own right.

During my three years working at St Augustine's, I developed the habit of arriving at the church early so that I could spend two hours practising on the piano. This became part of my routine until it dawned on me one day that my piano playing was becoming obsessive.

★

After my time based at the cathedral, I was appointed assistant priest to St Francis Xavier's parish in Box Hill, where Fr Dan Conquest was parish priest. Dan had a reputation as being hard to get on with, but I never found him that way at all. In fact, we became very good friends. He had served for many years as Inspector, and later as Director, of Catholic schools. In these roles Fr Conquest is rightly remembered as a tireless worker. However, he found the task frustrating as Dr Mannix made sure his authority, and that of the small Catholic Education Office he headed, was quite limited. The Archbishop depended on the religious orders to build and run new secondary schools in the archdiocese. Most of these groups had a base in Europe where they had struggled to win a degree of independence from clerical control. Mannix was sensitive to this reality, hence his limitation on the power of the Director. Despite the constraints he had to work under, Dan's achievements were considerable. He was an impressive educator and, despite his time-consuming responsibilities, also a great reader.

We lived and worked together in the years immediately after the Second Vatican Council (1962-65). Dan would have been one of the first priests in Melbourne to track down and read the documents of the Council, which he regarded as 'fabulous'. He encouraged me to read them as well. We discussed the consequence of considering the Church as the 'people of God' or as 'a pilgrim people', and the implications for Catholic practice of acknowledging 'freedom of conscience'. At the time we thought the most notable of the documents was *The Church in the Modern World*. In both tone and substance it was so different from anything that preceded it that it left people either amazed if they were for change, or aghast if they were against it. The prospect that the Mass might soon be said in English was hard to believe.

Dan and I shared the excitement of engaging with the new ideas and perspectives that emerged from the Council once its documents became available in English. I was fortunate to have met someone like Dan at that time, as he understood the significance of what was happening.

*

In 1963 Archbishop Mannix died, aged ninety-nine, and four years later Archbishop Justin Simonds, also died. James Knox was a surprise appointment as the new Archbishop of Melbourne. In 1973 Pope Paul VI made him a cardinal. Of all the leaders I have worked under, he had the greatest impact on my life and the course it has subsequently taken.

Knox was born in Bayswater, Perth. Although not accepted for the priesthood for the archdiocese of Perth, (it was the practice at the time to take the cheaper option and recruit priests from abroad), he applied for and was accepted in the territorial abbacy of New Norcia. Because he showed such promise, he was sent to Rome to study. World War II broke out while he was in Rome, and this prevented him from returning to Australia. On completing his studies and being ordained, Knox taught for a period in Rome and was later invited to join the Vatican Diplomatic Corps. He served in many places including Japan, East and West Africa, and India. This posting was followed by others in south Asia. In 1953 he was consecrated bishop and in 1967 succeeded Justin Simonds as Archbishop of Melbourne.[1]

At the time of his appointment to Melbourne Knox lacked practical pastoral experience. He arrived with very little knowledge of the local scene, and so faced an immediate challenge in getting to know the local clergy. He was however a born administrator and quickly won Rome's agreement to re-organise the archdiocese. Four auxiliary bishops were appointed, each with control of a region, and the local curia was re-structured into twelve departments, each headed by an episcopal vicar.

Knox got the nod for Melbourne to host the 40th International Eucharistic Congress in 1973. He was a 'can-do' ecclesiastical administrator of no mean talent. His was the unenviable task of leading the Church in Melbourne as the changes introduced by the Second Vatican Council were introduced.

*

The new Archbishop found out about my interest in Australia's Aborigines. In the late 1960s I wrote a small pamphlet for the Australian Catholic Truth Society called *My Fellow Australians*. Fr Greg O'Kelly SJ (later Bishop of Port Pirie) read this and asked me to contribute a chapter to a book he was editing on what Jesuits in Australia should be doing in their ministries in the next twenty years. The Jesuits were among the first Catholic orders to establish missions for Aboriginal peoples in northern Australia. Their missions

---

[1] For an account of Knox's life and many achievements, including as Archbishop of Melbourne, see Ian B. Waters 'Knox, James Robert (1914-1983)' first published in hard copy in the *Australian Dictionary of Biography*, Volume 17, http://adb.anu.edu.au/biography/knox-james-robert-12752

there had failed. The book aimed to help Jesuits articulate a vision for their ministries that captured the insights of the Second Vatican Council. Many Catholic groups were then engaged in this type of imaginal activity.

My chapter set out what the Jesuits had done, the reasons that led to their lack of success, and went on to suggest the shape a future ministry might take. In putting this chapter together, I had the advantage of knowing something of the history from my visits to the Northern Territory during my seminary days. The Jesuits presented Archbishop Knox with the book, and when he looked down the *Table of Contents,* he saw to his surprise that 'one of my priests' was included among the contributors. He rang and asked me to come and see him. I went along not really knowing why I was invited. Such invitations were not always welcome events!

I arrived at the Archbishop's office just as the dust was settling on an altercation between the Archbishop and one of his high profile priests over the latter's indiscretions. In the late 1960s many priests were beginning to put into practice their own interpretations of what the Council said and how this should be translated into Church practice. Cultural change was in the air for Catholics, but there were still few guidelines as to how best to manage it. Bishops sometimes had to lay down the law.

Having just passed a somewhat deflated colleague on the stairs, when I arrived in Knox's office I decided to get in first, so I asked, 'What have I done?' The Archbishop replied, 'Nothing,' at which I was relieved. What he wanted to see me about was what I had written. He had been impressed by my contribution. 'Hilton, would you like to go into this work a bit more?' Rather surprised, I replied: 'Yes, but I have not really had much opportunity to do so.'

The Archbishop then let me in on what, up until then, had been a well-kept secret. In four years' time the 40th International Eucharistic Congress was to be held in Melbourne. Such congresses were global events that would bring hundreds of bishops and religious from all over the world to Melbourne. The scale of the event can be gauged from the fact that the Melbourne Cricket Ground and the Sydney Myer Music Bowl had already been booked to stage the main public events.

Knox wanted the Australian Aborigines highlighted in the event, but did not have someone who could handle such an assignment. 'Then I came upon your article. I want you ready to undertake this role. We will put you in another parish where you will not have so much to do, and from there you can go to the university and study anthropology. We won't make any more decisions about Aboriginal involvement in the Congress until you have your degree.'

To say I was stunned by this development would be something of an understatement. It was quite rare for priests to study at the university in those days. We chatted about other matters for a while and then I left. I did so with the strong impression that Knox would not be satisfied with a token involvement of Aboriginal people in the event. So there was a big challenge ahead.

When the priests' transfers came out in 1969, I found myself at Glen Iris where Fr Jim Murtagh was parish priest. In addition to being parish priest, Jim was one of Australia's leading Church historians and editor of the Catholic newspaper, *The Advocate.* His strong academic interests created an environment at Glen Iris that was congenial for a student.

Michael Chamberlin, then the Deputy Chancellor of Monash University ensured I received some credit for my seminary studies and was admitted to the first year of the BA Degree as a part-time student. I was apprehensive about attending university having been away from study for so long, but when my first year results were good, I was permitted to enrol full-time in second year. This was my first step on the road to becoming a priest-anthropologist.

CHAPTER 7
PRIEST AND ANTHROPOLOGIST

When the Indonesians invaded East Timor in 1975 I was completing the second year of my PhD fieldwork at the Kalumburu mission in a remote section of the Kimberley ranges in Western Australia some 500km away. As part of my research I had to carry out an ethnographic study of people living in a particular culture, which required me to live in the culture for up to three years. My principal task was to record as many aspects of the culture as I could in precise detail, and then to try to interpret the worldview that gave significance to the activities I had observed.

I had been living among the Aboriginal community at Kalumburu for only a short time when Dili was attacked. The indigenous people listened to their transistor radios as events unfolded not too far away. The older members of the community spoke of 'the Japanese war' and thought the conflagration in Timor might soon reach the Kimberley as had happened in 1943 when Japanese bombers destroyed the mission, killing a number of their people and forcing the rest to evacuate. They were quite ready to move into the hills in case of attack! The situation in East Timor did not concern me a great deal at the time, as the news seemed fairly garbled, and my focus was elsewhere.

★

Social anthropology includes the study of customs, worldviews, and how people organise themselves in the societies in which they live. One of the most interesting aspects of social anthropology is the comparative study of cultures, that is, of how cultures are similar and how they are different. In the late 1960s and early 1970s anthropology was still a relatively new field, and the methodologies used to study culture and the dynamics shaping social life were still being forged. The practice of ethnography was being systematised. As a student doing fieldwork, you had a sense you were working at the cutting edge of knowledge.

A major figure in the field, Bronislaw Malinowski, had been stranded in Australia during the First World War. Malinowski held that the task of the anthropologist was 'to grasp the native's point of view, his relation to life, to realise *his* vision of *his* world.'[1] If an anthropologist is to analyze a new culture then he or she must first be able to describe it. This requires detailed observations and recording of the minutiae of daily life to see how relationships and exchange systems work. Cultural 'insiders' are often quite unaware of the

---

1   Bronislaw Malinowski *Argonauts of the Western Pacific* (London: Dutton, 1961 edition), 25.

existence of these systems and the way they influence people's behaviour. The task of the social anthropologist is to uncover these systems.

Anthropology is therefore an inductive study that sets out to reveal how human nature works in particular contexts. It is interested in how systems change, to what extent they change, and why they change. The belief at the time was that, as a result of empirical study, the ethnographer could come to an objective assessment of a culture. This belief gave the field its scientific aura.[2]

Franz Boas was another seminal social anthropologist who challenged the notion of 'cultural evolution'. This doctrine held that European culture provided the endpoint of cultural development and so was the high point of 'civilisation'. Boas introduced the notion of *cultural relativism* into anthropology. For him, cultures cannot be ranked as higher or lower. All humans see the world through the lens of their culture, and judge it according to their culture's norms and values. The aim of social anthropology in Boas' perspective is to understand how culture conditions a people's worldview and so shapes how they make sense of their world and their interactions with it. In his understanding, Europe provides only *one* model, rather than *the* model, for doing this. He suggested that 'cultural evolution', then widely assumed in Europe, illustrated the danger inherent in all ethnocentric worldviews.

*

As studies of culture began to accumulate, mostly carried out among peoples living on the periphery of colonial enterprises, the scope of anthropology began to expand, and move further into the mainstream of academic endeavour. Claude Levi-Strauss played an important role in this development.

Levi-Strauss had an encyclopaedic knowledge of ethnographic studies that enabled him to identify common patterns ('structures') that transcended particular cultures. In his view these structures reflected something common to all human societies, precisely because they were human.[3] Initially, he saw these as transcending historical periods, but later acknowledged that the studies he had consulted were largely carried out at an important point in time - when the colonial enterprise was teetering on the edge. This realization led him to conclude that human cultures are historically determined because human consciousness itself is historically conditioned.

'Historical consciousness', to use Bernard Lonergan's term, shapes the way in which cultures are created, sustained and evolve. Levi-Strauss argued that the process by which this happens is rarely arbitrary. Past, present and future are linked for a particular people by a mythology[4] that underpins all legitimate change. To understand a people and their

---

[2] In the 1980s and 1990s this view was roundly challenged by the post-modern critics who pointed out that many ethnographic reports told one more about the cultural biases of the person doing the study than about the culture being studied.

[3] Levi-Strauss did not have the empirical background in ethnography taken as *de rigeur* by most schools of anthropology. He spent a year in outback Brazil studying tribes he came in contact with there in what was more adventure than a detailed study.

[4] Mythology, as an anthropological construct, is perhaps best understood as a set of beliefs captured in symbols with currency in the culture. In some cultures the mythology is carried in oral narratives, in others by written narratives, in others as dance, or as totems etc. The symbol system is usually particular to a culture.

culture, it is therefore necessary to delineate the mythic structures that provide coherence to the manner in which different groups respond to innovation and changes within their immediate milieu. Stripped of this mythical core, a people soon loses its identity and reason for existence. Aboriginal peoples provide a classic example of Levi-Strauss's point.

For Levi-Strauss, myth represents the highly specific ways in which different social groups at various points in history have understood and responded to the demands placed on them to change.[5] In this perspective it cannot be said that one culture is necessarily better than another, since all represent particular ways of addressing the challenges of living together in a particular milieu and responding to the demands made as this changes. There is therefore something important to be learned from every culture.

*

This was all heady stuff for someone like myself who had been thoroughly enculturated into the Catholic Church and its theology. My training was infused with a Catholic identity developed during the 19th century and the first half of the 20th century. This identity was based on the idea that the Church stands outside history and outside 'the world' in which history is created. The Church should be understood as an entity complete in itself and so able to pass judgment on all other groups because it alone held a mortgage on 'the truth'.

Anthropology helped me understand that Vatican II was a cultural event within the life of the Church, as well as an important religious event. The assembled bishops at the Council strove to hammer out an alternative identity for the Church and redefine its mission. This goal is best summarised in the *Pastoral Constitution on the Church in the Modern World*. The operative word in the title here is 'in'. To be 'in the modern world' is to be in history and in culture, and to have a mission of service to people without reservation or exclusion. This is a truly 'catholic' perspective.

To make a change of this magnitude, given the understanding that had prevailed for at least two centuries, was from an anthropological perspective, no simple matter. It meant cutting through much of the cultural detritus accumulated in Catholic thinking since the Reformation, interpreted as 'the Catholic tradition'. At the end of often acrimonious debates, some of which lasted from 1962 to 1965, the bishops were forced to focus on the central elements of Catholic mythology, and in particular to acknowledge that the Church is best understood as 'the pilgrim people of God'. From an anthropological perspective 'pilgrim people of God' is best understood as an organizing symbol.

In their searching to identify the principles of change at the Council, the bishops, employed three notions: '*ressourcement*' '*aggiornamento*', and 'development'.[6] The term *aggiornamento* or 'updating' was introduced by Pope John XXIII and was not controversial. Questions concerning updating centred on its limits: 'how much?' and 'to what pastoral effect?' 'Development' was acceptable since it viewed change as occurring in organic continuity with what had been. This fitted well with the notion of the Church as the holder of 'the truth'.

---

5   The development of Levi-Strauss's thinking is very well traced in a recent biography by Patrick Wilcken *Claude Levi-Strauss: The Poet in the Laboratory* (London: Bloomsbury, 2010).
6   John O'Malley *What Happened at Vatican II* (Cambridge: Harvard University Press, 2008), 36-43.

The real problem was with the French notion of *ressourcement* that can best be translated as going 'back to the sources'. The principle seeks to skip what is presently the case, and return and re-appropriate something from earlier in the tradition that can be regarded as more appropriate to the present times, or more authentic to Jesus' mission and message. The problem at the Council, and since, is that this principle can be interpreted in two ways. From one perspective it means canonising selected aspects of the past. This is the 'restoration' route to change.

From another perspective it means recognizing that at some point in the past a fork in the road was reached, and that the lesser of two available choices was made. In the light of the human consequences and costs of this decision a new path now needs to be taken. There will be discontinuity between the present and the past. This understanding seems to undermine the earlier contention that the Church has a mortgage on 'the truth' and so severely qualifies the notion of inerrancy in regard to Church teaching even where this clearly fits the historical record.

At the Council the crucial test of *ressourcement* occurred when the bishops addressed Church teaching on religious liberty. The major opponents of change here were the Iberian bishops, including the future Bishop of Dili, Jose Ribeiro. These bishops voted as a block against the Declaration on Religious Liberty *(Dignitatis Humanae)*. The Declaration marked the Church's official abandonment of previous teaching that church-state relationship be formulated on the premise that 'error has no rights'. This meant, as happened in Spain and Portugal, that civil authorities in a Catholic state are responsible for enforcing Catholic Church teaching because such teaching embodies 'the truth'. The Catholic state had no responsibility to support other Christian churches since these are in error, and so had no rights. Implicit in the Church's *volte face* is recognition that freedom of religion is a basic human right. Further, 'rights' are associated with people, not with abstract entities such as 'the truth'.

As I wrestled with these issues at the time, I had no idea that they would all come together for me with new force in the 1990s in the context of East Timor and the Church's response to the situation there.

*

In my undergraduate years at Monash University my earlier experiences with Aboriginal people in Finley, and my first-hand association with Aboriginal communities elsewhere, gave me a big advantage over fellow students. I was able to fly through my undergraduate degree. When my professor invited me to move to BA Honours, I hesitated telling him that I needed to write a report for the Archbishop on *The Church and Aborigines*. He immediately suggested that I make this the subject of my BA Honours thesis. When I completed this in 1972 I was invited to go directly into doctoral studies. I was quite thrilled to be offered this opportunity. It came at some cost to the archdiocese as accepting the invitation meant that I would be away on fieldwork for the best part of three years. Archbishop Knox seemed undeterred by this, for which I am still very grateful. He thought on a bigger canvas than most of his Australian contemporaries.

The time I had spent with the indigenous groups provided an important window into the cultures of Aboriginal peoples. Slowly I was developing an appreciation of what is culturally significant for them. However, my major assignment before moving to Kalumburu was the Aboriginal Mass at the 40th International Eucharistic Congress in February 1973. I wanted to tap into the best aspirations of Aboriginal cultures and really break some new ground, raising Church-Aboriginal relationships to a new level. This was an admittedly ambitious goal, but one in which Knox encouraged me.

No one to that time had attempted to adapt the Catholic Mass to Aboriginal cultures. In making such an attempt, there were three main hurdles to overcome. In order to be authentically Aboriginal, the ritual had to contain elements that had significance for Aborigines across a range of indigenous cultures. At the time most Australians, and most visitors to the Congress, assumed that all Aboriginal peoples belonged to one cultural group. Nothing could be further from the truth. The majority of Aboriginal groups were independent of one another, so winning agreement about what would be 'meaningful' to them all was a major task in itself.

Secondly, the White-Aboriginal cultural divide had to be crossed. Europeans place great store on words and images in conveying meaning through ritual. Aborigines do not. They convey meaning through song and ritual dance. Words in Aboriginal languages do not always have fixed meanings. This has made recording the languages difficult, and has made learning them particularly so. Europeans, used to words having precisely defined meanings, find the 'slipperiness' of Aboriginal languages difficult to adjust to. Getting the cultural balance right within what Aboriginal peoples would see as an essentially European and 'white' ritual was never going to be easy.

Finally, there were also issues within Church culture that had to be negotiated. Until 1969, when the major changes to the ritual introduced by the Second Vatican Council came into effect, the Mass had always been said in Latin in the Roman Catholic Church, and there was very little participation by the congregation. From 1969 onwards the Mass was said in the local vernacular, and there was considerable scope for the congregation to become involved. For most Catholics this was the principal outcome of the Council, and by late 1972 when we were developing the Aboriginal Mass, people were still getting used to the changes.

The Catholic Church had not introduced change to its essential rituals for many centuries. In the 1970s Church leaders tolerated some experimentation, which gave us discretion in developing the Aboriginal Mass. However, breaking new ground in front of an international audience was nerve-wracking for everyone involved. We felt the pressure, and I was relieved when I showed Archbishop Knox our proposal and, far from taking a conservative line, he was very excited by it. He was not sure if he could get permission from the Vatican for what we suggested. I can remember saying to him at the time, 'You've got friends in Rome, haven't you?' Whether he contacted them or not I never found out, but Knox won the necessary approval.

★

While some people adapted quickly to changes in the Mass, many did not. In any culture, change to what is held as sacred, be it ritual or myth, involves also changes to key meaning systems, and this is never easy. In the early 1970s there were too few opportunities for ordinary Catholics, or priests for that matter, to process how they felt about the changes that had been mandated by the Church following the Second Vatican Council. There were even fewer processes that allowed new meanings to be negotiated. As a result, a good deal of bullying went on in the Church as one group or another sought to impose its meaning on others. The result was that the Mass had become needlessly politicised. This was an issue we had to negotiate in planning the Aboriginal Mass and why Knox's support was so important.

Anthropology highlights the relativity of cultures. Different people approach the sacred by a variety of paths. As my work in anthropology proceeded, I was being challenged to re-construct my worldview in a way quite different from the absolutist treatment of human life and its defining relationships that formed the basis of my seminary training. I was discovering that Jesus' message is mostly addressed to these defining relationships, and that different cultures understand them differently. In particular, in Australia white people and Aborigines understand them differently.

★

At the Congress Mass, the scripture 'reading' about the Last Supper was not read; it was danced. We incorporated an aboriginal gift-giving ceremony, and all the music and prayers outside the central ritual were indigenous. Aboriginal women from different states played major roles in the service. As the homilist, I took the opportunity to preach on the need to adapt the rituals of the Church to the meaning systems and symbol systems of the people living in different cultures, and not to impose Eurocentric symbols and understandings without reflection. It was one of the few times my homily has drawn public applause![7]

The 'Aboriginal Mass', as it was called at the time, was widely viewed as 'a hit' at the Congress.[8] Priests from India and Africa could not believe what we had attempted. The ABC televised the event at a packed Myer Music Bowl and the visitors wanted a copy of the tape to take home with them to show their own people. The initiative had been a bold venture by Archbishop Knox. He was prepared to make a large investment in ensuring it was authentic, including freeing me to study and travel, and I appreciated his support.[9]

After the Congress the forces of liturgical darkness moved in and effectively throttled all attempts to incorporate local cultural elements in the celebration of the Mass, except in very peripheral ways. To the best of my knowledge, the Aboriginal liturgy has been used only once since that time, in 2013.[10]

---

7   In the language of theology this process is called inculturation. It implies a form of mutual critique and interaction between the culture in which the Gospel is presented (in our case European) and the culture in which it is to be received (indigenous). As a consequence of inculturation properly carried out, both groups (giver and receiver) come to own a richer understanding of what the Gospel can mean, which in turn can be passed on to others.
8   I was pleased, subsequently, to see the Mass described in the official record to the Congress as 'one of the most memorable occasions of Congress Week........which broke new ground in the Church's liturgical renewal'. Michael Costigan (ed) *Congress of the People* (Melbourne: Advocate Press, 1973), 37, 58-59. The Mass, celebrated in the Myer Music Bowl on Saturday 24th February, was attended by approximately 30,000 people. To this day, Aboriginal communities hold and treasure video recordings of the event.
9   Just two years later, Knox was appointed head of the Roman department that looks after liturgy.
10 I used it again at the ATSICC conference in 2013. The Catholic Aborigines attending the conference were delighted.

When Pope John Paul II began his long reign, the message from Rome (and therefore from the Australian bishops) to the Aboriginal communities seems to have been that 'if you wish to become Catholics you must do so within the worldview, symbol system, and sense of what is sacred as held within European culture'. Such a stance is anthropologically naïve.

Institutional leaders in the Catholic Church struggle to see any worth in expressing 'the sacred' in a symbol system and worldview other than the European one in which they were trained. The struggle between Eurocentric Church leaders and those on the periphery is long-standing, and far from resolved. While Church leaders use the language of inculturation, they interpret the concept within too limited a cultural horizon. One consequence is that, despite one hundred and fifty years of missionary effort among Aborigines in Australia, there were no indigenous priests.

'Inculturation' is a battleground in the Church as people from local cultures seek to express their deepest religious beliefs freed from the hegemony of the European culture and a symbol system that dominates thought and practice in the Catholic Church.[11] It is a battle that results from conflating European culture with 'the Catholic tradition', and it is being fought out around the world. In this battle the abuse of institutional power plays no small part. In the minds of indigenous peoples, it relegates essential elements in Christianity to the category of 'white man's business'.

Things do not become 'sacred' in a culture through the use of power exercised by outsiders to that culture. Appreciation of 'the sacred' emerges from a people's experience and is expressed through the symbol system of the culture, which includes its use of language, its sacred places, its narratives and myths, and its ritual life. Moving the Mass into vernacular languages is only a *first step* in revitalising this central ritual of the Church. There are still other necessary steps to follow.

While Catholic theology now recognises that God plays a mysterious role in the formation of any culture, Church leaders face serious challenges in dealing with the consequences of this realisation. Indigenous peoples often feel that the Church has let them down, that it does not understand them, does not speak their language, and does not have answers to the questions important to them. Poor anthropology results in inadequate pastoral practice.

*

When the Eucharistic Congress was completed, my clerical colleagues more or less assumed that I would return to parish duties. It therefore came as a surprise to them when I 'disappeared' to Kalumburu. With the blessing of Archbishop Knox I commenced my fieldwork in social anthropology, and the challenging task of producing a doctoral thesis as a student of Monash University. The minimum time for the task was five years.

---

11   It is worth noting that the Catholic Church is made up of 24 different churches in communion with the Pope. The Latin (Western) Church is the largest. Only a small number of these churches mandate celibacy for their clergy.

CHAPTER 8
KALUMBURU

I chose to do my fieldwork at Kalumburu because I had some association with the mission, and the Kwini people from there had been participants in the Aboriginal Mass. The mission there had other advantages as well. It was so isolated that there were still Aboriginal groups there who had not been detribalised. The community therefore provided a unique, and quickly disappearing, chance to study what Aboriginal tribal life, and its associated culture, had been like before white settlement.[1]

There was a second element to this choice. Most of the Aborigines at Kalumburu lived in a long-standing mission situation under the control of Spanish Benedictine priests and nuns who had a unique approach, best described as patriarchal, to Aboriginal-white relationships. So my second research interest was to discover what progress Christianity had made in penetrating the culture of indigenous peoples living under these conditions. How compliant or, on the other hand, resistant, was the native culture to the culture into which the missionaries sought to induct them, and what were the social mechanisms at play in bringing about change? This aspect of my study dealt in microcosm, and under highly controlled conditions, with many of the issues that had surfaced in the Eucharistic Congress Mass. Ironically many of these same issues would arise when the Indonesians occupied East Timor, and attempted, from a position of total control, to impose Javanese culture on the native peoples there.

★

Kalumburu is situated in the far north of Western Australia. In 1974 the mission could be accessed by road only in the dry season. It had an airstrip that could take light planes, and barges came up the river twice a year with supplies. The community was composed of about two hundred people. The native peoples belonged to two groups: the Kulari whose homeland was to the west of the mission, and the Kwini who lived mainly east of the mission. From its inception, the mission contained members of both groups, although when I was there the latter were in the majority. In recent years people from the Western Desert have also made links with the Kalumburu community. Also there has now emerged a majority group with non-Aboriginal as well as Aboriginal parentage.

---

1 Twenty-seven of the older Aborigines at Kalumburu had not encountered a white person until they were in their thirties, which gives some idea of how remote this part of the Kimberley remained in 1974.

At Kalumburu my daily routine centred around recording the details of life within the mission to build up a bank of data from which I could piece together the social system and begin to establish the dynamics by which it worked. I made detailed descriptions of what the two groups of people – missionaries and Aborigines - said and did. The task included travelling out into 'the bush' with different Aboriginal groups. I became known among them as 'the man with the book and pencil'.

Although I stayed as guest of the Benedictines, I was careful to maintain a certain distance from the missionaries so that the Aborigines did not identify me with the mission group. The line of demarcation was strengthened when I asked the elders if someone could teach me *pela* which served as a kind of *lingua franca* among the two Aboriginal groups living at the mission.[2] My request marked the first time in the community's memory that a 'white' had asked an aborigine to teach them something!

My lessons went on for four months, by which time I knew enough *pela* to follow a conversation, insert a comment, or ask a simple question. The learning process created a bond between the community and myself, so that the men felt comfortable in inviting me to rituals and secret places to which no white person had ever been invited before. Later, when people understood why I was there, I was invited to similar places and events for the women. My fairly humble efforts to learn the local language gained me an extraordinary entrée into the Aboriginal culture at Kalumburu.

I soon discovered that a process of *'ressourcement'* was underway within the Aboriginal culture at Kalumburu. Modern communications and travel had helped Aborigines strengthen the traditional *Unan* or exchange system by which knowledge, cultural goods and economic benefits had been passed from one group to another across the Kimberley and beyond, from time immemorial. The rituals and knowledge of traditional ways were in the process of being re-asserted and passed from group to group. Greater ease of travel, and the availability of the tape-recorder were key elements in this re-assertion.

There was a 'back to the sources' movement occurring there, not dissimilar in intent from that occurring in European Catholic culture at that time. This development was of interest to me as an anthropologist, but I could see, as a Catholic priest, why it was of great concern to the missionaries who regarded it as a reversion from Christianity to paganism. I did not see it in this light at all.

What surprised me greatly was the limited nature of the missionaries' understanding of Aboriginal culture. They made great efforts in the area of the local dialects, but rituals, myths and customs were another matter altogether. Despite much goodwill, the missionaries belonged to the colonial school of missiology where the aim in dealing with indigenous peoples was to 'civilise' and Christianise them. Consequently, the relationship between Aborigines and missionaries was a complex one. I found that the Aborigines had a high regard for the women missionaries, and appreciated the many services they rendered them. For their part, generally speaking, the missionaries seemed blinded by the assumptions of their own Spanish colonial culture, and as a consequence, the Aborigines were rarely, if ever, active participants in shaping their own future. They were powerless in the face of the powerful.

---

2   Pela is a Kwini dialect spoken almost exclusively by older members of the community. Only the younger ones spoke English and even this was a dialect.

*

As my records accumulated I began to identify patterns that revealed two interacting, but quite separate, cultural systems at Kalumburu – that of the missionaries and that of the native peoples. While there were differences between the Kwini and the Kulari, these were minor compared to those between the whites and the Aborigines on the mission. It became apparent that *perception played a key role* in shaping social relationships. How the missionaries *thought of themselves,* their self-image, influenced how they saw the native peoples and vice-versa. Both the Aborigines and the whites held worldviews in which their own group was central and the other peripheral, or even excluded. Reading back through the history of the mission revealed that this cultural patterning had persisted unchanged for almost a century.

The self-identity of the missionaries was shaped by the *founding myth of the mission.* The founding myth was that of European pioneers showing amazing courage and self-sacrifice in order to brave the harsh conditions and incredible hardships involved in establishing the mission in a remote part of Australia. This often involved them in epic journeys to get supplies to the mission or the sick to medical treatment. Through their dogged persistence, the land around the mission had been tamed.

The present-day missionaries saw themselves standing within this tradition. For them the early male missionaries were folk heroes. The women's image was different. It was one of service and subordination, secondary always to the men in all key decisions. This mythology is deceptive in that it masks the attitude of the early missionaries to the Aborigines, rendering it invisible.

In reading the extensive diaries of the missionary pioneers, I discovered that almost no appreciation was ever expressed about Aboriginal culture. As one of the missionaries at Kalumburu put the matter to me at the time: 'The Church is a civilising agent, freeing natives from the bondage of barbaric customs, and leading them to a more humane and enlightened way of life.'[3] I would hear overtones of this statement two decades later from Javanese Catholic clergy working in East Timor.

*

Aborigines had little or no say in the development of the mission. In the missionaries' mythology a major source of the hardships they faced was 'the ungrateful and aggressive blacks'.[4] The biggest challenge facing the early missionaries was to make the mission self-sustaining in food. However, as they attempted to plant gardens and fruit trees local Aborigines raided them and helped themselves to the fruit. They were then perceived not only as ungrateful and unresponsive to the efforts of the missionaries, but also as thieves. From the outset, the missionaries distanced themselves from the Aborigines and their culture. Their aim was to transform the people into something different without themselves having to adapt in any way. Their missionary strategy was not inculturation,

---

3   Hilton Deakin *The Unan Cycle: A Study of Social Change in an Aboriginal Community* Doctoral Dissertation, Department of Anthropology and Sociology, Monash University, 1978, 51.
4   The Aborigines at Kalumburu did not see themselves as 'black' but as 'brown'. For them 'black' was a term of derision taken across from the white culture.

but replacement. This was driven by their assumptions about European cultural superiority.

This mission strategy began to fall apart when, in 1972, the year before I arrived, the Whitlam government insisted that Aborigines have a say in the development of communities receiving government assistance, including Catholic missions. From the missionaries' perspective the government's policy of 'Aboriginal advancement' was a step backwards. However, the mission was left with little choice but to establish a local council of elected members. This was not effective. It failed to recognise the cultural reality that real power in the community lay not with elected representatives but in the hands of the elders. The 'coming of democracy' had little influence on the cultural life of the locals. It simply reinforced the missionaries' view that the Aborigines were incapable of managing their own affairs.

★

In the Aboriginal mythology, the missionaries were settlers who claimed land that was not theirs. They were thieves. The outlook of the Aborigines was culturally determined, and they took the same attitude to the missionaries as they did to any other whites, or indeed other Aboriginal groups, who trespassed on their territory. Their aggressive response was also culturally determined. Since the Aborigines did not share the European concept of private ownership, when the whites grew things on their land they helped themselves. They did not see this as stealing. The world as understood by Aborigines in the Kimberley at the time was very small. Most had no idea that there were major Aboriginal groups in other states, or even in other parts of Western Australia, such was the isolation of the Kimberley.

★

In the aftermath of World War II leprosy, not present a decade earlier, became a serious issue, and a leprosarium was set up in Derby to which people were sent from all over the Kimberley. The police were assigned the task of identifying people with leprosy, often on the basis of inadequate diagnoses. The outbreak of this epidemic had two effects: as indigenous peoples visited their relatives in the leprosarium it helped renew Aboriginal contacts across the Kimberley that had been lost for decades, and re-ignited interest in traditional ways. It also consolidated tensions between the Aboriginal communities and the police so adding to the sense of grievance felt by the Aborigines who increasingly began to reject and resist 'white ways'. These two developments led them to re-affirm their self-identity as a people. They also shaped how they saw themselves, how they saw whites, and how they related to them. The missionaries, as representative of a white society that ignored and placed little value on their culture, were caught up in this dynamic.

A sense of grievance always lurked just below the surface of community life, ready to surface at any moment. It was a defining part of the community's self-image, and fed off their mythology in much the same way as a sense of superiority operated unconsciously in the white culture of the missionaries. Both groups were oblivious to the presence of these subconscious dynamics.

※

The patterns of interaction I uncovered at Kalumburu I was to see repeated later in Indonesian-East Timorese relationships. The Indonesian motivation there was to impose their perceived superior Javanese culture on the Timorese. From the Indonesian perspective, the Timorese were sullen and ungrateful. From the Timorese perspective, the Indonesians had rendered them powerless in their own country, and as a consequence they held a deeply ingrained sense of grievance that led them to define themselves against the Indonesians. The Catholic Church provided them with a legitimate means of adapting their traditional ways to a new and threatening situation so they chose to become Catholic. It was a way of re-asserting their collective identity.

In Kalumburu the missionaries controlled all aspects of community life, but even from this position of power, my research showed conclusively that they had changed traditional Aboriginal life only at the margins. Their efforts to suppress the local culture simply drove it underground for it to reappear later. Likewise, the Indonesians failed from a position of power to change Timorese culture. Javanese brutality only marked them down as inferior human beings in Timorese eyes.

The two situations hold a number of important anthropological parallels. Both dominant groups believed that power could bring about the cultural transformation of others, without ever being open to this themselves. Neither group had any anthropological insight into the situation of the other, blinded as they were by their own cultural biases.

※

I completed my fieldwork in late 1975 and returned to Melbourne to begin writing up my dissertation. In 1977 I returned to Kalumburu for a further nine months to finalise my study, so ending a very demanding time. I had managed to get through my doctoral work in the minimum time of five years. I did this by setting up a study regime where I would work till one or two in the morning and start again at six. I found I could function effectively on four hours sleep. It was a work pattern that I maintained for over twenty-five years.

While living and working with the Aborigines and missionaries at Kalumburu was rewarding, it was physically demanding and mentally very draining. The nature of the task committed me to living in a social no-man's-land. Added to this were the exacting and often frustrating demands that accompany PhD study. When it was over, I needed some time to recover and re-acclimatise culturally in order to make a return to 'normal' ministry.

※

While I was in Kalumburu, Frank Little succeeded James Knox as archbishop. When I visited Frank on my return, he advised me to take a year's sabbatical leave, after which he expected that I would take up a parish appointment and perhaps teach anthropology at one of the universities.

I decided to travel and spent the first three months in Paris at the *Ecole Practique des Hautes Etudes (EPHE)*. The EPHE is a prestigious institute for post-doctoral research. Here

I attended classes given by Claude Levi-Strauss who lectured twice each week. This was a fabulous program that gave the participants, drawn from all over the world, plenty of time to see and appreciate the rich cultural history that Paris offers a visitor. I also took the opportunity to make my first pilgrimage to Lourdes.

After France I moved to England which, given my English ancestry, I had always wanted to visit. I had arranged to stay at a B&B in central London, but soon after my arrival I collapsed. I spent three weeks in hospital recovering from viral pneumonia. Finding yourself alone and ill, and a long way from home, is not an experience I would recommend. The doctors kept me in hospital a little longer than was strictly necessary simply because I had nowhere to go and no one to look after me. Fortunately, my hospital costs were met by the National Health Scheme in England, otherwise I would have been in a desperate position financially. When I was discharged I moved into a London hotel and later travelled around England which I loved. I gave some seminars at the University of Kent, almost next door to Canterbury Cathedral. The academics I met in Kent thought it somewhat exotic to have a priest-anthropologist from 'Downunder' address them!

★

I left England buoyed up by the prospect of fulfilling two boyhood dreams. The first was to visit Israel. This, like my visit to Lourdes, had great religious significance for me. I also wanted to look up distant relatives on my mother's side of the family. In this I had no luck.

My second boyhood dream, shared by many young people of my generation, was to 'dabble in Egyptology'. This dream was inspired by great European archaeologists of the early twentieth century such as William Petrie and Howard Carter who worked in Egypt, and Heinrich Schliemann in Greece. These archaeologists had heroic status among young people of my generation. I spent three wonderful months in Egypt, including some time lecturing at the American University in Cairo.

1978 had been a marvellous year. Freed from the pressures of the previous five years, I had the opportunity to do things that I really liked, and to begin to piece together a worldview that integrated what was best in both my theological and my anthropological training. This process raised a number of questions for me about Catholic theology and its methods. These questions remained unanswered at the time. My time in Europe enabled me to make important contacts in the world of anthropology, a field in which I was beginning to feel quite at home. As I returned refreshed to Australia and to my friends and family, I felt really blessed.

CHAPTER 9
FINDING MY VOICE

When I got back to Australia at the beginning of 1979 I met with my former colleague, Frank Little now the archbishop, who told me that my new appointment would be as parish priest of the relatively new working-class parish in Altona North. This would place me relatively close to Melbourne University where I could continue my work in anthropology, if I desired. Frank suggested that I drive out to Altona and have a good look around the area. When I did this I discovered that there were a number of state schools within the parish boundary. So I began to assemble the resources needed to get a catechetical program up and running in these schools. However, two weeks later Frank rang again and said that 'after consulting my advisors', which is archbishop-speak for 'I've changed my mind', I would have to take on a much harder assignment. I was to be parish priest to a new Catholic parish at Mt Eliza.

Mt Eliza had once been an area to which the Melbourne establishment, predominantly Protestant, retreated to enjoy the serenity of rural village life and the magnificent views out over Port Phillip Bay. It was planned by the architect who planned Canberra – Walter Burley Griffin. When I arrived, this enclave of the privileged was under attack with new housing estates encircling it and gradually strangling the privileged lifestyle that had existed there for decades.

The newcomers, including most of my new parishioners, were not particularly welcome. I found myself confronted with an unexpected and quite daunting form of tribalism, one in which the chiefs held multiple academic degrees. The hostile reception was something I did not expect, but was a challenge that I gleefully accepted.

When I arrived, the parish owned two important assets. The first was land. There was a huge block of land with a farmhouse and a cowshed. I took up residence in the farmhouse and parked the car in the cowshed. There was also a block of land in the town, which we subsequently sold. The second vital asset was the goodwill of the local Catholics, many of whom, like myself, were new arrivals struggling to cope with the peculiarities of the upward mobility complex afflicting many in the area. Working with these good people was the start of a new phase of my life, that of parish priest (PP).

One of the joys of starting a new parish is that you have to give the parish a name. At Mt Eliza many people were of English descent, so we decided to name the parish after an eminent English Catholic saint, Thomas More, who had been the Chancellor of England under Henry VIII, and who was put to death when he failed to approve of the latter's decision to divorce his wife and marry someone else.

When I had visited Canterbury, I was able to stay with the Anglican vicar, Hugh Albin. I returned his hospitality when he visited Australia and stayed with me in Mt Eliza. He preached in our church. Hugh had been the vicar of St. Dunstan's, which is the very old Saxon church where Henry II took off his kingly robes and put on sackcloth, and from where he set out to Canterbury Cathedral to do penance for the murder of Thomas Becket.

St. Thomas More's head was buried in St Dunstan's church by his daughter, Margaret Roper. Hugh told me that the Roper vault was being renovated. I asked if I might have a stone from the vault for the new Mount Eliza church. A stone was sent out to Australia courtesy of Qantas airlines, at no cost. As part of the formalities I had to sign a declaration for the Archbishop of Canterbury that I would not use the stone for 'Popish' or 'superstitious' purposes! Of course I signed the declaration assuring him I would not do so. The stone, appropriately embossed, is part of the wall in St. Thomas More's church, Mount Eliza.

I spent seven happy years at Mt Eliza as parish priest, and in that time the parish expanded enormously. When I left Mt Eliza in 1985 about 1200 people attended Mass on Sundays. It is no small task to work with a group of that size, providing the sacraments of the Church at life's important junctures, establishing schools and putting other parish infrastructure in place. As well as this there was the additional task of situating a growing Catholic community in the wider municipal community so that the parish contributed to the development of that community.

The irony of my efforts with respect to this last challenge was that someone who has hardly ever kicked a football has a local football oval named after him. As they say: 'In Heaven, even God laughs!'

I found the people in Mt Eliza parish very generous, and their support continued after I left and became involved in the East Timorese cause. The tiny village of Tequimata lies on the north coast of East Timor between Baucau and Los Palos. The Mt Eliza community, with the support of successive parish priests, provided the funds necessary to build and equip both the local church and primary school there. Naturally, both are named after St Thomas More. This has created something of a puzzle for the local Timorese more used to the Portuguese style of naming parishes.

A challenge in effective pastoral leadership at the parish level is to assist the community *look beyond itself and its own needs* to those who are more needy. Outreach then becomes an important element in the parish community's mindset and priorities. In supporting the school and mission station at Tequimata the Catholic community in Mt Eliza has clearly demonstrated its vitality.

★

While trying to build up the parish and its infrastructure, both physical and social, I kept my hand in at anthropology, teaching one day a week at Melbourne University. I lectured in the Middle Eastern Studies Department, and my students were mostly Master of Arts candidates wanting to include some anthropology among their units. My best students were women. I was amazed at the dedication that led so many of them to cut short promising academic careers to start a family (often much to the frustration of their mentor). In the early 1980s 'career' was not the big priority for many women that it is today.

My other abiding frustration at Melbourne University was the dysfunctional impact of intra-departmental politics. Academic politics did not interest me and so, after having spent seven years working at the University, I resigned. However, I have always retained my interest in anthropology, even if I was no longer active in the field. My training gave me a unique view of the world and a quite different frame of reference in looking at issues from that shared by many of my clerical peers.

*

Across the early 1980s I became progressively drawn into the affairs of the Archdiocese, first looking after the Maintenance Fund and later as chair of the Senate of Priests, and occasionally as stand-in for auxiliary bishops. When the Vicar General, Fr Peter Connors, was appointed auxiliary bishop in Melbourne, Frank Little asked me to step into the vacancy, which I did.

Vicar General is often seen in clerical circles as a stepping-stone to becoming a bishop because of the level of involvement the vicar has in the diocesan administration. However, there is a huge gulf in clerical status between being a vicar-general and being a bishop. As vicar-general you are very much the junior member of the administration of an archdiocese. My two predecessors as vicar general had both been made auxiliary bishops. I remember Frank saying when I accepted the role, 'Hilton, don't expect to be made a bishop, because you are too old!' I was not sure then if he was joking, as I was only fifty-five, but his remarks gave me comfort nevertheless. I assured him, rather tongue in cheek, that 'I will continue to behave as I always have!' at which he just smiled. The role of vicar general carried with it the title of 'monsignor' so I was now 'Monsignor Deakin' which took some getting used to.

A short time after I took up my appointment early in 1986, Frank Little became ill and was hospitalised for three weeks. As his right-hand man on matters administrative, I used to visit him every day, and he asked me to take over most of the day-to-day responsibilities associated with running the archdiocese as he was simply too sick to cope. It was a new experience to find myself signing very large cheques on the Archbishop's behalf! I found Frank Little a conscientious man who did not like to delegate, and who held important matters close to his chest. I think he learned something from the experience of being quite ill and so forced to delegate. Later in the year I ran into my own health problems, and our roles were reversed. I always got on well with Frank and, as we had a good team around us, my years as Vicar General were happy ones. However, clouds were gathering on the horizon. As archbishop, Frank had considerable difficulty in dealing with members of the clergy who behaved badly, including those who abused children. He sought to avoid or contain scandal. In doing so he ran into major difficulties. The professional advice from counsellors in his time was that priests who offended against children could be rehabilitated.[1] Legal advice on how to deal with abuse cases, in retrospect, proved less than helpful. The Archbishop also seemed to fear that if he stood down priests accused of abuse,

---

1   The advice available to Australian bishops up until 1993 was that priests who were abused children could be 'cured'. This advice changed subsequently as the realization grew among professionals treating them that paedophilia is an almost incurable condition.

the Vatican would not support him. Whether this was true or not was never put to the test as far as I know. For the victims of sexual abuse and, in many cases for their parents as well, tragedy and unnecessary suffering ensued. As has become clear in testimony before the Royal Commission into Institutional Responses to Child Sexual Abuse, prior to the mid-1990s Australia's bishops were simply out of their depth in dealing with the issue, and this is a matter of deep regret for which we all share some measure of responsibility.

★

In 1986, with absolutely no warning, I experienced excruciating chest pain. My aorta ruptured. I was on my own at the time, and totally debilitated. Unable to walk, I crawled up the stairs to my bedroom, fell on the bed and went to sleep. I woke up four or five hours later and could not get off the bed I was so weak. I rang a doctor friend of mine. His wife answered the phone, and learning of my sorry plight said she would contact him. It was a Saturday and he was at the races. He came immediately and within half an hour I was on my way to hospital where the problem was diagnosed as an aneurism of the aorta that required swift and major surgery. In the course of the operation I stopped breathing three times and had to be revived.

The third time this happened, the medicos decided to attach me to a respirator. In attempting to clip this into place under emergency conditions, they damaged my vocal chords badly. When I woke up after the operation I found myself in the intensive care unit with wires and tubes everywhere. I was to stay for three weeks, too sick to care about much at all. However, to my horror, I soon discovered that I could not speak. I was forced to communicate with the nurses and interns by writing on a pad and wondered what was going on.

When I had recovered a little, one of the specialists came to talk to me about my 'problem'. He told me that most likely I would never speak again because one of my vocal chords had been cut accidentally when the respirator was being inserted during the surgery. This news was devastating. I was left in shock. My first thought was, 'This is the end of me!' After all, what use is a priest who cannot talk? The most encouraging thought I could muster at the time was, 'Well, at least I am still alive, and that is something to be grateful for! It's a beginning.'

When the doctor returned the next day I grabbed my pad and wrote 'I want to get another opinion about my voice.' So the hospital arranged for an ear, nose and throat specialist to examine me when the swelling in my throat had abated. Here my luck changed, as the specialist who arrived was Frank Little's brother, Gerry. His assessment of the situation was more optimistic. I drew new hope when he said, 'Hilton, I think we can get you talking again.'

When Archbishop Little came to see me I had to communicate with him using my pad. I offered to resign as vicar-general. He read what I had written, looked up, smiled, and said, 'Hilton, don't even think about it! You just concentrate on getting better.' He had probably been talking to his brother and knew more about my condition at that stage than I did, if the truth be known, but I have been forever grateful to both of them.

I soon discovered, like many before me, that recovering from major thoracic surgery is not easy. After six weeks in bed I found I was so weak that I had to learn how to walk again. I slowly regained my strength and was eventually able to go home, but I still could not speak. It took another six or so weeks to be able to get back to something approaching normal mobility. I then went to see Frank and let him know that when I was mobile again I intended to drive up to my old 'home' for a while to rest and recover. Home for me is Finley. I am very fortunate in having a good friend there who had a couple of farms with residences on them. I was able to camp in the old homestead on one of them. From there I could go for walks in the bush among the river gums, irrigation channels and wheat fields for as long as I wanted. The wonderful vistas of the Riverina were good for the soul as well as for the body, and I had the chance to observe the bird life and enjoy the peace.

Over the next few weeks I began gradually to recover my strength to the extent that I no longer felt terminally tired all the time. The remoteness of the place meant that few people were around, which I found a blessing as I did not have the constant worry of communicating by pad. Phone calls were simply out of the question, since there was no phone.

★

One morning I got up early to have a shave and shower, and in the process of shaving I cut myself. In a more or less reflex reaction I said out loud, 'Oh! Bugger' and then realised what had happened. I had actually spoken. So I repeated, 'Bugger, bugger bugger…!' till my throat was too sore to continue. From that point on I knew that Gerry Little had been right and that I was on my way back.

I stayed on at the farm for another fortnight, and although my voice gradually improved, it was still very weak. When I got back to Melbourne I saw a speech therapist and, of course, the rest is history.

The experience of spending years finding your voice, metaphorically, and then nearly losing it, literally, is life changing. When such an experience is combined with recovering from major surgery, the impact is decisive. The fact that I had made a good recovery and regained my voice not only made me feel I had been given a second chance at life, but also that I needed to use this chance very well. So I resolved to speak out, both as matters required, and when the need arose. It is a resolve that I have tried to maintain.

I returned to work after several weeks and the archbishop, aware of my frail condition, reduced my responsibilities as vicar to the basic minimum. I appreciated this kindness.

★

My illness happened five years before I met the Timorese. As I stood among them in the Cathedral in December 1991 sharing their tragic story, I could not help but reach back into my own story and sense intuitively that, 'This is the moment to speak out in a totally new context.'

In many respects the funeral Mass following the Santa Cruz massacre marked a new beginning for me, or rather, the end of the beginning. When the East Timorese subsequently asked me to be their spokesperson I said 'yes' without hesitation or reservation.

Being given a second chance at life, when you thought all you had striven for was about to collapse, is enormously freeing. You lose that sense of fear that holds most people back. The realisation often sustained me in the days and years ahead, and still does so today. It was not something that others easily understand or appreciate, but as I have now come to realise, it is an important part of who I am – because it is part of my story.

PART I

THREE STORIES

2. The East Timor Story

CHAPTER 10
EAST TIMOR'S PORTUGUESE LEGACY

When I began reading about the Timorese, the questions that first came to mind reflected my bias as a social anthropologist: Who are these people? Where do they come from? How do they organise themselves? And what is it about East Timorese culture that enabled the people there, in the face of savage violence, to resist Indonesia for nearly two decades?

There were a number of helpful studies available in 1992, and I read them with more than a passing interest. While books by Jill Jolliffe and James Dunn provided useful starting points, I found the work of English imperial historian, John G Taylor, of particular interest since he told the 'East Timor story' from an anthropological perspective. The question Taylor explores can be put simply: What resources did Timorese culture contain that enabled a seemingly backward people to unite and withstand all efforts to impose Indonesian culture on them in the face of the most oppressive violence and abuse of their human rights?

In the outline that follows I draw on all three sources. I want to trace the legacy of four centuries of Portuguese influence on the make up of the population, the administration of the colony, the changing influence of the Catholic Church and developments in the local culture. This legacy is a defining part of the East Timor story.

★

Historically, Timor has always been a melting pot of peoples. The original inhabitants resided in what is now West Timor. Later the Bellos arrived and settled in the central highlands and to the East. There were other migrations from the Indonesian archipelago and from Melanesia, including from New Guinea. Overlaying this base was a mestizo population, the result of four centuries of contact with Portuguese arriving from Europe, Goa, Malacca, Mozambique and Angola. The consequence of its migration history is that East Timor has no dominant racial group and racial discrimination is quite rare.

The exception here is the Hakka-speaking Chinese who migrated from Taiwan and came to dominate commercial life so creating a situation that has long been a source of friction in East Timor. For most of the 20th century the Chinese provided local farmers with access to markets for major agricultural products grown in East Timor such as coffee, wood and rice. This gave the Chinese a dominant position in the quite primitive business world of East Timor. As a group they became relatively well off when compared to the local peoples.

The sympathies of the Chinese population are oriented to Taiwan rather than to mainland China. As a social group they kept to themselves, operated their own schools and spoke their own language. In colonial times this made it hard for the Portuguese authorities to censor information coming into the Chinese community from the outside world. Its members were much better informed about world events than the native Timorese, particularly developments in Indonesia.

There were two other groups with important links to the outside world. The first was political exiles from Portugal and other Portuguese colonies, known collectively as the *deportados*. These were well-educated people who had been exiled for their political views or activities. They shared a worldview quite different from that of the native Timorese who had grown up in a colony where political activity was banned. The *deportados* were articulate and had links to political movements in Portugal, Angola and particularly in Mozambique. They were able to radicalise younger members of the local elite.

Catholic clergy and religious constituted a second group with extensive outside contacts, particularly those clergy belonging to religious congregations. The Jesuits and Salesians were the main groups of religious men while the Canossian and Salesian sisters were the main groups of religious women. Through their contacts with wider Church networks, members of these groups were often better informed about world events than the local clergy and the East Timorese elite running the colony.

The Portuguese used censorship to control the flow of information within the colony, and in this they were so successful that life in East Timor proceeded largely in isolation from what was happening even in the region. While Indonesia and Australia were East Timor's nearest neighbours, the local people were largely ignorant of developments occurring in these two countries. The Timorese elite was blinkered by an education that emphasised the glories of the Portuguese-speaking world largely unaware that this world was imploding.

Among the villages an indigenous communication system existed built around kinship ties. This system paralleled in many ways the exchange system I had studied at Kalumburu. News, goods and even people were exchanged from village to village setting up extensive communication networks. These were an important part of Timorese culture and played a key role in shaping the loyalties that often transcended language differences. While normal communications systems were non-existent, the local word-of-mouth system played an important role in sustaining cultural identity.

*

The people of East Timor are divided by language. There are at least nine native languages spoken, the most common of which are Tetum and Makassae. Tetum is the *lingua franca* of ordinary people, but until relatively recently had no official form and no literary legacy. The language existed as an oral tradition spoken in a number of dialects.

When political activity was sanctioned in East Timor in 1974 the FRETILIN party immediately began a literacy campaign based on teaching people Tetum. In their view an independent country needed to be united by a common language. Secondly, FRETILIN endeavoured, as a matter of strategy, to use literacy programs as the means to raise the political consciousness of village people.[1] Its members taught Tetum to conscientise ordinary people and make them politically aware so that they could take increased responsibility for changing the economic and social conditions under which they lived. FRETILIN recognised the importance of language in forging a national identity.

The Catholic Church pursued a similar direction but for different reasons. Its motivation was liturgical and cultural. Successive bishops sought to have the Mass celebrated in Tetum. However, as long as the language had no specific form this was not possible. The groundwork had to be laid to give Tetum a recognised form. Lacking this, the Mass was celebrated in Portuguese, the language of the elite, not of the ordinary people known as the *maubere*. As the agency of the state with responsibility for education the Church authorities made Portuguese the language of instruction in Church-run primary schools. The consequence was that the local people placed very little value on education. This is an unfortunate part of the Portuguese legacy that still endures.

Following the Indonesian invasion Church policy changed. It began to promote the formal development of Tetum. The use of Tetum in Catholic schools made education more accessible to the *maubere* during the Indonesian occupation and a powerful cultural force in forging a national identity. This was all part of a cultural war waged by the Timorese Church as a counterpoint to the physical war being waged by FRETILIN across the 1980s.

During the Indonesian occupation, Bahasa was mandated as the language of education in government schools as well in business, law and government. The Indonesians did not recognise Tetum as a language, so for the Timorese speaking in Tetum became a form of clandestine resistance countering Indonesian attempts to subvert their culture.[2]

Language plays an important part in all cultures as a marker of identity and the suppression of language equates to suppression of culture. East Timor remains a linguistic mess even today and the Portuguese, including early Church leaders, bear some responsibility for this.

★

As a traditional society, the social organisation of the peoples of East Timor centred around loosely federated tribal 'kingdoms' that varied in both size and composition. When the Portuguese attempted to establish sovereignty over the territory in the 19th century, the governor found himself dealing with forty-five kingdoms, many of which were at war with one another.

Each kingdom was ruled by a hereditary leader called a *liurai*. If calling these local leaders 'kings' is an overstatement, naming them as 'warlords' is an understatement. A *liurai* combined both these roles. As the occasion demanded, he could be called on to supply either warriors or a 'voluntary' workforce.

---

1 FRETILIN's literacy campaigns in 1974–75 were based on the work of Paulo Freire as set out in his classic text *Pedagogy of the Oppressed*. This first appeared in Portuguese in 1968. Freire holds that in a truly liberated society the oppressed have to become agents in their own liberation. For him, all pedagogy is political since what students are taught and how they are taught serve political aims.

2 The pioneering work of the MacKillop Centre founded in 1993 by the Josephite Sisters under the leadership of Sr Josephine Mitchell has also been significant in the development of Tetum, and of education in the Tetum language. Currently, the Timor Leste National Institute of Linguistics, based in the National University of East Timor (Universidade Nacional Timor Lorosa'e - UNTL), holds official responsibility for developing and codifying the language. Its work is carried out with the support of Macquarie University in Australia.

Long-standing tensions between rival kingdoms, often as a consequence of feuds based on historical memories, sustained hostilities across generations. The Portuguese exploited tensions between groups by forging alliances that enabled them to establish a system of governance based on indirect rule. They did not challenge the existing cultural arrangement but exploited it to their own advantage. An important aspect of their strategy was to have the children of *liurai* attend Portuguese schools in Timor or Portugal and over time these developed a lusophone sensibility. This educated elite became an integral part of the colony's administration.[3]

★

The Portuguese first settled at Oecusse in 1515. It was not until 1702 that the first Portuguese Governor arrived. As pressure from the Dutch East India Company and its troops increased, the seat of colonial government moved east to Dili. In the 18th and 19th centuries the colonial administration often found itself at war with local warlords, and for long periods the Portuguese lived under siege in Dili. A major rebellion began in the late 1880s and was not finally put down until 1912, demonstrating the capacity of the *liurai* to resist invaders.[4]

The Portuguese sought to co-opt the local culture rather than to fight it as the Indonesians later chose to do. This resulted in a form of social organisation in which the administration recognised the position of the *liurai*, often according them military rank, and in turn, the *liurai* provided support (and protection) for the local representatives of the Portuguese administration. In this the Portuguese showed good anthropological sense.

In the traditional social structure a 'kingdom' was composed of different tribal groups living in a region called a *suco*. Each of these regions had a *chefe de suco* who was appointed by the colonial administration and approved by the local *liurai*. The *chefe de suco* was responsible for collecting taxes, keeping a record of population, cattle numbers etc and reporting to the regional administrator. The *chefe de suco* was responsible to the Portuguese administrator of the district. To this end, the Portuguese set up *postos* (or bases) from which the district administrator, always a Portuguese citizen but only rarely a European, operated. The *posto* system overlaid an existing cultural order. For the local population, the *chefe de suco* provided the Portuguese administration with a local face. Few Timorese had direct contact with the Portuguese themselves.

While the *posto* system had immediate advantages, it hindered strategic development across the colony because its focus was on revenue generation in a relatively small group of villages. As a consequence, there was little development of infrastructure prior to World War II.

When the Portuguese returned to East Timor after World War II, the colonial administrative structure was changed to permit better planning. The *sucos* were combined into thirteen districts each of which had a district council. The district administrator was responsible for infrastructure development within his region. His other responsibilities included economic development, the operation of the law, and the supervision of the local militia. Basic elements

---

3   It was from this group that the leaders of all three political parties formed in 1974 would be drawn.
4   See Jill Jolliffe, 35-37.

of this system (that is the sucos or 13 administrative areas) still exist today.

The Japanese invasion had substantially weakened the power of local *liurai* and the new regional structure compounded this effect. While the district administrator remained Portuguese, an increasing number of East Timorese moved into subordinate positions at the district level. By 1974 nearly sixty percent of positions in the district administration were held by native Timorese. These were generally the relatives of the *liurais*, or of the *deportados*.[5] The presence of the latter group meant that there was a significant mestizo component in the Dili elite.

*

In the colonial period the presence of a small educated elite and a very much larger illiterate public led many outsiders to take the view that East Timor was a backward place whose people 'had just come down from the trees'. The lack of development and infrastructure in the country compounded this perception. The adoption of the district model promoted much needed change. The most notable was in education, where the number of schools increased dramatically. Portugal's chronically underdeveloped economy meant that, while 'five-year plans' were developed for East Timor's thirteen districts, administrators rarely had the funds needed to implement them.

Portugal's economic malaise stemmed from the fact that it remained neutral during World War II and was not a beneficiary of efforts to rebuild Europe after the war. As a consequence its economy remained depressed. The fascist Salazar regime was seen as an anachronism when new democratic governments arose in Europe. The regime endeavored to revive its declining economy (and international image) by trading in resources produced in its African provinces. When this option was jeopardised by independence movements, Portugal attempted to suppress them by force. The cost of these operations further weakened the economy. To fight wars overseas the government resorted to conscription at home which was very unpopular.

There was no independence movement in East Timor and little in the way of economic benefits to Portugal, so the colony commanded scant attention from the metropolitan government. This resulted in a legacy of neglect. After nearly three centuries of colonial administration, East Timor had few roads, and those that existed were passable only in the dry season. Dili, the commercial and administrative centre of the province, had an unreliable electricity supply, no reticulated water system, a very limited telephone system, and no sewage system.[6] The colony rightly seemed to qualify as 'the land time forgot'. For the bulk of the population life went on as it always had closely geared to survival.

*

Government officials appointed to the colony generally regarded their appointment as a penance to be endured and, with some notable exceptions, left as soon as their term

---

5   The *deportados* included journalists, army officers, communists, socialists and even liberals who had criticised the Salazar Government. Ramos Horta, for instance, was deported from East Timor to Mozambique for a year for an article that he, as a very young journalist, had written in a local newspaper.
6   It is worth noting that conditions were hardly better in Indonesian West Timor at the time.

of office expired. Military officers saw appointment to East Timor as a safe haven when compared with the other colonies. The words commonly used to describe the lifestyle in Portuguese Dili were 'inertia' and 'boredom'.

The Portuguese military quickly recognised that the native Timorese made good soldiers, particularly as guerrillas. The locals could move quickly across the rugged terrain and live off the land. With the demand for troops in other colonies high, the Dili garrison was manned by local recruits. Portuguese troops were reassigned to Angola and Mozambique rather than East Timor. However, all commissioned officers in East Timor were Portuguese. Many of these were conscripts who had completed tertiary studies in Portugal before joining the army. A number avoided the endemic boredom of life in Dili by running education programs for their East Timorese troops. Their efforts provided a valuable form of adult education.

By 1975 there were some two thousand East Timorese serving as regular troops and these were backed up by a trained reserve of around seven thousand. As a member of NATO, the Portuguese army, including its troops and reserves in East Timor, were re-equipped just prior to the Carnation Revolution in 1974. This was to prove an important and valuable component in the Portuguese legacy.

★

The Catholic Church was an integral part of the colonial legacy. It formed part of Portugal's 'civilising mission' to East Timor. The Catholic community has been part of local cultural and religious life for nearly four hundred years. The Catholic community in East Timor is some two hundred years older than that in Australia!

The message of the Gospel first reached the 'Spice Islands' when Dominican missionaries established a base on the present Indonesian island of Solor in 1566. To protect themselves and Portuguese traders from Muslim raiders, the missionaries established a stone fort there. From this base they ventured forth to the other islands of the Lesser Sunda group and so came to Timor the most remote island in the group. For the next two hundred years Oecusse in West Timor remained a mission outpost and a staging post for Portuguese traders making forays further north and east.

Since Portuguese merchants, soldiers and sailors rarely brought women with them, they married local women and their descendants, the *Topasses,* became in time the dominant warrior tribe in Timor. The descendants of the *Topasses* give East Timor much of its Portuguese cultural bias even today.

The Dominicans followed the classic missionary strategy, *cuius regio, eius religio,*[7] and directed their efforts at converting *liurai* to Catholicism. In this they were quite successful. In 1974 some thirty percent of the population were Catholic including the bulk of the elite.

★

The indigenous religion is a form of animism. Indigenous people hold mystical beliefs about the power that the spirits of places and objects (*luliks*) have over human beings

---

7   This can be translated loosely as 'The religion of the ruler becomes the religion of the ruled'.

and events. In this worldview spirits have to be placated using various forms of ritual performed by the local shaman. Rituals for the dead are particularly important in East Timor. Sacred objects were kept in a special location in the village called the *lulik* house.[8]

The early missionaries seized on the notion, common across East Timorese cultures, that physical objects can have a spiritual significance, to explain the Catholic notion of sacramentality. As a result there has been, almost from the outset, a ready marriage between animism and traditional Catholic belief giving Catholicism in East Timor its own special character.[9]

★

The Church's relationship with the Portuguese colonial administration in East Timor has tracked the ups and downs of its relationship with successive governments in Portugal. The restructure of the Portuguese administration after the World War II had its parallel in the Catholic Church whose leaders, mostly foreign missionaries, had been also forced into exile by the Japanese invaders, a story which we will come to in a later chapter.

After 1945, one of the main goals of the first Bishop of Dili, Jaime Goulart, was the development of a local clergy. As a young priest he had been responsible for establishing a minor seminary as Soibada. As Vicar Apostolic before the Japanese invasion he ensured that local seminarians, such as Martinho da Costa Lopes, continued their studies in Macau out of harm's way. At war's end these returned to East Timor as the vanguard of an indigenous diocesan clergy that would expand rapidly in subsequent years. This is an important part of the Portuguese legacy.

Native Timorese clergy played an important role as protectors of the people from the more outrageous demands of *liurai* and the blunders of local colonial administrators. As a consequence they were well-respected by the *maubere*. Many of them suffered from the lack of further education once they were ordained. This left them out of contact with developments in the Church following the Second Vatican Council. The Catholic Church in East Timor even today operates from a spirituality that placed great store on externals: processions, Marian devotions and so on. In many respects it models forms of Church practice found in Australia in the 1940s and 50s.

★

When the Salazar regime came to power in Portugal in 1932, with episcopal support, its leaders attempted to set up a 'Catholic social order'. The Vatican entered into a *Concordat* with the regime in 1940 under which Catholicism became the religion of the state. The *quid pro quo* was that the regime had the right to veto the appointment of bishops (who became salaried public servants).

---

8   *Lulik* items found in villages are Portuguese flags some hundreds of years old. These are often souvenirs of battles in which the local liurais sided with the Portuguese against another kingdom and were victorious. Jill Jolliffe *East Timor: Nationalism & Colonialism* (St. Lucia: University of Queensland Press, 1978), 16.
9   Animist beliefs still sit just below the surface in East Timorese customs, even today. It is not uncommon to find graves marked by inverted water buffalo skulls mounted on posts at gravesites. Their purpose is to protect the dead from evil spirits. For some Catholics, crosses and pictures of the Virgin Mary mounted above graves seem to serve much the same function.

The Portuguese bishops considered Portugal a 'Catholic' country and argued successfully that the privileged status of the Catholic Church enjoyed in Portugal be extended to the Portuguese Federation. As a consequence of the Concordat, the Church assumed responsibility for education in East Timor and the meagre salaries of its clergy were paid by the government.

Under the Concordat East Timor became a diocese in its own right and Fr Jaime Goulart was appointed Vicar Apostolic[10] of the newly defined ecclesiastical region.[11] When the Japanese invaded Goulart was forced to escape to Australia where he was consecrated Bishop of Dili in Sydney in 1942. Goulart's success as a leader stemmed in large part from his great respect for Timorese culture. He was a fluent Tetum speaker and so could communicate with all levels of Timorese society. When he resigned in 1967 due to declining health, his loss was greatly felt by the Timorese who had developed a great affection for a man who had spent his life with them.

Goulart's successor, Jose Ribeiro, was a man of quite different outlook. Ribeiro had been an auxiliary bishop in Portugal and like many ambitious bishops in this situation was impatient to be in control of his own diocese. He had a formality of manner that did not sit well with the native clergy used to a more encouraging, friendly and sympathetic leader. Ribeiro's inability to learn the local language isolated him from ordinary people.

As a Portuguese bishop Ribeiro attended all sessions of the Second Vatican Council. When he attempted to introduce its teachings and reforms into the diocese, the local priests, trained in an older style Catholicism, actively resisted his efforts. This may have been a subconscious reaction on their part to Ribeiro's lack of empathy for the often dire conditions in which they were forced to live and work particularly in rural areas. In order to win a modicum of co-operation from his alienated clergy, Ribeiro appointed Martinho da Costa Lopes as Vicar General and used him as a go-between. Da Costa Lopes was well-connected to local clergy, having taught a number of them in the seminary, and was skilful at getting people onside. He was also well connected with the administration having served two terms as East Timor's representative on the metropolitan government in Portugal.

Ribeiro initiated a project to have the liturgy translated into Tetum. However the Church lacked the linguistic expertise needed to make this change, so it lapsed. Instead, liturgical reform in East Timor saw the language of the Mass change from Latin to Portuguese. This had little impact locally as the ordinary people did not understand either language.

★

After five centuries in East Timor the Portuguese left an important legacy in terms of law, architecture and outlook. The Portuguese Catholic Church was part of this legacy. For its leaders, cultural life began and ended in Portugal. This was an attitude they shared with the Timorese elite. The attitude was perpetuated among the local clergy through their clerical

---

10 Vicar Apostolic is the lowest rank on the hierarchical ladder. It stands below Apostolic Administrator, which, in turn stands below that of Bishop.
11 Jaime Goulart was born in Portugal and ordained priest in 1931. He travelled to East Timor in his role as secretary to his uncle, the Cardinal Archbishop of Goa, and later requested to be appointed there in a missionary capacity.

education. In looking for ways to solve the problems of the day, the bishop and clergy looked first to Portugal for inspiration and help.

The Portuguese legacy in East Timor has been and remains principally at the level of culture and religion. The Catholic Church played a significant role in the development of this legacy. It is hard to make any sense of the East Timor story without taking its Portuguese legacy into account.

CHAPTER 11
DE FACTO INDEPENDENCE

Events in Portugal in the early 1970s precipitated East Timor into the modern world at breakneck speed. The *Estado Novo* established by Salazar went into decline with his illness and death in 1970. Under *Estado Novo* Portugal had become a one-party state. Political opposition of all types was repressed by the secret police (PIDE) and opponents exiled to the Portuguese provinces[1] where the local PIDE kept them under close surveillance. However, these exiles and students returning from studies in Lisbon brought ideas with them to East Timor about freedom, independence, democracy, and a future different from the past. Few had any real political experience. Political parties, as such, had been illegal in Portugal and, by extension, in East Timor, where colonial rule at its best was paternalistic, and at its worst, oppressive and corrupt.

The *Estado Novo* survived with the support of the military. By the late 1960s a younger generation of officers began to respond to a deep-seated desire among ordinary people for Portugal to become democratic. There was also a strong desire to withdraw from costly colonial wars that drained the metropolitan economy, and had caused a generation of young Portuguese men to lose their lives for no material gain. Portugal was also being pilloried in the United Nations for maintaining its colonial ambitions. These officers formed a loose-knit political grouping known as the *Movimento das Forças Armadas* (Movement of the Armed Forces or MFA), which pursued two strategic objectives: the restoration of democracy to Portugal and the decolonisation of the country's African provinces. East Timor did not initially figure in their discussions.

★

On 25th April 1974 troops loyal to MFA officers took control of major government installations in Portugal. This bloodless coup received strong popular support in demonstrations held on the 1st May. Since communist countries celebrated that day as a public holiday, the timing was unfortunate, and raised suspicions that a 'communist coup' had taken place in Portugal, which was not the case. However, the government had moved from the far political right towards the left. When the country prepared for elections, the

---

1 It was in this way, for instance, that Ramos Horta's father arrived in East Timor, as did the father of the Carrascalao brothers, all of whom were to become important players in East Timor's struggle for independence.

Communist Party was prominent, and this became a matter of concern for a number of Western governments.

While the revolution initiated major changes the MFA did not pursue a coherent political agenda. The coup generated uncertainty and made things quite chaotic at the policy level, when groups within the transitional government pursued their own agendas.

While it should have been recognised that decolonising Portugal's African provinces, Angola, Mozambique and Guinea-Bissau, would have implications for East Timor, this did not seem to have bothered Lisbon greatly. However, it certainly caught the attention of the East Timorese, as information flowed back into the province.

★

As noted earlier, at the time of the April Revolution there was no independence movement in East Timor. There was, however, a good deal of clandestine political discussion among young Timorese.

A major avenue for political commentary in the early 1970s was the Catholic paper, *Seara,* which under the editorship of Fr Martinho da Costa Lopes published articles by Timorese nationalists, many of whom would soon become leaders in political parties.[2] *Seara* had a degree of immunity from government censors, since the Church was regarded as an arm of the state. However, the latter took exception to an article by Ramos Horta on the *Maubere* of East Timor. Bishop Ribeiro, under pressure from the PIDE, closed down *Seara* early in 1973, almost a year before the MFA revolt in Portugal, and this meant that political discussion was again driven underground where it grew in intensity.

Within two weeks of revolution occurring in Portugal, three distinct political groups emerged in Dili differentiated by the ways in which each saw the relationship between East Timor and Portugal unfolding.

First into the field was the *Uniao Democratica Timorense* (Timorese Democratic Union), known as the UDT. Members of the group shared the view that East Timor was simply not ready for self-government, and that any act of self-determination (a necessary requirement for decolonisation under UN protocols) needed to take this into account. They therefore argued for a slow decolonisation process, supervised by the Portuguese, which would result in East Timor becoming part of a lusophone federation. The British Commonwealth provided them with a model for this type of development. Since many of the supporters of UDT depended on the colonial administration for their livelihood, such a strategy protected their position. It would be unfair to say that their thinking was shaped only by self-interest; it was also shaped by a real affection for the long-standing Portuguese cultural influence in East Timor.

The second political group grew out of a strike on the Dili waterfront, where poorly paid workers formed the first union in Timorese history. The union won a hundred percent increase in wages. The *Associacao Social Democratica Timorense* (Timorese Social Democratic Association) or ASDT, emerged as an offshoot of this industrial action.[3]

---

2   Jill Jolliffe lists among these, Nicolau Lobato, Jose Ramos Horta, Manuel Carrascalao, Xavier do Amaral, Domingos de Oliveira, Francisco Borja da Costa, Inacio de Noura, and Mari Alkatiri (who is Muslim). Jolliffe, 1978, 56.
3   ibid, 62-3.

ASDT, like UDT, called for an act of self-determination leading to independence after a transition period supervised by the Portuguese. In the interim, it demanded that the new MFA administration in Dili put an end to corruption and ensure greater participation by native Timorese in the administration of the colony. This group acknowledged that any decolonisation had to be carried out in a way that posed no external threat to East Timor's important neighbours and potential trading partners, Australia and Indonesia. ASDT did not see East Timor's future as tied to a Portuguese federation, but saw it as an independent country living in harmony with its neighbours.

The third party formed in May 1974 took a different direction again, calling for East Timor to be integrated into the Indonesian Republic as an autonomous province. This group called itself the *Associacao Popular Democratica* (Timorese Popular Democratic Association), or APODETI. Its platform was anti-Portuguese and pro-Indonesian. This group had its support base in Dili, mainly among the small Muslim population there. It also had a degree of support among educated East Timorese and expatriate Portuguese who considered that East Timor was economically too backward ever to be viable as an independent state. For this group, integration was the only realistic future for the colony, given the chaotic state of affairs in Portugal itself. This view corresponded with that view of the Australian government and the Vatican.

Two other minor parties also appeared, one proposing integration with Australia, and the other supporting independence for Timor (East and West). Neither of these commanded much support.

★

All three major groups faced common problems. In the first place their political base was in Dili, and the majority of the people lived in rural areas. Secondly, since the leaders were drawn from the lower levels of the administration or recently returned graduates, the parties had limited political education or practical experience of government. For this reason, both UDT and ASDT wanted the decolonisation process to be an extended one. By contrast, the APODETI position saw the Portuguese administration being replaced almost immediately by an Indonesian one. This was not a popular position to defend.

★

From the outset groups struggled to gain political traction either at home or internationally. If East Timor was to become an autonomous state, then its relatively small pool of lower echelon administrators had to take giant strides with very limited support and quickly. Portugal was not in a position to offer help, and Australia refused to do so.

The reality of their situation led political leaders in Portugal, Australia and elsewhere, to question whether independence was a feasible option for the colony once the Portuguese withdrew. Were a decolonised East Timor to become a failed state it would pose an unacceptable security risk for the region and threaten the national interests of neighbouring states. On the other hand, as part of Indonesia, East Timor would be in the anti-communist camp. Such was the logic of the Cold War era.

At the time the Vietnam war was grinding to a stalemate, and the 'domino theory' which envisaged Asian states falling one by one to communist movements was firmly in place, so ensuring that East Timor became part of Indonesia made sense, as it lowered the collective security risk.

The Prime Minister of Australia, Gough Whitlam, saw nothing but trouble ahead should the elites that ran the three political parties in East Timor ever get their hands on the reins of power.[4] ASDT, in particular, was a problem for external observers. While it had growing popular support, its leaders were not perceived as having the level of expertise in civil administration needed to run a country.

*

Of the major groupings in this early phase of political expression, ASDT proved the most astute in assessing the situation and working through its implications for the future of East Timor. Its leaders realised the necessity of establishing a broader political base than that provided by its union origins. Their idea was to form a 'coalition of the willing', or an umbrella group (front) that could speak for all those groups wanting independence, whether of the political left or the right, and embracing whatever views they held about future relationships with Portugal.

The model they had in mind was that of *Frente de Libertacao de Mozambique* (Mozambique Liberation Front), or FRELIMO in Mozambique. So in September 1974 the group changed its name to the Revolutionary Front of Independent East Timor (*Frente Revolucionara do Timor Leste Independente*) or FRETILIN for short. The inclusion of 'revolutionary' in the title sought to express solidarity with the independence movements active in Portugal's African colonies, and to serve as a rhetoric that could mobilise rural people to overcome the political torpor into which the colony had sunk under colonial rule. This goal was seen as a necessary condition for East Timor to survive as an independent state. The choice of title carried risks as the rhetoric of 'revolutionary front' had previously been colonised by Marxist groups in other developing countries.

Initially, there was little to differentiate FRETILIN from UDT either in membership or ideology. However this soon changed. FRETILIN leaders concluded that if East Timor was to become independent, the country needed greater social cohesion than was possible under the Portuguese. Social cohesion at the national level would have to be built, and built quickly. So FRETILIN advocated greater participation by East Timorese in the senior levels of the administration and the need to educate people, particularly those living in the rural hinterland.

*

To implement this ambitious program, FRETILIN leaders and sympathetic university students were formed into teams and sent into villages in rural areas as 'revolutionary brigades'. The immediate effect of this initiative was to raise the political awareness of

---

4 According to James Dunn, Whitlam single-handedly authored Australian policy on East Timor during 1974–75 allowing little involvement of either caucus or cabinet, (Dunn, 1996,131). In Dunn's view the Fraser Government did little to change this policy after it was elected in December 1975. (ibid, xii).

the 'ordinary people' and this quickly changed the political balance between UDT and FRETILIN very much in the latter's favour. By early 1975 political support for FRETILIN was significantly higher than that for the other two parties even when combined. FRETILIN's leaders positioned it as the party of the *maubere*, and support grew because FRETILIN was seen to be doing something for them. The term *maubere* came to hold almost mystical significance for some of FRETILIN's leaders.

As a 'front', FRETILIN brought together people of different political persuasions, but the majority of its leaders were Catholic, many strongly so as a matter of conviction. A number, including its first president Xavier do Amaral, had received their secondary education at the minor seminary in Dare where Martinho da Costa Lopes was one of their teachers.[5] Many had a good relationship with the East Timorese diocesan clergy, having studied together in secondary school. Da Costa Lopes, who was seen as sympathetic to the situation of the *maubere*, carried particular influence among FRETILIN's leaders. However, like all East Timorese priests he was determinedly anti-communist.

★

From the outset, FRETILIN leaders had a major problem with the Catholic Bishop of Dili, Jose Ribeiro. The latter was the product of his Portuguese clerical upbringing. His rise within the Church followed a common pattern: parish priest, to seminary staff, to auxiliary bishop, and finally to bishop. Having grown up in a fascist state, Ribeiro lacked any real feel for democratic politics. As a supporter of the *Estado Novo,* he had little sympathy for the change in national aspiration that led to its downfall, or for those who brought it about.

Ribeiro was a small man of modest talent that he masked by a firmness of manner, which unfortunately tended to alienate people. His austere personal lifestyle further distanced him from the local people. Ribeiro's problems were compounded by the fact that he had followed the diocese's foundational bishop, Jaime Goulart, whose friendly manner and dedicated service to the Timorese had won him widespread affection and appreciation. Ribeiro's conservative training and lack of background in politics led him to the view that the Church should stand above politics.

The irony in Ribeiro's position is that, while he was positioning himself 'above the fray' in Dili, the topic of the relationship between the Church and the modern world was explored at the synod on evangelisation in Rome, under the leadership of Pope Paul VI. In summing up discussion at the synod the latter would write in *Evangelii Nuntiandi (Evangelisation in the Modern World)* in 1975:

> …evangelization would not be complete if it did not take account of the unceasing interplay of the Gospel and of man's concrete life, both personal and social. This is why evangelization involves an explicit message, adapted to the different situations constantly being realised, about the rights and duties of every

---

5   Minor seminaries are used throughout the developing world to provide secondary education and so create the pool of educated young men from which aspirants to the priesthood can be drawn. Those who choose to continue beyond the minor seminary complete their studies in theology and philosophy at a major seminary. Clerical trainees in East Timor, for instance, on graduating from Dare completed their studies in either Macau or Portugal.

human being, about family life without which personal growth and development is hardly possible, about life in society, about international life, peace, justice and development - a message especially energetic today about liberation (#29).

When Paul VI spoke of 'liberation' in the mid-1970s he was doing so in the context of decolonisation. He was also doing so in a Church context, that he had helped create, which placed great emphasis *on dialogue as a necessary condition of peace*. In this pope's view the Church had a duty to work for peace. As he noted in his 1964 encyclical letter, *Ecclesiam Suam,* addressed to all Church leaders during the Second Vatican Council:

> *The Church must enter into dialogue with the world in which it lives. It has something to say, a message to give, a communication to make.* (#65).

Paul VI's interest was not only that the bishops see the Council itself as a forum for dialogue, but also that dialogue be promoted as an important aspect of the Church's mission to bring peace and justice into a troubled world. To drive home this message, Paul VI used the term 'dialogue' eighty times in this document which sets down the Church's foundational teaching on the matter.

★

Given Bishop Ribeiro's potential influence over the leaders of both the major political parties he was well placed to initiate a dialogue between them. However, instead of being proactive in the matter, he chose to go on the defensive, warning all Church communities in a pastoral letter against the 'communistic' influence at work in local politics, and urging them not to vote for parties that were communist or socialist. This letter, written on his return from Portugal, was seen as a thinly disguised attack on FRETILIN.

According to his colleague, compatriot and friend, Fr Julio Aco whom I interviewed in Sydney in the early 1990s, Ribeiro was not a reader. This may have contributed to his misconstruing the nature of FRETILIN as a 'political front' and his clear failure to understand the models on which FRETILIN leaders based their organisation and rhetoric. To loyal supporters of the *Estado Novo* these models would have seemed like the equivalent of today's 'terrorist' organisations.

In the circumstances of 1974 it was not possible for the Bishop to position himself above politics. His strong anti-communist views placed him in the UDT-APODETI camp. The latter exploited his anti-FRETILIN stance to the full. Ribeiro's personal view that the colony was too backward to survive as an independent nation was also used to make political capital. Thus, at a time when the Church might have exercised a strong influence for good, the Bishop rather naively sidelined himself. His refusal to talk with FRETILIN leaders, including those who were devout Catholics, stood in stark contrast to the position taken by Paul VI.

★

In October 1974 a group of Indonesian generals, led by Ali Murtopo and 'Benny' Murdani (a Catholic), launched a sophisticated campaign to covertly take over East Timor and integrate it into Indonesia under the name *Operasi Komodo*. The generals hoped to avoid military confrontation with the Portuguese and use APODETI to take over the colony peacefully. The project failed because the planners relied on faulty intelligence from their consul in Dili who, according to James Dunn, consistently overestimated the strength of support for APODETI.[6] A second strand of *Operasi Komodo* was to discredit FRETILIN, by then the most popular party, by identifying it as a 'communist' enterprise. This was to be done through a disinformation campaign emanating by radio from Kupang in West Timor.

As a 'political front', incorporating the political left and right, FRETILIN was open to this type of attack, and its leaders lacked the political and media skills needed to counteract it. Murtopo and Murdani had access to the government-controlled media in Jakarta, particularly the *Antara* newsagency, which was required to fabricate a series of stories about events in East Timor with little prospect of their ever being effectively countered. The old adage that 'if you tell a big lie often enough people will take it as the truth' was borne out. As a consequence, FRETILIN was so consistently labelled as a communist organisation that this became an accepted line even in the international press.

In addition to its local and international media campaigns, *Operasi Komodo* included three other initiatives. The first was an international diplomatic blitz that sought to isolate both the Portuguese and the two parties seeking independence in East Timor. The aim was to convince nations in the region that an independent East Timor was a threat to their interests, and that 'integration' was the only realistic option for the colony once the Portuguese withdrew. This soon became the accepted diplomatic wisdom.

A second initiative sought to influence the academic community that East Timor was not viable as an independent nation. This strand was assigned to the Centre for Strategic and International Studies (CSIS) headed by Yusuf Wanandi, an influential Catholic in Jakarta. The CSIS group had links with Bob Santamaria in Australia, and he became their mouthpiece and spokesperson in this country.

The initiative was to have Catholics holding senior positions in the Suharto government co-opt the Indonesian Catholic Church and the papal nuncio in the cause of integration. This was considered possible because the Vatican did not appear to have any clear policy position on the future of East Timor at the time and because of the Church's strong opposition to communism.

★

As concern mounted in Dili over external interference in the colony's politics and APODETI becoming a front for Indonesia, FRETILIN and UDT leaders entered into a coalition in January 1975 at the suggestion of the Governor. To head off the external threat, the coalition then demanded that the Governor give in-principle recognition to East Timor's independence from Portugal. They argued that once East Timor had its independence, an act of self-determination should decide the form this would take. This demand caught by surprise the Portuguese who had been negotiating with the Indonesians in London behind

---

6   James Dunn, 78-89 et al.

the backs of the East Timorese. Following the London talks the Indonesians concluded that the Portuguese government had no in-principle objection to East Timor being integrated into Indonesia, provided there was a suitable act of self-determination. However, the political situation in Portugal at the time meant that the government's left and right hands were often playing different games. The main game in Portugal was to get rid of East Timor as quickly as possible, while that in East Timor was to decolonise in as responsible a way as was possible; so confusion reigned. Had the Indonesian negotiators talked to other Portuguese representatives they may have drawn different conclusions!

★

On 7th May 1975 a Decolonisation Commission made up of representatives of the colonial administration and the major political parties met in Dili. APODETI, which had been invited, declined to attend. The UDT-FRETILIN delegation questioned APODETI's right to attend, since its political option - integration with Indonesia - closed off eventual independence as a possible outcome of an act of self-determination, and so frustrated the basic purpose of a decolonisation process. In their view, APODETI stood for re-colonisation by the Indonesians.

At the first meeting a timetable for decolonisation was agreed upon. It envisaged that a transitional government would be put in place by October 1975 with elections for a National Constitutive Assembly a year later. The Commission agreed to reconvene in Macau in mid-June.

Following the first meeting of the Commission the Indonesians stepped up their anti-communist propaganda using Radio Kupang to broadcast into East Timor. An anonymous pamphlet campaign broke out in Dili demanding that FRETILIN purge itself of all the 'left-wing supporters' named in the pamphlet. The attack was directed principally at Timorese students newly returned from Portugal who had joined FRETILIN.

The Indonesians invited UDT leaders to Jakarta where they stressed Indonesian objections to a FRETILIN 'communist' government in Dili, hinting that this would be unacceptable. The aim of these talks was to build distrust within the coalition, and so break it up.

At this crucial juncture Bishop Ribeiro made his most serious miscalculation. Relying on Indonesian disinformation relayed privately to him by the bishops of Kupang and Atambua, he informed UDT leaders that Vietnamese military advisors were providing military training to FRETILIN supporters. The Indonesians were then able to quote the bishop as a credible source in confirming that FRETILIN was communist, a view long publicised in the Indonesian press. His comments were grist for Bob Santamaria's *News Weekly* mill in Australia, and influenced the stance of bishops there. The comments enabled UDT to project itself as the Catholic, anti-communist, pro-Portuguese party, thus differentiating itself politically from FRETILIN. At this stage some of the Catholics in FRETILIN simply gave up on the institutional Church. In the atmosphere of crisis that developed the coalition collapsed.

That Ribeiro did not check facts before defaming the most popular political party, when such checking could easily have been done, was a serious error of judgment on the bishop's part. It was an error compounded by closing himself off from dialogue with key members of his own church. What seems even more surprising was that neither the papal nuncio in Jakarta, Vincenzo Farano, nor Vatican diplomats in Rome seem to have questioned Ribeiro's assessment of the situation, or the evidence on which this was based. Thus, from the outset, the Vatican's assessment of the situation in East Timor was flawed by biased intelligence.

★

Late in June 1975 a group of UDT leaders was invited to Jakarta by the Centre for Strategic and International Studies, headed by the Catholic Yusuf Wanandi, where they were told that FRETILIN was planning a coup with the support of the MFA officers heading the Decolonisation Commission. They returned to East Timor on the 6th August and events then unfolded quickly. On 9th and 10th August UDT staged large-scale anti-communist demonstrations in Dili. All the members of FRETILIN's Central Committee were condemned and demands were made for the expulsion of the two MFA officers on the Decolonisation Commission, on the grounds that they too were 'communists'. The UDT's intention was to discredit the Commission and the process of decolonisation.

The next day UDT leaders made what has proved to be one of the most disastrous decisions in East Timorese modern history. They staged a coup against the Portuguese Administration, taking over key installations in Dili.[7] They also began to round up and imprison FRETILIN supporters in the major towns. However, given the kinship networks that are integral to Timorese culture, word of the coup quickly leaked out and FRETILIN was able to ensure that the party's main leaders, many of whom were scattered across the colony participating in the literacy and agriculture programs, were safe. Leaders at lower levels were not so lucky, and some were subsequently killed.

★

When Governor Pires was told of the coup, he was at first disbelieving, but then ordered that all troops be confined to barracks. He did not want Portuguese troops embroiled in another colonial war of independence.

When UDT took control of the radio centre in Dili, it immediately began a campaign of disinformation broadcast to Australia which was picked up by an unsuspecting media there. While the UDT rounded up its opponents, the Portuguese sat on their hands, awaiting instructions from Lisbon. No envoy from Lisbon ever arrived. He was sent but was prevented from travelling beyond Denpasar by the Indonesians.

Lacking direction from Lisbon, the Governor tried to win time by sending the officers accused of being 'communist' home, ostensibly to report on the situation. However events were now out of his control. By 19th August, a week after the coup, the FRETILIN leadership had re-organised. Rogerio Lobato convinced soldiers based in the Dili garrison to come over to the FRETILIN side. The garrison at Aileu also sided with

---

[7] UDT 'troops' were armed with only the light weapons held in the police armoury. Many were young people co-opted by their employers and relatives with little or no prior training.

FRETILIN. This gave FRETILIN control of the province's two major armories, 2000 battle-ready troops, heavy weapons and effective transport. The subsequent battle for the control of East Timor was therefore very one-sided, given the difference in fire-power and combat-readiness of troops.

Whether or not UDT's leaders had sold out to the Indonesians at their meeting in Jakarta in exchange for places in an eventual Indonesian administration remains an unanswered question. The timing of events, the use of disinformation to throw the media off balance, the detention of the Lisbon envoy, all seem too co-ordinated to be other than damning.

By the 27th August FRETILIN had control of Dili, and the following week UDT's dispirited troops were driven west to the border town of Batugade where they made a short stand before seeking refuge in West Timor. The speed with which UDT collapsed caught the Indonesians by surprise. Having failed to use APODETI to achieve their end through democratic means, they also seem to have failed with UDT and the use of force. The ineptness of *Operasi Komodo* was becoming increasingly obvious in Jakarta.

★

FRETILIN leaders were drawn into a civil war by UDT's miscalculation rather than by design. Once in command of Dili they re-affirmed Portuguese sovereignty over the colony. The Portuguese flags were left flying over all government buildings which remained untouched. During the battle for Dili the Governor had moved members of his administration, Portuguese officers and their families, to the island of Atauro thirty kilometres off the coast of Dili.

As the fighting raged in the two weeks following the coup, the UDT leadership was scattered. Some fled to Australia, others to the hills where they met up with supporters, and some fled over the border into West Timor where they and their supporters were held in detention camps by the TNI (Indonesian Armed Forces).[8]

The quick FRETILIN victory forced the hand of the Indonesian generals. With FRETILIN now armed and in charge, it was clear to them that integration by stealth had failed. Tactics had to be re-thought. The first step in their revised strategy was to test the strength and resolve of FRETILIN troops in the west of the country. On 8th October Indonesian troops attacked the garrison at Batugade and quickly took it. The battle was portrayed as UDT and APODETI forces fighting back, whereas the reality was that the remnants of the UDT force and its leaders were under lock and key in Atambua in West Timor.

With FRETILIN in charge in Dili, a press contingent arrived from Australia. This included a Channel 9 camera crew. On suspicion that the recapture of Batugade was an Indonesian operation, and not a new chapter in the civil war, the party travelled west to get conclusive proof of this without realizing the danger they faced.

Indonesia's media strategy served its military strategy. An Indonesian invasion was being portrayed as the work of Timorese forces engaged in a civil war that the Indonesians would soon offer to resolve by intervening. This would thus win the Indonesians international approbation, and in the process pave the way for integration. The trick lay in perpetuating

---

8   Tentara Nasional Indonesia

two untruths: that FRETILIN was a communist organisation and therefore a danger to the region, and that the civil war did not end on 27th September when the UDT forces were driven across the border.

In line with their 'test and see' strategy, Balibo was attacked by TNI troops on 14th October and was soon abandoned by FRETILIN as the town was too easily encircled. When Indonesian troops arrived in Balibo, their leader was confronted with the question of what to do with five Australian journalists who could give the lie to the whole campaign. The pragmatic solution was simply to eliminate them. Not only would this preserve the integrity of the strategy, but it would also test Australia's reaction.

While subsequent events mark one of the most disgraceful cover-ups in Australia's national history,[9] the killing of the journalists played out differently in Timor. Radio Kupang branded them as Australian 'communists' killed while fighting with FRETILIN. This story was later changed, and the official story became that they were 'killed in crossfire' in a battle between FRETILIN and UDT-APODETI troops, an explanation that preserved the 'civil war' lie.

What seemed obvious as I read accounts of the 'civil war' was that the UDT coup was poorly planned and poorly executed. It let loose the dogs of war, particularly in the interior where the 'civil' war provided tribal leaders with an excuse to settle old scores, and in consequence over a thousand people were killed. The coup projected FRETILIN into a position its leaders did not seek.

The swiftness with which they took control of the colony generated confidence among them about the strength of their position vis-à-vis the Portuguese, and about their military capability. At the same time the covert war being waged in the west with Indonesian forces was a cause for concern. Still, November 1975 seemed a time of hope that the world would see that the goal was a just one.[10]

Unfortunately, in this they were sadly mistaken. They were small fish in the big pond of international diplomacy, and the predators were circling. Among these were Australian, United States, Japanese, Malaysian and British officials all of whom, along with Vatican diplomats, were eager to protect their respective 'self-interests' at the expense of the people of East Timor.

This chapter in the East Timor Story is certainly not its finest. The consequences were to be devastating. The events led directly to the invasion, but also created a measure of distrust between Timorese that would take a generation to mend. The chapter also represents the Catholic Church's worst hour. Its leader became a tragic figure who aspired to lead but when the hour arrived failed to do so.

---

9   Getting to the bottom of the story of the 'Balibo Five' has been a lifetime quest for Jill Jolliffe who, before she departed Dili, stayed at the Hotel Turismo with the journalists who were later murdered. Her authoritative accounts are to be found in Jill Jolliffe *East Timor: Nationalism and Colonialism* (St. Lucia: University of Queensland Press, 1978), 166-184 and *Cover-Up: The Inside Story of the Balibo Five* (Melbourne: Scribe, 2001).
10 Jill Jolliffe's *East Timor: Nationalism and Colonialism* provides an authoritative account of FRETILIN's outlook and situation at this time.

CHAPTER 12
THE TRAGEDY OF RE-COLONISATION

The path that led FRETILIN to political power in East Timor, and the colony to de facto independence, was strewn with miscalculations. The Portuguese seriously underestimated the strength of nationalist feeling in the colony. They also failed to assess the consequences of relying on local recruits to make up a shortfall in troop numbers as regular Portuguese units were moved to other theatres of combat. The Portuguese presence became so degraded that it lacked the capacity and the will to resist even a haphazardly mounted rebellion.

The Catholic Church's fear of communism led to miscalculations. This led Bishop Ribeiro to warn UDT leaders about Chinese and Russian support for FRETILIN and so rendered the Catholic Church an early victim of Indonesia's propaganda war.[1] There was a communist influence within FRETILIN but it was never a dominant force within the group.[2] This same fear motivated UDT leaders to withdraw from the coalition in May 1975 and to stage an abortive coup three months later.

FRETILIN's leaders seriously miscalculated the strength of the anti-communist sentiment allied against them. The Indonesians used the prevailing fear of communism in the West to successfully mobilise international opinion against FRETILIN. This tactic isolated the Portuguese colony diplomatically.

The Indonesians miscalculated on two important issues. They seriously overestimated the strength of support for integration within East Timor and they failed to gauge the consequences of denouncing FRETILIN as stridently as they did. When the quick victory they anticipated did not come, and the costs of the invasion escalated in both human and financial terms, their anti-communist rhetoric made it almost impossible for them to negotiate with FRETILIN without losing face. So the costs of the invasion continued to multiply.

The cumulative effect of all these miscalculations precipitated a human disaster that would cost many thousands of people – both Indonesian and East Timorese – their livelihoods and their lives. But that is to jump ahead in the story I was trying to piece together as I continued my reading and meetings early in 1992.

---

1   According to Dunn's account, when Ribeiro was asked by UDT leaders, 'How do you know?' his reply was, 'I am your Bishop, you must believe me!' (Dunn, 147).
2   In 2004 I asked Xanana Gusmao if FRETILIN had ever been communist. His answer was that, in trying to make sense of the situation, the group found that Marxist analysis proved more useful than any other form of political analysis, and for a time this was reflected in FRETILIN's rhetoric. While there were certainly some communists in the group, the group itself was a 'front' and it would not be unreasonable for some communists to be present, but they were never the dominant group and the group itself was not communist.

The speed with which FRETILIN forces took control of East Timor caught everyone by surprise, especially the Indonesians. They had backed APODETI and lost. They had then given the tacit go-ahead for the UDT coup, and lost again. Invasion became their third option. While the military had made preparations for this and trained for it, Suharto had resisted his generals thinking that an invasion would compromise Indonesia's position among the non-aligned nations.[3]

FRETILIN's declaration of independence making it the *de facto* government of East Timor convinced him that a good case could now be made for military action. The Indonesians believed that they had to act before FRETILIN could consolidate its position internationally.

The main purpose of Indonesia's propaganda war and its military operations in the west of East Timor was to sow doubts in the minds of neighboring countries about the status of the 'civil war' and so create the perception that there was need for intervention.[4] By early October the generals could assure Suharto that Indonesia had the support of all the countries that needed it to be onside if integration was to occur through military intervention. Against this formidable diplomatic offensive, battle-hardened in the annexation of West Papua (1962)[5] and in the *Confrontasi* clash with Malaysia (1963-6), were arrayed three part-time 'diplomats' with little travel experience outside East Timor, and almost no international diplomatic experience. FRETILIN's 'foreign minister' at the time, at age twenty-four, was Jose Ramos Horta, whom Foreign Affairs officials in Canberra simply refused to take seriously when he visited in 1975.[6]

James Dunn makes the telling point that Australian intelligence knew FRETILIN was not a communist organization. However, for domestic political reasons the Whitlam government was quite happy to promote the narrative that a 'civil war' was being fought in East Timor, and that it was a battle between moderates and communists which threatened Indonesia's security interests. There was no attempt to question Indonesian propaganda. Dunn is scathing in his critique of this stance:

> By encouraging the view that Indonesia was an innocent party to the conflict, a party whose legitimate security interests were under threat, and to whom

---

3   On 18 February 1975 the Indonesian military carried out, at Lampung in southern Sumatra, a joint exercise that mimicked an invasion force landing near Dili. John G. Taylor *Indonesia's Forgotten War: The Hidden History of East Timor* (London: Zed books, 1991), 201.
4   By 16 October 1975 General 'Benny' Murdani had some 3,500 regular Indonesian troops under his command on the East Timor border for this aspect of *Operasi Komodo*. Dunn, 204.
5   In the annexation of West Papua the Indonesians had been able to convince the international community that the act of self-determination they orchestrated was legitimate despite its many shortcomings. There seems little doubt that they hoped they could repeat this exercise in East Timor, despite the differences in each case, which was why, in the lead up to the invasion, they courted sympathetic *liurais* and made one of them the first 'governor' of the annexed twenty-seventh province. Jill Jolliffe *East Timor: Nationalism & Colonialism*, 50ff.
6   Seasoned political leaders, such as Whitlam, had great difficulty in taking the new leadership in East Timor seriously. In their view political leaders could not appear out of a vacuum. Here they miscalculated badly. Horta was to receive valuable tutelage from the former Australian consul in Dili, J.S. (Jim) Dunn, and also private tuition at the Development Studies Centre of the Australian National University, arranged by Professor Fred Fisk. Jolliffe, 111.

Portugal might consider turning for assistance in restoring order to the colony, Australia became an accomplice to the Indonesian conspiracy to bring about the incorporation of the territory, in disregard of the wishes of the Timorese people themselves.[7]

★

From August 1975 FRETILIN became the *de facto* power in the colony. The Portuguese, now camped on Atauro Island, still could not believe that they had been so comprehensively wrong-footed, first by the UDT and then by FRETILIN. The Governor refused to negotiate with FRETILIN on terms for a Portuguese return to Dili. To express his displeasure, he had removed Portuguese medical staff from the Dili hospital which left victims of the 'civil war', both UDT and FRETILIN, without professional medical attention until help arrived from Australia some weeks later. Trust between the Portuguese administration and FRETILIN leaders was non-existent.

FRETILIN leaders now regarded UDT leaders as traitors who had sold out to the Indonesian cause for their thirty pieces of silver and refused to give them standing in negotiations about the future of the colony. This position was not acceptable to the Portuguese or the Indonesians now holding some of these leaders in West Timor.

FRETILIN was willing for the Portuguese to return to Dili but insisted that they provide in-principle recognition of East Timor's independence. With the Governor refusing to come to Dili and FRETILIN's leaders refusing to go to Atauro for fear of being arrested, a stalemate which served no one's interests ensued.

FRETILIN was forced to put a caretaker administration in place which proved remarkably robust given that the colony was left with few people outside the military with administrative and technical skills. The Chinese, who controlled the business sector, had fled taking their money with them, so there was a currency crisis, and no operating bank. In many ways the military challenge was less daunting than the civil challenges.

FRETILIN leaders also had to respond to Indonesian provocation in the west. The battle in the west went badly for the Indonesians once the wet season arrived, and they lost the advantage provided by their light armored vehicles. When the fighting moved into the mountains, the situation suited FRETILIN fighters because they knew the terrain, and were well trained for guerilla warfare.

★

The Portuguese held talks with the Indonesians in Rome in early November 1975. In FRETILIN's eyes they were more interested in negotiating the release of twenty-three Portuguese soldiers held by the Indonesians since September than in the fate of their colony.[8] FRETILIN'S leaders knew the colony had been isolated diplomatically, and since they lacked the resources to engage in an outright war with their powerful neighbor, the most likely scenario was now a protracted guerilla war. From October 1975 onwards arms and supplies were moved to selected strategic locations in the mountains.

---

7   Dunn, 173.
8   Their release had become a major political issue in Portugal. Dunn, 234.

The Indonesians attacked again from the west in late November. This action caused FRETILIN to finally abandon negotiations with the Portuguese and make a unilateral declaration of independence. The leaders hoped that if East Timor could quickly win recognition as an independent nation, they could appeal for support from the United Nations. The move was an act of desperation based in the vain hope that East Timor could win the instantaneous international recognition that had happened in Angola.[9] However the geopolitical cards were all stacked against them. James Dunn records the overwhelming sentiment among FRETILIN fighters at this time quoting one of its leaders as saying:

> It is not that we want to be independent yet, or that we are ready for it. But if we are going to fight to the end we can at least die independent.[10]

★

On 2nd December, well aware of the impending invasion, the Australian government warned its citizens to leave Timor. With the example of Balibo still fresh in their minds, few expatriates needed a second prompting. Radio Kupang reinforced the government's message by declaring that any Australians found in Dili would be killed when 'UDT-APODETI' troops arrived. This warning precipitated a general exodus of refugees from East Timor to Darwin.

The Indonesian invasion began at 4:00am five days later. An invasion force composed mainly of Javanese troops arrived in two waves. A parachute commando drop was followed by the seaborne landing of some ten thousand troops. The invasion was a technical disaster. Some of the commandos were dropped too early and landed in Dili harbor where, weighed down by their parachutes and packs, they drowned. Their colleagues angered at what had happened went on a rampage shooting indiscriminately.

APODETI supporters who came out to welcome the Indonesians were gunned down. Chinese who came out with gifts for the invaders were also gunned down.[11] The troops even fired on each other in the confusion. From a military perspective the invasion was an embarrassment.[12]

★

In 1975 Dili lacked a wharf. Cargo was loaded and unloaded onto barges at a jetty situated more or less across the road from the Bishop's residence. The jetty became a notorious

---

9   The MPLA which, with Cuban help, had become the victorious faction in the battle for independence in Angola, made its unilateral declaration of independence on 11 November 1975, and was recognised by thirty countries almost immediately. By contrast, East Timor's diplomatic efforts were doomed by the conspiracy of western and other south-east Asian nations wishing to do business with Indonesia.
10 Dunn, 242.
11 Quoting from the work of James Dunn *Tapol Bulletin* No 20, February 1977 refers to 500 Chinese being shot down in the first day of fighting, and an estimated 7000 being killed before the end of the year.
12 This disastrous enterprise is well covered from an Indonesian perspective in Julius Pour *Benny Moerdani: Profile of a Soldier Statesman* (Jakarta: Yayasan Kejuangan Panglima Besar Sudirman, 1993, 1st edition, 316ff). Pour makes it clear that Murdani was convinced that Indonesian troops thought they were fighting a Marxist-Leninist foe comparable to FREMILO in Mozambique.

'killing ground' in the days after the invasion. Here men and women were routinely lined up and shot. Their bodies were weighted with metal bars and thrown into the sea. Those remaining in the line on the jetty awaiting execution were forced to count aloud as the bodies fell. Roger East, the sole Australian journalist to remain in Dili, met his fate in this manner.

When Liquica and Maubara on the north coast were taken by Indonesian troops advancing from the west, the population in both towns was slaughtered. In the town of Aileu, south of Dili, all residents over four years old who had not fled were executed. The children were loaded into a truck and taken to an Indonesian orphanage.[13]

Church and community leaders tried to intervene and stop the indiscriminate killing but to little avail. Memory of the savagery associated with the Javanese invasion is so etched in the minds of the East Timorese that many still have an abiding hatred for all things Javanese. The behavior of the first two battalions to arrive in Dili was so rapacious and outrageous that they were both withdrawn two weeks later in disgrace. The brutality of the invasion cast the die for East Timorese-Javanese relationships subsequently, and seemingly forever.[14]

*

Bishop Ribeiro showed commendable courage during the invasion. He was one of the few Europeans to remain in Dili. He confronted the Indonesian commanders about the senseless killing and even conveyed the injured to hospital in his own car. He was knocked down and had his episcopal ring stolen for his effrontery.

The bishop and da Costa Lopes witnessed the executions on the Dili jetty from the Bishop's residence and went out at night, at considerable risk, to retrieve what bodies they could for burial. Ribeiro was quickly disabused of any enthusiasm he had for integration once he witnessed the barbaric treatment Indonesian troops meted out to the East Timorese. His new advice to his flock was 'to resist, but to do so intelligently'.

Ribeiro became more and more distressed at the turn of events, and at his own impotence as time passed. When this began to affect his health and he began to lose control of his anger, the papal nuncio, Vincenzo Farano, stepped in and announced to the assembled clergy that the bishop was resigning.[15] He was in ill health and close to a mental breakdown when he departed Timor in July 1977. On returning to Portugal, Ribeiro aged 59, retired to Braga where he helped train those Timorese diocesan seminarians fortunate enough to escape before the invasion. Carlos Belo was then completing his training as a Salesian priest and visited him there. The bishop encouraged Belo to return to East Timor, if this was at all possible. According to Jolliffe, Ribeiro could never be drawn to speak about his time in East Timor.[16]

---

13 For a detailed account of the atrocities which accompanied the Indonesian invasion see James Dunn, 250-254.
14 The East Timorese distinguish between Indonesians as a whole and the Javanese.
15 Fr Avo was a colleague of Ribeiro in East Timor and a compatriot who subsequently migrated to Australia where he served as chaplain to the Portuguese community in Sydney. I interviewed him there in 1994, about Ribeiro and events surrounding the invasion.
16 Jill Jolliffe wrote a sympathetic obituary for Ribeiro which was published in the *Sydney Morning Herald* 22 August 2002, on the occasion of his death, entitled 'Bishop kept Timor secrets to himself'.

With Ribeiro's departure, the clergy nominated Martinho da Costa Lopes to lead the Church in East Timor through what proved to be the darkest years of Indonesian re-colonisation. The darkness was more than figurative as during his time as leader East Timor remained almost completely cut off from the outside world. A communications blackout imposed by the Indonesians masked its 'pacification' activities from other nations in much the same way then as Indonesia does today in West Papua. Entry into the country was tightly controlled as was the press, and the mail.[17] NGOs, other than the compliant Indonesian Red Cross and US Catholic Relief Services, were not welcome. Foreign journalists were banned until the late 1980s. It became impossible for outsiders to form a reliable view of what was happening in East Timor.

Jill Jolliffe, based in Portugal, used information from the East Timorese refugee community there to report on events in Timor for the Australian press. However, the Indonesians made sure that they had plants among this migrant community to ensure that it could never speak with a coherent voice.[18] The Church became an important source of information that could be juxtaposed against Indonesian and migrant accounts of what was happening in East Timor. However, visiting clerics were carefully screened and their accounts of the situation in East Timor seemed to vary, often depending on their attitude to the perceived benefits of integration.

The Vatican took the opportunity afforded by Ribeiro's resignation to downgrade the status of the diocese, making da Costa Lopes, the first native Timorese to lead the diocese, an apostolic administrator directly accountable to the Vatican through the papal nuncio in Jakarta. While the nuncio who appointed da Costa Lopes, Archbishop Farano, was sympathetic to the situation of the East Timorese post-1975, his successor, Pablo Puente was not. Puente was personally cultivated by General Murdani as part of *Operation Komodo* and became so unremittingly pro-integration that he downplayed intelligence from the local Church and is 'not fondly remembered in East Timor'.[19]

*

Da Costa Lopes led the Church from 1977 until 1983 and was regarded as 'the Bispo' by his people (and the Indonesian military leaders in Dili as well), and so came to think

---

17 Letters going to or coming from overseas were suspect and most were dumped in Dili harbour. However, information still flowed within the country along the indigenous exchange system despite severe restrictions on movement.
18 Such migrants were most likely to be those with considerable means at their disposal. According to Taylor, drawing on information supplied by a refugee who left Dili in the mid-1980s, the standard payment for a visa to exit Timor at that time was between 4 and 5 million rupiahs (US$3636-$4545), an impossible amount for all except the elite to raise.
19 Patrick Smythe *The Heaviest Blow – The Catholic Church and the East Timor Issue* (Munster: LIT, 2004), 192. East Timor was Puente's first appointment as nuncio and he interpreted Vatican policy re integration in the narrowest of terms. At face value, his friendship with Murdani, who was one of the chief strategists in developing *Operasi Komodo*, and as military commander, was the man who unilaterally called off the ceasefire with FRETILIN in 1983, seems singularly unwise. However, as nuncio, Puente's primary responsibility was to establish good relations with the government of Indonesia, and so befriending one of the most powerful men in the country, who was also a Catholic, makes some sense. He may have hoped to influence events in this way, but there is little evidence that he did.

of himself in this light. However he was never ordained as a bishop. His appointment as Apostolic Administrator solved one of the Vatican's problems. Because Da Costa Lopes was not a bishop he could not be considered part of the Indonesian Bishops' Conference.

As a state with observer status at the United Nations, the Vatican did not wish to give East Timor an ecclesial status that could be interpreted by the Indonesian government as *de facto* recognition of annexation, particularly when the UN did not recognise this. Making the diocese directly accountable to the Vatican, and not part of the Indonesian Bishops' Conference, obviated this difficulty. However, it had the unfortunate consequence of leaving the papal nuncio with a *prima facie* conflict of interest once the human rights of the East Timorese were abused by the Indonesians and the Apostolic Administrator spoke in their defence.

In East Timor the local Catholic Church quickly became the only civil institution able to offer the local population a degree of protection from the arbitrary justice meted out by the armed forces and the police. When Archbishop Farano departed Jakarta in 1980, the pro-Indonesian stance of his successor meant that da Costa Lopes, the local clergy and members of the Church he led were totally isolated in the face of Indonesian hostility. When da Costa Lopes spoke out publicly against the abuse of human and civil rights in East Timor he was sacked by the nuncio and replaced by Carlos Belo whom as a Salesian religious the Vatican thought might be more compliant.[20]

As I read what limited information was available on East Timor from the period 1977 to 1983, I became intrigued by the situation into which da Costa Lopes had been projected, and was determined to find out more about this brave leader when the opportunity arose.

★

The brutality the Indonesian military showed towards the civilian population in areas they controlled in 1975-80 was fuelled by the fact that they had to fight so hard to win ground against FRETILIN forces, even to go beyond Dili. The troops did not expect this as they had been led to believe that the East Timorese were 'a backward people'. The Indonesian troops found themselves confronted by a well-organised, highly mobile force easily able to negotiate the difficult terrain, and one that had superior weapons. These factors led some commanders to believe that FRETILIN had to be getting external help.

Four years after the invasion, the Indonesian army found itself still confined to the readily accessible coastal strip and the river valleys while FRETILIN controlled the majority of the colony's rugged interior. At the time of the invasion, all the East Timorese who could fled to the mountains, as their ancestors had done since time immemorial when invaders arrived. There they believed FRETILIN fighters could and would protect them. This was true until 1983 when the US military provided the Indonesian military with new planes and ordinance such as napalm and defoliants rendering life vulnerable, even in the most inaccessible of mountains. The US also began training Indonesian military officers in the tactics for mass control of the population used in Vietnam.

---

20 Apostolic Nuncio Pietro Sambi told me personally that da Costa Lopes was told to vacate his role and then asked to resign so that it would seem that he stepped down voluntarily, which he did not.

★

In early 1976 the Indonesians established a civil administration in Dili and the larger towns. Selected UDT and APODETI leaders, previously held in West Timor or released from jail in Dili, were appointed to senior positions to give the administration some legitimacy. By 31st May 1976 a puppet regime known as the 'Popular Assembly' was in place. Its members immediately petitioned President Suharto to incorporate East Timor as the 27th province of Indonesia. A week later hand-picked representatives of the Assembly were flown to Jakarta to present this petition to Suharto in person.

The Indonesian Government labelled the petition an 'act of self-determination'.[21] However, the United Nations refused to recognise it as legitimate, so Portugal remained legally responsible for East Timor even though it had no presence.

★

Following the invasion the Indonesians set about building roads and schools in areas under their control. Army generals took control of the local economy.[22] Infrastructure development mainly served the military officers' commercial and military interests and little was done to improve the general living conditions of the East Timorese. Bahasa became the official language. Monuments to *integrasi* in the form of giant statues were erected in major towns. A program of transmigration was introduced that saw traditional lands taken over by the immigrants and the local people displaced. Some thirty thousand Indonesians came to East Timor as part of this program. This number quickly swelled when the relatives of the migrants followed them.

Traditional animist beliefs and practices were banned. A process of 'Indonesianisation' was underway that threatened to obliterate Timorese culture. While this was happening in the towns, FRETILIN consolidated its position in the interior in 1976-77, but fighting numerically superior forces supported by airpower was beginning to take a heavy toll and by the early 1980s FRETILIN could no longer provide protection for East Timorese living in the mountains.

★

FRETILIN leaders were divided over whether or not to negotiate with the Indonesians. People increasingly looked to Nicolau Lobato who favored struggle, rather than the FRETILIN president, Xavier Amaral, who favored making peace.

Up until the late 1970s the FRETILIN cause was helped by poor troop morale among the Indonesians. Indonesian troops rotated to East Timor were portrayed as 'volunteers' fighting alongside 'APODETI-UDT' fighters. In practice, they found themselves alone on the front line, with inferior weapons and poor logistical support. They were not paid

---

21 This was a repeat of a strategy that Indonesia had used in annexing West Papua. Suharto had been a major figure in the annexation of West Papua.
22 Taylor traces in some detail the way in which this occurred. General Benny Murdani and two of his colleagues controlled the coffee trade through the company they established and owned, P.T.Denok. This made them very wealthy men. See Taylor, 125-7.

for months on end. Many Indonesians were killed or wounded as the result of persistent guerilla attacks. Those who died received little acknowledgement in Indonesia. Reprisals against the local population were vicious but, far from discouraging further attacks, they only fed local hostility.[23]

In 1977 Indonesian authorities doubled troop numbers in an attempt to pacify its new and recalcitrant province. This proved a costly exercise. They also began to employ strategies used during the Vietnam conflict establishing 'strategic hamlets'. The strategy sought to isolate villages from FRETILIN influence and to cut off FRETILIN's food supply. Large groups of people were moved from villages to the outskirts of towns where all movement could be monitored. The strategy kept the population under constant surveillance in concentration camps set up to control the production of food. By 1983 the East Timorese living in the hills faced a stark choice: to starve in the mountains or to die of disease in re-settlement camps established by the Indonesians on the malaria-infested low lands. The result of this strategy was that fertile lands previously under cultivation had to be abandoned in favor of poorer land near cities. The strategy quickly created a famine condition.

★

The independence cause suffered major setbacks in 1978. FRETILIN lost its radio link with the outside world. Those involved in the struggle for independence outside East Timor lost contact with those fighting in East Timor. As well as this, FRETILIN's charismatic leader, Nicolau Lobato, was killed on the last day of the year in a fire fight with Indonesian troops. A new Indonesian strategy that targeted FRETILIN's leadership saw a number of them killed in a short time before the charismatic Xanana Gusmao took command in 1982. Xanana was to lead the military and the political fight in East Timor for a decade, and in the process become the mythic hero for his people. The Indonesians' failure to capture him until 1992 gave heart to an embattled and oppressed people, and enabled FRETILIN to rebuild its grass roots base.

In 1983 a new Indonesian commander sought to conduct a campaign to win over the 'hearts and minds' of the local inhabitants. As part of this strategy, he negotiated a ceasefire with Gusmao. However, this did not sit well with the generals in Jakarta, and when he was replaced by General Murdani, the latter immediately revoked the ceasefire and threatened to 'exterminate' FRETILIN. An uneven and bitter struggle ensued in which no quarter was given. Surrender became an illusory option for FRETILIN fighters as it led to almost certain death.

With better aircraft FRETILIN positions in the interior could now be bombed with impunity so there were no safe havens. Attack helicopters gave Indonesian troops greater mobility and more effective firepower against guerillas. The Indonesians also began to use East Timorese conscripts as human shields in their infamous 'fence of legs' operations, sweeping through FRETILIN strongholds with the result that FRETILIN's grasp on the interior was broken and its numbers savagely depleted. FRETILIN forces were gradually

---

23 In the first four months of the struggle the Indonesians lost about 2000 men, while some 60,000 Timorese perished in 1975-76. Taylor, 70-71.

being contained in the jungles around Los Palos in the eastern section of the province. However, the FRETILIN organization, which made use of the kinship networks existing across the country, remained intact.[24]

All of this came at a cost, as Taylor observes:

> ...Almost all social groups, economic classes and political elites from pre-invasion East Timorese society now defined themselves primarily through their alienation from the military project. The differentiated social structure of the pre-invasion period, with its divisions between colonial, rural and nationalist groups, reflecting religious, cultural, educational and economic cleavages, converged ideologically and politically as a result of military occupation. Furthermore, just as this opposition united previously disparate groups, so too did it include a growing number of students and young people, the so-called second generation, which the Indonesians had hoped to 're-socialise'. Consequently, there were increasingly fewer social groups and institutions on which the military could rely to achieve its objectives.[25]

In Taylor's view the growing opposition drove the Indonesians to increasingly drastic measures that in the end equated to 'eradicating all traces of indigenous society and culture'.

Gusmao reconfigured the resistance. He separated the armed resistance from the clandestine resistance. The former was now called *Forcas Armadas de Libertcao Nacional De Timor* (National Armed forces for the Liberation of East Timor), or FALINTIL. The latter became an urban movement embracing all levels of society that operated to subvert Indonesian intentions, publicise the situation in East Timor and support the armed resistance with intelligence and supplies. FALINTIL was re-organised as small highly mobile units that operated on a 'hit and run' basis avoiding pitched battles. The armed struggle thus took on a more symbolic role to the clandestine resistance which eventually extended down to school children.

★

In 1989, fourteen years after the invasion, the Indonesians judged the 'pacification' process to be sufficiently complete to lift their embargo on visitors. While at one level the 27th province was militarily contained, a major problem remained. Little progress had been made in winning over the minds and hearts of the East Timorese, particularly the youth. While students now spoke Bahasa, they remained as committed as ever to the ideal of national independence. This was made more than evident in the demonstration that sparked the Santa Cruz massacre.

The Indonesians now began to employ their ultimate 'drastic measure' – to contain the population through a program of sterilization under the guise of 'population control'. Church leaders objected strenuously. Sterilization occurred without women's knowledge during surgical procedures such as caesarian sections. The result was that the local women

---

24 The re-settlement camp strategy in East Timor functioned in the same way as the Derby leprosarium in the Kimberley in the 1950s in re-awakening kinship connections among peoples drawn from different areas.
25 Taylor, 157.

lost confidence in the public health system and came to rely on clinics run by Catholic sisters.

*

In December 1991 the head of Australian Catholic Relief (ACR)[26] Michael Whiteley, accepted an invitation from the Indonesian Bishops' Conference to visit East Timor as part of a delegation exploring how the Church in Indonesia could better provide material assistance to the East Timorese.[27] On his return he compiled a confidential report for the ACR Board summing up the situation in East Timor. His visit occurred a month after the Santa Cruz massacre. In view of subsequent events I found his comments very insightful:

> The situation in East Timor is as serious now as it has been at any time during the past 17 years. The tension and frustration among the East Timorese must be building up until it becomes intolerable. With no freedom and very little opportunity to build an acceptable way of life for themselves, more and more people, especially the young, will take actions – either as part of the organised resistance or independently – to change the situation in East Timor. The Indonesians appear to be taking a harder line on dissent and are prepared to take whatever action is necessary to repress it. More bloodshed and suffering can, most regrettably, be expected.[28]

He goes on to comment that Santa Cruz should be interpreted as the *consequence rather than the cause* of this tension and concludes:

> The Church in Australia, including ACR, should be prepared to accompany the Church in East Timor as it confronts the challenges facing it. This will require us to take those actions in the political, justice, development and relief area which the Church in East Timor requests.[29]

Two years later I found myself as deputy Chair of Australian Catholic Relief working with Michael to implement this multi-dimensional agenda. His description of the Church we would be accompanying together is as follows:

> The Church (in East Timor) was described to me as one that has been and still is in most cases, only ceremonial and sacramental. It is being challenged to become

---

26 To be officially renamed by the Australian Catholic Bishops' Conference as Caritas Australia on 1 July 1996.
27 The Indonesian bishops declined to take any steps to address the abuse of human rights in East Timor which might jeopardise the position of the Church in Indonesia. Their policy, first set out in 1983 (eight years after the abuse started), was to provide what material assistance they could for the victims. Letter to Monsignor Carlos Belo from the Indonesian Bishops' Conference, 17 November 1983, in Catholic Commission for Justice, Development and Peace (Melbourne Archdiocese), *The Church and East Timor*, (Melbourne, 1993), 18.
28 Whiteley Michael 'Confidential Report on Visit to East Timor December 15th -17th' (Sydney: ACR, 1991), 6.
29 ibid.

more involved in the issues facing the East Timorese. The way that it should do this is the basis of divisions in the Church. These divisions are focused on differences between the young and old; between the East Timorese diocesan clergy and religious and the expatriate clergy (including the Javanese); and on the role of lay involvement. I was told that even among the members of one of the religious orders there are … different approaches to the challenges facing East Timor.[30]

Importantly, he added:

There is a real effort being made to address these differences and I believe that the current crisis is playing a role in accelerating this. Bishop Belo is playing a crucial, but very difficult role in the process. His welcoming, open and relaxed manner certainly hides the pressure he must be under.[31]

It seemed to me, as I began to formulate in my own mind how I might be of assistance, that Belo must be a very lonely man facing both division from within and pressure from without, with little in the way of support in positioning the Church to achieve its mission. I felt there was at least an opening there for me to be of help if this help was required. So I began to explore what more I could find out about the Church in East Timor, its connections with Australia, and the way in which it had dealt with the crises created by the Indonesians' tragic and anthropologically naïve efforts at re-colonising the country.

---

30 ibid, 5.
31 ibid.

PART I

THREE STORIES

3. Catholic Church Story

CHAPTER 13
THE INDONESIAN CHURCH'S ORPHAN CHILD

As I put together the narrative of East Timor, I was struck by the prominent role the Church and its leaders had played. During the Portuguese period the Church was an arm of the government, and this gave its leaders a certain credibility among the East Timorese. While the political status of the Church changed under Indonesian rule, the credibility of its leaders did not. What changed was the reason why they were still seen as credible leaders.

In the Portuguese era people expected the bishop to assist them to address injustice and corruption perpetrated by *liurai* or by administration officials. Many of these officials were Catholic. The bishop operated from *within* the ruling system. This intercessory role continued under Indonesian rule (and became a matter of life and death for many individuals). But da Costa Lopes, and later Carlos Belo, operated from *outside* the ruling system.

The East Timorese people's long history of looking to the Church for protection lay behind efforts of those living here in Australia, especially those in Melbourne, to co-opt the Church here in their struggle for self-determination. I do not think they would have put the matter in those words, but this was a conclusion I was coming to. After the Santa Cruz massacre and that very moving Mass in the Cathedral which I have already described, I was more than ready to be co-opted as their spokesperson. However, I still needed to know more about the way in which the Catholic Church functioned, not only in East Timor but also in Indonesia, since the standing of the Church there clearly had an important bearing on its standing in East Timor.

In 1992 the Indonesian and East Timorese churches were caught up in Suharto's *Orde Baru* (New Order)[1] and functioned within the opportunities and limits of its espoused political philosophy – *Pancasila* – the foundational philosophy of the Indonesian state. Both churches predate the establishment of the Indonesian state by several centuries.

★

---

1   The *Orde Baru* (New Order) is the name given to the political order set up after Suharto succeeded Sukarno following the abortive attempt by the Indonesia Communist Party to seize power in 1965. Suharto's regime was, understandably, vigorously anti-communist, and as it became established, the new order limited participation in government to the military and a narrow band of civilian officials. The student-led pro-democracy movement of the 1990s was to overthrow this political order.

The Indonesian Catholic Church dates itself back to the arrival of the remarkable Franciscan friar, Odoric Mattiussi, early in the fourteenth century. At that time Church leaders in Rome knew very little about Asia, and Mattiussi's mission was to find out more. He was clearly an extraordinary character as is evidenced from his arduous and successful journeys.[2]

The first wave of missionaries arrived two centuries later, following the Portuguese capture of Malacca. They subsequently settled in various places in what was later to become Indonesia. The famous Jesuit missionary, Francis Xavier, was one of these early missionaries, visiting the islands on his missionary journey to Japan.[3] Christianity arrived in present-day Indonesia at approximately the same time as Islam, and almost a millennium after the introduction of Hinduism and Buddhism.

With the formation of the Dutch East India Company in 1602, Protestant influence became dominant in the region. In areas controlled by the Dutch, Catholicism was banned or confined to the ever-shrinking Portuguese-controlled enclaves in the east of the archipelago.[4] It was not until the second half of the nineteenth century that active mission work could resume unhindered on the islands that comprise present-day Indonesia. Flores and West Timor became Catholic centres. They remain strong centres to this day with over half the population Catholic.

Present-day Indonesia is a secular state. Although the population is predominantly Muslim, Indonesia is religiously diverse with long-established traditions drawing on Hindu, Buddhist, Catholic and Protestant histories, as well as the Islamic (predominantly Sunni) traditions.[5]

★

When Sukarno sought in 1945 to unify the many islands and peoples that make up Indonesia, part of his strategy was to formulate the political philosophy known as *Pancasila* (Five Principles). Subsequently, this became the ideology of Suharto's *Orde Baru* (New Order). Suharto gave this doctrine almost mythic significance, seeing it as the epitome of ancient Javanese wisdom.

The five principles have been articulated in a variety of ways since 1945. Under the *Orde Baru* regime they had the status of 'moral principles' and constituted the foundation on which human rights in Indonesia rested. Officially the five principles were expressed as follows:

---

2   Mattiussi departed from Rome in 1318 and journeyed overland via Constantinople to the Persian Gulf. From there he set sail for India, landing near present day Bombay where the Franciscans had a mission. He then ventured into the unknown by junk, arriving in Java en route to his eventual destination, China. He completed the journey back to his native Italy via the Silk Road, arriving home in 1330.
3   He visited and worked in the present day Maluku Islands (Moluccas) which are west of New Guinea.
4   Under the Dutch, Catholicism was banned and priests jailed. In 1624, one priest, Fr Egidius d'Abreu SJ, was executed for saying Mass while in jail. With the resolution of Catholic-Protestant tensions in Europe, the proscription of Catholicism was lifted and Indonesia became a major mission field for the Catholic Church in the Netherlands.
5   In 2010 data on the various religious groups was a follows: Islam 87%, Protestant 7%, Catholic 3%, Hindu and Buddhist under 1%. The overall population is now of the order of 245 million which makes Indonesia the country with the biggest Muslim population in the world. The Government recognises Catholicism and Protestantism as two distinct religions.

- *Belief in the one and only God.* Every Indonesian citizen, no matter which religious denomination or faith they follow, should respect each other's belief for the sake of the harmony and peace of mankind. This Principle contains the precept of religious tolerance and the freedom of all to adhere to the religion or faith of his or her choice.
- *Just and civilised humanity.* Fundamental individual human rights and freedoms need to be balanced with the individual's obligation toward society and state.
- *The Unity of Indonesia.*
- *Democracy led by the wisdom of representatives.* Democracy is conceived in a way that is consonant with Indonesia's traditional and social values which emphasise consensus and imply not only political equality, but economic, social and cultural equality.
- *Social justice.* The common endeavor to build a just and prosperous society, materially as well as spiritually, in which any form of exploitation of human beings is prohibited.[6]

The affirmation that a person's religion should be respected is, however, qualified. In practice, the government recognised only six religions – Islam, Catholicism, Protestantism, Hinduism, Buddhism, and Confucianism. Each citizen was expected to nominate one of these official religions on his or her identity card. This practice was adopted not only as an effective way to implement the 'moral principles' but also as a means to proscribe communism and other atheistic ideologies. Religion is an integral aspect of Indonesian culture.

★

When East Timor became the twenty-seventh province of Indonesia, it came under the *Pancasila,* which had two immediate effects: the Catholic Church had to be respected as a civil institution in East Timor, as it was in Indonesia, and all Timorese had to nominate their religion.

The indigenous religion of the East Timorese is best described as animism which is not officially recognised by Indonesia. When the East Timorese were asked to nominate their religion, the majority had to make a choice, and they chose Catholicism. Clearly, they had no wish to take on the religion of their oppressors. Also, they had had considerable exposure to the Church and its practices under the Portuguese, although only about thirty percent had become Catholics during Portuguese colonial rule. The fact that so many embraced Catholicism after 1975 can be interpreted as a form of protest against the invaders most of whom were Muslim. The consequence was that Catholic numbers in East Timor exploded. Although spurred on, initially at least, by political necessity, their motivation would change as their suffering deepened, and their respect for Catholic Church leaders as champions of human rights grew.

The annexation of East Timor as a province of Indonesia created diplomatic and practical problems for both the Vatican and the Church in Indonesia. The question for the Vatican was: Where does the Church in East Timor fit into episcopal arrangements now that it is cut off from Portugal? If it was included in the Indonesian Bishops' Conference, the Vatican would be giving de facto recognition to the annexation. The Vatican temporised by not appointing da Costa Lopes as bishop, instead appointing him Apostolic Administrator

---

6   These interpretations are paraphrased from the Indonesian Embassy website London, July 2013.

accountable to its Secretary of State through the papal representative in Jakarta.

In his capacity as Apostolic Administrator of East Timor da Costa Lopes was invited to attend meetings of the Indonesian bishops' conference, but merely as an observer. This left the question of whether or not the Church in East Timor was part of the Church in Indonesia deliberately ambiguous.

Vatican policy was, however, unambiguous. Its diplomats were decidedly of the view that East Timor should be integrated into Indonesia, and this was the view put to the other episcopal conferences in the region by nuncio after nuncio, including the nuncio to Australia. Vatican policy seems based on three sets of considerations. Firstly, the general diplomatic wisdom of the 1980s was that East Timor was not viable as an independent nation. Secondly, weighing on the minds of Vatican diplomats were the likely costs that speaking out about human rights abuses could have for the Church in Indonesia. Thirdly, they were also concerned about the relationship between Christians and the followers of Islam more generally. The third of these considerations carried more weight under Pope John Paul II.

★

Each year the Vatican compiles and publishes data on selected aspects of Church life in its various cultural regions. The numbers are cumulated from locally sourced figures. Data for the churches of Indonesia and East Timor is instructive in understanding the moral and political dilemmas that the abuse of human rights in East Timor posed for Church leaders. The two tables below show the comparative developments in the churches of East Timor and Indonesia in the period 1975-2009.

	1975	1985	1995	2005	2009
National pop	659,000	660,000	860,000	889,000	1,115,000
Catholic pop	197,000	513,000	732,000	800,000	972,000
%	29.9%	77.7%	85.1%	90.0%	87.2%

Table 1: Growth of the Church in East Timor 1975–2009[7]

Growth in Church numbers in East Timor in the two decades after the Indonesian invasion is staggering.

	1975	1985	1995	2005	2009
National pop	136.04m	163.04m	193.98	219.95m	231.37m
Catholic pop	2.86m	4.10m	5.39m	6.54m	7.08m
%	2.1%	2.5%	2.8%	3.0%	3.1%

Table 2. Growth of the Church in Indonesia 1975–2009[8]

Most Australian Catholics, aware that Islam is the dominant religion in Indonesia, are quite surprised at the sheer size, in absolute numbers, of the Catholic Church there.

The following table provides further detail of the Church's ministry in East Timor.

---

7   Compiled from the *Statistical Yearbook of the Church*. (Libreria Editrice Vaticana: 1975, 1985, 1995, 2005 and 2009). The numbers here are conservative. For instance, the World Bank Report for 2005 gives the Catholic population figure as 98%.
8   ibid

	1975	1985	1995	2005	2009
	Ministry			Data	
Staffed Parishes	19	21	31	39	53
Bishops	1	0	2	3	3
Priests	43	38	93	160	201
Religious Women	51	52	199	365	441
Catholics/Priest	4,581	13,500	7,871	5,000	4,836
	Education			Data	
Primary Schools	51	85	114	130	187
Primary Numbers	8,819	18,064	19,407	25,891	44,638
Secondary Schools	2	21	46	32	71
Secondary Numbers	562	3,860	7,076	9,874	15,314

Table 3. East Timor: Key Aspects of Church Ministry 1975–2009[9]

The data on East Timor in the table above indicates that the Church has played a significant role in the expansion of education that took place under Indonesian rule and which has continued since independence. It also indicates the challenge that both da Costa Lopes and Belo faced as Church leaders in the decade after the invasion. While the number of clergy and religious remained unchanged, the Catholic population exploded, as did the need to create the Church infrastructure required to cope with this explosion. The data also makes clear that the Church now plays an important role in secondary education. However, it has limited footprint in the tertiary sector besides the Catholic teachers' college founded by the Marist Brothers in Baucau and the teacher training institute associated with Colégio Santo Inácio de Loiola in Kasait and conducted by the Jesuits, along with the technical training facilities in the charge of the Salesian order in Dili, Baucau, Los Palos and Maliana.[10]

By comparison, the Catholic Church in Indonesia dwarfs that in East Timor and is substantially larger than that in Australia. This should not come as a surprise given that the Church in Indonesia is some two hundred years older than in Australia, and also given the size of Indonesia's population.

The data in Table 4 provides a clear idea of the differences in size. The table paints an impressive picture of the Church in Indonesia and its place within civil society. What has to be added to this information is the fact that the Church in Indonesia has a substantial footprint in tertiary education. In 2009, for instance, there were over sixty-five thousand students in Catholic institutions of higher learning and around eight thousand theology students.

---

9 ibid
10 There are moves afoot to establish a Catholic University in Dili, but, at the time of writing, this is proving a controversial and divisive proposal.

	1975	1985	1995	2005	2009
	Ministry			Data	
Staffed Parishes	469	665	829	1,162	1,256
Bishops	24	26	26	27	39
Priests	1,464	1,747	2,585	3,363	3,935
Religious Women	3,811	4,230	6,708	8,363	8,456
Catholics/Priest	1,952	2,348	2,084	1,944	1,800
	Education			Data	
Primary Schools	2,984	2,675	2,682	2,396	2,497
Primary pop	596,380	607,816	545,334	573,239	505,865
Secondary Schools	1,019	1,216	1,407	1,255	1,278
Secondary pop	210,779	377,840	395,643	323,651	349,484

Table 4: Indonesia: Key Aspects of Church Ministry 1975-2009[11]

The data above makes it clear that the Catholic Church in East Timor is minute compared with that in Indonesia. Secondly, the data also points to the fact that the Church in Indonesia represents one of the few instances of Catholics being able to function effectively within, and contribute to, the development of a society which has a population largely Islamic, albeit living within a secular state. At only three percent of the national population, the Church's position remains vulnerable, despite the fact that Catholics are well placed within the government, the military, the civil administration and academic circles.

★

The situation of Catholics in East Timor created a major moral dilemma for Church leaders in Indonesia and Rome, none of whom wanted to compromise the interests and position of Catholics in Indonesia or their place in society there. This seems evident from their actions. The Indonesian Bishops' Conference did not make any public statement on East Timor until 1983, eight years after the invasion. Their failure to act was not the result of any ignorance of the situation. They knew what was happening there from the Apostolic Administrator. They also had the witness of an open letter written by the religious of East Timor to their superiors in Indonesia in 1981, of which the Bishops would have been well aware since a number of them were members of religious congregations. The letter calls the Church in Indonesia and the global Church to account. It paints the situation as follows:

> That which was feared has truly happened: the people's way of life has been turned upside down and the basis of the community life has been destroyed. Masses of the population have been forced to shift in large numbers to places far away and unknown. This has already happened several times and in the last few months many East Timorese have been exiled from their homeland. Consequently, apart

---

11 ibid

from having lost all their possessions, there is alienation and disintegration of families... People who have been concentrated in certain areas and who live in dire poverty in an atmosphere of false peace, have been forced to accompany the army to the mountains...morning and night for months on end without any medical care and food at all. They were aged 12 to 55. The seriousness of the health problems and the rebellious mood of those who return to their huts can no longer be denied....

The letter continues:

The people are now experiencing oppression without end, their rights are not acknowledged. The people do not have a voice and live in fear. Indeed the people live in a situation of continual war and thus must be silent and submissive. The produce of their soil is seized, such as coffee, teak, cattle and even their property rights. The army monopolises everything...

Cut off from the rest of the world, the religious acknowledge that they are now part of 'the silent Church of East Timor' which yearns for social justice. In an appeal to their superiors in Indonesia they go on:

We cannot put to one side or consider unimportant the misunderstandings and great difficulties which are a consequence of the actions of the government against the people, against the religious, the faithful and the Bishop (da Costa Lopes).

They conclude with a cry for solidarity:

We must understand and acknowledge that we do not yet understand why the Indonesian Church and the Universal Roman Church have not up till now stated openly and officially their solidarity with the Church, people and religious of East Timor. Perhaps this has been the heaviest blow for us...We feel stunned by this silence which seemed to allow us to die deserted.[12]

The response from the Indonesian Bishops came in March three years later, by which time da Costa Lopes was in exile and his nemesis General Murdani was in command of the army in East Timor. In 1983 Murdani voided the ceasefire that his predecessor had established with Gusmao, without reference to Suharto - a measure of his growing authority - and scaled up the offensive against FRETILIN.

The Bishops' statement employs the Vatican style with many quotes from the major Church documents about the need for 'solidarity' with the East Timorese. The reply continues:

---

12 Quotations above taken from 'Letter of the Timorese Religious to the Indonesian Religious Superiors in 1981' in *The Church and East Timor* (Melbourne: Catholic Commission for Justice, Peace and Development, 1993) 14-15.

> The sympathy and solidarity of the Church of Indonesia… with our brothers and sisters in East Timor who are suffering, is expressed not only in our prayers, but also in the form of material assistance, although from our hearts, we must confess that this has been a drop of water when compared to the ocean of pain that has been suffered by our brothers and sisters.[13]

The letter goes on to list the various limited forms of this material assistance that the Indonesian Church has provided and expresses its willingness to provide more if asked.

At no point in the letter does the Indonesian Church commit itself to entering into dialogue with the government on behalf of the East Timorese. Clearly the bishops saw that any moral obligation to the Church in East Timor was resolved by prayer, material aid and the provision of personnel. The wider and more important issue of finding a just solution to the situation in East Timor was largely ignored. While the letter anticipates that the bishops have left themselves open to the criticism in that they have acted in self-interest, the omission of any concrete steps to seek a just resolution to the conflict is quite damning.

★

The frequent references to 'solidarity' above require some explanation. As the world became more interdependent across the last two decades of the twentieth century, and as communication technology improved, the notion of 'solidarity' became more nuanced. Today, an issue in one country can quickly gather large numbers of signatures on a petition worldwide. This was not the case in the 1980s before the age of email and the internet.

The concept of 'solidarity' has its popular roots in Poland in the Gdansk shipyards where in 1980 Lech Walesa created the *Solidarność* movement, the first independent trade union in the communist bloc, and a major tear in the Iron Curtain. Pope John Paul II played no small part in this development as Walesa acknowledged: 'The Holy Father, through his meetings, demonstrated how numerous we were. He told us not to be afraid'.[14] The same pope was later to formally incorporate solidarity in Catholic social teaching in his 1987 encyclical, *Sollicitudo Rei Socialis*. The Indonesian bishops in 1983 did not have access to this development, one that the East Timor dilemma helped shape.

The notion of solidarity is understood in Catholic social teaching as having two senses: a general sense and a particular sense. In the general sense solidarity means a commitment to the common good brought about as a consequence of interdependence. Used in this way the concept can mean, for instance, people in one nation stand in solidarity with the victims of a natural disaster in another; or the St Vincent de Paul Society providing help to the marginalised in the local community. In a later development, this way of understanding solidarity underpinned the idea of exercising a preferential option for the poor and marginalised when seeking to promote the common good. When choices have to be made due to limited resources, solidarity in the general sense provides a criterion of judgment – to stand with the poor and marginalised first and then work out what to do next!

---

13 'Indonesian letter to Bishop Belo and the priests, religious and laity of Dili', 1983, *The Church and East Timor*, 19.
14 Jan Repa 'Analysis: Solidarity's Legacy' (London: BBC News, 12 Aug 2005).

The concept can also be understood in a more particular sense. In this understanding groups combine together to augment the strength of each in working for the common good. This was the way in which *Solidarność* used the concept. This understanding finds secular expression in the oft-used union mantra, 'workers united will never be defeated'.

When the Indonesian bishops spoke of 'solidarity', they were clearly operating from the first of these two meanings. When the Portuguese bishops and the religious of East Timor used it, they were clearly thinking in a different frame of reference. It is unlikely that this confusion would exist today, but it is certainly part of the East Timor story and the Catholic Church's role in that story.

★

Vatican policy on East Timor was shaped by geo-political considerations – the need to maintain constructive relationships with the governments of Muslim-majority societies in order to protect Christian minorities elsewhere, for example, in Egypt and the Middle East.

In the early 1970s, Lebanon and Indonesia provided two examples of Christians and Muslims living peacefully together and building a mutually beneficial society. However, early in 1975 Lebanon began to self-destruct. This left the Church in Indonesia as the sole example of constructive co-existence so creating increased pressure to ensure that the Indonesian government maintained its commitment to religious tolerance.

The Vatican's pro-integration stance has to be understood against this bigger picture. Its dilemma lay in working out how to help the people in East Timor without adding fuel to fires smouldering in Muslim societies where Christians were a minority.

The Vatican was determined not to endanger the advantages – economic, social, and political – Catholics had gained in Indonesia, and the influence they were capable of exerting there. If the people of East Timor had to be sacrificed for this objective then their sacrifice served a 'higher good'. Such a stance sits awkwardly with the Gospel!

The fact that after 1983 a Catholic and known friend of Nuncio Puente in Jakarta, General Benny Murdani, was leading the military oppression in East Timor presented Vatican diplomats with a nightmare scenario.

CHAPTER 14
EAST TIMOR:
THE CHURCH AND HUMAN RIGHTS

Pancasila's provisions on social justice and human rights must have seemed ironic to most Timorese. However *Pancasila* provided Church leaders with a publicly shared moral base and rhetoric when interceding with the Indonesian commanders on behalf of those who had been arrested. While some Indonesian commanders took the view that 'we are at war and so anything goes'; others did not.

Increasingly discussion about East Timor was becoming cast in terms of human rights, and this was not something the Indonesians could easily deflect in the post-colonial era when, during the Cold War, they were trying to position Indonesia as a leader among non-aligned nations.

The permanent council of the Portuguese bishops drew attention to this in a statement expressing their solidarity with the Church in East Timor in March 1984:

> …Timor aspires to the full expression of its own individuality and to hinder it signifies not only a physical genocide, but also we can say a 'cultural' genocide, this last one is more grave because it affects as much the people who are dying as those who survive, and not only the present generations but those of the future….
>
> …we welcome all sincere efforts already undertaken to find a just solution to the problem (the abuse of human rights in East Timor)…

The statement continues:

> We appeal to the Portuguese government to which historically, morally, and juridically this task is being entrusted, and we appeal to the Indonesian government, the occupying power, as well as to international organisations, which could act as intermediaries, and finally we appeal to the political leaders of Timor, in their homeland or in exile, asking them to dedicate their forces to obtaining rapidly and efficiently the end of this painful situation which seems to be lasting forever…[1]

---

1 Permanent Council of Portuguese Bishops, 28 March, 1984, in Catholic Commission for Justice, Development and Peace (Melbourne Archdiocese), *The Church and East Timor*, 1993, 20-21.

The contrast in both substance and tone between this and the Indonesian Bishops' statement of the previous year is marked.

★

In July 1984 Pope John Paul II took up the human rights theme with the new Indonesian ambassador to the Vatican when he presented his credentials. He rather pointedly observed:

> ...the Holy See continues to follow the situation in East Timor with preoccupation and with the hope that particular consideration be given in every circumstance to the ethnic, religious and cultural identity of the people.

He goes on to note that the Holy See has made many efforts 'to contribute to helping the people of that area' and 'it has earnestly recommended (to the ambassador's government) respect for human rights'. The Pope concludes by saying that it is

> ...the ardent wish of the Holy See that all rights of individuals be respected and that every effort be made to lighten the sufferings of the people by facilitating the work of relief agencies and ensuring the access of humanitarian aid to those in need.[2]

While the Pope's remarks were supportive, they were made in the context of a difficult change of leadership in East Timor in response to Indonesian diplomatic pressure. The previous year the Nuncio Puente had dismissed da Costa Lopes[3] who was replaced as Apostolic Administrator by Carlos Belo. According to Belo's biographer, Arnold Kohen, Pope John Paul II personally chose Belo despite his young age and lack of pastoral experience.[4] Da Costa Lopes was not permitted to stay in East Timor and was exiled to Portugal. There he became an advocate for the East Timorese cause while his health lasted. He died in poverty largely abandoned by the Church he had served so loyally. His dismissal was resented by local clergy and Belo was forced to bear the brunt of their anger.

★

Despite his inexperience Belo quickly realised that the Pope's statement could be put to good use in two ways: firstly to put pressure on the Indonesians, and secondly to build bridges with senior clergy put offside by the Vatican's shabby treatment of his predecessor whom they regarded as a national hero.

On New Year's Day 1985, Belo and the Council of Priests in Dili published a statement that took up the Pope's call to defend the rights and identity of the East Timorese. Catholic

---

2 Pro Mundi Vita Dossier *East Timor* (Brussels: 1984), 31-32. PMV is quoting from *Osservatore Romano*, 13 August 1984, 5.
3 In 1992 I had a conversation with the papal nuncio to Jakarta, Archbishop Pietro Sambi. In response to my direct question about the fate of da Costa Lopes, he admitted to me that da Costa Lopes had been 'sacked' by the nuncio of the time, Archbishop Pablo Puente Buces.
4 Arnold Kohen *From the Place of the Dead* (New York: St. Martin's Press, 1999), 113.

social teaching, as developed to that point in time, provided a basis on which to rest their case.

The opening section makes the document's intentions clear:

> Conscious of its mission, the Church wishes to set down what it feels to be vital and urgent for the defence and safeguarding of the fundamental values and human rights of the people of East Timor as well as their identity at this historical moment in time.

Fundamental to this project is the right of a people to be 'sovereign over their own destiny'. The local church can speak on this matter because it lives in solidarity with the people of East Timor sharing their suffering as the war, 'which they would have us believe to be a civil war', goes on with the arrival of ever more Indonesian troops. The statement makes the point that, while the people of East Timor have a right to their own identity, the Indonesians have failed, after nine years of occupation, to create the conditions in which this can find expression. This has led to a situation in which the majority of the population do not see their future as being part of Indonesia. A necessary condition of peace, social harmony and wellbeing is that people effectively enjoy all their basic human rights.

The balance of the statement spells out in considerable detail the ways in which the ethnic, religious and cultural identity of the East Timorese is being suppressed, and concludes:

> The attempt to Indonesianise the Timorese people through powerful Pancasila (Indonesian State ideology) campaigns, schooling and media, by divorcing the people from their own Weltanschauung (worldview), represents a slow assassination of Timorese culture. To kill their culture is to kill the people themselves.

It ends with a plea for dialogue:

> We also appeal that conditions indispensable for an open, frank and fruitful dialogue between the different parties involved in the problem should be created, in which especially the People of East Timor, represented by the active movements, whether inside the country or abroad, should take part free from any form of coercion.[5]

Belo was setting out a position arguing from Catholic social teaching – a tactic he would use again and again. It was a brave move that won him respect, and annoyed the Indonesians who at first denied that he had even written the statement. As I would discover later, in his dealings with the Indonesians, Belo was always prepared to roll the dice and live with the consequences. He was fearless in this. The 1985 statement set a pattern for future years.

★

---

5 Statement of the Apostolic Administrator and Council of Priests of the Diocese of Dili (English translation), 1 January, 1985. (Carlos Filipe Ximenes Belo Apostolic Administrator),

'Human rights' provided Church leaders in East Timor with an understandable rhetoric in defending their people against oppression. I had to admit that in 1992 my own knowledge of human rights was quite limited. I was aware that the topic of human rights was a relatively late addition in Catholic social teaching, but that was about the extent of what I knew.[6]

I subsequently discovered that this important area in Catholic social teaching emerged in explicit form in the last two decades of the 20th century and is articulated in the teaching of Pope John Paul II on solidarity, preferential option for the poor and the defence of civil rights, among which is the right to culture. The complexity of the Church's situation in East Timor provided a catalyst for this development, and the contribution of Belo and his clergy in standing up to the Indonesians on the matter should be acknowledged.

Belo's stance was never going to be a popular stand in Indonesia since East Timor was not the only place in the archipelago that indigenous people were resisting Javanese cultural imperialism. Arguing for cultural rights in this context could be interpreted by the Javanese controlling the country as arguing against 'the unity of Indonesia', one of the basic planks in *Pancasila*.

*

Acknowledgement that a people has a right to their culture is relatively recent in Church thinking and practice. Up until the middle of the 20th century, the Church's anthropology was both Eurocentric and elitist. This was a legacy of an era in which missionaries travelled to all parts of the known world as an integral part of colonisation projects. East Timor was typical of this development. Colonisation there, as in so many other places, was justified on the grounds of Portugal's 'civilising mission'. The Church's mission was construed within this broader ambit.

In this era culture was interpreted in terms of 'civilisation'. All other 'civilisations' were judged according to European civilisation taken as the gold standard. According to this standard Portugal's 'civilising mission' in East Timor was to share the glories of Portugal with the local population including its Catholic faith. Since this 'high' notion of culture is transmitted through education, the Church was assigned this responsibility, which it took up with enthusiasm. Secondary education in particular became the vehicle for 'civilising' upper-class Timorese introducing them to the Portuguese heritage in art, language, literature, architecture, law and so on.

*

By the early 1970s the Catholic Church was beginning to rethink its understanding of culture, largely through the pioneering work of mission anthropologists such as Louis Luzbetak SVD who was strongly influenced by contemporary developments in anthropology.[7]

---

6   In 1963 Pope John XXIII became the first pope to use the language of human rights in his encyclical letter *Pacem in Terris* where he fulsomely endorsed the UN's *Declaration of Human Rights* (1948). Prior to this human rights was frowned on by the Vatican as an idea sourced in the Enlightenment which it had duly condemned.

7   Louis Luzbetak *The Church and Cultures* (Techny Illinois: Divine Word Publications, 1963) has been updated and republished several times since it first appeared, in response to the added need for practitioners to understand cultural milieus.

Catholic missiologists pointed out that missionaries did not bring the 'pure' Gospel to mission churches, but a version of the Gospel strongly influenced by the culture in which they had grown up and in which they had been educated. Missiologists also challenged the notion that local cultures were 'pagan' and devoid of any worthwhile religious content. The evangelisation of peoples too often had become a form of cultural imperialism. I had encountered this phenomenon myself during my fieldwork in Kalumburu.

As noted earlier, in the late 1970s Pope Paul VI expanded the rather ambiguous teachings of the Second Vatican Council on culture, moving Catholic teaching away from the classicist model towards the modern understanding. Culture in this perspective is the possession of a people that provides them with a means of living together in harmony within their environment. Cultures are built on a shared worldview that finds expression in a variety of ways. European cultures function no differently.

From a missiological perspective God is at work affecting God's mission in the world, so God is present in all cultures. The task of the missionary is not to bring something entirely new to a culture, but to work with what is already there. All cultures are therefore relative.

*

The argument can be taken further. To be human is to be a person-within-culture in much the same way as to be human is to be a person-within-history. Respect for persons and respect for their cultures therefore go hand in hand. If people are to be evangelised, then so too are the cultures in which they live. This means the Church should seek to have a presence in the public square where culture is shaped. In moving into the public square in East Timor and staking out a space there on human rights, Belo seemed instinctively to understand this, as did his Council of Priests. His stance differed from that of da Costa Lopes who saw his role in more prophetic terms expressing moral outrage at what was happening without offering a way forward. Both differed from Ribeiro's approach which was to reject the need for the Church to be present in the public square.

*

As I began to understand these issues, I realised that my knowledge of human rights and developments in Catholic social teaching was somewhat out of date, so I was fortunate to come across the English translation of a work by a French priest and human rights activist, Jean-Francois Six. In 1992 his book, *Church and Human Rights*, had just been published.[8]

Six gives a 'warts and all' account of the development of human rights as a central element in Catholic social teaching, and does not fall into the trap of seeing the Church as having 'always been a champion of human rights', a commonly-held revisionist view. The book was written in response to the failure of the Catholic hierarchy in France to acknowledge the bicentenary of the *Declaration of the Rights of Man and of the Citizen* (1789), a document foundational in the development of Western thinking about human rights.[9]

---

8   Jean-Francois Six *Church and Human Rights* (Slough: St Paul's Publications, 1991).
9   Six's treatment, which I follow loosely here, is presented in narrative form. For a critical, analytical exposition of Catholic social teaching see Charles Curran *Catholic Social Teaching 1891-present: A historical, theological and ethical analysis* (Washington: Georgetown University Press, 2002).

★

Six begins his treatment by pointing out that the concept of human rights does not belong exclusively to anyone, and did not originate with one particular individual or group, or in one particular era. It has emerged as the consequence of a long process of discovery tenaciously carried on within humanity, and across human history. In his view, the political affirmation of human rights is part of the long struggle to define what it means to be human. It reflects developments in our anthropological understanding. As such, religious beliefs have played no small part in its development.[10] I studied Six assiduously. Through my efforts I came to see how the notion of human rights has developed across time, taking a somewhat different trajectory in different societies. It is a story with its roots in both faith and culture. Later, I was to gain further insight from the work of Charles Curran.

★

The United Nations *Declaration of Human Rights* (1948) was a giant step forward in the legal and moral definition of universal human rights, a development about which the Vatican had reservations despite the fact that leading Catholic philosopher Jacques Maritain was part of the drafting team. Its reservation centred on the use of civil law as the *sole* justification of human rights.

The Church's critique was that civil law is open to interpretation and political influence, whereas human rights are inherent, universal and not granted by the state. They are a matter of moral concern. There is clearly merit in this position.

Pope John XXIII brought Church teaching into phase with secular developments in his encyclical *Pacem in Terris* (1963). There he acknowledges a comprehensive list of 'human rights' and in commenting on the *UN Declaration of Human Rights* acknowledges its main achievement:

> It is a solemn recognition of the personal dignity of every human being; an assertion of everyone's right to be free to seek out the truth, to follow moral principles, discharge the duties imposed by justice, and lead a fully human life.

John XXIII encouraged Church leaders to recognise worth in the aspirations of the modern people encouraging them to 'read the signs of the times'.[11] His efforts bore fruit at the Second Vatican Council (1962-5). There the assembled bishops redefined a number of positions. Importantly, human rights were formally recognised in Church teaching as ascribed to *people* rather than to abstractions such as 'truth'. This change in stance acknowledged that all people have the right to freely seek the truth and any constraints that limit a person's ability to exercise this right need to be removed.

The implications of this position are then set out unequivocally in the Council's *Declaration on Religious Freedom (Dignitatis Humanae)* which holds that all individuals are equal before the law in matters of religion, and so freedom of conscience must be granted

---

10   Ibid, 31.
11   Pope John XXIII Apostolic Constitution *Humanae Salutis*, promulgated 25 December, 1961.

to all. This was a major development in Catholic social teaching and redefines the Catholic position not only on the relationship between religions, but also between Church and state. It took Church leaders a long time to realise that 'freedom of religion' can be interpreted as either 'freedom for religion' or 'freedom from religion'!

*

In the fifty years since the Second Vatican Council, Catholic social teaching about human rights has become more sophisticated as it has progressively accepted new insights from anthropology and historical experience. People always search for truth at a particular time and in a socio-cultural context. All constructions of truth, including the truth about human rights, emerge from historical experience and a socio-cultural context. This is 'bread and butter' for anthropologists, if not for theologians. The implication is that truth is discovered in a qualified rather than in absolute form, and so its formulation over time can and does evolve or change. How truth is expressed is always a product of culture and is therefore limited by the tools of culture that must be employed to express it.

The deep human aspiration to be free from oppression in all its forms runs as an undercurrent through the narrative of human rights. This aspiration surfaces, is suppressed, and then re-surfaces in cultures at different times in their development. It is expressed in multiple ways in different cultures. In this context the *UN Declaration* which sets out to specify *universal human rights* represents a major achievement in the moral development of the human race.

Catholic social teaching has played a role in this important development as the Catholic Church is certainly one of the most significant religious bodies capable of developing a coherent set of teachings dealing with the spectrum of human experience covered by human rights. The teaching has credibility because it has been formulated against the background of actual historical and cultural developments, rather than as a matter of ideology. As a consequence, Catholic social teaching has an audience much wider than simply the Catholic Church. It must also be acknowledged that despite the fact that the Judeo-Christian understanding of the human person provides a basis for human rights, and the aspiration to be free from oppression, Catholic Church leaders have at different times been the determined enemy of those seeking to realise this aspiration. As Six notes, it is important that the Church, which today is a vigorous supporter of human rights, avoids hubris.[12]

The requirement that Catholics 'read the signs of the times', that is, to be sensitive to and discern the best aspirations of the age, has the potential to avoid the mistakes of the past. In particular, it provides clarity in the confusion caused when Western experience and assumptions are taken as definitive for all cultures, and all times. Six concludes his study by observing that, if the Church wishes to speak with an authentic voice about human rights, it must 'sweep its own front porch and satisfy the human rights doctrine within its own organisation'.[13] This remains an ongoing challenge.

---

12 Six, 116
13 ibid

★

The story of East Timor cannot be told without reference to development in Catholic social teaching. When Belo and his Council of Priests stood up for the cultural identity of the East Timorese, they opened up a new dimension in this teaching, incorporating important anthropological insights. Their understanding of 'culture' is much broader than that found in the UN *Declaration of Human Rights* or its associated covenants.

They also opened up a new front in the war being waged in their own country. Here victory did not depend on the power of guns, but on the power of a people bonded by a strong culture in which the aspiration to be free from oppression and to assert their rights increasingly took central place.

CHAPTER 15
AUSTRALIA AND THE CATHOLIC CHURCH IN EAST TIMOR

The word most commonly used to sum up the relationship between Australia and East Timor is 'betrayal'. James Dunn makes a powerful case that, while this is true of the Australian Government, it does not generally apply either to the Australian people or the Australian Catholic Church.[1] It has been the reactions of ordinary people that have moderated the unprincipled actions of successive governments in pursuing national self-interest at the expense of the East Timorese people.

Standing against this sorry tale of government duplicity are the actions of individual Catholics and the Church in Australia that enabled the Church in East Timor to survive World War II. This narrative stands alongside the story of the East Timorese helping Australian commandos survive there while fighting the Japanese. While the latter story has been well covered, in this chapter I want to focus on the role Australians and the Australian Catholic Church played in helping the East Timorese Church survive during World War II. This is very much part of our story.

*

As the sun rose on 17 December 1941, the Australian soldiers standing on the deck of the Dutch gunship *Soerabaja* got their first view of Dili. They saw for themselves the beauty of its beaches and the gumtree-lined hills beyond in what was still largely unmapped terrain.[2] The cathedral, which had only recently been completed, with its white stucco façade and its magnificent twin bell towers, dominated all other buildings in the settlement. It was a symbol of the colonial Church and its links to the Portuguese state. As the soldiers waited for their officers to return from a visit ashore to the Governor, they were unaware that across the next year a relationship would develop between themselves and the Portuguese that would become a matter of life and death for each group. Two priests would die as a consequence of this relationship.

The arrival of the Australian and Dutch troops was in flagrant violation of international law. Portugal was a neutral country and not involved in World War II. In planning the

---

1   See James Dunn *Timor: A People Betrayed* (Sydney: ABC Books, 2001).
2   For a detailed account of the campaign conducted by the 2/2 and 2/4 Independent Units in Portuguese Timor see Paul Cleary *The Men Who Came Out of the Ground: Timor 1942 – Australia's First Commandoes* (Sydney: Hachette, 2010).

defence of Australia in the face of Japan's military push into South East Asia, the Allies set out to secure all airfields on the ring of islands to the immediate north of Australia. This included those on Timor and Ambon.

Sparrow Force was assigned this task, and the 2/2 Independent Company, commanded by Major Spence with Captain Bernard Callinan as second-in-command, was assigned the task of securing Dili airport. The deployment was part of a disastrous plan that saw 22,000 Australian troops stationed in South-east Asia. By the middle of 1942 of this number only the 143 surviving members of the 2/2 Company were still in the field. However, military commanders in Australia did not know this. They thought that the 2/2 Company had been wiped out or captured, and members of their families were duly informed that their loved ones were 'missing in action'.

★

The Governor of Portuguese Timor was not impressed when the Allied troops arrived, nor were his superiors in Lisbon when he contacted them. As he did not have either the troops or the firepower to resist what was a *de facto* invasion, an 'arrangement' was made whereby the Australians and their Dutch counterparts could land to the west of Dili near the airport and the Portuguese troops would remain in their barracks.

The 2/2 Company had drawn the proverbial 'short straw' because in the wet season Dili airport, far from being a forward airbase, was in fact a boggy swamp on which it was impossible to land anything but the lightest of military aircraft. From the outset, planning for the operation had been haphazard. The troops had no maps of Timor and lacked a communication system capable of reaching Australia. They were incorrectly dressed for the climate, and soon fell prey to malaria for which they had no medicine. Additionally, they had no transport and discovered, to their surprise, that there was only one truck in the colony, and few roads on which it could be driven.

They sought to redress a bad situation by sending out patrols to make accurate maps of the regions around Dili. These patrols soon moved further inland scouting and mapping the terrain. The troops also began the arduous task of moving equipment and military supplies from the beach into the hills where they would be less vulnerable to surprise attack. Due to the lack of transport, equipment had to be manhandled, and the Australians began recruiting the local Timorese to help them.

Many of the Australian commandos were bushmen, and were accustomed to dealing with indigenous peoples. They quickly picked up the basics of Tetum with the result that the Australians could communicate with the locals, whereas most of the Portuguese still could not. News that the Australian troops treated the local people well quickly spread across the colony.

Major Spence and Captain Callinan collected intelligence on how the colony was organised, and determined what local support was available. Callinan, a staunch Catholic and student of my alma mater, Parade College, made contact with the leader of the Church in East Timor, Monsignor Jaime Goulart, and a rapport was established. Goulart proved to be a useful contact because he was well respected by both the Portuguese and the Timorese.

★

Jaime Goulart was born in a small village in the Azores in 1908. When he decided to become a priest at the age of fourteen, he was sent to study in Macau where his cousin was the bishop. While still a seminarian, he was appointed as the bishop's secretary and travelled back to Europe with him, where he completed his clerical training and was ordained in 1932. The following year he returned to Macau and accompanied the Bishop to Timor on a pastoral visit. When the priest heading the mission asked the Bishop if his young assistant could remain, Goulart agreed.

This first pastoral assignment lasted three years during which time Goulart established a junior seminary (secondary school) for local Timorese. In 1937 he resumed his duties as the bishop's secretary and accompanied his cousin to Rome where he spent a good deal of his time researching the history of the Portuguese mission to Timor. It came as little surprise when, on his return to Macau, he was asked to head the Catholic mission in Portuguese Timor, which he did in 1940 the year the Vatican signed a concordat with the Salazar regime.

Goulart as Apostolic Administrator, headed a local Church with thirty thousand members served by twenty-two priests. While not all the priests were ethnic Portuguese, they were Portuguese citizens hailing from Goa and Macau. At the time three local Timorese seminarians were completing their training in Macau.

The colonial Church was composed of nine missions and forty mission stations. Timorese Catholics were seen as loyal to the missionaries and to the Portuguese.[3]

The mission stations were effectively networked for gathering local intelligence, and Callinan was keen to access this once he understood how extensive it was. Information flowed from mission station to mission station and back to the centre so that Goulart had a very good idea of what was happening across the colony quite independently of the Portuguese administration.

★

In 1941 Portuguese Timor was divided into five provinces divided into smaller administrative areas called *postos*. Here the local Portuguese administrators lived in characteristic Portuguese-style *pousadas* whose stucco walls and tiled roofs became symbols of Portuguese culture and rule.

The district administrators were all Portuguese citizens and exercised considerable power. Most treated the local people well and were respected; some treated them harshly and were resented. Thus, there was always a sub-text in play whenever the Australians sought the help of Portuguese administrators in mobilising the local people. While Portugal was neutral with respect to hostilities in Europe, many of the district administrators were pro-British and so were supportive of the Australian presence. A number would lose their lives because of the support they offered to the Australians.[4]

---

3   *Catholic Weekly* 'Bishop Goulart of Dili Peasant Boy in Azores, Seminarian in China, Missionary at Dili, Friend of Timor's Commandoes … Colour has never been lacking' Oct 25, 1942, 2-4. This article provides an extensive account of the Church in Portuguese Timor in 1942, sourced to Goulart, which I draw on heavily in this chapter.
4   In 1941 some 600 Portuguese were secretly evacuated from Timor to Darwin as Japanese attempts to turn the Timorese against them intensified.

★

Spence and Callinan attempted to co-opt the *deportados*, some of whom had previous military training. These also proved useful in providing intelligence and negotiating relationships with local tribal groups.[5]

The Christmas-New Year period was a busy one for the newly arrived troops. The work was hard, the heat oppressive, and the conditions generally trying. By early January 80% of the group had contracted malaria. Communications were so bad that troops in Dili were out of contact with each other and with the Sparrow Force HQ in Kupang. They had to rely on the Portuguese for radio news about how the war was proceeding. As a contingency, patrols were sent further west to see if they could link up with those from Kupang and so make contact with HQ.

In early 1942, Japanese planners had been inclined to ignore Portuguese Timor in the drive south. However the presence of Allied troops there changed the situation.[6] Fearing that neutral Portuguese territory could be used as a base for guerrilla attacks, they decided to take the whole of Timor by landing at Dili in the East and Kupang in the West.

In late January the Japanese took the nearby island of Sulawesi. This gave Japanese fighters control of the air space over Timor. In response, the RAAF quickly withdrew its bombers from Kupang to Darwin, leaving Sparrow Force with no air cover. As Cleary observes, Sparrow Force might then have been better named 'Sitting Duck Force', as without aerial reconnaissance capacity its commanders had no way of knowing if or when its units would be attacked.[7]

As events turned out they did not have long to wait. Singapore fell on the 15th February and three days later a Japanese force sailed from Sulawesi to Timor. The aim in sending Sparrow Force to Timor had been to secure the airports there. The withdrawal of the RAAF meant there was no point to the troops remaining. The Australian troops in Dili were simply abandoned to their fate in the general chaos following the fall of 'impregnable' Singapore.[8]

On the 19th February, the Japanese bombed Darwin in order to neutralise any Allied air capacity in preparation for the attack on Timor. In Dili people were oblivious to the impending invasion. The Japanese landed at night and immediately attempted to take the airfield. However, they were driven back and the Australians were able to blow up the airfield and withdraw. Those in the hills above Dili did not know what was happening as the settlement below was enclosed in fog. Unaware of the invasion, a group of Australians set off for Dili next morning to replenish supplies. They were captured by the Japanese and summarily shot. One survived his wounds and was nursed back to health by a Timorese woman who then got a message to the Australians.

★

---

5   They went on to form the 'international brigade' of Portuguese partisans, a unit that continued to operate after the Australians withdrew in 1942. See Cleary, 118.
6   Dunn argues that, since the Japanese respected the neutrality of Portuguese Macau, it was the presence of the Australian troops that drew the Japanese to Timor and that the Timorese subsequently paid a huge price for their presence. Dunn, 19.
7   Cleary, 39.
8   When the Commander in Kupang asked Darwin for instructions he received no reply (Cleary, 45.) Even if he had received one it could not have been relayed to the troops in Dili's hinterland.

The 2/2 Company as a whole was not surprised by the Japanese as its base was in the hinterland behind Dili. Australian troops in Kupang were not so lucky and, while most were forced to surrender, a number managed to escape and lived off the land as they wandered aimlessly in the hills of central and south Timor.

The 2/2 Company remained a fighting force, but its leaders were faced with the difficult question: What do we do next? With Dili taken the Japanese set up a base there but showed little interest in moving into the hinterland. So a stalemate ensured. Spence and Callinan realised that they had two options: to escape or to stay and fight. The problem with the first option was that they had no means of escape. The second option raised other questions: What strategic purpose would staying and fighting serve? And for how long would this be feasible?

For three weeks patrols kept a watching brief ascertaining what the Japanese were doing. There were a number of attempts to engage small contingents of Japanese troops as 'amateur hour' continued.[9] The Australians knew the theory of guerrilla warfare but had no experience of applying it in combat conditions, so they were lucky that casualties remained light as they gained experience.

On the 6th March, Callinan while on reconnaissance made contact with the mission priest at Laharoes in West Timor. Only then, weeks after the event, did he discover that Kupang had fallen and that there were Australian and Dutch troops now wandering in the hills.

★

In Dili, the Japanese were annoyed by Australian raids, and so sent the Australian consul David Ross, who had remained in Dili when it fell, up into the hills to advise the Australians that if they did not surrender they would be executed if captured. The senior officers met with him and sent back the message: 'We are Australians. Australia is still fighting and so are we!'[10] So began a second phase of the campaign begun under 'Timor rules'.

The Australians, with Timorese help, moved ordinance stored in the hills above Dili further inland.[11] The troops used the Timor ponies owned by one of the Portuguese for the purpose. The 'ponies were guided across the mountain tracks by the Timorese. Those who helped in this operation were given promissory notes for their services, although no one knew when these would be honoured. Each soldier adopted a young offsider – a *criado* – who negotiated with locals for food and acted as his interpreter. The pony trails were to become a feature of the campaign as Australians, with the help of the Timorese, moved munitions strategically around the colony for safe-keeping. The *criados* enjoyed new freedom as they were now allowed to move around the colony, which had not been possible under the Portuguese.

★

---

9   Cleary, 93.
10 ibid, 104.
11 The same strategy was used by FRETILIN three decades later.

By April 1942 the Australian commandos were using their guerrilla tactics to inflict serious casualties on the Japanese. Operating in small units they hit the enemy hard and then withdrew quickly.[12] Observation posts around Dili enabled them to know when the Japanese were moving, and so to plan attacks. As the attacks mounted, the Australians' munitions were depleted, and without resupply, Spence and Callinan knew the battle was unsustainable. This made it imperative to make radio contact with Darwin.

With considerable ingenuity the parts needed to build and power up a radio transmitter were sourced from all over Timor, and on the 17th April a message was received in Darwin that the 2/2 Company was still fighting. The news was received with amazement and joy in Australia. The Australian Army Chief wanted to bring the troops home immediately, but he was overruled by General MacArthur who wanted them supplied and kept in the field.

So began a third phase of the campaign in which the 2/2 Company continued to harass the Japanese but were now supplied by ship from Darwin. The wounded were repatriated on the return trip and the health of those remaining improved with access to medicines, food, clothes etc. The Timorese played a major role helping the Australians to move supplies quickly off the beach, so preventing Japanese reconnaissance planes from discovering how the Australia troops were being re-supplied.

By May 1942 troops on Timor had the capacity to relay information back to Australia about Japanese shipping and deployment around Timor. This enabled bombing raids to be conducted at opportune times. By June these attacks were proving so effective that the Japanese, who then had around 8000 troops on the island, were forced to act. Ross was sent into the hills again with an offer of conditions for an Australian surrender, but this time he did not return to Dili and was evacuated to Australia.

The Japanese now had little option but to increase the number of troops on Timor to get rid of the Australians. The massive increase in Japanese troops that followed rendered the 2/2 Company's situation precarious, so planners in Darwin supported them by massive air strikes. In one of these strikes a Hudson bomber was shot down with the pilot the sole survivor parachuting to safety, but badly burned. The Timorese rescued him and Monsignor Goulart used his car to ensure he was delivered safely to a 2/2 Company patrol.

*

The behaviour of the Japanese troops towards the locals was often bad. However, initially they respected the priests and the nuns. The Catholic Church was left alone as it was seen as part of the Portuguese establishment. However, this soon changed, and the Bishop's residence was ransacked as the Japanese looked for evidence of the Church's collaboration with the Australians.

When the Allies' heavy bombing campaign began in May 1942, the Japanese initially refused to let the Portuguese leave Dili, but as casualties mounted they were allowed to go. The Bishop moved to Ossu and was there when two of his priests, Frs Norberto Barros and Antonio Pires, were killed by the Japanese on 2nd October.

The priests had briefed the Australian commandos on the condition of Japanese troops who had stayed in their village shortly before they were ambushed at Nunamogue where

---

12 Cleary, 127.

over 100 were killed.[13] Two weeks prior to this event two other priests had been arrested in Ossu.

Goulart was interrogated in his house about the presence of the Australians and the Dutch. The interrogation was not easy as the Japanese officer did not speak Portuguese or Tetum and had to work through a Javanese who spoke Malay. The Monsignor was asked if he was in contact with Australians, to which he replied that he was, as some were Catholics and needed his spiritual assistance. He was asked if he had given them food and tobacco to which he again replied he had because Portugal was neutral and this did not infringe Portuguese neutrality. After all, the Portuguese also helped the Japanese in this way.

In the middle of this tense exchange the phone rang. The interpreter answered it and informed the interrogator that he had someone on the phone asking in English if the missionaries could advise on the whereabouts of the Japanese. The interrogation continued but in a higher key. The phone rang again. The caller repeated his earlier question. By now the Japanese interrogator was really angry. When the phone rang a third time things became even more tense. Goulart apologised for the interruptions and said he could not be held responsible for people telephoning him. At this stage the interrogator seized him by the throat and threatened to hit him. Fortunately, the Japanese commander arrived and, after apologising to Goulart, said he and the two priests being held were free to go.

The next day the local *liurai* advised Goulart that Japanese intelligence officers had approached them and offered them weapons if they would kill the Portuguese including their priests. Goulart decided that it was too dangerous to remain in Ossu, and so he set out under cover of darkness leading a party of eleven Portuguese priests and ten nuns to find the Australians.

After a tense fifteen hours they arrived at Callinan's hide-out where they were warmly welcomed by the Australians. The group then travelled night and day for the next few weeks to reach Betano on the south coast from where they were evacuated at midnight on 15th December 1942. The group was evacuated on the same boat as the 2/2 Company, now relieved and returning home to a heroes' welcome.[14]

With the knowledge that the Japanese planned to use their Timorese supporters to wipe out the Portuguese, Callinan set about rescuing those who had helped the Australians, together with their families. In all, some six hundred people, mostly Catholics, made the hazardous boat crossing from the beach at Betano to Darwin. The White Australia policy meant that those East Timorese who had also helped the Australians were left to their fate.

★

While the Australians had saved the members of the Portuguese colonial Church in East Timor, they destroyed its greatest symbol, the Dili cathedral. Dili had been bombed continuously since May, but the cathedral had been spared. However, on the 3rd November, as Goulart and his companions were making their slow trek overland to safety, the RAAF

---

13 Cleary, 214.
14 *The Catholic Weekly* October 25, 1945, 2. The heading of the article, under the label, *Life Story*, captures something of the flavour of the life of this remarkable man – 'Bishop Goulart of Dili – Peasant boy in Azores…Seminarian in China…Missionary at Dili…Friend of Timor's Commandoes…Colour has never been lacking.'

conducted a raid with the specific purpose of bombing the cathedral that it suspected was being used to billet soldiers. After five sorties little was left of the cathedral!

The sun was setting on the Portuguese colonial Church. A local Church would rise from the ashes, built around the local Timorese clergy whom Goulart had taken care to nurture. One of the first of these to be ordained was Martinho da Costa Lopes. He had been sent to Macau to study at the outset of the war and returned to his homeland in 1945. Goulart ordained him in 1948.[15]

The priests and nuns rescued by the Australians were hosted in Australia for the duration of the war.[16] In 1945, with the war over, Goulart was named the first bishop of Dili and was consecrated in a ceremony held at St Patrick's seminary in Manly NSW. He returned to Timor later that year and began the onerous task of rebuilding the Church there. Bernard Callinan went on to become very distinguished for both his contributions to civil society and to the Catholic Church.

★

It might be expected that, having formed an important bond during World War II, collaboration between the churches in Timor and Australia would continue. This did not happen, largely due to the tyranny of culture and of language.

Following the war, the Australian government quickly lost interest in Timor. Many of the IOUs issued to the Timorese for services rendered were never honoured, and in fact during the war possession of these became death warrants if found by the Japanese. The 2/2 Company had created chaos in Timor. In the mayhem that it initiated resisting the Japanese drive southward, some 60,000 Timorese died and the country was devastated.

The Australian troops abandoned in Timor would not have survived or been effective without the assistance of the Timorese and the Portuguese. However, the Australian government demonstrated no sense of obligation to the Timorese either during or after the war. The Timor story went largely untold to future generations, and it was not until the events of 1975, and 1999 in particular, when World War II veterans who had fought there began to publicly disown their own government, that the story was revived and action taken. By then a vast number of East Timorese had perished.

---

15 Rowena Lennox *Fighting Spirit of East Timor: The Life of Martinho da Costa* Lopes (London: Zed Books, 2000), 34.
16 Goulart was hosted by the Redemptorist Fathers in their monastery at Pennant Hills in Sydney.

CHAPTER 16

THE ROAR OF SILENCE: AUSTRALIAN BISHOPS' RESPONSE TO THE DEVELOPING CRISIS

If the Australian Government failed the people of East Timor in their long hour of need beginning in 1974[1], did the Australian Catholic Church do any better? This is the question I want to explore in this chapter.

How the Catholic Church functions is exceedingly difficult for most people to understand. A common stereotype views the Church as the last of the absolute monarchies with an organisational structure still reminiscent of the Roman imperium. Like all stereotypes there is some truth in this image, and certainly at times the institutional Church has corresponded to it.

The issue of how power is exercised within the Church provided a largely unacknowledged sub-text that runs through all of the documents of the Second Vatican Council. Noted Church historian John O'Malley has rightly observed '…the so-called politics of the council were not an interesting sideshow. The drama of the politics was part of the council's substance, intrinsic to its meaning.'[2] Because the use of power operated as a sub-text, the matter was only partially addressed. As a result, after the Council the Vatican quickly re-asserted its control when local Church leaders, often fearful of the energy liberated by the Council within local Church communities, looked to the centre for guidance. The centre was also able to consolidate its power by carefully controlling the appointment of bishops in the two generations after the Council and by controlling the operation of the newly established national episcopal conferences.

★

Episcopal conferences, as national gatherings of bishops, were established by Pope Paul VI to give expression to the notion of 'collegiality', that is acknowledging the collective role bishops play in the leadership of the Church. An emphasis on collegiality offsets the excessive centralisation of authority and gives pragmatic recognition to the fact that, in a world of instant communication, what a bishop teaches in a particular situation can easily

---

[1] In a sense 'failed' is a euphemism; 'betrayed' is the term more commonly encountered term in the political literature on East Timor.
[2] O'Malley, 10.

be construed (or misconstrued) as applying everywhere.[3]

The Australian Episcopal Conference was established in 1966[4], the year following the Vatican Council, but its statutes were not given definitive form until 1979, so that the limits of its authority were still quite unclear at the time Dili was invaded. The dilemma associated with the authority of these assemblies stems from the fact that each bishop is directly accountable to the Pope for what happens in his diocese. Who then is accountable for what happens on the national stage?

In 1985 John Paul II called an extraordinary synod to review the impact of the Second Vatican Council twenty years on. There the bishops sought clarification about the authority of episcopal conferences.[5] This was not provided for another thirteen years.[6] So in dealing with the East Timor issue, the Australian bishops were operating in a lacuna about who could speak authoritatively for them *as a group*.

Against this background it becomes possible to make some sense of why the Australian bishops collectively had so very little to say about East Timor in the fifteen years from 1976 to 1991. In that time a vast number of East Timorese had died and thousands had fled to Australia, Portugal and other parts of Indonesia. This tragedy was not occurring on the other side of the world, but across the Timor Sea from Darwin, a lesser distance than from Melbourne to Sydney. Furthermore, policies and actions of the Australian government were among its significant causes.

By the mid-1980s Timorese refugees living in Australia were marginalised by Australia's immigration regime. Most of them were Catholics. The bishops' collective silence seems incomprehensible. What was happening that led to this situation?

★

The efforts of the Australian Church to support the Church in East Timor have to be considered in the context of other events in Australia itself and what was possible at the time. When the Indonesian invasion took place on the 7th December 1975, Australia was in a state of political disarray. The Whitlam Government had been dismissed a month earlier and Malcolm Fraser headed a caretaker administration until the election scheduled for 13th December. Realistically, there was little anyone could do until a new government was elected.

In 1974 the Australian Episcopal Conference (AEC) had acted. Its Secretariat made a formal request for the Whitlam Government to act as mediator in East Timor. At the practical level, it sent $10,000 to the Church in Timor via the St Vincent de Paul Society to alleviate suffering. These were small but practical steps. The AEC also requested the Catholic Commission for Justice and Peace (CCJP)[7] to brief it on the situation in East

---

3   Brian Lucas, Peter Slack, William d'Apice *Church Administration Handbook* (Sydney: St Paul's Publications, 2009), 110.
4   Its statutes were approved by the Holy See on 21 June, 1966. Thus was created a more formal association of the bishops than had existed previously, one which recognised the necessity and anticipated the fruitfulness of official and public collaboration of the bishops. http://www.catholic.org.au/
5   The Final Report of the 1985 Second Extraordinary Synod, ##4-5
6   Pope John Paul II's motu proprio *Apostolos Suos* 21 May, 1998.
7   The CCJP had a number of names in its formative years. Founded in 1969 it was first called the Interim Justice and Peace Commission. This changed in 1972 to the National Justice and Peace Commission and finally to the Catholic Commission for Justice and Peace (CCJP) in 1976. It retained this name until it was dissolved in 1987.

Timor. The resulting CCJP report placed blame for the crisis at the feet of both the Portuguese Government (for its neglect of the colony) and the Australian Government (for its inaction). The report advocated UN intervention, and recommended that the bishops provide public support for a UN-supervised plebiscite on the future of East Timor. It also suggested that the bishops make a plea to all sides in the conflict to act with both humanity and justice until such time as the future of the colony could be decided.[8] The AEC did not choose to act on this advice at the time.

★

The deteriorating situation in East Timor in the late 1970s raised an important issue for Church leaders. What role, if any, should or could the Church in Australia play in addressing the violations of human rights occurring in East Timor? With thousands of refugees now in Australia, this was no longer a hypothetical question. The bigger question was: What role should the Catholic Church play in the formation of public policy?

In the 1970s there was little consensus among the bishops about how such questions should be answered. The reasons for this situation were both historical and theological.

★

Priesthood combines three dimensions: proclaiming the Gospel, sharing the spiritual mysteries of the Church, and the ministry to the poor. While all priests understand proclaiming the Gospel as a primary responsibility of their calling, how they make sense of their priesthood seems to depend on the relative emphasis they place on the other two dimensions. What is true of priests is equally true of bishops, except that the latter exercise their ministry in a wider social milieu, one in which justice, people's rights and the structures of society at the local and national levels, are interwoven.[9] Also as we have seen above, the episcopal ministry inevitably projects bishops into the public square whether they wish to be there or not. Not all bishops accept this aspect of contemporary reality. Some choose to interpret their role mainly in cultic terms.

Theological outlook also shapes the relative importance Church leaders give to issues such as peace, justice and development, and their importance in the mission of a local Church. Some see this mission as directed locally with its focus on Church matters, while others see outreach as one of its integral components.

★

In the 1940s and 1950s the Australian Catholic bishops did enter the public square united behind Catholic lay people attempting to eradicate Communist influence from the trade unions and from the Australian Labor Party (ALP). Bob Santamaria was a key figure in this

---

8   Confidential Briefing: CCJP to AEC, 12 January 1976. CCJP archives.
9   By the 1970s press and TV coverage of the Church meant that what a bishop did in his diocese could instantly become a national matter.

struggle and gained a high standing among sections of the hierarchy as a result.[10] By the early 1950s this battle had been largely won.

When members of Santamaria's Movement attempted to use tactics developed in the union fight to gain control of the Australian Labor Party in 1956, its support among many of the Australian bishops collapsed.[11] Bishops in Victoria, Tasmania and Western Australia continued to support the Movement, while those in New South Wales, Queensland and South Australia did not. Rome was called on to intervene, and as a result the Movement lost its recognition as a Catholic body. Undeterred, Santamaria established the National Civic Council (NCC) as an organisation of Catholics that operated outside episcopal control and which gave him a powerful platform from which to influence Catholic opinion through its magazine, *News Weekly,* which continued to be sold in many parishes particularly in Victoria. As well, Santamaria had a regular time-slot on the TV station Channel 9 called *Point of View,* personally funded by the station's owner, Kerry Packer. Using these twin platforms to good effect, he remained an influential Catholic voice in the public square, one consistently pro-Indonesian when it came to East Timor.

★

Catholic social teaching sets out general principles, but it also raises difficult questions: What do these principles mean in practice in particular socio-cultural and political contexts? How should Catholic social teaching shape the way the Church leaders, and groups view particular issues?

Bishops used to interpreting their priesthood primarily in cultic terms, sometimes struggled to grasp the Church's service role in a modern society. Responsible leadership in society requires a commitment to action. Paul VI put the matter clearly when he wrote:

> …It is not enough to recall principles, state intentions, point to crying injustices and utter prophetic denunciations; these words will lack real weight unless they are accompanied for each individual by a livelier awareness of personal responsibility and by effective action.[12]

However, it is not possible to take *effective action* in a society without doing some analysis of the structures within society that marginalise people. Secondly, any commitment to action means that choices have to be made and these bring with them the risk of failure. Finally, no one can guarantee success when it comes to addressing structural injustice. Justice is a particularly messy virtue and it is hard to keep the mess off your hands!

★

The two structural justice issues contributing to the marginalising of the East Timorese in the 1980s were Australia's foreign policy and its immigration policy. To address either

---

10 In the years leading to the Second Vatican Council (which began in 1962) Santamaria had made himself *the* Catholic spokesperson in the public square. As a protégé of Archbishop Mannix his influence among the bishops in dealing with social matters was extraordinary, at least until 1956.
11 The name 'Movement' is an abbreviation for the *Catholic Social Studies Movement.*
12 Paul VI, *Octogesima Adveniens*, 1971, #48.

of these, a social justice ministry had to project itself into the public square with all the controversy that this entailed. Put simply, controversy is the coin of the realm in the public square and without it no effective contribution is likely to be made to either policy development or action.

In the circumstances of the time, there was silent consensus among the bishops that their newly formed national agencies, Australian Catholic Relief and the Catholic Commission for Justice and Peace, would deal with any thorny issues in applying Catholic social teaching to a rapidly changing Australian and world context (including East Timor).

Australian Catholic Relief (later renamed Caritas Australia) commenced operations in 1966, and three years later the Interim National Commission for Justice and Peace (NCJP) met for the first time. Until 1972, NCJP operated as a subsidiary of Australian Catholic Relief (ACR). In 1976 it was renamed the Catholic Commission for Justice and Peace (CCJP). ACR and CCJP were the two agencies charged with the task of interpreting Catholic social teaching in the context of Australian society.

Both organisations operated through councils chaired by a bishop appointed by the Australian Episcopal Conference. The discretion given their principal officers in setting priorities and determining functions usually depended on the bishop in charge. The fact that both organisations were based in Sydney reflected the wish of the Australian bishops to distance ACR and CCJP from Santamaria and his episcopal supporters in Victoria.[13]

CCJP itself constituted a type of 'Catholic public square' as its members were drawn from across the nation and included bishops, clergy, religious and lay people. While CCJP was never commissioned to speak on behalf of the Catholic bishops, in the minds of most people it did, and this led to serious misunderstandings about the role of the Commission as its work proceeded.[14]

★

In 1972 the AEC asked NCJP to revive the earlier practice of issuing annual social justice statements that Bob Santamaria had pioneered on their behalf in the 1940s and 1950s. This it did, beginning in 1973 with *Population in Perspective*. Preparing annual social justice statements became the major public focus of the Commission's work until 1986, by which time fourteen had been produced covering a wide range of topics.[15] The CCJP's statements received wide acceptance within the parishes and nationally. The topics discussed were of interest to other Christian churches and some statements were jointly sponsored.

The annual social justice statements were among the best-selling religious publications

---

13 Michael Hogan (ed) *Option for the Poor: Annual Social Justice Statements of the Australian Catholic Commission of Justice and Peace 1973–1987* (Department of Government and Public Administration, University of Sydney, 1992), 3.
14 CCJP Social justice statements included the disclaimer: *The Bishops recognise that not all people, even within the Church, will necessarily agree with the positions taken by the CCJP on all concrete social issues to which it has addressed itself and which are often open to different approaches. However the Bishops ask the Catholic people and with respect their fellow citizens, even though they may not agree with these positions to examine and discuss them in a Christian spirit of justice and charity.*
15 The topics included: population, affluence, the social side of sin, women in society, multiculturalism, aborigines, unemployment, poverty and power, Australia and its region, housing, change in Australia, young people in Australia and reconciliation. A proposed statement on industrial relations in 1986 was deemed to be too contentious in the political climate of the era.

in Australia in the 1970s and 1980s, sometimes selling up to 100,000 copies. The launch of each statement became a media event. As a result of this success and the controversy the statements generated, the CCJP became an increasingly prominent player in the Australian public square. Chris Sidoti, National Secretary of CCJP (and later Australian Human Rights Commissioner), notes of this development:

> The Social Justice Statements more than anything else established the reputation of the Commission. They took people by surprise - the institutional church was not expected to be able to comment with such weight on controversial and topical issues. Their insights and analyses were considered significant, even if they were not accepted. More often than not their views were validated by subsequent events.[16]

Despite this, in the 1980s the Australian Church was seen by the public to have a divided voice - the official CCJP from Sydney and the unofficial, but nevertheless influential, Santamaria in Melbourne who used *News Weekly* and his regular TV appearances to castigate CCJP for its 'Marxist analysis'. His words carried weight among the clergy as I found out when a Melbourne parish priest refused my request to speak to his congregation about the situation in East Timor on the grounds that I was 'supporting communists'!

There is much truth in Catholic academic Fr Patrick Smythe's summation of the Australian Catholic Church as events unfolded in East Timor:

> As an institution the Church in Australia cannot be said to have had a coherent and unified policy in respect of the people of East Timor at any stage. The bishops themselves had different viewpoints and various perceptions were evident within ecclesiastical agencies that addressed the matter on behalf of, or independently of them, and among the laity as a whole. Thus segments within the Church aligned with Australian government policy, some remained idle while others were highly committed to a just and peaceful resolution of the issue.[17]

The result of these divisions was that in the fifteen years from May 1976 to November 1991, the only Church statements on East Timor came either from the CCJP or ACR. No additional statement was made by the AEC.

*

In the empty space created by episcopal silence, solidarity movements began to take shape. In 1976 the CCJP helped set up the Australian East Timor Association in Sydney. The same year the first National East Timor Consultation took place. This attracted sixty

---

16 Chris Sidoti 'From the General to the Particular: Achievements of the Catholic Commission for Justice and Peace' in *Australian Politics Catholic Perspectives* (Uniya, Jesuit Social Justice Center: Occasional Paper No 6, undated), 32.
17 Patrick Smythe *'The Heaviest Blow'- The Catholic Church and the East Timor Issue* (Munster: Lit Verlag, 2004), 106.

representatives from the churches, the unions[18] and NGOs represented by the Australian Council for Overseas Aid (ACFOA).[19] The meeting recommended a protest march modelled on the Vietnam moratorium marches to draw public attention to the plight of the East Timorese. *News Weekly* immediately questioned the political motivation of those involved, claiming that most were communists.[20]

The CCJP and Santamaria accessed different sources of information on East Timor and these coloured the nature of their commentaries. Santamaria's sources were confidential Vatican briefings given to the bishops by the Nuncio in Canberra. He was able to access these through his episcopal supporters. Santamaria also had contacts in the Jakarta-based *Centre for Strategic and International Studies* (CSIS) headed by prominent Indonesian Chinese Catholics, Harry Tjan and Jusuf Wanandi.[21]

The genesis of the CSIS and the influence it came to exert on the development of Indonesian policy adds to the complexity of the Catholic story as it affects East Timor.

★

In 1936 Joop Beek, a Dutch Jesuit trainee, aged 19, was assigned to Indonesia. When war broke out he was interned and it was not until after the war that he could return to Europe, complete his studies, and be ordained in 1948. Beek was influenced by the European Catholic Action Movement which had its parallels in Australia in the various movements such as the Young Christian Workers (YCW), Young Christian Students (YCS), and the National Catholic Rural Movement (NCRM) in Australia, which sought to give practical expression in public life to the principles of Catholic social teaching.

When he was re-assigned to Indonesia in 1952, and with the co-operation of Jesuit institutions across Indonesia, Beek set about training young Catholics to participate in public life. This happened in the context of the demise of the Sukarno regime and the three way political contest that ensued between the Communist Party, radical Muslim groups and the secular nationalists, all of whom had their representatives in the all-powerful armed forces.

When Beek's trainees, who Frank Mount calls 'the Beek organization' returned home they formed a network of groups across Indonesia which over the next decade morphed into a Catholic intelligence organisation sending back information about local political developments each month to Beek.[22] Wanandi and Tjan who sat at the centre of this operation, had political connections to the secular nationalist cause and in particular General Ali Moertopo, Soeharto's top political operative.

Moertopo recognised the value of the Beek organisation and tried to co-opt the Jesuit to his cause but Beek rejected these overtures. However, Wanandi, his chief organiser did not. Through Wanandi, Moertopo had access to the intelligence generated by the Beek

---

18 Union involvement stemmed from solidarity with Dili workers involved in the 1974 waterfront strike which gave birth to FRETILIN.
19 ACFOA, based in Melbourne, was the umbrella organisation for Non-Government Organisations (NGOs) dealing with overseas aid.
20 *News Weekly* 17 March 1976.
21 Smythe, 64.
22 See Frank Mount 'The Beek Organisation in Indonesia' in *Wrestling with Asia: A Memoir* (Ballan: Connor Court Publishing, 2012), 253-263.

organization which he used to good political effect. He established and financed the CSIS as a front organization with the brief to monitor political developments in South East Asia. Frank Mount had a similar brief from Santamaria and the NCC here in Australia which he executed under the cover of being a freelance journalist. Mount became the go-between between Wanandi and Santamaria. The two were joined at the hip, so to speak, in terms of their political ideology and methodology. A mutually beneficial partnership developed.

The CSIS's Church connection gave credibility to intelligence sourced to Wanandi. Wanandi and Tjan sought and valued Santamaria's advice on political matters and his 'take' on political developments in Australia. However, the CSIS was also playing a double game in advancing the secular nationalist political agenda which at the time included the integration of East Timor into Indonesia. It is not hard to see why the addition of a province that was largely Catholic would be attractive from a Javanese Catholic perspective, even if East Timor was generally viewed as something of a backwater.

As part of the game, the CSIS fed Santamaria information designed to counter that from pro-autonomy sources. The security situation in East Timor during the occupation meant that most reports coming out of the country were anonymous and so their authenticity could be challenged. This Santamaria did when they did not fit his ideological agenda.

In 1982 a letter from da Costa Lopes, addressed to the Chair of ACR, Bishop John Gerry, was smuggled out of East Timor. In it da Costa Lopes indicated that famine was likely to hit some areas of East Timor in the months ahead if the rains were poor. At the time people were being moved in large numbers into resettlement camps and so food production was affected. The Apostolic Administrator was signaling the likely need for ACR's support.

Bishop Gerry released the letter to the Australian media and East Timor support groups then quoted it extensively. The appearance of this letter in the Australian media sent the CSIS machine into overdrive. It sponsored a visit to East Timor by Gough Whitlam. The intention behind Whitlam's visit was to discredit da Costa Lopes. Whitlam did this subsequently in testimony before the Senate Foreign Affairs and Defense Committee, calling da Costa Lopes a liar. His comments were given extensive coverage in the media and a two-page spread in *News Weekly*. Santamaria used the occasion to attack ACR, implying that it had manufactured the crisis to raise money for East Timor.[23] This drew a vigorous response from its Director, Michael Whiteley.

★

Because of the communication blackout imposed on East Timor between 1975 and 1989, the world knew very little about what was happening there other than the elaborate storylines of the Indonesian press. The Australian Government connived in maintaining this blackout by closing down independent wireless operators in Darwin who were sending and receiving signals from FRETILIN. This made it hard for the independence movement in Timor to link up with operatives such as Ramos Horta who were operating outside Timor, and so frustrated the possibility of a genuine peace process getting off the ground.

---

23 SMH 6 Feb 1982 'Monsignor Accused over Timor'; *News Weekly* 19 February 'Report of Famine False'; and 7 April 1982 carried the text of Whitlam's testimony.

In the circumstances, accessing reliable data was important since both the Indonesians and the independence movement had a vested interest in minimising or maximising, as the case was, the scale of the atrocities and violations of human rights.[24] The main source of credible information was that provided by refugees repatriated from Timor to Portugal where Australian journalist Jill Jolliffe was based. Church personnel also moved in and out of East Timor and these provided a second source of information. Indonesian clergy could move about the country quite freely, but the East Timorese clergy were restricted, so it was difficult for them to verify the accuracy of information passed down the indigenous exchange system, even though the sheer volume made its thrust incontrovertible.

Successive papal nuncios in Jakarta (Pablo Puente, Francesco Canalini and Pietro Sambi) further muddied the waters by casting doubts on the veracity of information provided them by Belo and other clergy based in East Timor. They too were victims of the well-oiled Indonesian propaganda machine.

*

CCJP tapped into reliable networks in gathering information on East Timor. The first was *Christians in Solidarity with East Timor* (CISET), an Australian group originally founded by the religious congregations in 1982. CISET had links to similar solidarity groups in the U.S. Its monthly newsletter disseminated information on East Timor as it became available, which included news commentary from around the world relayed by fax.

CCJP maintained close links with the UK-based *Catholic Institute for International Relations* (CIIR). CIIR issued a number of reports on East Timor beginning with its *Declaration on East Timor* in May 1985, which set out the minimum conditions for a just peace: involvement of representatives from East Timor in UN negotiations; provision of international access to East Timor; and an act of self-determination by the East Timorese. CCJP publicly endorsed this *Declaration*. In 1987 CCJP reprinted the CIIR's 1987 *East Timor: A Christian Reflection* in toto.

CCJP also accessed data from *Pro Mundi Vita* based in Brussels. *Pro Mundi Vita* was a research institute concerned with disseminating information on issues that impacted on the Church's mission around the world. It produced a number of well-documented 'dossiers' including its authoritative *Dossier On East Timor* in April 1984. This bulletin set out and assessed all the information then available in the public domain. In Holland, the Dutch CCJP was also active in promoting the East Timor cause and in 1983 produced its own detailed report on the situation, a report which it updated in 1986.

The Australian CCJP contributed to these networks using information it had accessed from refugees arriving in Australia.

*

---

24 The leadership of the independence movement outside East Timor was not always coherent, as people remained divided about what independence would mean and how it might come about. For this reason neither Belo nor da Costa Lopes, whilst having their own views about the desired course of events, allowed themselves to be drawn into these discussions. The leadership in Melbourne was particularly coherent, and it was with this group that I became closely connected.

In 1986, the year Pope John Paul II visited Australia, the Secretary of the AEC Monsignor (later Bishop) Kevin Manning contacted the nuncio to enquire whether or not the AEC should issue a new statement about East Timor. His confidential reply dated the 22nd July gives some insight into Vatican thinking at the time.

The nuncio urged caution in making a statement since sources of information from East Timor were 'unreliable', and lest the Indonesians retaliate against the local Catholic community there, 'so adding to their suffering'. The briefing went on to acknowledge that Indonesia had made little progress in winning the confidence of the people; that 'Indonesianisation' and transmigration were well underway; that FRETILIN had become unpopular; and that UN support for East Timor was weakening. The nuncio acknowledges that the clergy in East Timor were standing up for the human rights of the people and that restrictions on Belo's movements had been lifted. The letter implied that this positive development could be compromised by an imprudent intervention by the Australian bishops.[25]

The briefing provides a powerful reminder of just how effective Indonesia's misinformation campaign had been in influencing Vatican thinking. Not surprisingly the AEC took no action in response.

★

CCJP followed the example of Catholic organizations overseas such as CIIR and became involved in justice and peace education. An adult education package was developed for parish peace and justice groups and instructional materials were produced that could be used in Catholic schools for teaching in religious education and the social sciences. These materials introduced Catholics to social analysis, enabling them to understand for themselves how social structures contributed to, and often institutionalised, injustice. Social analysis – seeing and judging – was seen as a necessary skill to participate and act effectively in the public square.

CCJP's materials suggested that, while helping the victims of injustice was vitally important (a role that ACR fulfilled through its relief and development work funded by its annual Project Compassion appeal), by itself it was not enough. What also had to be addressed were the structural issues that created the victims.

A new generation of Catholics was taught to appreciate the fact that marginalization can be the consequence of the social systems in which they live and over which they seem to have little control. Christian responsibility requires good social analysis. They were also taught that, in an increasingly interconnected world, the causes of poverty in one country result from options chosen by people living in another.

In this education project the situation in East Timor provided a case study right on Australia's doorstep.

★

In addition to its educational and advocacy roles, CCJP also made a number of direct interventions on behalf of East Timor, beginning as early as 1975. In December 1976,

---

25 Confidential note from Archbishop Brambilla to Bishop Manning 18 July, 1986.

for example, it castigated the Fraser Government for abstaining from the UN vote on East Timor. In March of the following year it wrote to all federal politicians seeking a parliamentary enquiry into East Timor. In 1982 it appeared before the Senate Committee on Foreign Aid and Defence demanding that the Australian Government step up its efforts to assist East Timorese refugees in Australia, and re-affirming the need for an act of self-determination in East Timor. In 1983 members met with Monsignor da Costa Lopes during his ill-fated visit to Australia to plead the case of his people, and later criticised the report of the parliamentary delegation sent to East Timor. The next year it urged the ALP national conference to retain its commitment to human rights in East Timor. In 1985 it again briefed the AEC on the situation in East Timor. In 1986 it sought unsuccessfully to have the AEC invite Bishop Belo to Australia, and contested the Australian ambassador's statement that the human rights situation in East Timor was improving. In 1987 CCJP issued a CCJP Issues Paper (No 10) entitled *East Timor: A Forgotten People*.[26]

By 1985 a number of bishops were concerned with the advocacy role of CCJP, and were disturbed by the level of criticism this necessarily attracted, particularly from its opponents *within* the Church. At the time CCJP was preparing a paper on peace and nuclear disarmament. After much controversy, *Work for a Just Peace* was published as the annual social justice statement for 1985.

The following year CCJP embarked on the preparation of a statement on industrial relations. This was abandoned following a decision of the AEC at its May 1986 conference. The controversy generated by an early draft of this paper was the trigger which led to the bishops' decision that the time had come for the Church to retreat from the CCJP's model of participating in the public square. The Bishops themselves would, it was intended, thenceforth take a more prominent leadership role. The CCJP's mandate was not renewed and it was replaced by the *Australian Catholic Social Justice Council* (ACSJC) which would opt to follow the model set up by the US Bishops Conference in developing major policy statements.

The manner in which the CCJP was disbanded was a public relations disaster for the Australian bishops. It had provided a model of involvement in the public square that commanded attention. Like all models for such Church participation, the CCJP model had its limitations and in due course, might have been expected to reach its 'use-by' date. Its work was extensive, but much of its public profile came from the annual social justice statements that addressed in depth issues having national import. Sooner or later the pool of such major national issues would become exhausted. What then?

The best construction to be put on the AEC's actions is that, rightly or wrongly, the bishops thought that the times called for another model, one with which they were more closely involved. In a sense the CCJP was a victim of its own success. It had helped create the critical mass of people needed to establish local justice and peace commissions in a number of dioceses so that in the time following the CCJP's closure, the ACSJC was just *one* player among many. This subsequent 'localisation' of issues meant that the impact of the Catholic presence in the public square diminished to such an extent that, when I began to

---

26 The original brief was to produce a paper on industrial relations at the time of the Hawke/Keating accords but this was later withdrawn. The CCJP then adopted the CIIR's 1987 statement *East Timor: A Christian Reflection* as its own. Included with the paper was a chronology of CCJP interventions on East Timor from 1976.

speak out on East Timor in the early 1990s, I was seen as quite radical.

Bishop Bill Brennan, the initial Chair of the ACSJC, was strongly committed to helping East Timor. He visited privately in 1991 and again in 1993 and I met him there on several subsequent occasions. He sought to support Bishop Belo, which I believe he sincerely wanted to do. However, Belo could not afford to accept the support of someone known to have an agenda favouring Indonesia without being compromised in the eyes of his own people. Brennan seemed incapable of understanding this and became very frustrated in consequence.

★

So did Church leaders in Australia fail the East Timorese in the period 1975–1991? This is not an easy question to answer definitively since, as I hope I have shown, bishops operated in a Church milieu that did not favor collective action on almost any issue. They were too divided and had delegated responsibility to less authoritative bodies.

In 1975–87 a divided Catholic Church had limited its capacity to respond to *any* peace and justice crisis. Some of the difficulties were internal, others were imposed by Rome, while some were the result of inexperience. It is a measure of the ineptitude of the Australian Church's institutional response to a crisis affecting hundreds of thousands of Catholics that, fifteen years after the Indonesian invasion, and with thousands of Timorese refugees in this country, and despite the efforts of its official national justice agency, the CCJP, few Catholics in Australia were aware of events unfolding to our immediate north and in their own country. Until 1991 I had to count myself among the ignorant.

Part 2
CONVERGENCE

CHAPTER 17
VISITING SANTA CRUZ WITH CARLOS BELO

During the past two decades I have made more than thirty visits to East Timor in a variety of capacities. Over time some of my memories of these visits have tended to merge into one another. However, this is not the case with my first visit in 1992. That remains singularly engraved in my memory.

When I went to East Timor, I did not go as a representative of the Australian Bishops' Conference. My own passion for social justice, and a growing sense of the terrible suffering that the people were enduring, were my motivation. I was also responding to the challenge of the East Timorese in Melbourne who had asked me to visit their country and, as one of them put it, 'to see the cause of our pain'. I was also keen to meet Bishop Belo and other Church leaders in East Timor whom I suspected trod a very difficult and lonely path.

While I had travelled a good deal prior to 1992, I had never visited a militarised state, which seemed the most appropriate way to describe Indonesia's twenty-seventh province. So it was with a certain amount of excitement that I bade farewell to Archbishop Frank Little, and caught my taxi to Tullamarine airport for the flight to Denpasar.[1]

*

My public association with East Timorese refugees in Melbourne meant that I had become a 'person of interest' to Indonesian officials in Australia. As it turned out, they had notified Dili of my impending visit to East Timor. I was also aware that some of the Australian bishops were in touch with the people in the Indonesian embassy. They had been there as dinner guests for example, and of course the embassy people do not provide dinners without requiring something in return. A small number of bishops were also in contact with the papal nuncio in Jakarta, and some of the Indonesian bishops. Very early I knew I had to be very careful what I said, and whom I spoke to. There were some bishops in Australia with whom I simply could not discuss my work on behalf of the East Timorese.

At the time of my visit, Indonesia was attempting to re-build tourism in East Timor. While journalists were still banned, there was no longer a ban on Catholic clergy visiting

---

1   While Archbishop Little was unsure about the wisdom of my visiting East Timor, he did not put any obstacles in my way. This was also true of his successor, Archbishop George Pell. I kept up my rate of visitation to East Timor once Bishop Pell was appointed as archbishop of Melbourne.

the territory – the exception being Portuguese clergy - as many were quite supportive of Indonesia's efforts to 'develop' what they saw as a 'neglected' former Portuguese colony.

I had been warned in advance by Timorese in Australia that my visit would attract the attention of INTEL, as the Indonesian intelligence service was known, and that I could expect that my room in the Hotel Turismo in Dili would be bugged. With all the well-intentioned advice I had received about being spied upon, I was determined not to become paranoid or to be intimidated.

★

In 1992 there were two possible routes from Australia to Dili. The direct route went via Denpasar, Bali. The second route went from Denpasar to Kupang, the capital of West Timor, and then on to Dili. I was booked on the latter. My trip with Qantas to Denpasar was uneventful. I was just another Aussie making his way to Bali. However, things changed the next morning when I arrived at the Merpati Airlines counter to check in for the flight to Dili. When I presented my ticket I was referred to another desk around a corner, where a man in military uniform questioned me about my visit to East Timor. 'Why are you going? Who are you meeting?' and so on - all very unusual for a tourist! This questioning went on for some time so I asked if there was some type of problem, to which the reply was 'No, just routine security'.

Over successive visits this form of interrogation became something of a game, and I eventually developed a strategy that seemed to work. If I was asked 'Why are you visiting?' I would reply 'I am interested in the theological principles and catechetical methods being used by the local Catholic priests in East Timor to evangelise their congregations'. This, or some version of it, had the usual effect of dissuading further questions. Anyway, it was not far from the truth.

Once my passport had been stamped, an INTEL employee was assigned to escort me to the plane. His job was to make sure no one spoke to me before I was aboard. I decided to engage him in conversation and quickly found out that the young man's name was Yusuf. He was a Catholic from Flores and had attended a Catholic school. His mother, two sisters and a brother still lived there. He stayed with me the whole time, taking me right up to the plane. Sadly, I later found out that Yusuf had been killed by the Indonesian military, but I could never establish why this had occurred.

The Merpati plane was dirty and filled mostly with Indonesians and a few Timorese returning home. After a short stop at Kupang we flew on to Dili arriving at about 1:00pm. Prior to leaving Melbourne I had been in communication with Bishop Belo who had indicated that someone would be there to meet me at the airport. However, when no one appeared I caught a taxi into town to my hotel. Taxis in Dili then, as now, were yellow jalopies, mainly Mercedes in those days, serving their last sentence before making their way to the scrapheap.

The trip into town was uninspiring. The airport is at Comoro, a suburb about five or six kilometres to the east of the city centre. At first glance Dili looked drab, untidy and decaying. I checked in at Hotel Turismo and found I had a first floor room overlooking the bay with a great view out to Atauro Island, thirty-eight kilometres or so off the coast.

From the outside Hotel Turismo looked tacky. Its white paint had been challenged by the local climate, and had given up the battle. However, on the inside the facilities proved fairly modern. Because my room overlooked the ocean, the breeze blowing through the windows off the sea came as a most welcome relief from Dili's steamy heat.

I did a quick check of the room to see if I could find any 'bugs'. I decided that they were either too well hidden or simply did not exist. However, I was later told by an insider that the room was indeed bugged. I had a shower, went downstairs, and asked the way to the Bishop's house. It turned out that the residence was just a few doors further up the road so I set off to introduce myself to Bishop Belo. However when I knocked on the door of his residence I was told that he was not in - he had gone to the airport to pick up someone from Australia!

The visit gave me the chance to look around Belo's compound. This had been the site of a major stand-off between the Bishop and the Indonesian military following the Santa Cruz massacre. My visit to the compound gave me the opportunity to meet Belo's housekeeper, Josephine. She was a lovely woman who had been with Xanana Gusmao in the hills. Josephine remained with Belo under his protection.

On the day of my visit the only occupants of the compound were hens and a few geese all sheltering from the sun in the tranquil shade of a large mango tree. The Bishop's residence was located in a more or less square piece of ground about an acre in size, and was surrounded by a solid fence, two metres high. The residence is elevated with a veranda approached by a wide flight of steps that were dazzlingly white in the midday sun. The veranda provides the visitor with an uninterrupted view of Dili Bay. The residence is built in the Portuguese style, solid white stucco walls with overhanging red tile roof, no guttering, and deep drains surrounding the entire building.

The compound is located on the beachfront road and has a small park opposite the main gate. The park is dominated by a large shrine, dedicated to the Virgin Mary, that has long served as the site for Marian festivals in East Timor. At the climax of a procession ending there on the 13th October 1982, Monsignor da Costa Lopes had addressed a crowd of about twelve thousand East Timorese, and denounced Indonesian atrocities against his countrymen and women. By doing so he drew down upon himself the wrath of both the Indonesians and the Vatican.[2]

★

Having failed to meet Bishop Belo, I returned to the hotel and sought the refuge of Hotel Turismo's beer garden, where tall palm trees provided leafy shade and a welcome escape from the heat. As I sat at one of the colourful tables enjoying a cool drink, I went through what I had been able to find out about Belo before I left Melbourne.[3] Since the Dili Massacre he had been frequently in the news and on television in Australia.

---

2   At the time of his denunciation tens of thousands of Timorese had died as a result of the Indonesian occupation. There was widespread famine due to Indonesian resettlement policies and its infamous 'fence of legs' operations in which large numbers of men and boys were used as human shields ahead of Indonesian troops to flush out FRETILIN fighters.
3   For a comprehensive biography of Belo to 1999 see Arnold Kohen's *From The Place Among the Dead: The Epic Struggles of Bishop Belo of East Timor* (New York: St Martin's Press, 1999). Kohen, a respected US journalist, was an important political activist on behalf of the East Timorese, particularly in the United States.

Carlos Belo was born in 1948 in a small hamlet Wailakama near Vemasse. Belo was not his surname. It was the surname of his godfather, and was adopted after he was born. This was a common practice. His father's surname was Filipe, and his mother's surname was Ximenes. He was called Carlos Filipe Ximenes Belo.[4] His family belonged to the *liurai* class among the Makassae, a Melanesian tribal grouping originally hailing from New Guinea. Carlos's father was a catechist and as a Church worker was able to move freely around the colony, a privilege that few Timorese enjoyed under Portuguese rule. His mother, whom I met several times, was one of the few Timorese girls of her generation to receive any education at all. Belo's family lived in the standard bamboo and thatch cottage still prevalent in the villages around Baucau. They were very poor by Western standards.

As a young boy Belo was regarded as a keen student with a good ear for languages which he picked up by talking to tourists staying at the Majestic Hotel.[5] At age fourteen Carlos attended the diocese's minor seminary where he studied for the next four years. Towards the end of that time he decided to become a Salesian rather than a diocesan priest, much to the annoyance of Bishop Ribeiro. The Salesians then sent him to Portugal to complete his secondary education and begin his theological training.[6] Carlos was the second member of his family to join the seminary. His elder brother Antonio died suddenly in Portugal before completing his studies.

Belo was in Lisbon when the April Revolution took place there in 1974, and so experienced at first hand the chaos that reigns when an authoritarian state collapses. This was an important part of his political education. He was one of a group of young Timorese studying in Portugal, a number of whom would go on to become FRETILIN leaders. Almost all perished in the fight for independence.

Late in 1974, as part of his Salesian training, Belo returned to East Timor as a teacher. He taught a range of subjects at the Salesian College in Fatumaca which is situated a few kilometres outside Baucau. However, his time there was short. While he was attending a teacher in-service program in Dili in August 1975, the UDT coup occurred. As the road back to Fatumaca was in UDT hands, it was deemed too dangerous for him to return to his school. When Belo sought the advice of da Costa Lopes on what to do, he was advised to join those fleeing to the west and make his way through Indonesia to Macau.

Belo set out with others for the border region of Bobonaro where he hid for about a month before crossing the border into West Timor. He spent some months in a refugee camp there and, being quick at languages, got a good grounding in Bahasa before making his way, with the help of the local bishop, to Indonesia and then on to Macau. From Macau Belo was sent back to Portugal to complete his priestly training. He was ordained as a Salesian priest in 1980 at age thirty-two.

Belo returned to East Timor late in 1981 where he was responsible for the formation of young Timorese training at Fatumaca to become Salesians. The following year he was

---

4   Belo was also the name of a people who lived on the south side in the area between East and West Timor.
5   Now re-named the Pousada de Baucau. During the Indonesian occupation the hotel was taken over by the military and many Timorese were tortured there.
6   The Salesian order has had a long presence in East Timor beginning after the Second World War. They have major technical colleges in Dili, at Fatumaca south of Baucau, and a third near Lospalos at Fuiloro. They also run other educational institutions including primary schools. From these centres the Salesian priests, brothers and sisters operate an extensive pastoral ministry to surrounding villages.

appointed head of the large Salesian community serving the college. Much to his own, and everyone else's surprise, the Papal Nuncio from Jakarta, Pablo Puente, who had been involved in the dismissal of da Costa Lopes, announced Belo's appointment as Apostolic Administrator. He was installed on the 12th May 1983.

★

The appointment was not well received by the local diocesan clergy who in protest refused to acknowledge him at the social function celebrating his appointment. They saw Belo as too young and far too inexperienced for the role, and resented the fact that more senior and experienced diocesan priests were passed over. There was also some resentment at the fact that he had been out of the country when the worst of the Indonesian atrocities took place. A senior and well-respected diocesan priest, Martinho da Costa Lopes, who had been treated quite unjustly by Rome, had been replaced by a relatively junior priest from a religious order. In the eyes of these diocesan priests, Belo was seen as a 'Vatican plant' appointed because he was unlikely to upset the Indonesian authorities in East Timor. These factors made Belo's first year in the role a very difficult one.

In a later visit I was to ask Belo about this time. He said that the hurt resulting from the hostility of the diocesan clergy following his appointment as Apostolic Administrator had affected him deeply. He had been given a clear message that he was not 'one of them'. His prayer to God had been 'Is this the price I must pay?' The conversation gave me a clue about what I might do to support him. I could simply be a listener if he wanted to talk. He didn't always want to talk, but sometimes he did, and would say things that he was not willing to share with others.

Undeterred by rejection Belo quickly developed his own style in dealing with the Indonesians. His fluency in Bahasa was a considerable help. His strategy was to act as mediator between the people and the occupiers. He attacked the abuse of human rights in East Timor, the lack of respect shown for the local culture, and the marginalisation of Timorese people in their own land. He was effectively turning Indonesia's national doctrine of *Pancasila* against them, much to the annoyance of Vatican diplomats. I also noticed over the years how he knew who to help and when to help. He was at home with the complexities of relationships within the culture in a way that an outsider could not be.

Pope John Paul II provided him with a measure of protection and support in the face of hostility from the Vatican bureaucracy. He had another friend in the Vatican bureaucracy, Cardinal Roger Etchegaray who headed the Pontifical Council for Justice and Peace.

Belo was consecrated Bishop of Dili in 1988. As a further measure of his personal support, Pope John Paul II included East Timor in his itinerary when visiting Indonesia in 1989.[7] He arrived there on the 12th October 1989, and celebrated Mass at Tasi Tolu which had been a killing field. The Pope asked the master of ceremonies about the killings and where people were buried. I spoke to that man later, and in private conversation he was

---

7   Pope John Paul II, who knew how to demonstrate his message symbolically as well as deliver it verbally, deliberately kissed the ground in both East Timor and Indonesia during these visits. Given this was his public practice whenever he visited a country, he was thereby demonstrating that he saw East Timor and Indonesia as two separate countries. In East Timor, he did not do this on alighting from the plane, but rather, when he arrived at Dili cathedral. Kohen, 141-7.

to tell me that he had been forced to tell the truth to the Pope! The man was at that time pro-Indonesian.

★

As I was to discover in the years ahead, Belo was always prepared to roll the dice if he thought the situation demanded it. For instance in 1989, totally frustrated with the lack of progress on the part of the Indonesians in recognizing the human rights of East Timor's people, he had taken a huge gamble and written directly to the Secretary General of the United Nations seeking a democratic act of self-determination to determine the fate of East Timor. He did this unilaterally without consulting either the Vatican or the nuncio. This initiative was not well received by the Vatican Secretariat of State, nor by the Indonesian authorities. As a direct consequence Belo began to receive death threats. However, Pope John Paul II reinforced Belo's message about human rights during his visit later that year.

Belo lived in an uneasy truce with both the Indonesians and the Vatican's diplomatic arm, protected from the latter by the support of the Pope. Vatican diplomats had snookered themselves in bending to Indonesian pressure to dismiss da Costa Lopes over the human rights issue.[8] They could not play that hand a second time without losing face internationally, given growing awareness of the scale of the injustices being perpetrated in East Timor.

Belo was a very courageous leader with enemies outside the Church, but also within it. He was isolated in that he had no episcopal conference to support him. He did attend the Indonesian episcopal conference, but this ambiguous situation would have added to his sense of isolation rather than alleviate it. As apostolic administrator and later as bishop, he reported directly to the papal nuncio who lived in Jakarta, and who was a known friend of the notoriously hard line General Murdani. Clearly Belo was in an invidious position. I did not know if I could help him at all, but I was certainly prepared to offer any support I could.

★

I had hardly finished my drink when I noticed the Bishop standing at the hotel entrance opposite where I was sitting. He was dressed in his white episcopal soutane and was accompanied by another man who turned out to be his driver, Antonio.[9] He did not come in. Instead he sent Antonio to get me. Belo's first comment after greeting me was: 'You can't stay here Monsignor Deakin. The place is full of Indonesian spies.'

When one thinks of heroic leaders, one sub-consciously pictures them as being tall and self-assured. By contrast, like many of his countrymen and women, Belo is quite diminutive and, for a bishop, at least by Australian standards, was extraordinarily youthful

---

8   Da Costa Lopes had been having meetings with FRETILIN, because it was his view that there would be no progress if people did not talk with one another. FRETILIN was regarded in some quarters within the Church as communist.

9   As a young man Antonio had been exiled to Atauro where the families of known FRETILIN supporters were often detained. Belo had secured his release and Antonio lived at the Bishop's residence and acted as his driver.

looking in 1992. He did not seem like someone who by this time had carried the burden of leading the Church in East Timor in the most trying of circumstances for almost a decade. Even at first meeting, Belo came across as someone who was naturally courteous, but also a person of great resilience. I was quite taken by surprise, and wondered how he kept going.

He quickly explained in passable English that he had not been at the airport to meet me because of a mix up about flight times, and had only just then returned. With a chuckle he told me that authorities had already contacted him twice that day about 'the general' arriving from Australia. The Indonesian consul in Melbourne had clearly got his wires crossed.

Belo suggested that I move to his residence for the night. He had arranged for me to stay with the Salesians at Comoro and they would help me with my travel to the east of the province. I thanked him for his invitation but said that I wanted to stay at Hotel Turismo for just one night because of its historic connections with Australia.[10] We agreed to meet the next day and, as I had time on my hands, I decided to go for a walk along the foreshore. This turned into a very enjoyable two-hour exploration of the local culture. It is amazing how much one can pick up about a culture by simply observing and listening. When I returned to the hotel, I changed and had little difficulty in identifying the INTEL agents posing as tourists who wanted to be my friends. Their efforts to get information from me certainly lacked subtlety.

★

As arranged, Bishop Belo picked me up in his four-wheel drive the next day. When I got into the vehicle he pointed out that we were being followed. As we drove past his residence a man was sitting in the shade of the shrine opposite his gate recording who came in and out of the compound. Such was the daily life for the Catholic Bishop of East Timor! As I was to find out many times during the next two weeks, the Indonesians used surveillance as a means of intimidation and harassment. This meant that knowing whom one could trust was a critical survival skill.

We paid a quick visit to the magnificent cathedral that had been built by the Indonesians at Indonesian expense as part of the *Pancasila* policy. It has a huge stone in the porch with the signature of Suharto on it. We then went across town to the large white parish church at Motael which had played a key role in events leading up to the Santa Cruz massacre. This event was still very raw in Belo's mind.

The Motael church is located on the foreshore road facing the sea. Following the Japanese invasion during the Second World War, it had become the main Catholic church for Dili after the cathedral was destroyed by allied bombing. Given the rather exclusive area in which it is located, the church grounds are quite extensive and include a large open area where major religious ceremonies were often held.[11]

In the sanctuary I noted a stone marking the burial site of Bishop Jose Antonio Medeiros, the Portuguese bishop from Macau, who used to come to Dili when it was a

---

10 The Australian journalists who were killed by the Indonesians at Balibo in 1975 had stayed at Hotel Turismo prior to their ill-fated journey to Balibo.
11 It was not uncommon, given the large Catholic population, for the Bishop to confirm over a thousand children in the one ceremony.

small village. On one of his visits he died and was buried there. I stopped and said a prayer of thanksgiving for this man's great love for the Timorese people, and the part he had played in their early journey in Catholicism.

We then drove the short distance from Motael to Santa Cruz. Bishop Belo began to outline the events of the 12th November 1991 once we were back in the car.

★

In October the clandestine resistance movement had intended to use the arrival of a protest ship, *Lusitania*, and later the visit of a UN special representative, to draw attention to their cause. When the Indonesians turned the *Lusitania* back and cancelled the UN visit, people's hopes were dashed and some sporadic protests took place. Sebastian Gomez had been involved in a student protest, and with some companions sought refuge in the Motael church grounds when hunted by the military. After some time spent hiding in the church, and believing the coast was clear as night was falling, Gomez decided to go home to his mother who lived nearby. He was shot at the gate leading out of the church by a soldier and died in the arms of passers-by who bravely came to his aid. His death marked the beginning of the end for the Indonesians.

The custom in East Timor is to hold a memorial service for the dead a short time after the burial. People meet at a church for Mass, and then process to the cemetery where they place a cross on the grave. A large crowd gathered in the grounds outside the Motael Church after the 6:30am Mass for Sebastian, and then moved in procession across town to Santa Cruz which is about two kilometres from the church. Along the way they were joined by members of the resistance who saw the procession as an opportunity to make up lost ground. What followed was a very large demonstration – perhaps two thousand people – complete with banners in English for international consumption.

Along the route of the procession there was also a certain amount of provocation in the course of which an Indonesian soldier was stabbed. The bishop believed the aggravation could be traced to agitators planted by the Indonesians for this purpose. As he noted: 'That is their way!' The provocation failed to deter the group from its purpose of protesting the cold-blooded killing of another young Timorese at Indonesian hands, and calling for independence.

★

When Belo and I arrived at Santa Cruz, my immediate impression was that I was visiting a killing field. It was an eerie experience and, unfortunately, it would not be my last during this visit to East Timor.

The cemetery is surrounded by a high besser-brick fence and is entered through an arch just big enough to take a car. There is a large open area in front of the cemetery where people assemble for funerals and where cars can be parked. There is very limited room in the cemetery itself as the graves are closely packed and paths between them very narrow. On the other side of the road is the cemetery for Indonesian soldiers, and one periodically saw newly turned graves indicating more had been killed.

As Belo told the story, the crowd approaching the cemetery banked up as the protesters collected in front of the cemetery gates. Some went inside to take part in the religious ceremony and others waited their turn outside to get in through the gate. While this was happening, Indonesian soldiers from the local barracks formed up on the two ends of the open area and behind the wall of the Indonesian military cemetery, so that they surrounded the protest group on three sides. At a signal from a military commander dressed in civilian clothes, the troops opened fire. As I stood in the car park, I realised how hopelessly vulnerable people would have been.

Caught in the open the Timorese had two options – to rush through the gate and risk being stomped on, or to climb over the cemetery wall. In both cases they were sitting ducks for the troops positioned immediately opposite the gate. The chaos that followed is grittily captured on journalist Max Stahl's film shot from inside the cemetery after the firing started.[12]

During this my first visit to Timor I met a number of people who had fled the slaughter. These were mostly Timorese, but also included an American reporter, and a New Zealander of Indian origin. They told me how they had run down to the back of the cemetery, got over the fence and ran and ran till they could find shelter and stayed in hiding for some days. Their fear was immense.

★

As we walked through the arch and to the open-air chapel about forty metres inside the gate I found myself standing right where I knew from watching Stahl's film that wounded people had been crowded. I was struck by how unnaturally tidy it now seemed. We found Sebastian Gomez' grave marked by the cross placed there on 12th November. Together we prayed not only for him but for all those who died that day. The bishop continued his story when we got back into the car.

Belo had not found out what had happened till late in the morning, and when he did, went straight to the cemetery arriving around 11:00am, about an hour after the shooting had started. He first visited the chapel where some of the wounded still remained. These were later taken away in trucks and killed. When Belo arrived, soldiers were hastily washing the blood off the road and the paths in the cemetery with buckets of water. He saw bodies piled up in the back of trucks. He was told they were going to be taken to the public hospital down the road. One of the military men told Belo that over three hundred people had died in the incident, most in the cemetery. Another accosted him saying 'We should shoot you, since you are the leader of these trouble-makers!'

He then visited the hospital where many wounded were taken by relatives. There he saw 'dozens and dozens and dozens' of mainly young people lying in corridors waiting to be attended to. In fact hundreds were wounded on that day. Belo wanted to minister to them, but those in charge, Indonesian doctors and others, told him to leave as he was in the way. He also saw fifty or sixty lined up along the fence. He was later told Indonesians went up on the road above and dropped rocks down on people. That can never be proved, but it is what was being said.

---

12 Max Stahl's original footage can be seen at https://www.youtube.com/watch?v=7HkktBcIDzg

The next day Belo returned, and discovered that all the injured had disappeared. He was told by East Timorese Catholics working in the hospital in an ancillary capacity that they had all been killed, some with injections of phenyle. Belo was unable to verify what he had been told, but the indisputable fact was that all the wounded had disappeared without trace.

I was deeply impressed not only by what Belo had said, but by the obvious depths of the compassion he had for those who had perished. In the range of pastoral experiences, this went well beyond anything I had encountered.

*

My sense at the time was that Belo, being a Salesian, had a special concern for the rising generation who were now part of the protest movement. The odd thing about East Timor in 1992 was that it was a country seemingly without old or middle-aged men. Whole generations had been wiped out. Belo's concern was that this not happen to another generation. In some respects he saw the younger generation as their own worst enemy. He had regular tussles with leaders in the protest movement when the latter sought to co-opt the Church and Church services in the cause of their protest activities. Belo was keen to ensure that the Church not be compromised in this way, as it too easily played into Indonesian hands, and reduced both his and other clergy's ability to play a mediating role. I was to see him in action in this role several times during my stay when people came to the residence seeking his help in assisting relatives who had been taken into custody by the military or the police.

In 1992, Belo's position on East Timor's future was that the people were entitled to a genuine act of self-determination supervised by the United Nations, and that the Church would live with whatever outcome resulted. However, the Indonesians, by the way they treated the East Timorese, were digging a deep grave for the integration option. This was made clear to me when we paid a courtesy call on Mario Carrascalao who was nearing the end of his second term as Governor. I was surprised when he openly admitted that a major problem in the province was that 'the Indonesians do not understand the East Timorese'. How often is this the case with invading powers. Invaders always underestimate the enduring power of culture which can be suppressed and driven underground for decades, only to re-emerge transformed at a later date.

*

Across the next two weeks Belo had arranged for me to travel around the province and meet up with various religious groups. This was my cover story with the security people, but it was also a good way to gain an insight into the Timorese people and their culture, and also into the Church. In the next chapter I try to capture further life under the Indonesian occupation, and the role played by the Church as I listened and observed. It was my privilege to meet and talk with many people during that extraordinary time in my life. I still recall those meetings vividly, and recount the stories with a sense of awe, gratitude and humility.

CHAPTER 18
TIMORESE PERSPECTIVES 1992

A decade and a half after the Indonesian invasion of East Timor the Catholic Church lived in an uneasy tension with the Indonesian authorities. When in 1975 the people fled to the hills a number of the local clergy went with them. They returned with the people in 1983 because FALINTIL fighters could no longer provide the people with protection. The priests' action created the impression in Australia that some of the Catholic clergy in Timor were members of FRETILIN. However, the picture I uncovered was much more complex. One of my aims in going to East Timor was to discover how Catholic leaders, clerical and lay, saw the future of their country. This was not an easy task at a time when trust was almost universally in short supply.

It often happened during my visits that, after I had spoken with ordinary people in the street or students in a college, they would subsequently be questioned by INTEL agents about what we had discussed. In one case I was wishing a teacher well as she was about to set off for a study program in New Zealand. Her nervous husband asked me to leave as we were being followed by a known INTEL agent. In this sort of atmosphere one had to win people's confidence and trust before they would speak about what was close to their hearts. This took time, and time was not on my side.

Belo tried to overcome this difficulty by travelling with me himself when he could. This gave many people the very clear message that I was someone they could trust. He was keen that I meet a number of the local Timorese diocesan clergy as well as the members of religious congregations, a good number of whom had been in East Timor prior to the invasion. They had remained because leaving would, in all likelihood, mean they would not be re-admitted.

The experience with the teacher and the INTEL agent was not an isolated incident. On my second visit I was invited to Soibada to give some talks to about fifty people gathered in the beautiful church there. They were young people preparing for marriage, and the talks were held over three nights. My input was translated, but I could see from the people's demeanour and the questions they asked, that they were finding the material relevant and were engaging with the points I made. A week or so after I arrived back in Dili I had a visit from one of the participants who told me that the Indonesian police had arrested a number of people present at the talks, in order to find out what I had said. The man himself was one of those arrested. He had been deprived of food for two days, and beaten with rods. I thought to myself: 'My God. I am playing with fire.' I wondered if I should be doing anything at all.

★

In the course of our travels together, Belo and I met a surprising number of Timorese who had relatives in Melbourne or other parts of Australia. They tended to be more open than others. Belo had asked the Salesians to look after me, and in the course of the fortnight that I spent with them, I got to know a number quite well.

What became clear very early on was that the members of the Church in East Timor held a range of views about the future of the country, depending on their general assessment of the Timorese and the situation in East Timor. These perspectives were often shaped by their views about the FRETILIN leader, Xanana Gusmao.

It was Belo's practice to take me to visit the Indonesian commander wherever we went. Some were cold, and some friendly. Belo always introduced me as 'the Vicar General from Melbourne'. This posed protocol issues for the military commanders. On one occasion, I was asked how many people were under my command. I gave the number of Catholics in the Melbourne archdiocese where I was vicar general. When I said 'about nine hundred thousand' this created a considerable impression!

★

My understanding of Belo cumulated across a number of visits to East Timor. I grew in admiration of his fearless defence of the people. One example that stays with me was his action on behalf of six young men picked up and taken away by the TNI. The military would cut off the power to a section of Dili, and send in their 'ninjas' to raid houses and take away those they wanted for questioning. Sometimes those taken would never be heard of again.

The distraught mothers were waiting for Belo after morning Mass. He listened to them and then went immediately to the military headquarters and demanded to meet the commander. He was granted prompt access. Belo explained that three of the young men were the only support person their mothers had. Furthermore, all the young men were loved members of their families who were anxiously awaiting their return. As events transpired, three of the young men were returned to their families by the end of the day. The others were released some days later, having been tortured.

★

To convey the atmosphere of the times I want to profile some of the people I encountered on my first visit to Timor in the balance of this chapter. This provides a way to understand the complexities that the local Catholic Church had to deal with under the Indonesian occupation.

CRISPIM NICOLAS HORNAY

Belo provided me with the services of a driver to take me around while I was in East Timor. He was Brother Crispim Hornay, an East Timorese Salesian brother originally from Lospalos. Crispim had contacts with FRETILIN. He carried messages to them which was very problematic for him as a Church person (and also very dangerous). I vividly recall travelling with Crispim from Dili to Baucau on my first visit. The blue sea was on one side and the hills on the other where lookouts manned by Indonesian soldiers recorded the passing cars and their number plates.

As we were travelling along, Crispim pointed out where four people had been killed, and where he had buried them. He could do so as he was known to the military, and the relatives were too scared to reclaim the bodies. As we drove along, it was common for him to say something like: 'Two people were killed here and they are buried over there'. By the time we reached our destination the body count was in the forties!

Because he had the cover of the Church, Crispim could do this where others could not. His was an unusual, but clearly necessary, part of the local Church's mission.

Crispim's main concern about the future was the marginalisation of the young people within their own country. While the government had built a major polytechnic at Hera, which we had passed, the majority of places in it went to Indonesian students, not to Timorese. Many Timorese now went to study in Indonesia but they rarely returned as there was very little work for them in Timor where Indonesia now controlled everything. In Crispim's eyes, FRETILIN and its associated protest movement seemed to represent the best hope of reversing this trend. I owe much to Crispim.

WALTER VAN WOUWE

Fr Walter, a native of Belgium, was head of the Salesian community at Comoro at the time of my first visit. Walter had previously been the parish priest in Lospalos, in the eastern part of Timor. The jungles around Lospalos were a FALINTIL stronghold long after the fighters had been cleared from the central part of the country.

The presence of FALINTIL presented some interesting challenges for Church leaders there as most of the FALINTIL and their supporters were Catholic. How does one serve one's people while not aligning the Church to FRETILIN? This was the ongoing dilemma facing the parish priest of Lospalos. The scale of the challenge was amplified as the Indonesian military, who were largely Muslim, had little appreciation of the dilemmas faced by Catholic clergy.[1]

Following a clash in 1986 the military's frustration boiled over and Walter was badly beaten for being a FRETILIN sympathiser. Belo's response was immediate. He forbade all Catholic institutions in East Timor from participating in any program promoting the Indonesian national doctrine of *Pancasila* as attacks on Church personnel contravened its principles. The ban was to continue until 'Church personnel can exercise their duty in complete freedom'.[2]

★

On my first visit I went for a long walk with Walter to discuss the situation in East Timor. I had noted that the topic of conversation at community meals in Comoro changed quickly

---

1   Although most of the Indonesian military were Muslim, a number of those sent to East Timor were Catholic, and some were very respectful of the Church and its personnel and religious practices.
2   Belo quoted in *CISNET Newsletter* July 1986, 1.

whenever one of the kitchen staff entered the room, or if there was a stranger, cleric or layperson, at the table.

Walter held decidedly anti-communist views. In his eyes FRETILIN was 'communist' and Xanana 'no good'. FRETILIN's leaders had, as young people, been taught a godless ideology that supported terrorist methods and people control. Xanana may have changed his political colour, he acknowledged, but this did not cause him to rise in Walter's estimation. He did, however, acknowledge grudgingly that Gusmao had successfully tapped into the national spirit.

As we walked, Walter pointed out the Indonesian observation post on the hill near the college. He explained that they recorded who came into the college and who went out. The person observing at that time, he told me, was an East Timorese who had 'sold his soul to the Indonesians'. He also explained that if I went out walking someone would be following me, although most likely I would not know that this was occurring. Although later I was able to joke about all this, at the time, I found it most oppressive.

Fr Walter thought the demonstration that preceded the Santa Cruz massacre was not spontaneous as was presented in the Western press. He thought it was well-organised with the leaders hiding behind religion in order to create a space for protest. He acknowledged that this did not justify or explain the sheer horror of what had happened.

When I asked Walter about independence he thought that if it came it would bring little peace as ethnic groups would jostle for power. These included people of mixed race, Chinese traders, and native Timorese, including Timorese who had been seen to betray their people. It would be an explosive mix. In his view, if the Indonesians departed, then so too would about 200,000 of their Timorese sympathisers. However, the *real politik* was that the Indonesians were not going. They had settled many people in East Timor, and were not about to lose face by changing direction, having risked and faced down international disapproval generated by annexing East Timor in the first place. The only possible scenario under which change might come to East Timor would be 'change in Jakarta'. In the light of subsequent events, Walter's assessment of the situation was prescient, to say the least.

★

I thought a great deal about Walter's comments, and often spoke about them later in Australia. Our chat is one of the things I most remembered about my first visit. I would explain to people that the East Timorese on their own could not win out against the Indonesians, but they could keep alive the sense of possibility. This could only be actualised if there was a collapse of authority in Indonesia.

A most serious blight on Indonesian rule in Walter's view was the economic marginalisation of the local population. While there had been improvements in local administration and the beginnings of a monetary economy, most Timorese were systematically excluded from participating in economic growth. They were still poor fishermen and agricultural workers on poor land. They were seldom to be seen in any business, or in whatever middle management positions there were in the country. Walter could contrast Portuguese and Indonesian rule in East Timor and clearly preferred the former. While Portugal lacked the resources to develop East Timor, they respected the local people and their culture.

With the Indonesians this situation was reversed. Indonesia was sponsoring a new form of colonialism and simply repeating the errors made by former colonial powers. East Timorese were not given the same opportunities as those migrants from Indonesia who were being settled in large numbers in the country.

DEMETRIO SUAREZ

Demetrio was the Parish Priest of Aileu which is a short distance south of Dili as the crow flies, but which is accessed by a much longer journey, over an appalling road. I visited there with Belo.

In the Portuguese times the area had been noted for its strawberry farms. The village contains the remains of Australian troops from the 2/2 Company who died in East Timor in 1942–3. The surviving members of the 2/2 Company sponsored an anti-malaria program for children in East Timor, for many years supplying drugs and mosquito nets. As their numbers thinned, the program has been taken up by Rotary. At the time of my visit the program was temporarily suspended due to Indonesian insistence that all aid programs operate only through their agencies.

Belo was welcomed very ceremoniously by several *liurai* on horseback in traditional dress. I was welcomed as 'the general'. There were also senior Indonesian soldiers present for the welcome ceremony. The people performed a very traditional dance known as the *tebe tebe*.

Later my conversation with the Indonesian commander went as follows:

> *'How is it that they do this for you? I have been here for three years, and have been wanting to see this, and the people would not perform it for me.'*
> *'Do you really want to know?'*
> *'Yes that is why I ask'.*
> *'Well, you don't offer them an important enough occasion'.*
> *'Do you mean you are more important than me?'*
> *'I suppose so'.*

Belo was laughing!

In earlier years the area around Aileu was the scene of many battles between FALINTIL and Indonesian forces, and the villagers suffered as a consequence. The area had been 'swept' just before the Dili massacre (also known as the Santa Cruz massacre) and the inhabitants, now mainly old men and women and middle-aged widows, had been threatened.

Belo's purpose in taking me there was to show me the pastoral situation in which local diocesan clergy operated. Unlike religious, such as the Salesians who had the support of a community and an international organisation, the local Timorese clergy lived with very few resources, in the midst of a people who were poor and thoroughly oppressed. I noted particularly that there was very little reading material in any of the priests' houses so that the possibility of their knowing what was going on in the Church outside East Timor was limited. They seemed to exist in a kind of theological limbo, which partly explained their very conservative views.

Demetrio did not speak English so communication was awkward. He told me he had a brother living in Melbourne and another who was active in FRETILIN. We went on a short tour of the village and he introduced me to some of his parishioners. One has stayed in my mind, a young woman of about twenty-four who had six children, all boys. Demetrio told me that, when it had been suggested to her that she have a rest from pregnancy, her reply was 'My husband lost nine brothers, all shot by the army. I want to replace them. Then I will stop'. To find such resilience in a village which, in the words of one of the Maryknoll sisters who live there, is a 'military hamlet', was remarkable. Aileu at the time had one policeman for every fifty people, so everyone lived under constant surveillance. The feeling of hatred towards 'the occupiers', and refusal to accept the present situation as final, were palpable.

We met one young person on this visit, a man of striking appearance, who spoke English quite well and was very pleasant. However, Demetrio later warned that he was suspected of being an INTEL agent. This seemed the condition of life – one never knew whom one could trust.

JOSE VATTAPARAMBIL

Jose is a larger-than-life Salesian priest from Kerala in India responsible for the agricultural college at Fuiloro near Lospalos. As too many of the students joined FRETILIN following the invasion, the college was closed in 1975 and remained so till 1986. One of its past students was Xanana Gusmao.

I first met Jose in Dili when he came to collect supplies for the college, and later at the college itself. Jose's views on FRETILIN were almost diametrically opposite to those of the Salesian parish priest of Lospalos, Spanish missionary Fr Cervantes, whom I also met, and who was decidedly anti-FRETILIN and pro-Indonesian.

I stayed with Jose for a few days. At the time he had two FALINTIL fighters recuperating in the priest's residence. The very few who knew about this were sworn to secrecy. The fighters spent about two weeks with Jose who provided them with good food, and then they returned to the jungle. I did not speak with them because they could not speak English. I was quite aware as I went around the place that I was being looked at all the time, and that they were wondering who I was, and if they were still safe. When I spoke to Jose about having wounded FALINTIL fighters on the property, his reply was 'Where else could they go?'

While Jose acknowledged some of the good things the Indonesians had done, particularly in improving East Timor's infrastructure, he did not think that the future of the country would really unfold until after they left. Unlike many of his colleagues, Jose was quite optimistic that this would occur as 'the Indonesian's had grossly underestimated both the resilience and tenacity of East Timorese culture'.[3]

---

3   When I visited Fuiloro again in 1994 I was advised not to visit what is now the library building. It was only in 2000 that I found out from Jose the reason for this. Two FALINTIL fighters were staying there while they recuperated after being wounded. For Jose this was a humanitarian rather than a political act. He reminded me of Bishop Jaime Goulart's approach to the Australians in 1942. In response to my query, he answered 'Where else could they go?'

FLORENTINO SARMENTO

Fr. Jose introduced me to Florentino, and Belo was keen that I keep in touch with him. He was a great friend of Belo. Florentino was a prominent Catholic lay man who worked for the East Timor Agricultural Development Program (ETADEP), a non-government development agency with strong links to the Catholic Relief Services.[4] He later became the Chair of the Peace and Justice Commission of the Dili diocese, a position that Belo could not fill when I was there because of the harassment that all the lay members of the Commission endured from INTEL. Florentino's good standing with the Indonesians enabled the Commission's work to get off the ground. His was a brave decision to take up the role.

Florentino, like many of East Timor's leaders, was a graduate of the minor seminary system in Portuguese times and went on to become a primary school teacher before being drafted into the Portuguese army. After the invasion he was talent-spotted by the Indonesians and sent to the Catholic Teachers' College in Yogyakarta where he studied English and English Literature and so became one of the first indigenous Timorese to hold a tertiary degree.

On returning to Timor in 1981 he became interested in development work and joined an ETADEP project sponsored by Catholic Relief Services as a cook. Six years later he was heading the organisation which was trying to re-energise local agricultural production that had fallen off badly after a decade of Indonesian occupation.

We met in Dili where he took Jose and me to lunch at a local restaurant. He knew the owner so we could talk privately. I remember the restaurant well. Florentino had lost two relatives in the 'present troubles'. When his father-in-law, who lived in Portugal, saw pictures of the Dili massacre on television, he had a heart-attack and died.

The restaurant owner's son, Toni, who served us, carried three bullet wounds from events at Santa Cruz and was lucky to still be alive. Florentino said that over two hundred had been killed in the massacre and that the bodies had initially been buried in three mass graves around Dili at places he named. However, when the international spotlight fell on the Indonesian military over the matter, the army disinterred some of the rotting corpses, put them in bags and dumped them at sea. One bag later floated ashore with three bodies in it. People living near the three sites knew what was happening as the stench associated with the disinterment was unbearable.

Florentino's work took him out of the country, and although he could have left East Timor and lived elsewhere, he chose not to do so. He had recently visited Australia, and in his words 'enjoyed sucking in the freedom'. He admitted to being often very depressed about the state of affairs in his home country. I sensed that commitment to improving the lot of his people is what kept him going. On this score he has a significant record. The ETADEP Foundation was helping some 15,000 rice growers lift production in just one of the development projects he was overseeing. He invited me to join him in visiting one of these. They were introducing a new form of rice seed which could produce two, and sometimes three crops, in a year. The next day we journeyed west and had the chance to talk away from prying ears.

---

4   See interview with Florentino at http://www.library.ohiou.edu/indopubs/1996/10/22/0042.html

Florentino talked of the war, policies, suffering, and the future. He was in favour of integration, but was appalled by Indonesian brutality. He was always guarded in expressing his views. Florentino was typical of some of the young Timorese who were caught between the reality of Indonesia's presence and power and what it might offer East Timor, and love for his people. Despite their differences in outlook, Belo liked and supported him, and recognised him as a man of faith.

I met Florentino again just before I left in 1992. He asked me for my impression of the Church in East Timor and I told him. He then told me he was not the flavour of the month with the local clergy who saw him as a Church leader who peddled materialistic aims and ends (at the time Florentino was the chair of the Motael parish council). For his part he saw the clergy, and Belo in particular, as 'too unworldly'.

He was critical of the local clergy for not marshalling Church resources to support businesses run by Timorese. I was quite taken by Florentino's level of commitment to his people and his forthrightness. He highlighted for me the dilemma many talented East Timorese faced in the current political climate.

MARIO CARRASCALAO

Belo set up a meeting for me with Mario Carrascalao, the Governor of East Timor. For a Timorese, Mario Carrascalao was quite tall. He was bespectacled, greying and impressive, articulate and had a good command of English. His family owned coffee plantations, and was quite wealthy. When I greeted him in the Governor's palace in Dili, he surprised me by saying 'Monsignor, I am and always have been a Timorese Catholic'.

We discussed the situation in East Timor at some length particularly the role of the Indonesian army. He made no bones about the fact that much of what the Indonesians tried did not work since they did not attempt to understand Timorese culture. In his words, 'We are different!' He considered *Pancasila* a policy that simply did not work.

Carrascalao shared Fr Walter's view that any change in East Timor would be precipitated by events in Jakarta, not Timor. In his view, the local young people would eventually settle for some version of regional autonomy within Indonesia. The only real pressure for independence was coming from the UN, and its position was weak and compromised by the fact that UN votes on East Timor could be too easily bought!

The governor favored developing tourism, but acknowledged that the present system of military checks and restrictions was a major impediment. We spoke of his pending retirement and of his family. His son was studying engineering in Australia, but he did not expect that Pedro would ever return to East Timor.

MARKUS WANANDI

Markus Wanandi, a member of the Jesuit order, is the final person I will mention. His brother Jusuf was co-founder of the Centre for Strategic and International Studies (CSIS) in Jakarta which, as has been noted previously, played such an important role in *Operasi Komodo*.[5] I met Markus only once. He was teaching at the Catholic school in Dili. Our conversation was polite, but guarded. He wondered about my interest in the East Timorese who, in his words, 'had only just come out of the trees'. I spoke to him about the Santa Cruz massacre, the aftermath of which he had witnessed first hand. He expressed his horror at all the blood, death and destruction that he saw. He claimed that FRETILIN fired on the Indonesians and that the other people had got in the way!

As someone so clearly linked to the Indonesians I wondered what Markus was doing in East Timor and how he construed his priestly ministry there. As we spoke I gathered that Markus saw the role of the Indonesian army in all-encompassing terms, as if they had a 'civilising mission' to an under-developed people. For him the East Timorese were lacking in education, nutrition and sanitation. We chose to avoid politics. However, I could not resist giving him a vivid description of my various 'social visits' from INTEL.

Markus seemed a pleasant man in his forties, who freely admitted to sending information to newspapers in Jakarta for home consumption. At the time his reporting of the numbers killed and injured was very far from accurate. He subsequently returned to Indonesia to work in education.

*

Belo invited me to dinner on my last night of my 1992 visit and we went to a Javanese restaurant. There were no Timorese serving. This was increasingly the pattern with employment. That day sixty-five students had been sent to Jakarta for further studies, only six of whom were Timorese, this despite the fact that many more had qualified to go. As our meal was ending I suggested that Belo might visit Melbourne. He said that leaving the country was problematic for him as he had to get permission from the Nuncio, the Vatican and the Governor. There was a real risk that if he left, even with guarantees, he might not be allowed to return.

I could not help but reflect once again that the bishop was a lonely man who had no one to share his burdens with. During my visit he had been extremely helpful, courteous and encouraging. His position was very difficult given the diverse attitudes of his senior clergy to autonomy, independence and integration. The situation was not helped by the glaring differences between the resources and support available to clergy who were members of religious congregations and those who belonged to the diocese.

It seemed to me that the clergy's attitudes were shaped in part by judgments they made about the capacities of the Timorese to run their own affairs. Where this was pessimistic

---

5 The CSIS was formed in 1971 as an advisory group to the Catholic Party of Indonesia and to the Conference of Bishops. For an account of the Catholic fight against communism in Indonesia see Jusuf Wanandi *Shades of Grey: A Political Memoir of Modern Indonesia 1965-1998* (Singapore: Equinox Press, 2012). Wanandi's account makes it amply clear why those fighting communist influence in Australia, such as Santamaria, would see as highly credible what Wanandi, and his fellow Catholic associate, Harry Tjan Silalahi had to say about East Timor.

(as it often was with Javanese and European ex-pats) the dice came down on the side of integration. Where it was more optimistic, it moved first towards autonomy and then to independence. Belo, on the other hand had stood above this divide opting, in public at least, for an act of self-determination.

A second factor shaping Church attitudes was the fact that, while the country was moving, albeit in fits and starts, to a new place, the clergy were on the whole locked into a religious sensibility that was still very Portuguese in its orientation. Like the many *posedas* we had passed on our travels, they risked becoming a relic of the colonial era if the national consciousness changed and independence were gained. I was left with the question: Is it possible to operate with a colonial religious sensibility in a post-colonial world?

It seemed to me that Catholics in East Timor had still to find their own expressions of faith. The history of their recent suffering, and the memories stored about this, were surely creating the crucible in which such expression could be forged. My concern was whether a clergy, so cut off from developments in Catholic thought in the second half of the twentieth century, would not allow this to happen.

As I reflected on what I had heard and seen, I was struck by the fact that, despite having different views about the future, people shared a common concern about the present which did not focus on violence, even though the Dili massacre was still very much on their minds. Among the Church leaders what they saw as the most appalling aspect of life in East Timor was the attempt on the part of the Indonesians to destroy their culture. In this the Indonesians were being singularly unsuccessful. Hope *was* being maintained, even among those who had only ever known the *status quo* of occupation. Ironically, as students in schools learned more about Indonesian history, they learned about the role student movements had played in the formation of the Indonesian nation. These lessons were not lost on them. The realization began to grow in me that, given the hope alive in the students' hearts, the Indonesians could somehow be defeated. How I did not know, but then neither at the time did anyone else.

FINLEY DAYS 1932–41

John Francis Deakin ventured to Australia seeking opportunities denied to Catholics in England 1897 © Hilton Deakin

Stan Deakin at work with his team at Finley 1927 © Hilton Deakin

Off to war Hilton Deakin aged 7, his father & sister Nanette 1939 © Hilton Deakin

Hilton Deakin aged 3 1935 © Hilton Deakin

Catholic Church at Finley 1933 © Hilton Deakin

EDUCATION

Move to Melbourne Hilton Deakin aged 11 and his mother, Ruby 1943
© Hilton Deakin

Lead singer Parade College Annual Concert, Melbourne Town Hall, 1950
© Hilton Deakin

Studying in the seminary 1953
© Hilton Deakin

Following Fr Leo Griffin out for seminary Grand Final 1956 © Hilton Deakin

With Stan and Ruby following first Mass, St Raphael's, West Preston 1958 © Hilton Deakin

LEARNING THE ROPES 1958–1970

Curate to Monsignor Willis, Moonee Ponds, 1959
© Hilton Deakin

Assisting Archbishop Simonds, opening of St Bernard's College Campus at West Essendon 1963 © Hilton Deakin

Appearing on *Epilogue* GTV9 1961 © Hilton Deakin

Monash Uni student with Fr Dan Conquest at Box Hill 1967 © Hilton Deakin

On holidays at the Jesuits' Daly River mission 1963
© Hilton Deakin

PHD FIELD WORK, KALUMBURU, 1971–74

Local Aborigines outside main building, Kalumburu Mission 1972 © Hilton Deakin

Hilton Deakin (second right) with Spanish Missionaries at Kalumburu 1971 © Hilton Deakin

Hilton Deakin story-teller 1972 © Hilton Deakin

Hilton Deakin & friend Kalumburu 1972 © Hilton Deakin

Hilton Deakin Anthropologist 1971 © Hilton Deakin

EUCHARISTIC CONGRESS 1973

Hilton Deakin admiring Aboriginal art presented to Archbishop Knox 1973 © Hilton Deakin

Aboriginal Mass Sidney Myer Music Bowl 1973 © Melbourne Diocesan Historical Commission, Catholic Archdiocese of Melbourne

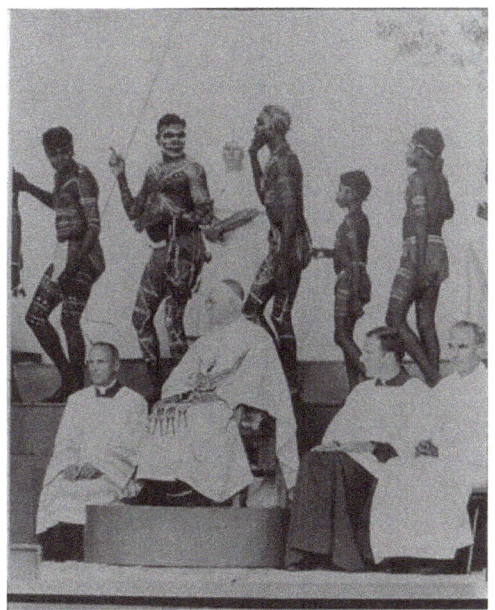

Aboriginal Mass Sidney Myer Music Bowl 1973 © Melbourne Diocesan Historical Commission, Catholic Archdiocese of Melbourne

Dancing the Gospel 1973 © Melbourne Diocesan Historical Commission, Catholic Archdiocese of Melbourne

Aboriginal Ministry Continues 1997 © John Casamento

MT ELIZA YEARS 1978–1985

St Thomas More's takes shape 1981 © Hilton Deakin

Archbishop Little opens the Church
© Hilton Deakin

The new parish's interim base at Greyfriar's chapel 1979
© Hilton Deakin

Becoming a local landmark 1984 © Hilton Deakin

St Thomas More's - consecration ceremony undated © Hilton Deakin

VICAR GENERAL 1985–1992

Hilton Deakin with friends during recovery from major illness 1989 © Hilton Deakin

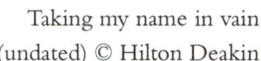

Taking my name in vain (undated) © Hilton Deakin

Hilton Deakin welcoming Bishop Belo 1993 © John Casamento

AUXILIARY BISHOP 1993–2007

Ordination as bishop 1993 © Kairos 1993

Hilton Deakin preaching in vestments featuring indigenous design 1993 © John Casamento

Hilton Deakin, Cardinal Clancy meet Pope John Paul II
© Hilton Deakin

Hilton Deakin in Rome with Bishops Peter Connors and Bill Brennan (2nd right)

Archbishop Little and his Auxiliary bishops, George Pell, Denis Hart and Hilton Deakin, (undated) © Hilton Deakin

CARITAS IN RWANDA 1994

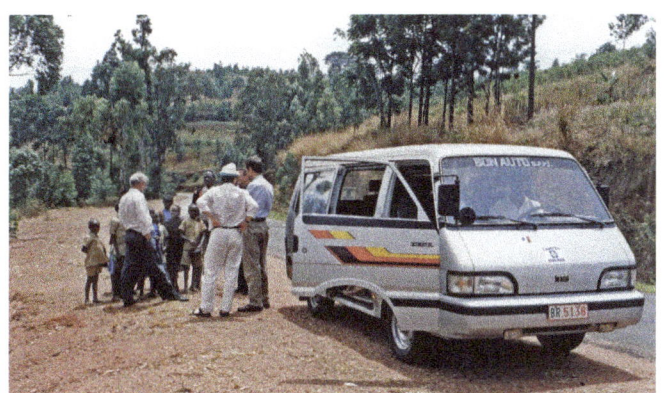

Caritas group encounter man leading orphans on way to Butare 1994 © Hilton Deakin

Hilton Deakin with Bishop Jean-Baptiste Gahamanyi sharing what little food he had with the visiting team 1994 © Hilton Deakin

Hilton Deakin in the refugee camp at Goma 1994 © Hilton Deakin

Caritas team meet up with Caritas workers in the Goma camp 1994© Hilton Deakin

FIRST VISIT TO EAST TIMOR 1992

Br Ephrem Hilton Deakin's driver (on right) 1992
© Hilton Deakin

Hilton Deakin and youthful Bishop Belo at Aileu 1992
© Hilton Deakin

Salesian HQ in Dili, Hilton Deakin's base in East Timor 1992 © Hilton Deakin

ETAP staff, Florentino Sarmento on Hilton Deakin's left.
1992 © Hilton Deakin

Hill beyond Comoro from which
INTEL agents spied on College 1992
© Hilton Deakin

EAST TIMOR STORY

Bernard Callinan (R), liaison between the 2/2 commandos and Bishop Goulart, in Dili 1942, courtesy of Australian War Memorial

The Cathedral in 1945, courtesy of Australian War Memorial

Martinho da Costa Lopes, churchman, patriot and sad victim of Vatican policy on East Timor © Jim D'Orsa

Hilton Deakin and Paul Stewart (brother of Tony Stewart, one of the 'Balibo Five') at an East Timor Association fundraiser, Melbourne 1994 © John Casamento

Dili Cathedral today 2013 © Jim D'Orsa

SANTA CRUZ MASSACRE

Motael Church in 1992 © Hilton Deakin

Inside Santa Cruz Cemetery 2013 © Jim D'Orsa

Car park, entrance gate and fence - site of the massacre 2013 © Jim D'Orsa

Hilton Deakin at grave of Sebastiao Gomes 2013
© Jim D'Orsa

SALESIANS IN EAST TIMOR – FATUMACA

Salesian College at Fatumaca 2013 © Jim D'Orsa

Hilton Deakin with Fr Eligio Locatelli, founder of the Salesian College at Fatumaca 2013 © Jim D'Orsa

Workshop at Fatumaca 2013 © Jim D'Orsa

Prefabricated materials ready to build/repair local Catholic churches and schools © Jim D'Orsa

HILTON DEAKIN WITH EAST TIMORESE LEADERS

President Taur Matan Ruak 2012 © Hilton Deakin

Travelling with Belo 1998 © Hilton Deakin

With Xanana Gusmao undated © Hilton Deakin

With Jose Ramos Horta undated © Hilton Deakin

THE BISHOP VISITS

Village visit. 1998
© Hilton Deakin

Reception at Kailaco, a remote village near the West Timor border 2013 © Jim D'Orsa

The ubiquitous mobile camera recording the visitor! - Kailaco 2013 © Jim D'Orsa

Bishop presented with *tais* as a mark of respect, Kailaco 2013 © Jim D'Orsa

Hilton Deakin visits St Thomas More's church in ET built by donations from St Thomas More's parish, Mt Eliza © Jim D'Orsa

HILTON DEAKIN AND FAMILY

Ruby Deakin on holidays with Hilton Deakin in Alice Springs 1998 © Hilton Deakin

Hilton with his sisters Val and Nanette 1993 © Kairos

Hilton Deakin with East Timorese attending World Youth Day, Sydney 2008 © Hilton Deakin

Robin Deakin 2015 © Robin Deakin

Hilton Deakin in typical pose (undated) © Hilton Deakin

Bishop emeritus! 2012 © Hilton Deakin

CHAPTER 19
A VOICE IN THE WILDERNESS

By the mid-1990s the narrative of East Timor had reached a stalemate. There were a number of threads slowly interweaving, but it was impossible to see any real pattern in events. The situation had been so bad for so long that the sense developed that things could only get better. That hope drove those of us active in helping the Timorese. For the East Timorese themselves hope and despair seemed to alternate in rapid succession. Looking back I see these as the 'wilderness years'.

By 1993 it was clear that Indonesian hopes of reviving the tourist industry were wishful thinking, given the poor way overseas visitors were treated. When tourists did come they were shocked at the outright criminality sanctioned by the armed forces and police in East Timor. Not only did those entrusted with law and order not protect the local people, they sponsored much of the crime and violence. In the chop logic of the occupiers, a person protesting the violation of his or her human rights committed a criminal offence! To a Western visitor this was an incomprehensible position. The Timorese themselves had lost all confidence in the province's legal and law enforcement systems. With no protection expected from the forces of law and order, the people went to the only institution capable of providing any degree of protection, the Catholic Church.

Bishop Belo, like da Costa Lopes before him, was quite fearless in intervening on behalf of people taken into custody. What Belo was doing in Dili, many other clergy were doing in the villages and towns.[1] The fact that the clergy chose to play this mediating role contributed greatly to the respect people had for the Church. This was really obvious when Belo and I visited villages.

His visits were regarded locally as 'state' occasions and people came from all around to celebrate the event. The local military commander was usually invited as well. Belo was well aware that he was giving people something to celebrate and that this helped sustain their hope.

The mediation role became very problematic if the local military commander was unsympathetic. Then advocacy on behalf of those detained could be misinterpreted as 'the Church supporting the resistance' and lead to retribution, not against the clergy, but against

---

1 By way of illustration, a young man named Salvador Sarmento was arrested in Ossu and charged with making contact with FRETILIN and planning a demonstration to coincide with my visit in 1992. He was tortured and after representation by the local parish priest was released. It later emerged that the purpose of his arrest was to implicate the parish priest and the Church. In 1994 I met the young man who then lived under the protection of the Divine Word missionaries in Dili.

their parishioners. On my early visits to Timor I spoke with a number of parish priests who had been harassed because of their advocacy on behalf of their parishioners who were faced with arbitrary torture and imprisonment, if not worse.

Many priests were angry with the Papal Nuncios who they believed contributed to the harassment by accusing them 'of being more interested in politics than the care of souls' as if body and soul existed in different planes! The degree of unreality in the nuncios' criticism alienated many local priests.

★

By my third visit to East Timor in 1995, Belo had made sure that I had the chance to meet and to know a number of his diocesan priests. I could then begin to ask them questions that earlier on would have been greeted with suspicion.[2] In particular, the priests opened up on events surrounding the invasion, the Vatican's sacking of da Costa Lopes and tensions within the clergy, and their struggle to balance the demands of their pastoral work with commitment to seek justice for their people. It was one thing to read about these events; it was altogether something else to discuss them with the people who had lived through them.

As I listened to their lived accounts, da Costa Lopes began to emerge as a heroic figure and it was easy to see why he is now regarded as a national hero. At the same time Bishop Ribeiro became a more tragic figure. Whenever his former colleagues visited him in retirement in Portugal and talked about East Timor, he almost immediately broke down. He seems a broken man who lived with regrets.

★

In the period 1993-95 trust was in very short supply in East Timor, not only between the Indonesians and the East Timorese, but also among the Timorese themselves. Even among Church leaders there were major differences of opinion and trust issues, particularly once priests and religious began to arrive from Indonesia and seminarians were sent there to complete their training. With the withdrawal of Portugal from the administration of East Timor, responsibility for the seminary in Dili was transferred to the Jesuit province in Indonesia. This meant that seminarians came under the influence of pro-integration mentors, some of whom were expatriate missionaries from Europe. In my experience ex-pat clergy, with some notable exceptions, were generally more favourable towards integration than their local counterparts. In the local mind the Church in Indonesia was colluding with the central government to preserve its influence, so Indonesian clergy and religious were often regarded as agents of the occupying power, and not trusted. This was not always a fair assessment of their intentions and efforts, but it was the lived reality at the time.

The Church situation was extremely complex. As an illustration, Belo was always keen that Markus Wanandi SJ, then running the minor seminary in Dili, be moved on because

---

[2] Approximately 50% of the priests in East Timor were diocesan, the rest being members of religious congregations, and many were ex-pats. Most of the diocesan priests were native-born Timorese. Their views covered a wide range of ideas, so that it is not accurate to generalise about the views of the priests serving in East Timor.

Wanandi's strong pro-integration sympathies and close links with the military in Dili were an embarrassment. The matter was not simple as Belo was a friend of Wanandi's brother, Jusuf, a leading Catholic in Indonesia and head of the Centre for Strategic and International and Strategic Studies (CSIS). Belo stayed with Jusuf when he visited Bali for medical treatment. Jusuf, in turn, cultivated, and was cultivated by, the papal nuncio in Jakarta as a conduit for information on East Timor.[3] In these circumstances one had to be very careful whom one trusted, to what extent, and with what information. Few things could be taken at face value as even key Catholics were playing a double game.

The general lack of trust among the East Timorese made it all the more remarkable that the National Council for the Maubere Resistance (CNRM) leader, Xanana Gusmao, was able to evade capture for over a decade. By 1992 Xanana had become something of a legend to his people. The following story illustrates why this was so. When Belo and I were returning from Lospalos to Dili, a long journey was made even longer by a series of new road blocks. These had been set up because Xanana had unexpectedly arrived at a party in the vicinity and had been photographed with the hosts there. When INTEL got wind of this they descended on the party and the unsuspecting host was badly beaten. In the meantime, and despite the road blocks, Xanana had simply 'disappeared into thin air'.[4]

It must be said that some Indonesian religious were heroic in their support of the East Timorese. I have in mind one group of Indonesian nuns whose convent was well off the beaten track between Lospalos and Fuiloro. These brave women remained through all the atrocities, and are still there. The sisters nursed injured FALINTIL soldiers in their convent. The military would not dare go in there and if they did would not have expected to find men, and certainly not FALINTIL soldiers. The Church situation in the early 1990s was very complex.

★

When he took command of the resistance in 1982, Xanana initiated a significant shift in the way FALINTIL operated. Though still a potent force, FALINTIL scaled back its military activity.[5] While this change in strategy still tied up large numbers of the Indonesian military,[6] senior commanders seemed quite happy with the new *status quo* that developed. For them a posting to 'Tim Tim', as they called East Timor, provided an accelerated path to promotion. They used East Timor rather cynically to 'blood' ordinary troops in guerrilla

---

3   According to Wanandi, Suharto declared the CSIS *persona non grata* in 1988 after it suggested that he consider a succession plan for the transition of power after 20 years in office. (Jusuf Wanandi *Shades of Grey: A Political Memoir of Modern Indonesia 1965-98* (Singapore: Equinox Publishing, 2012), 231. He also notes that in meetings with Australian diplomats he and his associate Harry Tjan deliberately exaggerated the CSIS's influence in the planning of *Operation Komodo*. Their version of events was accepted and fed back to Australia in diplomatic cables and thus influenced how authors such as James Dunn constructed the narrative of East Timor. In reality, the CSIS ceased to be a player once the intelligence operation mounted by Generals Murdani and Murtopo in 1974 was abandoned in favor of a military operation late in 1975 (ibid, 193).
4   Xanana's luck ran out later in the year when he was captured at his safe house in Dili and taken to Indonesia.
5   The Indonesian military had access to the military tactics developed by both Australia and the United States during the Vietnam War, including the use of napalm. Indonesian officers were being trained in both countries. In response to the Dili massacre President Bill Clinton terminated training in the US. Australia took no comparable action.
6   When I visited the Ermera region in 1995, there were six battalions operating trying to mop up FALINTIL forces in the area. The jungle around Lospalos was still a 'red zone' for the Indonesian troops.

warfare by rotating units of the territorial army command though East Timor.[7] The commercial companies controlled by the generals funded this operation.

Xanana moved the struggle in East Timor from a military battle to a political battle by setting up resistance cells across the country, the role of which was to thwart the Indonesians at every available opportunity, and to publicise the East Timor situation whenever opportunity arose. By the late 1980s and early 1990s the efforts of the 'clandestine' resistance were beginning to bite. One of their tactics was to use religious celebrations as the opportunity to protest. This put Belo and Xanana on a collision course since Belo did not want the Church's position compromised by resistance activities over which he had no control.

*

As a matter of policy, the Indonesian administration in East Timor had written off the generation of people alive at the time of the invasion, and a decade later were concentrating their efforts on the young in their quest to bring about integration. By 1994 the province's educational infrastructure had been upgraded significantly and young people were better educated than ever before. A large number could speak and read Bahasa. While the guerrilla threat was more or less contained, it had been replaced by a new form of resistance from a rising generation that spoke in fluent Bahasa. To many Indonesians this situation was simply incomprehensible.

As an anthropologist looking at the situation in the early 1990s, I found it hard to avoid the conclusion that the Indonesians were committed to a strategy that was inevitably going to be 'lose-lose'. They showed little or no interest in understanding what was important in Timorese culture, and lacked any understanding of the power of traditional cultures. Their lack of cultural sensitivity was blatant to an observer. By contrast the East Timorese seemed somewhat more culturally aware. For instance, they rarely spoke of 'the Indonesians' as such; rather their anger was directed at 'the Javanese' whom they regarded as barbaric, cruel, belligerent, and bent on dispossessing them of their land, their culture, and their future. Thus they distinguished between the Javanese and people from other parts of the archipelago. Their resentment, directed at the Javanese, sustained the clandestine resistance.

The Indonesians' cultural incomprehension, and frustration caused by the clandestine resistance's thwarting their every effort, seems to have simply boiled over in 1991 so precipitating the Santa Cruz massacre. The military commander in Dili at the time decided to employ 'shock treatment' on them. Suharto had used this tactic in Jakarta to remove 'hoodlum gangs'.[8] He did not anticipate that the press would be present, and draw world attention not only to East Timor but to what was happening in other parts of Indonesia as well.

*

---

7   Wanandi, 215.
8   Wanandi, 219.

With the Cold War ended and the Berlin Wall down, the West's need for an aggressively anti-communist bulwark in South East Asia had passed. Once the focus in international relationships moved from containing communism to the quality of democracy in developing countries, Indonesia's *Orde Baru* (New Order) came under increased scrutiny. The Santa Cruz massacre projected Indonesia up the list of democratically recalcitrant states. Its position was further weakened in 1994 when Amnesty International, in a damning report, pointed out that events in East Timor were not an isolated instance of a military acting with impunity, but were the consequence of state policy operative in other parts of Indonesia.[9]

The report pointed out that the abuse of human rights in Indonesia was blatant. It concluded:

> A fundamental problem is that the international community has focused almost exclusively on the human rights problem in East Timor and, even there, only on the most dramatic incidents such as the Santa Cruz massacre. Grave violations committed by Indonesian forces throughout the archipelago have gone virtually unnoticed…
>
> The reality is that human rights abuse is not confined to East Timor, and that the killing, torture and political imprisonment reported from various parts of Indonesia are far from isolated incidents; they are part of the pattern of gross and systematic human rights violations which have unfolded over more than a quarter of a century.

The climate of dissatisfaction in Jakarta is well captured by Indonesian novelist Pramoedya Ananta Toer who wrote:

> Twenty-seven years is enough time for the rulers of any state to restore human rights. And 27 years is far too long for those who have suffered such theft to have to defend and uphold their dignity.[10]

Following the election of Bill Clinton, the United States began to ratchet up pressure on the Indonesian Government to do something about its human rights record.[11] When I spoke to Indonesian bishops about this record, as I did from time to time, they claimed to be ignorant of both the nature and scale of the atrocities occurring. I found this hard to believe. If they did know, their silence is reprehensible.

★

Jusuf Wanandi provides a key in understanding the mindset of Indonesia's leaders running the country in this era. Discussing the outlook of his friend, General Benny Murdani, the

---

9   Amnesty International Briefing *Indonesia and East Timor* (London: Amnesty International Publications, September 1994), 2.
10 Pramoedya Ananta Toer cited in *Indonesia and East Timor*, 8.
11 Their first action was to make the Indonesians pay for military training previously provided free. In 1996 the sale of arms used in crowd control was banned.

most influential Catholic in the Suharto regime[12], he notes:

> Benny was a very close friend and I loved him very much because he helped us a lot. He was very bright on one hand and very brave also as a soldier. But in politics, he was so limited. It was not his field – he was not comfortable with it.
>
> I am convinced that if one day Suharto had told him, after 1988 when he was still in the cabinet and we were out of favour, 'Hey this chap Wanandi talks too much, just get rid of him' – then Benny would definitely be sorrowful and would ask me to come to see him at night. He would have said to me 'I have to do this. What I can do now for you is to tell you that you have to disappear this evening or this night because tomorrow, I am looking for you and if I find you, then we have to kill you'.
>
> This is how it would have happened, I'm sure. Even with Benny as a close friend, that was the whole mentality of the military and that's why you could not – and perhaps cannot - trust them. What is going to come out depends on the order. Who is going to give the order and what the order is going to be. And so that is not how we should organise this country. So that is what I have learned after 35 years of working with them.[13]

This assessment of the state of law and order in Indonesia at the highest levels is telling, and perhaps explains why the military could act with such impunity in East Timor.

★

One aspect of the Santa Cruz massacre that was little reported in the English-speaking press, but which had a profound effect in Portugal, was that as film of the massacre played, the soundtrack has a group of women who were caught up in the event continuing to pray rather than running away. What hit the consciences of people in Portugal most starkly was that they were praying in Portuguese so long after the Portuguese government had effectively abandoned them to their fate. The emotional impact of this footage galvanised Portuguese efforts to assist the Timorese. I was caught up in this development.

At the end of 1993 I co-hosted Belo's first visit to Australia. Following this, I received an invitation from Professor Barbedo de Magalhaes of the University of Oporto in Portugal to speak at a symposium on East Timor being sponsored by the university. I consulted Jose Ramos Horta and when he thought it was a good idea I accepted. The reception I received in Lisbon was amazing.

The Portuguese had not heard a member of the Church speaking about East Timor. During my ten-day visit I was on radio or television most days. I was also a dinner guest of the President, Mario Soares, who spoke to me at length on how the Indonesians had 'booted the Portuguese out of Timor'. It was a different account of events from the one

---

12 Murdani took part in the campaigns in New Guinea and Malaysia and served as diplomat (intelligence) in South Korea. As intelligence chief he was responsible for *Operation Komodo* and co-ordinated important aspects of the invasion. Later, he headed the Intelligence Coordinating Agency in East Timor before becoming army chief in Indonesia. Following his military career he went on to become Minister for Defense.
13 Wanandi, 262-3.

with which I was familiar, and I soon realised that, the political scene was moving in Portugal.

In my discussions with the press, and people more generally, I was struck by the fact that the Portuguese had a very limited understanding of the situation on the ground in what had once been part of 'their empire'. I found myself outlining a vision of what could happen there, contrasting the realities of life under *integrasi* with the hopes embedded in the prospect of 'self-determination'. The visit helped lay the groundwork for an important visit by Belo the next year following the first All Party Timor Talks held in Salzburg. Belo emerged from this round of talks as a highly credible spokesperson for his people. His positive reception in Europe alarmed the Indonesians who doubled their efforts to discredit him.[14]

★

When I returned to Melbourne I met Jose Ramos Horta at a function in St Kilda. We adjourned to a pub in Windsor to discuss what more could be done at the practical level to reduce the violence in Timor. We agreed that at some point in time the suffering of the people in East Timor would have to be acknowledged if reconciliation was ever to be achieved among them, or between them and the Indonesians. Reconciliation requires an accurate portrayal of events, one not coloured or manipulated by ideology. The immediate question facing us then was how to create the necessary records. We believed that if the military commanders in East Timor and elsewhere knew that such a database was being put together, this in itself might curtail some of the grosser violations of human rights. What we needed was *an organisation* that could record and validate witness statements; *a process* to obtain reliable witness statements; a *strategy* to disseminate the information collected, and *secure premises* to store the records as they accumulated. Above all we would need staff, and this meant having access to ongoing funding.

Jose said that if I could find a suitable office, he had contacts among human rights groups in Scandinavia whom he thought would provide the necessary financial backing. In this he was as good as his word, and the East Timor Human Rights Centre (ETHRC) was born. I became Chair of its Board. While later ETHRC was claimed as a CNRM (National Council of the Maubere Resistance) project[15], it was in fact an independent operation, and I was always keen to keep it that way.

The East Timor Human Rights Centre operated from a secure room in the Uniting Church complex in Napier Street Fitzroy. Maria Britt was responsible for assembling human rights records and producing press releases publicising serious violations of human rights in East Timor. Ramos Horta devised a training program for *rapporteurs*, first in Australia and later in East Timor, and across the next eight years the Centre accumulated enough files on human rights abuses to fill three large filing cabinets.

The ETHRC published an annual report that was disseminated widely among human rights groups, politicians, embassies, Church Justice and Peace Commissions, and NGOs with an interest in human rights. The embassies were particularly important because it

---

14 Kohen, 203.
15 See http://www.ci.uc.pt/timor/cnrm.htm

was from there that the information was fed on to governments, for example, those of the U.K., Australia, Japan, France, South Africa and Ireland. With the advent of the internet these were circulated around the world to advocacy groups.

★

When East Timor was opened to the wider world in the early 1990s Bishop Belo came to international prominence. The Catholic Church's role as protector of people in the face of human rights violations by the military was becoming more widely recognised and the international press sought out Belo for comment. Despite having no training in this area, he quickly became quite adroit at handling the press, but he also realised he was dealing with a two-edged sword as his words could easily be twisted.

The Indonesians now allowed him to travel, but always under the threat that if he was too outspoken he could be refused entry when he returned. Belo travelled to the United States and Canada in June 1993 and to Australia later in the year. He travelled to Austria, Portugal and Rome in 1995 and returned through the United States where he had meetings at the UN. People meeting him for the first time quickly realised that he was no human rights firebrand, but a pastor who cared for the welfare of his people, particularly the younger generation who by now demonstrated a recklessness born of despair in protesting the situation in East Timor which could bring disastrous consequences on their heads.

His visit to the United States drew attention to East Timor just prior to the Asia-Pacific Economic summit in 1995 hosted by Indonesia. It was not welcome attention for the hosts. Things then went from bad to worse for them when twenty East Timor students scaled the walls of the US embassy in Jakarta to protest the situation in their country.[16] The stand-off that ensued commanded the attention of the world's media who sought Belo out for comment.

The irony at the time, as his biographer Arnold Kohen points out, was that Belo could speak much more freely in interviews he gave in Dili than he could when travelling overseas.[17] A new facet of the Church's role in East Timor was rapidly opening up – using the international media to defend the human rights of the East Timorese.

In pursuing this role Belo was never interested in confrontation with the Indonesians. He saw this as a no-win option. His preference was for dialogue and reconciliation. His problem was that the Indonesian government believed it was so powerful, and had such powerful friends, that dialogue was unnecessary. In consequence it held out against UN efforts to bring the contending parties (Portugal, Indonesia and representatives of the National Council of Maubere Resistance) together.

Belo matched his words to his actions when a group of young protestors took over the cathedral grounds in Dili to protest in solidarity with their colleagues in the US embassy in Jakarta during the APEC Conference. The military quickly surrounded the cathedral grounds. The protesters were asked to give themselves up, but refused. When the dean of the cathedral and the military commander could not resolve the impasse, Belo was asked to

---

16 These students, some of whom had been on the run in Indonesia since the Dili massacre, were eventually flown to Portugal where they were welcomed by the President, Mario Soares.
17 Kohen, 179.

intervene. His condition for doing so was that the protestors be able to disband and return home safely. The military commander angrily refused. The standoff continued.

Belo resolved the matter by driving his car between the two groups. He and his driver sat there till darkness began to fall. With the spotlight on Indonesia it was the commander who blinked first, and the protestors were allowed to go home, but not before Belo had given their leaders a dressing down for embroiling the Church in their protest.

★

Belo could mobilise the press in support of his people because he was beholden to no group, including the Vatican. He chose an independent path and this non-plussed both his friends and enemies alike, so that everyone sought his views. However, it was a very lonely path to follow and this was one of the main reasons I made so many trips to East Timor to support him as best I could.

In my view Belo, along with Xanana, were symbols of hope shining in an otherwise bleak landscape. The local people wanted a say in where their country was heading, and hoped fervently that this would mean independence. I knew this at first hand because on my visits I attended many youth camps and listened to the discussions. The young people attending them had all been born since 1975 and had been through only the Indonesian education system. They had been taught Bahasa and the culture of the Indonesians. They had learned about the cultural heroes who had fought for Indonesian independence from the Dutch and the Japanese. They rejected all that. They talked about their own heroic leaders like Nicholas Lobato. They also talked about their rights, and their desire to be free, but first there would have to be a referendum. These were very young people, in their teens. It was the same around the country, and I became convinced that independence was really only a matter of time.

★

Belo's public statements were now being disseminated through a growing network of international human rights groups appalled at the situation in East Timor. The network brought together people of very diverse backgrounds and interests: human rights activists, Church people, trade unionists, university students and so on.

The East Timorese diaspora in Melbourne were part of this network. The group had good intellectual capacity and leadership potential. They were particularly effective in winning support from within the universities. I used to meet them at the various rallies and protest meetings that took place in Melbourne. I spoke at some of the gatherings. The number attending varied from a few hundred to many thousands. They also made and cultivated their contacts in the Australian Broadcasting Commission. They were building up an extraordinary support system. It was a strange coalition of interests that brought people together to object to the thrust of Australian Government policy and its 'Indonesia-at-any-cost' emphasis.[18] There were many who were ashamed of how Australia

---

18 Changes of Government in Australia made little difference to the stance of Australia's official representatives when it came to Indonesia.

had treated the East Timorese following their role in assisting Australia during World War II. The Government seemed to have written off the historic debt this country owed to East Timor, a fact that many of the protestors viewed as immoral.

*

The Indonesian reaction to Belo's growing international standing was not encouraging. The Indonesian Government complained to the nuncio in Jakarta, and then directly to the Vatican, seeking his removal. When this failed, it sought to weaken his influence by having the Dili diocese divided. I talked with him about this many times. There were two major problems in dividing the diocese. The first was that the local clergy did not want the Vatican to allow such an obvious divide and rule ruse to weaken Belo's position. The second was the lack of suitable candidates for bishop. If East Timor had to be divided, the clergy's wish was that it should be divided into three dioceses, not two. This would mean that East Timor could have its own episcopal conference. However, such a move would be tantamount to acknowledging East Timor's independence. That would offend the Indonesians, something Vatican policy sought at all costs to avoid. So the matter remained unresolved.

When it became clear to the Indonesians that the Vatican was stalling on the matter they embarked on new campaign to discredit Belo. They began fomenting religious division by having soldiers desecrate holy places and core Catholic symbols. When riots broke out in response, these were portrayed as evidence of 'Catholic-Muslim conflict' for which they tried to blame Belo. To their credit religious leaders in the Muslim community refused to exploit the situation.

However, the systematic nature of these incidents made members of the Catholic Church feel they were being persecuted for being Catholic. The actions of the military ran counter to Indonesia's national ideology of *Pancasila* and Belo condemned them as such. This futile strategy alienated the East Timorese and the prospect of integration retreated still further.

*

When I visited East Timor early in 1995 Belo had just returned from Rome and his first *ad limina* visit.[19] His treatment at the Vatican was dispiriting, and I found him somewhat disillusioned by the experience. Secretary of State Sodano had let it be known that he was too busy to see him. His only meeting with Pope John Paul II was in a normal *ad limina* audience with eleven other Bishops. He felt frozen out and more alone than ever.

The reason for his 'cold shoulder' treatment may well have been official displeasure at an interview he gave to the Portuguese newspaper *Publico* late in 1994. Here he was quite forthright in responding to questions:

---

19 A visit 'ad limina Apostolorum' (literally 'to the threshold of the Apostles') is the visit to Rome required to be made at regular intervals (currently every five years) by each bishop in charge of a diocese. The purpose of the visit is to give an account of the affairs of his diocese to the pope of the time.

> The Holy See does not want problems with Indonesia which is a huge nation and whose Catholic community is influential in schools and hospitals. In 1985 when I met the Pope, His Holiness said to me 'I understand your position. I pray for Timor. I suffer with Timor. But, on the other hand the Church in Indonesia needs our attention.' ... Even though we are few, I believe that over the years we have all contributed towards a Church which is on the side of the poor and oppressed which the Indonesian Catholic Church has not done because, just like in the times of fascism in Portugal, it is a Church that collaborates with the authorities. This is what happened in Chile, Brazil and Portugal. Only a democratic revolution (in Indonesia) will change things....The Church is not here to be a political instrument or to be politicised. The Church is here to carry out its mission as an intermediary. It is here with everyone and for everyone...[20]

Commenting on the recent riots in Baucau he added:

> It was the first time that this happened – an uprising throughout the city, with everyone in the streets shouting that the Timorese are also a people with their dignity. It means that the patience of the Timorese is running out. The government says that everything is all right and the Governor makes promises, but they have not taken steps to correct the errors. I think the government understood the message, but it will not sit down at the table to talk to the people because it is an arrogant, military dictatorial Government, and only they can be right. As long as there is no democratic spirit in midst of the military ranks, nothing will ever be achieved.[21]

Belo could never understand how people in authority could put abstractions such as 'the welfare of the Church in Indonesia' in the place of the welfare of real people in East Timor. 'How many people' he asked 'need to be killed before the Vatican can take a view that transcends politics?' He kept a keen but critical eye on the activity of Pope John Paul II in Poland and pointed out the contrasts with the Vatican's attitudes towards events there and towards East Timor.

If Belo was *persona non grata* at the Vatican for his unflattering commentary on its stance towards East Timor, he had important supporters. His international standing had grown to the point where he received a nomination for the Nobel Peace Prize in both 1994 and 1995. One of his supporters, President Mario Soares, let it be known in a press interview that his removal as Bishop of Dili 'would not be tolerated by Catholics throughout the world'. Soares then went on to criticise Pope John Paul II's 'double-faced attitude to the East Timor issue and the Bishop', so compounding Belo's problems with the Vatican.[22]

★

---

20 Belo quoted in Paulo Nogueira 'Bishop Belo Speaks Out' *Publico*, 23 March 1995.
21 ibid
22 David Shanks 'Soares Backs East Timor Bishop' *Irish Times* March 28, 1995.

During these wilderness years change was afoot but its direction was hard to discern. In East Timor despair was breeding recklessness. Internationally, pressure was slowly mounting on Indonesia to address the human rights situation in the country, but a tired regime prevaricated. Australia made muted human rights protestations to its neighbours, whilst ensuring these did not compromise its burgeoning trade interests with Indonesia. Bishop Bill Brennan, acting as an agent of the Catholic Church in Australia, prodded the government to act, but ever so gently.

In this most confusing of times Belo was literally a 'voice in the wilderness' and I took my lead from him. To a much lesser extent I found myself cast in a similar role in Australia when I was made a bishop in 1993, and attempted to take up the East Timorese cause with the Australian hierarchy.

CHAPTER 20
A WIDER MISSION: A BIGGER CHALLENGE

After I returned to Australia in 1992 my activities publicising the plight of the East Timorese attracted a good deal of attention in both the secular and the Catholic press. When I received a letter from the nuncio's office on the last day of the year, I assumed it was a reprimand of some sort, so I put it in my pocket, closed up the office, and forgot all about it. I came across the letter again when I resumed work after the New Year break.

To my great surprise, rather than a reprimand the letter was my formal appointment as auxiliary bishop of the Melbourne archdiocese. The appointment was a life-changing event and marked my entry into what, for many people, is the arcane world of the Catholic episcopacy. In March 1993 I joined the three bishops assisting Archbishop Frank Little: Joe O'Connell, Peter Connors and George Pell. Since I was already part of Frank's administrative team, I knew my episcopal colleagues quite well. At sixty, I considered myself rather 'long in the tooth' for such an appointment.

★

Auxiliary bishop is the bottom rung on the Catholic Church's episcopal ladder, although one is no less a bishop than any other holder of episcopal office. As an auxiliary bishop you tend to create your own authority. It does not come with a role created by Rome to get certain things done. For older appointees, the role is an invitation to put one's talents at the service of the diocese or the national church and its agencies in a range of leadership roles. For younger appointees, it serves as an apprenticeship for higher office. Teaching is an important component in the role of any bishop and one that I have always taken seriously. The attitude one brings to teaching is important.

All cultures are defined by the way in which people living in them come to balance out competing claims. Catholic Church culture is no different in this respect. It has been shaped and re-shaped by the way in which *the claim to certitude* and the *need to search for the truth* of things are held in balance. Go too far in one direction and you find yourself offering false certitude, or at least extravagant claims; go too far in the other, and people no longer know what the Church stands for.

Philosophers Bernard Lonergan and Charles Taylor remind us that historical consciousness plays its part in how this crucial balance point is determined. Historical consciousness is an awareness shared by people living in a particular age of core beliefs and aspirations that create the demand for change. The centralisation of authority in Rome, especially over the past two centuries, has in my view moved the Church too far in the direction of false certainty, with the centre providing answers to questions from all over the world, as if the one answer can play out in all cultures in the same way equally well.

While the process of centralisation has been unfolding in the Latin Church, the Eastern churches have continued as faithful and faith-filled communities, going about their lives together in a quite different way. My long association with Eastern and Orthodox Church leaders has forced me to challenge the value of the *imperium* model of Church governance.

The *imperium* model reached its zenith during the pontificate of Pope Pius XII. The model lost ground at the Second Vatican Council, only to be re-asserted under Popes John Paul II and Benedict XVI. Its major weaknesses have been exposed by the sexual abuse scandal where the all-controlling centre has sought to distance itself from responsibility for what has occurred, as if this is merely 'a local matter' and of only local significance. Vatican officials cannot have it both ways – central control when it suits, and designating something as 'a local matter' when it does not! Neither is it helpful to have power so concentrated at the local level that even auxiliary bishops had quite limited influence in affecting important decisions, and lay Catholics including those heading major agencies, virtually none. Women simply did not figure in this equation at all! The latter situation greatly complicated any capacity the Church had to respond to the issue in Melbourne or elsewhere.

As a human system, the *imperium* model of Church governance is anthropologically naive. The power (and intransigence) of the model comes from the fact that too many clerics have their careers tied to its operation. However, change is in the air. With a new papacy comes hope that a different future is possible and that an alternative model might emerge. Its birth will be painful.

Pope Francis's major reform to date lies in moving the certitude-searching balance point back towards the searching end of the spectrum. I find it encouraging when he writes:

> …Nor do I believe that the papal magisterium should be expected to offer a definitive or complete word on every question which affects the Church and the world. It is not advisable for the Pope to take the place of local Bishops in the discernment of every issue which arises in their territory. In this sense I am conscious of the need to promote a sound 'decentralisation'.[1]

While this comment was made in the context of discussing issues surrounding the way in which the Church engages in its mission, it contains a much greater truth, viz that *false certitude encourages people to stop searching*. It suggests that, rather than being a pilgrim people, the Church has somehow arrived at its destination.

My own study has taught me that searching is a condition of all life, and is celebrated in all vital cultures. It involves a healthy awareness of limits. Developing this theme, Pope Francis writes:

---

1   Pope Francis *Evangelii Gaudium* (Strathfield: St Paul's Publications, 2013), #16.

We see then that the task of evangelisation operates within the limits of language and circumstances. It constantly seeks to communicate more effectively the truth of the Gospel in a specific context, without renouncing the truth, the goodness and the light it can bring whenever perfection is not possible. A missionary heart is aware of these limits and makes itself 'weak for the weak…everything for everyone' (1 Cor 9:22). It never closes itself off, never retreats into its own security, never opts for rigidity and defensiveness. It realises that it has to grow in its own understanding of the Gospel and in discerning the paths of the Spirit, and so it always does what good it can, even if in the process, its shoes get soiled by the mud of the street.[2]

For those of us who have struggled for so long to address the dysfunctional impact of the *imperium* model of Church governance, the words of Pope Francis offer the prospect of a much-needed change in direction.

In an interview with the editor of a major Italian newspaper, *La Repubblica,* he is explicit in naming the problem:

> You know what I think about this? Heads of the Church have often been narcissists, flattered and thrilled by their courtiers. The court is the leprosy of the papacy.

When asked by the interviewer does he mean the Curia when he uses the word 'court', Pope Francis goes on

> No, there are sometimes courtiers in the curia, but the curia as a whole is another thing. It is what in an army is called the quartermaster's office, it manages the services that serve the Holy See. But it has one defect: it is Vatican-centric. It sees and looks after the interests of the Vatican, which are still, for the most part, temporal interests. This Vatican-centric view neglects the world around us. I do not share this view and I'll do everything I can to change it.[3]

★

George Pell and I have a history as sparring partners because we hold quite different views on many issues. Despite this we have always got on agreeably. As fellow auxiliary bishops George and I always stood on opposite sides of the certitude-searching spectrum. When he was my 'boss' in both Australian Catholic Relief (subsequently Caritas) and later as Archbishop of Melbourne, and despite our differences, George to his credit never put obstacles in my way when it came to helping the East Timorese, even though he closely followed Vatican policy on the matter.

---

2   Ibid, #45.
3   Eugenio Scalfari 'Interview with Pope Francis' *La Repubblica* 1st October 2013. http://www.repubblica.it/cultura/2013/10/01/news/pope_s_conversation_with_scalfari_english-67643118/
    Not surprisingly, members of the 'court' soon hit back seeking to discredit Scalfari's version of the interview or to qualify the Pope's quoted remarks.

The fact that we are both Catholic bishops points to the pluralism that is possible within the Church, and this is a sign of health.

★

I was formally ordained bishop on 3rd March 1993. My elderly mother was chief among the guests. One of the first people I invited to the ceremony was Carlos Belo. I hoped the invitation would give him a valid reason for visiting Australia. However, he could not get a clearance to come at that time. Archbishop (later Cardinal) Francis Xavier Nguyen Van Thuan was visiting Australia at the time and was a welcome guest. He told me at the ceremony that he knew about my work for the East Timorese.

Nguyen was appointed Archbishop of Saigon just six days before the city fell. He was immediately arrested and spent the next thirteen years in prison, nine of them in solitary confinement. I met Nguyen a number of times in later years. He lived in Trastevere not far from where Caritas Internationalis is based in Rome. He succeeded Belo's great supporter Cardinal Roger Etchegaray as President of the Pontifical Council for Justice and Peace. On my visits to Rome we would meet to discuss events in East Timor and Australia, and have a meal. It was a very lovely friendship. Nguyen was a deeply spiritual man, and is held in high esteem as a witness to faith in and beyond Vietnam. He died in 2002 and his cause for canonisation is already well advanced.

★

While Belo was unable to leave East Timor to attend my ordination as bishop, the situation changed later in the year when he was invited to the United States by a member of the Foreign Relations Committee whom the Indonesians did not want to offend. In November 1993, we hosted his first visit to Australia where he visited Melbourne, Sydney and Wagga. Belo felt quite constrained in what he could say during this visit, and maintained a very low press profile.

The visit did, however, have a number of practical outcomes. Belo's fight for human rights in East Timor included the right of his people to their culture. This battle was being fought on a number of fronts both in Timor and in Australia. The challenge in East Timor was to keep Tetum, the local *lingua franca* alive, given that all school instruction was in Bahasa. If Catholic schools were to continue the momentum for Tetum, they desperately needed teaching programs and resources and texts so that the young could be given a formal introduction to a widely used native language.

During his visit to Sydney, Belo invited the Sisters of St. Joseph, who have their headquarters in North Sydney, to provide assistance. Given that the Sisters have a long and successful history of primary school educators in this country, he asked whether they might take on the challenge of producing resources in Tetum. He wanted the teachers in Catholic schools in East Timor to help the rising generation learn to speak and write the widely spoken native language (which at that time still had no agreed form). As I knew from my own work with Aborigines, language is central to culture, and without it a culture soon loses its imagination, its stories and the memories that help define collective identity.

The Sisters of St. Joseph took up the challenge. Sisters Josephine Mitchell and Susan Connelly did wonderful work heading an inter-congregational team of sisters and lay people based in Sydney. Wisely, the team tied its aims very closely to the *United Nations Charter on Human Rights*. In line with this, it specifically aimed 'to preserve and strengthen the Tetum language as a means of safeguarding the culture and identity of the East Timorese people'.[4] The program provides literacy material and a range of catechetical materials in Tetum. Mary MacKillop East Timor (MMET), the institute founded by Sister Josephine Mitchell, 'a woman of capable hands and expansive heart', as Cardinal Clancy described her,[5] has been incorporated into the work of Mary MacKillop International Inc. (MMI), and has played a significant role in defining the content of primary education in East Timor.

The work done by MMET is perhaps the most significant contribution the Australian Catholic Church has made to the development of Timor Leste. MMET built on earlier work done by the Australian Catholic Social Justice Council (ACSJC) under Bishop Bill Brennan's leadership. The ACSJC had sponsored the work of linguist Geoffrey Hull and his associates to give the Tetum language a definitive form.[6]

Loss of language was not only a problem in East Timor, it was also a problem for the rapidly expanding generation of young Timorese born in Australia.[7] The local challenge was to help this younger generation growing up in Australia not only to learn Tetum, but also to help develop a literature in Tetum. The East Timor Association sponsored Tetum poetry, drama and music events to keep their culture alive. I was both willing and proud to be the guest of honor at many of these evenings.

★

My change in role from vicar-general to auxiliary bishop brought both opportunities and surprises. The earliest surprise was finding myself more or less excluded from clerical circles where I had once been very welcome. This was in no way personal. It was simply the way clerical culture plays out within the Church. Bishops are shown a degree of respect that isolates them from their fellow priests to a surprising degree. This is something that you have to get used to, and get over. Being a bishop can be a very lonely experience, and having good family support along with a close circle of friends helps in negotiating the isolation that comes with the role.

As a bishop you are, however, presented with many opportunities. It is up to you to choose whether to take them up or not, and how seriously you want to be involved. I was fortunate in having previously worked with two good role models who, while they represented contrasting styles, were both effective. Bishop Joe O'Connell epitomised all that was best in the Irish-style clergy who had anchored the development of the Catholic Church in Australia. Joe had an extraordinary pastoral sense. He loved people and sought

---

4   Margaret Press & Susan Connelly *Mary MacKillop East Timor 1994-2006* (Sydney: Mary MacKillop East Timor, 2007), 16.
5   Cardinal Clancy 'Introduction' in ibid.
6   The situation of language in East Timor remains fluid and volatile despite the inclusion of a statement in the national constitution recognising Tetum and Portuguese as the two official languages.
7   In the early 1990s there were about 16,000 East Timorese living in Sydney and a comparable number in Melbourne, the latter mainly drawn from around Dili. There was a much smaller group living in Darwin.

them out. While he was very supportive of the priests in his care, he could be quite tough on those with a propensity to clericalism. Bishop Eric Perkins, whom I replaced when he retired, had a gentler style, one that enabled him to engage easily with people from all walks of life. Eric was particularly effective in working with political leaders. I learned much from observing both these men in action during my time as Vicar General.

When the meeting of the Australian Catholic Bishops' Conference (ACBC) was held in the latter part of 1993, I was still finding my feet. The ACBC's work at the national level occurs through a committee system. The conference agenda at that time was created around reports from these committees. These were circulated prior to the conference and the bishops were then free to question their content. The report-question format made the event tedious, and some of my new colleagues came to refer to it irreverently as 'the half-yearly meeting of the Catholic Church's gas works'.

*

The ACBC report that interested me the most at my first conference was that covering Australian Catholic Relief's work with Aborigines. Bishop Joe O'Connell came to me after this session and asked if I would be interested in taking over his job as the bishop's representative on ACR. He wanted to step down because of the travel involved, and his poor health. I said I was interested, and that is what transpired. I was appointed as Joe's replacement as Deputy Chair. Bishop George Pell was the Chair.

I found George Pell a most difficult man to work with in an organisational setting, as usually he has already decided, prior to the meeting, what was to happen. I have always found this style problematic. Despite this, I was glad to be working on the Aboriginal component of ACR's work because at the time I was trying to provide official Church support for the Aboriginal Catholic groups who were already meeting, and get an official archdiocesan Aboriginal Catholic ministry up and running in Melbourne.[8]

*

As a relatively new bishop, I had to invest time in finding my place in the episcopal sun. I came to realise that, as a very junior bishop, I was a pussycat thrown in among lions. It was a case of learn quickly or be eaten!

Finding my place meant coming to grips with the work of ACR and how this articulated with Catholic social teaching. One of my earliest ambitions was to change the name of the agency from Australian Catholic Relief to Caritas Australia so that the public saw us as part of the world-wide Caritas organisation (to which ACR already belonged). I was keen that the Australian agency be seen as an expression of the global Church's concern for the marginalised through the provision of aid and relief where the needs were greatest.

When Bishop Pell's term as chair of ACR ended, I succeeded him. My first goal was to

---

[8] The Melbourne Aboriginal Catholic Ministry (ACM), which flourishes at the time of writing, had its origins in the initiatives of dedicated Aboriginal lay people who, over a period of time, had been meeting with the support of certain religious and priests. Information about its development can be found in *Invisible No More: The story of the foundation and development of the Aboriginal Catholic Ministry Melbourne 1984-1996* (Thornbury: Aboriginal Catholic Ministry, 1996), and on ACM's website. www.cam.org.au/acmv

change the style of leadership. Working to address social justice issues is challenging since the environment is quite unpredictable, and thus differs from that of many other Church ministries. ACR/Caritas personnel rarely have control over an agenda set by changing political priorities, or when natural or man-made catastrophes strike. There is also a constant tension between the short-term help needed to negotiate a crisis, and sustainable recovery in the medium to long-term.

In this context, values-based policy setting is crucial to be effective. A tension exists between giving a person fish in order to survive, and teaching that person how to fish. However, that is not the end of the matter. There is no point in teaching a person to fish if that person is already well able to do so and someone else has stolen all the fish or polluted the water so that there are no fish to be had! Advocacy for the rights of those whose livelihoods are being destroyed is an imperative in social justice ministry. Advocacy and development need to operate hand in hand. Social justice education is an important part of advocacy. The scope of Caritas's educational role was therefore necessarily and wisely expanded.

*

To be effective in this ministry the leader has to be prepared to listen in order to find out how people think, how they feel, how they see the problem or issue, and what they perceive the possible solutions to be. Social justice requires unremitting hard work for which people receive little in the way of positive feedback. Victims are often so lost in their suffering that they fail to appreciate the assistance on offer. The powerful interests that create victims do not want to be called to account and actively seek to discredit social justice agencies. In the parlance of young people, social justice ministry is 'a hard gig'.

My leadership style has sometimes been described as 'ponderous', but in the social justice field it works. Because it was so different from my predecessor, initially it took ACR people some time to adjust. Over the next six years it was wonderful to be among the community of Caritas people, whether at home or abroad. I came to value their willingness to get on with the job and not look over their shoulder for preferment.

*

My first visit to Rome as Deputy Chair of Caritas Australia in 1993 was something of a mind-blower. People were there from all over the world dealing with pastoral problems we didn't even dream about in Australia. For instance, the people from El Salvador were talking about their extraordinary archbishop who had been murdered (Oscar Romero). Other priests had also been murdered and nuns raped to stifle Church opposition to the oppression of the poor. Just as I had found in East Timor, it is one thing to read about things in the newspaper, but altogether something else to be talking to people directly affected by what is happening. Another participant was a bishop from the north of Brazil who talked about the institutional racism that existed in his country. He was eloquent about the greed of American capitalism that was swallowing up local forests to create more land for cattle in order to provide the mince needed for hamburgers in the U.S. I began to read up on the Church in Latin America so that when I returned to Rome for later meetings I could speak with these people from a more informed perspective. They appreciated this very much. I also met the Bishop of Johannesburg and listened to him talk about Soweto. I just could not believe what he was telling me. Ten people living in little tin sheds with no privacy, no toilet, no water, nothing! This was the world of the poor that Caritas dealt with, and I was proud that Caritas Australia was making a constructive contribution to the overall effort. Later I was to visit Soweto and see for myself the conditions there.

★

I quickly slipped into a routine as auxiliary bishop. I found that my role had three components. A third of my time was spent on diocesan business, and an equal amount was spent on pastoral work in my region which had eighty or so parishes in the east of Melbourne. My principal pastoral tasks were administering confirmation and supporting the clergy in the region. This meant visiting parishes, discussing issues with the priests and lay people and encouraging them in their work. Combined with this work was my involvement with the Aboriginal ministry as I was the ACBC representative on the National Aboriginal and Torres Strait Islander Catholic Council (NATSICC). At NATSICC conferences I was always proud of the Melbourne contingent. Most of the delegates were women.

It was especially delightful that increasingly indigenous people were taking leadership in looking after their own affairs. I told them that I was always available to listen and to provide advice or critique if needed, and many groups took up this offer as they moved ahead. The groups I met with found it hard to deal with certain bishops in the north of Australia whom they saw as operating out of an outmoded mission paradigm. I had earlier encountered a version of this paradigm at Kalumburu.

The third element of my role as auxiliary bishop involved international commitments. My role in Caritas included visits to project teams, needs assessments and attending meetings and conferences. Caritas Australia was involved in East Africa, Southeast Asia and the Pacific, so these areas were my focus and I visited them all. These responsibilities and my pastoral work in Australia had to be juggled so that I could meet my commitments to East Timor. Over time the international and East Timor commitments interweaved. Caritas provided me with an international platform to speak on behalf of the East Timorese, and the chance to extend their support network.

★

Across the 1990s, the ACBC had two groups endeavouring to support the East Timorese. Caritas worked from a relief/development perspective and the Australian Catholic Social Justice Council (ACSJC) worked from a justice/human rights perspective. Bishop Bill Brennan who was responsible for ACSJC was much senior to me as a bishop and thought I (and Caritas Australia) should defer to him and to the ACSJC. However, we operated in quite different ways. He was an institutional man, well connected within the episcopal ranks and to the Apostolic Nuncio. His line was always the Roman line and he worked only though official channels which meant that in dealing with East Timor he did so through the Indonesian embassy and the nuncio in Jakarta. He did not choose to come and stand with the Timorese in a demonstration when people were fighting for their lives. He was totally focused on getting an official Church delegation to visit Dili without ever being at all clear about what such a visit would or could achieve, let alone how the East Timorese themselves might view the ACSJC's approach.

Because I am a network man who believes in creating and maintaining alliances across institutional lines, I had no problem in making connection with either the Indonesian consul in Melbourne or FALINTIL representatives in Dili. I was as keen to talk to trade unionists about East Timor and seek their help as to any other group. In turn, there were times when they sought my help. This is how networks operate. They function around mutually shared values and do not require that people take sides. The aim is to provide help where it is needed and as it is needed. Networking operates to forge a consensus that defines areas where and how people with differing worldviews can work together. Such consensus building recognises that there are 'no-go' areas and thus limits to co-operative action.

The approach leads to genuine dialogue and provides a much more flexible way forward than institutions generally allow.

★

Bishop Brennan put his proposal for an official delegation to visit Dili to the ACBC Central Committee where it was approved. Subsequently a small Church delegation went to East Timor via Jakarta where it was wined and dined by the Indonesians and later by the nuncio before leaving for Dili. When I heard that the visit was to take place, I contacted FALINTIL people I knew to inform them that two Australian bishops were going to East Timor as part of a formal delegation of the Australian Church. FALINTIL said they would track them wherever they went to keep tabs on what the Indonesians were up to.

As events turned out the Indonesians were up to their usual games. Three days before the bishops visited Becora prison in Dili (where many East Timorese were tortured), prisoners under interrogation were moved out and the place completely hosed out. These were replaced with 'happy people', prisoners due to be released in the next few days. Rooms where the torture was carried out were blocked off for the visit. Such conduct was *de rigeur* for international visitors.

When the delegation returned, it produced a report that was presented to the Indonesian Ambassador. The ACBC was not given a copy of the report. This was forbidden under the terms of the visit. I later learned the report was sent to Rome as 'the view of the Australian bishops'. It was not. It was a private report that the bishops did not even see. In my view the two bishops who went had allowed themselves and the Church here to be manipulated by the Indonesians.

Needless to say the visit went down like the proverbial lead balloon with the Timorese, both here and in Dili, and did little to improve the image of the Australian hierarchy. After this visit, Belo and the priests in East Timor were always courteous to Bishop Brennan when he visited, but suspicious of his judgement. Looking back it is hard, given the nature of the man, to see how else he could have acted given his unbounded faith in institutions.

We found ourselves in opposite camps on the East Timor issue for the next decade.

Caritas Australia knew of my interest in East Timor and fired up to help without too much prompting on my part. We were able to do some good things in partnership with Caritas Indonesia providing food and medical supplies.

★

International commitments took me overseas three times a year, usually corresponding to school holidays when my pastoral duties eased. These visits gave me a new perspective on justice issues and the way in which the Church in various parts of the world seeks to address them. To say there is a high degree of pluralism in approach would be an understatement. I found that interest in, and commitment to, human rights varied depending on how closely matters impinged on the Church's own interests. This seems true whether 'Church' is understood as the global Church centered on the Vatican, or local churches. There is often a clear mismatch between Church rhetoric on social justice and human rights and Church action, particularly when the Church's own interests are involved.

The notion that the Holy Spirit somehow guides those in charge of the Church so that they can never make serious mistakes is a very dangerous aberration of doctrine that simply does not stand the test of historical fact. A Church made up of fallible human beings will always make mistakes. Sometimes it takes the help of the Holy Spirit for those in charge even to acknowledge that this is so. Membership in the Church does not excuse Church leaders from membership in the human condition. This is why a realistic anthropology is so important to a successful Church leader.

★

That bishops can be as venal as anyone else was brought home to me in Rome where I encountered the politics of power and saw the Roman 'court' in action, 'up close and personal' as they say. Rome brings together the best and worst in the clerical world. With its many ecclesiastical universities turning out graduates, it is the epicentre of clerical ambition. It is also the refuge for clerics either not wanted in their own dioceses, or who need to be 'moved on' for one reason or another. Many of these people seek to establish a power base in Rome, and international organisations, such as Caritas, that control significant funds, are a prime target.

I was particularly disappointed that Lesley-Anne Knight, an English lay woman who held the role of Secretary General of Caritas Internationalis, during the time I was a Vice-President, was denied the opportunity of re-election by the Secretary of State, Cardinal Bertone. She had been treated badly during her term of office, having been studiously snubbed by the clerics to whom she was required to report and who accused her of not being explicit enough about her 'Catholicity'. Lesley-Anne's reply was: 'Whenever we met a hungry person, we fed them. We don't ask about their religion'. She was a very talented and experienced woman, and her treatment at the hands of Vatican bureaucrats must have been very painful. She was replaced by a cleric. That is how the power game is played at the Vatican. It is the culture that the present Pope has to struggle against daily.

★

As a bishop I was learning what was involved in being called to a wider mission, and that the challenges of the service dimension of my priestly calling had expanded. I was slowly developing an understanding of Belo's situation not as outside observer but as a participant.

My growing international exposure helped me put the situation in East Timor into context. While life there was bad, I soon came to realise that there were places and people even worse off. Much of the rottenness I encountered during my visits could be sourced to a failure to respect people's human rights. The good I encountered came from the efforts people made in Africa, Latin America, Asia and the Pacific to address this most fundamental of issues. On every visit I met the most wonderful disciples of the Lord – women, men, religious, priests. They understood the ministry of service their baptism requires of them. I also met suffering, despair, and so much that debases human worth and dignity.

Nothing, however, prepared me for the horror that was Rwanda which I visited as part of the international team sent by Caritas in September 1994, following the end of the genocide in which 800,000 people, the majority of whom were Tutsis, were slaughtered over a period of 100 days.

CHAPTER 21
EAST TIMOR AND RWANDA: CULTURE AT ITS BEST AND WORST

My visit to Rwanda with a Caritas team in September 1994, a few short weeks after the genocide had been halted, was one of the most formative experiences of my life. Rwanda remained a tragic and very dangerous place with sporadic episodes of savagery continuing. Australians had contributed most generously to Caritas for relief and rebuilding.[1]

There are few people more needy than the victims of a civil war that creates refugees on both sides of the conflict, leaves women raped or widowed, people maimed, and large numbers of children orphaned. The situation of the victims is more horrible when the war is fought along ethnic lines, with one side believing that their humanity is somehow superior to that of their opponents. The scale of the help needed is proportional to the level of violence perpetrated.

Events in Rwanda attracted only minor international attention until it became clear that the genocide of Tutsis being carried out by the Hutu government had re-ignited a slow-burning civil war. By this time hundreds of thousands of innocent people had been killed and well over a million displaced. The capacity of NGOs to help was exhausted by the scale of the unfolding tragedy.

The situation was unique in that the genocide was being carried out in a country that was nominally 80% Christian. Christians were killing Christians with ruthless efficiency.[2] Churches in Rwanda, mainly Catholic churches, became 'killing fields'. People who had been encouraged to flee there for safety were slaughtered in their tens of thousands, sometimes with the complicity of their priests. This is what was known on the eve of my visit to Rwanda in September 1994.[3]

A ceasefire of sorts had been in place for a month following the victory of the Rwandan Patriotic Front (RPF) over the forces of the former government and their French allies. Revenge killings were still occurring, but order of a sort had been restored which made

---

1   Within the first year of fundraising for Rwanda Australians had contributed $3.4 million for Rwanda.
2   Beginning on 6 April 1994 and ending 100 days later, the most conservative estimate put the number of people killed at 500,000, the vast majority of these being Tutsi killed indiscriminately and systematically by youth militias organised by the Hutu government of the day as it desperately sought to cling to power in the face of growing opposition within Hutu ranks.
3   An authoritative report covering many aspects of the Rwanda genocide is the Expert Personalities' Report commissioned by the Organization for African Unity, entitled *Rwanda: the Preventable Genocide*, 2000. See http://www.refworld.org/pdfid/4d1da8752.pdf

the journey dangerous, but not impossible. To people living in Western countries what was happening seemed unimaginable, and reinforced their worst stereotypes about Africa. If their support was going to be gained, then an alternative narrative would need to be constructed, one that gave people reason to hope that things could be better, and that they had a role to play in making them better. Many then believed this about East Timor, so why not about Rwanda?

★

While the immediate tragedy had unfolded in Rwanda, the refugee problem was on such a scale that it threatened to de-stabilise Rwanda's neighbours – Burundi, Zaire (now called the Democratic Republic of the Congo), Tanzania and Uganda.[4] It is beyond the scope of this memoir to deal in any detail with the tragedy that occurred in Rwanda.[5] However, parallels with the situation unfolding in East Timor were striking.

Rwanda is sometimes referred to as 'the land of a thousand hills' made famous by the films *Gorillas in the Mist* and *Instinct*. Australians find it difficult to envisage that the entire country which is just over one tenth the size of Victoria, could have a population almost half that of Australia.

Rwandan culture has developed around agriculture with cattle still regarded as a de facto currency. Since arable land has always been in short supply, local politics have tended to centre on who controls the land and how it is used. Here the parallel with East Timor is very clear.

★

Catholic missionaries came to present-day Rwanda (at the time part of German East Africa) in the late 19th century during the second great missionary movement from Europe. By papal mandate the 'White Fathers' (Missionaries of Africa) were the dominant missionary group in Africa. They followed the time-honoured missionary strategy *cuius regio eius religio* (which loosely translates as the religion of the king is the religion of the people), and sought to convert the king of Rwanda and his court, initially to little avail. However, with the backing of the colonial administration, the Catholic Church soon became politically powerful. The colony was composed of three cultural groups: Tutsi, descended from the cattle herders, comprised fifteen percent of the population; Hutu subsistence farmers comprised over eighty percent; and the Twa, descendants of a pygmy people, about one percent. The king and his court were Tutsi and it was to these that both the colonial administration and the missionaries were drawn.

---

4   Later in the decade these countries would all be caught up in Africa's first continental war fought around the Great Lakes region. The source of the conflict lay in the international community's lack of will to address the situation unfolding in Rwanda in 1990-1994.
5   There are many accounts and analyses available about the genocide in Rwanda and its aftermath. Here I rely on the report *Rwanda: the Preventable Genocide* cited above.
    Timothy Longman presents a more readable account in *Christianity and the Genocide in Rwanda* (New York: Cambridge University Press, 2010). See also Andre Sibomana *Hope for Rwanda: Conversations with Laure Guilbert and Herve Deguine* (London: Pluto Press, 1999).

After World War I German East Africa[6] became two mandates, one administered by Belgium (Ruanda-Urundi) and the other by Britain (Tanganyika). Under the new administration in the Belgian territory, the Catholic Church continued its 'civilising mission' and assumed responsibility for education. Post-World War I the Catholic Church became effectively an arm of the government, paralleling the role it played in East Timor under Portuguese rule. Belgium also employed a model of indirect rule similar to that used in East Timor relying for power on the support of local rulers. Its system of government could best be described as an 'adapted feudalism' with a social order, bordering on a caste system set firmly in place. This system was defined by prevailing European beliefs about 'cultural evolution'. This placed Europeans, Tutsi, Hutu and the Twa in order of their assumed cultural merit. In the pre-World War II period, the Catholic Church cultivated Tutsi leaders in order to gain influence, with considerable success. A mutually self-serving relationship developed that was to have important consequences.

As a result of mistaken cultural beliefs, colonial administrators and Church leaders preferenced the Tutsi over other groups in education and jobs as a matter of policy. As it was not immediately obvious to Europeans who were Tutsi and who were not, based on their racial features, in 1931 the administration introduced a now notorious identity card system. Everyone had to nominate which 'ethnic' group he or she belonged to, and from that point onwards heredity determined a person's ethnic identity.

Under this arrangement there was no longer room for any movement between the Hutu and Tutsi castes, as had been the case. The card system became the principal means by which Tutsi could be distinguished from Hutu. People marked as Hutu were then screened out of education and whatever jobs were available. Those nominated in 1931 as 'Tutsi', together with their heirs, soon came to dominate the political, social, economic and ecclesiastical life of Rwanda. The Catholic Church in the Belgian mandate was headed by ex-pat bishops and foreign missionaries supported by local clergy who, almost to a man, were Tutsi.[7]

★

In the post-World War II era, the marginalisation of the Hutu became a matter of concern for Church leaders who addressed it by opening up positions for them in seminaries and within Church organisations. As in East Timor, this provided potential leaders with a wider view of the world than they would otherwise be able to achieve. Apart from the seminaries, there was negligible opportunity for secondary education available at the time. Some seminary students went on to the priesthood, but as in East Timor, most did not. The latter took up roles within Church organisations and were able to parlay these into roles in the civil administration.[8]

In the decolonisation process in 1962 the Belgian colony became the two independent states, Rwanda and Burundi. However both had to struggle with the legacy of European

---

6 German East Africa encompassed present-day Rwanda, Burundi and continental Tanzania (Tanganyika). It was split between Belgium and Britain by the League of Nations in 1919.
7 Rwanda and Burundi were administered as a single colony until 1962.
8 The first president of an independent Rwanda, Grégoire Kayibanda (President from 1962–73), had previously run the Catholic press office and served as secretary to the Bishop of Kabgayi.

rule – the Tutsi–Hutu divide. In the years immediately prior to independence (1959-1962) elections were held and the Hutu, being the majority, came to power. In the violent wave of revenge killings that followed over fifty thousand Tutsis died and six hundred thousand were forced to flee to neighbouring countries - Uganda, Zaire and Tanzania. After independence the social order in Rwanda was reversed.

In the decade that followed, Hutu leaders in the various provinces conducted sporadic massacres involving the Tutsi, so expanding the number of refugees. When some wanted to return, they were refused entry on the grounds that Rwanda was 'over-populated'. A political movement developed among refugees in Uganda known as the Rwandan Patriotic Front (RPF). Its stated aim was to force the central government in Rwanda to overturn its policy of Tutsi exclusion as this denied Tutsi their human rights.

Many of the Hutu who came to power in 1962 had close connections with the Church, being the beneficiaries of opportunities that Church leaders had created for them. So the position of the Church remained largely unchanged in the transfer of political power from Tutsi to Hutu.

*

In 1973 Juvénal Habyarimana became President in a military coup. He won Tutsi support by promising to introduce a quota system in allocating education and employment opportunities. Once elected President he transformed Rwanda into a one-party totalitarian state. Over time, as in Indonesia, cronyism and corruption took its toll. When the price of coffee, the main source of Rwanda's international currency, collapsed in the late 1980s, Habyarimana was forced to court Hutu extremists to maintain his (and their) grip on power. The President had to accede to the request from countries providing foreign aid, on which the national budget now depended, to introduce multi-party democracy.

The Catholic Church in Rwanda had indigenised the local clergy during Habyarimana's long reign. By 1993 nearly all of the country's bishops were Hutu. Only three were Tutsi.[9] The archbishop in Kigali, Vincent Nsengiyumva, was deeply involved in national politics. He served as chair of the ruling party's central committee from shortly after his appointment as archbishop in 1974 until told to vacate the position by the Vatican fourteen years later.[10] The Church and the Government, the President and the Archbishop, faith and Hutu nationalism, formed dangerous liaisons.

*

Tutsis living in Uganda fought in the successful liberation movement there and some rose to senior ranks in the Ugandan army. These then provided the expertise needed to train and mobilise their compatriots. With arms supplied from Uganda, the RPF developed an armed wing, similar to FALINTIL in East Timor. The Ugandans were keen to see the Tutsis gone. As their numbers increased, they were becoming a political force in the country.

---

9   Mgr Jean-Baptiste Gahamanyi, Bishop of Butare; Mgr Wenceslas Kalibushi, Bishop of Nyundo; and Mgr Frederic Rubwejanga, Bishop of Kibungo.
10 'Rwanda 10 years on: not forgiven, not forgotten', *The Age* April 6, 2004.

In October 1990 an RPF force attacked from Uganda and, but for French intervention, would have succeeded in overcoming the Hutu government.[11] The invasion re-fuelled Hutu fears and the determination to enforce a 'final solution' that would remove not only the Tutsis, but the government's political allies among the Hutu as well. Death lists were drawn up and circulated. The nationalist ideology known as 'Hutu Power' was born at this time. This aimed to rid Rwanda of Tutsis once and for all. The extremist strategy was to agree to peace terms and invite Tutsis to return home, and then kill them all.

When the initial invasion failed, RPF forces regrouped and with recruits supplied by the Tutsi diaspora in Burundi, Zaire and Tanzania, a formidable army was formed in Uganda. Rather than engage in a direct assault that might again draw in the French, the RPF leader, Paul Kagame, opted for a low-intensity guerrilla war aimed at pressuring the government to recognise the rights of Tutsi exiles to return, and also to obtain political power in the country.

Tragedy unfolded when President Habyarimana's private jet was shot down as it came into land at Kigali airport on 6th April 1994. The government blamed the RPF for the assassination and this became the signal for Hutu militias to wipe out all Tutsis living in Rwanda, as well as any Hutu critics of the government. The groundwork for the subsequent genocide had been laid by months of incendiary anti-Tutsi rhetoric on two national radio stations. The similar role played by Radio Kupang comes to mind in regard to events in East Timor.

★

The killing had been carefully planned. In the months prior to the assassination the military had armed 'self-defence' Hutu militias called the *Interahamwe* on the pretext of defending the population against possible RPF attack. In the next one hundred days more than half a million Tutsis – men, women and children – plus their Hutu sympathisers, were killed often in the most barbarous manner. The killing was motivated by nationalistic ethnic hatred that extended even into the ranks of the clergy and religious.

When news of what was happening reached the RPF, they attacked from the north and quickly advanced south on the capital Kigali. The French seeing they could not stop the RPF's advance this time, and perhaps appalled by the genocide, set up a safe corridor for the Hutu forces to withdraw, taking hundreds of thousands of 'refuges' with them.

We arrived in Africa a month after these events. By then, the world was well aware of the genocide in Rwanda and the terrible conditions in the camps across the border in Zaire and other neighbouring countries where over two million refugees had fled, in some cases living under the control of armed Hutu militias. These would go on to destabilise Zaire and set the scene for Africa's first continental war in 1996.

When our team assembled in Nairobi, both Burundi and Zaire were awash with refugees. Rwanda was still littered with bodies. Visiting Rwanda in September 1994 was as close to visiting hell as I ever wish to come.

In order to reach Rwanda, I had to go via South Africa. My journey took me from

---

11 The French government saw the country as a part of the Francophone world under attack from English-speaking rebels based in Uganda.

Pretoria to Nairobi in Kenya to arrange visas for Burundi and Zaire. We were met at Nairobi airport by Fr Yvon Pomerleau who was himself a refugee in Kenya following the Rwanda genocide. A Dominican priest, Fr Yvon was asked by the then Secretary General of Caritas Internationalis to be his personal representative in regard to the Rwanda crisis. In that capacity he welcomed Terri Thrower and myself on September 18, 1994. We were to travel together in Kenya, Burundi, Rwanda and Zaire. His support for our efforts was very considerable.

The Caritas Internationalis group assembled at the Dominican house in Kenya and were briefed on the current situation in Burundi and Rwanda. The rough statistics I recorded in my diary at the time were stark. Before 6th April there were three hundred and fifty priests in Rwanda. Since then a hundred had been killed together with a similar number of religious Brothers and Sisters. Four ex-pat priests had been murdered trying to protect their Tutsi parishioners from their Hutu parishioners!

The best estimate of the numbers killed at the time was somewhere between half a million and seven hundred thousand. Only six of the eight Catholic dioceses in the country still functioned. The Archbishop of Kigali, two other bishops and thirteen of the priests had been murdered by RPF forces who were supposed to protect them. The Archbishop was a target because of his close association with the previous regime. The rest were killed in retaliation for the Church's perceived complicity in the genocide. This was all very sombre news to digest.

★

There were six people in the Caritas Internationalis team, four ex-pats and two Africans. We met at the Dominican house in Nairobi to plan our journey. There I met my first Rwandan priest. Fifty members of his extended family had been killed since April. The mind simply boggles at such numbers. He told us that the Rwandan Church as a whole was in crisis. Priests with Hutu connections were marked men and would never return.

To get to Rwanda, we flew to Bujumbura, the capital of Burundi, where violence following a military coup two years earlier had been bad, but things had now settled.[12] Our plan was to travel by minivan to the border and on to Butare, the main city in the south of Rwanda. From there we would travel north and then west to the refugee camp at Goma just across the border in Zaire, where Caritas had a major presence. Caritas had booked our flight from Goma back to Nairobi. All this in a week!

Caritas Internationalis had set up a temporary office in Bujumbura. Its main work was getting food and medicine to camps along the border. We soon discovered that the relief effort in both Rwanda and Burundi was chaotic. Nearly one hundred NGOs were operating, each doing its own thing, much to the frustration of the Government. I met two Australian nuns who were so disenchanted with Catholic efforts to help the refugees there that they were at that time working with CARE Australia.

The local Caritas groups were concerned that the NGOs were focused on short-term aid projects and did not care about what needed to happen in the longer term. Many

---

12 The plotters had killed the Hutu President and installed a Tutsi government. This created a Hutu refugee crisis in Rwanda which added to the growing sense of paranoia among government personnel.

NGOs were using media-driven fund-raising campaigns that, by highlighting the sensational, distorted the grim reality of local suffering. Local Caritas groups worried what would happen when these publicity-hungry NGOs pulled out and the locals were left to cope on their own.

★

The local church in Burundi was in disarray. The Hutu bishop's residence was a fortified compound. When we visited Mgr Simon Ntamwana, Bishop of Bujmumbura,[13] it was obvious that he was living in a permanent state of fear, and not without reason.

There was a good deal of disenchantment with the role Church leadership had played in the current troubles. In Rwanda, with the exception of the head of the bishops' conference, Thaddée Nsengiyumva, Bishop of Kabgayi, Church leaders were seen as too close to and too uncritical of the Habyarimana regime. Catholic churches had become the killing fields of Rwanda. Tutsi parishioners had fled to their local churches seeking protection only to be trapped and killed there in their tens of thousands. Church personnel were now targeted by the RPF. As a consequence the new government was seen locally as anti-Church and anti-Catholic. We needed to be very discrete during our visit.

★

Our immediate concern was to determine who was most in need of the limited help *Caritas Internationalis* could offer. There were a number of very pressing candidates: Tutsis returning from refugee camps; displaced Hutus living in fear of the RPF; Hutus fleeing back to Burundi; Hutus fleeing to Zaire; Tutsis held hostage by Hutu militia and now living in the disease-ridden camps in Goma; victims with horrific injuries; orphans, both Hutu and Tutsi; the many rape victims trying to get on with their lives while living in a traditional society. The catalogue of human misery was vast.

We needed to see the situation on the ground, talk to people and then make some quite tough and pragmatic judgements about what was possible, what was likely to be helpful and, more importantly, what would be sustainable. My experience dealing with similar issues in East Timor proved of benefit in setting up workable policy parameters and developing protocols with government officials who were less than impressed by the self-serving actions of many NGOs.

★

The road trip to Butare was sobering. We stocked up with food before we left as the situation in Rwanda was so desperate at the time that we could not expect people there to feed us. After a long holdup at the border, we passed through a countryside that had been depopulated and its villages vandalised or totally destroyed. Bloated bodies were still lying where they had fallen. The countryside was depressing beyond measure. One of our team, Fr Michel Descombes, a White Father who had previously worked in Rwanda, and was

---

13 Bishop of Bujumbura (1989-1996). He later became Archbishop of Gitega (1997-).

Secretary General of Caritas Rwanda, murmured: 'Mon Dieu. Rien!' When he had been here some years earlier the road had been crowded with kids. None of us could talk. I got out at one village. No one wanted to come with me. As I moved around I counted five or so bodies, one was that of a child with his head missing.

Twenty or so kilometres further on we came across a man leading a group of nine lads, all nine- or ten-year-olds. There was fear in their eyes when our car stopped. I got out to greet them. One of our team spoke to the group in French and we found out that they were 'orphans' who had not eaten for days and were not even sure where they were heading.[14] They were just trying to survive from one day to the next. We all sat down and shared what we had with them and then left them some of our rations. This positive action lifted the cloud of depression that had been steadily settling on our group. It also had a big effect on the young people as well. They started to smile, and that memory has always stayed with me. When it was all over they came around and hugged us.

★

Butare was a scene of devastation with houses burnt and shops blown up by hand grenades and looted by soldiers. We stopped at what was left of the diocesan centre to meet the local bishop, Jean-Baptiste Gahamanyi. He kindly shared with us his meal which consisted of a watery soup, a dry biscuit with a boiled egg, and a cup of tea. He told us that his diocese had lost thirteen priests. It had been comparatively fortunate. In another diocese, Nyundo, thirty-one priests had been killed.

We stayed the night at an abandoned religious house which had been the home of the Pallotine Fathers. Two weeks prior the *Interahamwe* had shot its two caretakers and then hacked their bodies to bits in the shower area. The blood was still caked on the walls! There were bullet holes in the main door and some of the windows had been shot out. This made a big impression on the team as we gathered for Mass that evening.

When we settled down for the night, I called on lessons learned from dealing with the ninjas in East Timor. I advised everyone to sleep in a different room, and under the window, so that if intruders came they would step on the sleeper in the dark, and the noise would raise the alarm. Needless to say, no one slept very well that night.

Towards dawn I heard the sound of persons running and torches flashing. They were looking for someone. A torch flashed in my window. I then heard the call 'Arretez' (stop), followed by shots. I waited for a while and then went out. There was a dead body on the veranda. We were shocked to be caught up in the violence. When we tried to tell the authorities about the dead body, no one wanted to know. It was terrible.

★

Our next stop was at Kabgayi where our host was Fr Andre Sibomana, the administrator of the diocese. His bishop, who had been the only Hutu Church leader to speak out against the violence, had been murdered by RPF troops. As the editor of the main Catholic

---

14 The term was used for children whose parents were missing. They might or might not have been orphans in the sense commonly used.

newspaper, Fr. Sibomana had become something of a legend in Rwanda for his intrepid defence of human rights. He had been hunted and in danger of losing his life on several occasions for exposing government corruption under the previous regime. His survival had been something of a miracle.

Of the twenty-one parishes in the diocese Andre was leading, only seven were still functioning. The diocese had been a Hutu Catholic stronghold and had lost fifty-nine of its seventy-one priests. Fr Andre spoke of the need for 'a moral reconstruction' in Rwanda. People had to admit what they did and try to come to terms with the way in which they had been manipulated into believing that it was right. A total suspension of moral judgement led people to attend Mass before going out killing, apparently blind to the fact that this was totally wrong. When we visited, Andre was setting up a reconciliation program for parishioners. Participation in it was a condition for being re-enrolled in the Catholic community.

The dilemmas of reconciliation were enormous. If Hutu parishioners had killed members of your family it was no simple matter to be reconciled with them. It was an enormous 'ask' for Tutsi women to have to sit in church with the people who had raped them, or students to sit with teachers who killed their classmates. This was the reality of Catholic life in Rwanda in 1994. Re-building the shattered community was complex as both sides had now committed atrocities, as we were finding out. In Andre's view the military defeat of the Hutu had led to their cultural defeat as well, rendering communication within parishes very difficult.

Andre was proud of the fact that at the height of the genocide some thirty thousand Tutsis had fled to Kabgayi and most had survived. However it seemed clear to us that he was a marked man. Everywhere he went RPF soldiers followed, even when we went to visit the cathedral. As we left we all wondered if he would survive.[15]

Looking back I see so many parallels between Andre Sibomana and Carlos Belo. Both were very brave men, who faced the prospect of death constantly, both were totally committed to the marginalised and to the Church, and each was possessed of singular gifts in defending the defenceless.[16]

★

On our way out of Kabgayi we stopped at Kivumu parish, run by a Croatian missionary Franciscan, Fr Vjeko Curic,[17] known to one of the team. He lived in a simple house with a dark secret. When the RPF had swept through in August, they had rounded up around two hundred men suspected of being members of the militia who were responsible for most of the local killing. Many were young Hutu who thought that killing Tutsi would open up opportunities for them in a world that otherwise offered little hope. These were

---

15 Fr Andre Sibomana administered the diocese until 1996 when he returned to his job as editor of the Catholic newspaper. His premature death at age 43 in 1998 was a great loss for the Church in Rwanda and for the human rights cause.
16 Andre Sibomana's book *Hope for Rwanda* provides an excellent account of the background, events and consequences of the Rwandan genocide as experienced by one of the Catholic Church's most outstanding leaders.
17 This Bosnian Croat Franciscan priest was subsequently recognised internationally for his heroic work on behalf of both Tutsi and Hutu. He was murdered in 1998.

taken one by one into the priest's house where they were questioned and then mercilessly bludgeoned to death with a steel pipe. The blood flowed out the door inches deep. The bodies of the victims were all buried nearby in a shallow grave. One can only imagine the terror of the victims as they awaited their fate. This was revenge on an industrial scale. We visited the site and as the soft ground gave way, could see limbs poking up out of the ground.

★

Fr Michel Descombes had been based in Kigali, the capital of Rwanda. The devastation there was similar to Butare. We stopped at what had been his office. The place had been wrecked and he was much affected by what he saw. We discussed how to get the archdiocesan infrastructure up and running again. Without this, Caritas and other Church agencies centred in the capital would have no base from which to work. We also visited the Australian soldiers who were working in the hospital at Kigali. They were part of the United Nations Assistance Mission for Rwanda (UNAMIR).[18]

From Kigali we headed to the northern centre of Ruhengeri, once an epicentre of Hutu power. The road took us through lush forests and while the villages seemed badly damaged and deserted, some people were again working in the fields. From the hills we could see Lake Kivu which marks the border with Zaire in one direction, and an active volcano spouting steam in another. The beauty of the view stood in stark contrast to the squalor in which people now lived. Déjà vu East Timor! When we stopped to look at the ruins of the Nyundo cathedral, RPF soldiers quickly appeared and moved us on, so we continued on to Nyundo on Rwanda's western border with Zaire.

The bishop's residence and diocesan centre there were both in chaos with papers and books scattered everywhere and appliances ripped off the walls. The meeting room was full of bullet holes and dried blood. When chaos descended the bishop called a meeting of priests to discuss what to do for Tutsis seeking sanctuary. Halfway through the meeting the bishop left the room to go to the toilet in his house, and was there when the Hutu arrived. The Hutu shot everyone in sight. Suddenly the diocese had no priests! The bishop could see what had happened and headed into the bush.

We found that the cathedral, one of Rwanda's most notorious 'killing fields' was locked. In April some twelve hundred Tutsis had taken refuge there in the belief that they would be given sanctuary in the church. When the Hutu troops arrived they surrounded the church, barred the doors, and told the people inside to say their prayers. They then used ladders to access the roof and prised up sections of the corrugated iron. They hurled in hand grenades until all inside was quiet. The local *Interahamwe* were then given the task of finishing off any one who was still alive. The carnage must have been unimaginable.

An Australian army medical team from Kigali was given the task of clearing the cathedral. I asked one of the team how many had died. He told me they determined the number by counting the skulls as so many of the bodies had been dismembered and

---

18 Diary notes kept by Fr Yvon Pomerleau O.P. who was accompanying us as representative of the Director of Caritas Internationalis, have been very helpful in complementing my own diaries in preparing this account of our work.

he said over half the skulls were those of children. We were able to support this crippled diocese by building houses for displaced people to get things going. A small light of hope shining on a great hill of despair!

That night we were glad to eventually arrive at our hotel after a harrowing day spent listening to victims and seeing the results of experiences that almost beggared description. I did not sleep. I was haunted by what I had seen and heard. Sunday 25th September 1994 is stamped indelibly on my memory.

★

Crossing from Rwanda to Zaire the next day was a tedious process and despite starting early we found ourselves entangled with NGO vehicles on the move. Once in Zaire we headed for the Bishop's house near the Goma airport. Transport planes were landing in rapid succession as the Vicar General greeted us. We then made our way to Caritas headquarters where we were expected, and after being formally welcomed, we were whisked off to the Caritas section of the refugee camp at Mugunga.

As part of its responsibilities, Caritas ran an orphanage there for some twelve hundred children. There were over a quarter of a million people in the camp living in blue UN tents that seemed to stretch to the horizon. The logistics of running the place were mind-blowing. Members of the defeated Hutu army, still in uniform, seemed to be everywhere. The Zaire government had threatened to move the camp away from the border region but lacked the means to achieve this without considerable outside help.

★

We returned to the bishop's house in Goma where the Bishop, Mgr Faustin Ngabu, greeted us. He had delayed a trip to Kinshasa specifically to speak with us. His concerns mirrored those of the people with whom we spoke in Burundi: 'What would happen when the NGOs pulled out?' Help without long-term policies would stop people dying only in the short term. They would still die later, but away from the cameras.

The bishop hoped that Caritas would take up the slack when other NGOs moved off to a new tragedy. I found the general cynicism of locals towards NGOs and their operation hard to hear, but seemingly justified.

In the afternoon we returned to a decidedly Catholic part of the camp which had a tent chapel and section names like Bethany, Nazareth, Bethlehem and so on. There was one tent for handicapped children. Another was for mothers dying of AIDS, often the result of rape by soldiers. Since there were no drugs, these women could not be treated. Their children, about eighty of them, lived in the next tent. Many of these too had AIDS and, according to the French doctor caring for them, probably most would die.

The doctor, whose name unfortunately I did not record in my diary account, was thirty-four years of age. He had left his wife and two children in the south of France. His grandfather had worked with the Belgian army in the Congo and was his hero. When he said to his wife that he should go there and help, she had replied 'I knew you would come to this decision. It was only a matter of time'. As he was leaving he said, 'I hope I come back. That is the risk I take', to which she replied 'When you go shopping you might get hit by a car!' The doctor said he was a Catholic and that every night he knelt with the kids and said a prayer with them believing this was the best therapy he could give them. 'That is as good for them as any medicine I can give them. It does something for them'.

Many children in the camp were classified as orphans when they had in reality just been abandoned or become separated from their families as they fled. Each day parents arrived looking for their children, and if they found them, took them back to their own camp. We visited one tent set aside for malnourished children. When one little girl, who would have been about twelve years old, stood up and read a welcome to us in French, it was just too much. There was not a dry eye among our team.

We stayed on discussing with the Caritas workers what was happening and what was needed almost until dusk. As we began to head back to our hotel in Goma, people in their thousands began crowding down the narrow roads to collect food and water from distribution centres set up by various NGOs all advertised by colourful flags.

That night we met up again with the Caritas people working in the camp and had a simple meal with them. You could not but be impressed by the quiet way in which they went about their life-saving work. Next morning we found out that a group of ex-pat Caritas aid workers wanted to see us. Their immediate concern was the lack of long-term planning by Caritas that led them to actually question the value of what they were doing. They had come to help on humanitarian grounds, and had a religious edge to their convictions. They questioned the local Church's *bona fides* after encountering Hutu priests in the camps with means, but no visible source of income. Were they, like the remnants of the Hutu army, simply biding their time, hoping to ride to power on the returning army? And, if so, where did that leave Caritas personnel working with them in the camps? The group had sought our party because they had heard there were two Australians in the team and thought that we would listen to them! After three hours of robust but enlightening discussion, we bade farewell to the group and headed for the airport and the Lutheran plane to Nairobi where I had a couple of days to wait for my return flight.

★

While in Nairobi I visited the Karen area where Karen Blixen of *Out of Africa* fame had her farm. Karen is home to the Catholic University of East Africa and many religious congregations have training houses there. As I was walking through the area, which is relatively safe, I found a young man collapsed in the gutter. When I stopped to help him, I discovered he was a refugee priest from Rwanda who had been on the move for a month, and had collapsed in total despair. He just wanted to die where he lay.

We were near a Jesuit house so I took him there, explained who I was, and asked the Jesuits to take responsibility for him which they eventually agreed to do. I gave them some money, which the Jesuit I dealt with said would keep him. I did not think any more about the matter.

Some years later I was giving a talk on East Timor in Melbourne and recounted this incident. The group was startled when one of the group yelled rather excitedly – 'So you're the one'. When we had all recovered, Sr Maryanne Confoy explained the reason for her excitement. She had just returned from teaching at the Jesuit University in Boston, and the Rwandan priest I had helped had been one of her students. He was there on a scholarship arranged by the Jesuits. The priest recovered in the Jesuit house in Nairobi, returned to Rwanda, and had been sent overseas to study. He had no idea who had helped him, but knew it was 'a bishop from Australia'. Our globalised world can prove very small sometimes.

★

The parallels and differences between the situation in East Timor and that in Rwanda seem obvious. In a worst-case scenario, East Timor could easily have become another Rwanda with pro-integration militia supported by TNI wiping out independence supporters and Indonesia spreading the balance of the population across the archipelago. Quick action by Australia's then Prime Minister, John Howard, probably thwarted this happening.

Belo belonged in a different category to the bishops in Rwanda in his unwavering defence of human rights. This put some limits on the Indonesian military's culture of impunity. In Rwanda there had been no such brake, and without it the Government had been able to kill with impunity while Church leaders, including successive papal nuncios, stood by strangely silent.

I met some very brave and impressive individuals in Rwanda, such as Andre Sibomana, for whom I had great admiration. But it was hard to avoid the conclusion that there was a serious failure of collective leadership by the Church there over many years. How did papal nuncios justify the abuse of human rights? Did they too seek refuge in arguments about a 'greater good' such as protecting the Rwandan Church against possible reprisals from a totalitarian government? I was left with a very uncomfortable feeling of *deja vu*.

My other reflection was on the power of culture and what happens when this is manipulated for evil purposes. The whole Tutsi-Hutu division is based on a distorted view of history propagated by misguided missionaries and seized on by an equally misguided colonial administration. The result has been untold tragedy and human misery that extends across Rwanda's borders into neighbouring countries. While the Vatican later maintained that clergy and religious who participated in the Rwandan genocide acted as individuals, the Church's earlier role in setting the course of cultural development in Rwanda must be acknowledged.

Culture is a powerful force in human affairs that can be co-opted in the cause of good and evil. In Rwanda the local culture was co-opted in the cause of evil. I was growing increasingly confident that in East Timor it was being co-opted in the cause of good.

CHAPTER 22
1996 BECOMES A VERY GOOD YEAR

If there was ever a nadir in the East Timorese struggle for self-determination it was reached early in 1996. Then mysteriously, and quite unexpectedly, the wheel began to turn, first within the Church with several senior clerics going public in support of Belo, then in the international community when Belo and Ramos Horta were declared joint recipients of the Nobel Peace Prize.

By awarding the peace prize to Belo and Ramos Horta, the Nobel Committee effected a decisive change by drawing the attention of the international media to Indonesia, and what was happening within that country. Once the government there lost control over the flow of information about what was happening in the country, things began to spiral out of control even before the Asian financial crisis a year later tipped the Suharto government over the edge. Up until that time those of us who had been supporting the fight for human rights in East Timor found it difficult to get traction in the media.

★

At the beginning of 1996 spirits among the East Timorese in Australia were at a low ebb. Refugee communities in Melbourne and elsewhere were under pressure on a number of fronts. Early in the year a group of young adults had made the hazardous boat journey to Australia, and after being held at Port Hedland for some months, were released into the care of the refugee community here on bridging visas. This meant that they could not work or claim benefits, so the full burden of supporting them fell on an already impoverished group. The young people, totally dependent, having little English, and finding themselves with nothing to do, soon became disillusioned. The situation was ameliorated to some extent by the Red Cross, and changed for the better only later in the year when the Government provided them with a special allowance.

Morale among the refugee community was undermined by suspicion that some members were selling information to INTEL agents operating in Australia (some of whom used to park opposite my house in Blackburn watching who was coming and going). Trust within the community eroded to such an extent that even a person like Kirsty Sword[1] was suspected of working for the Indonesians.

---

1 An Australian East Timor activist, Kirsty Sword married Xanana Gusmao in 2000. She was First Lady of East Timor during the years 2002-2007.

Politically, there were major disagreements about the future of East Timor with four options in play: full integration; integration with special autonomy; autonomy within Indonesia leading to independence; and outright independence. While the first was rejected out of hand and no one really believed the last a likely option, people were divided on the other two. This caused divisions and made Ramos Horta's task in presenting East Timor's case to the international community all the more difficult. At the time CNRM was struggling for traction outside of East Timor and Ramos Horta was increasingly seen in diplomatic circles as a one-man-band.

Infighting within the community gave credence to Indonesian/Australian assertions that 'Timorese are always fighting among themselves and so could never run a viable state'. Early in 1996 I spoke at a meeting of the East Timor Refugee Association (ETRA) pointing out that the bickering and infighting had to stop or thousands of people would have died for nothing. I warned that disunity equates to death. It was a grim time. Even Jose Ramos Horta was close to giving up.

In late January I met him and the CNRM group, including Kirsty Sword, at Matlock in Victoria where we discussed how to deal with the morale issue and with Ramos Horta's principal detractors in Australia and Portugal. Jose confided that he thought the next two years would be crucial. If there was no change by then, all would be lost. At that time, he was subject to fits of depression – little wonder, given the load he had carried for so long! We all tried to jolly him along.

★

I visited Dili again late in January 1996 for the opening of the new seminary. The situation there was depressingly the same as it had been previously. The violence and provocation continued unabated. Ninja groups still roamed the streets at night. The war of attrition that had destroyed the local economy went on. New graves appeared regularly in Indonesian military cemeteries – this was how the locals knew that FALINTIL was still active despite propaganda to the contrary.

I was pleased to see that Belo had upgraded his technology. He now had a mobile phone and so was accessible to the international media, his overseas supporters and his own people at all times. This was to prove something of a mixed blessing. He now employed a lad to drive his new computer! His office contrasted with those in the main diocesan centre in Dili where the technology was still hopelessly out of date.

The opening of the seminary coincided with celebrations marking fifty years of the Salesians' presence in East Timor, fifty years of Indonesian independence, the feast of St Don Bosco, and Belo's birthday. He was forty-eight. There was much to celebrate. Belo invited a number of bishops to be present for the occasion. These included Bill Brennan, Kevin Manning and myself from Australia, Bishop Soma, the chair of the Asia-Pacific Coalition for East Timor (APCET) from Japan, the bishops of Atambua and Kupung, and Bishop Januario Ferreira, an auxiliary bishop from Lisbon. All attended with the exception of Bishop Soma who had been declared *persona non grata* by the Indonesians. The Papal Nuncio from Jakarta, Archbishop Pietro Sambi, presided.

As the first Portuguese bishop to set foot in East Timor since the invasion, Bishop

Ferreira was greeted like a returning hero wherever he went. When he spoke out strongly about human rights in East Timor his stocks rose even higher. This fostered the dangerous illusion that the Portuguese, who had abandoned the people to their fate in 1975, would somehow come to their rescue now. His visit enhanced a nostalgia for things Portuguese which has always run like a hidden stream just below the surface among the Dili elite and the local clergy.

*

Belo usually organised pastoral visits to coincide with my arrival, and 1996 was no exception. This strategy enabled me to move around the province delivering and picking up sensitive communications etc *en route,* so by-passing curious eyes. We travelled west to Oecusse, returned to Dili and then headed east to Los Palos effectively criss-crossing the country.

The trip west was not without its hazards as the road along the north coast is treacherous in the wet season when normally sedate streams become raging torrents that wash the road away or make it impassable. It is easy to be swept off the road, slide over a cliff, or be stranded mid-stream. We had some hair-raising moments on our way to Oecusse and without the Indonesian army winching Belo's SUV across one of the rivers, we would have had to turn back.

From Oecusse we headed south into West Timor to Atambua and stayed with Bishop Anton Ratu, an Indonesian, who looked impressive in episcopal garb complete with purple fez. Anton had a sharp mind and quick wit. His first question to me was 'Did you come to Dili to protest or to cheer?' He clearly knew who I was.

*

On our trip east we by-passed Bacau as Belo had learned that students there planned to stage a demonstration to coincide with our arrival. I stayed at the Salesian College at Fuiloro to join in the celebrations there, while Belo went on to join the Salesian community in Los Palos a few kilometres away. My host was the affable Fr Jose Vattaparambil. In 1996 the local situation was clearly difficult: Fuiloro was still a hotbed of rebellion. The army had three battalions stationed nearby and they patrolled the college perimeter at night. There were regular clashes with FALINTIL involving casualties on both sides.

At the time Jose had another FALINTIL fighter spirited away somewhere on the property. The man had been shot, betrayed when he sought help, imprisoned and tortured by the Indonesians, and then shot again while escaping. The local FALINTIL unit would not take him back, regarding him as a security risk despite the fact that he was being hunted by the Indonesians. The man's situation was impossible which was why Jose was helping him.

The college's standing in the local community was steadily improving. Its operation helped feed the local people who regularly stole from the crops it produced. While the students found the stealing discouraging, Jose's response had been to plant more seed to accommodate the theft. His attitude was: 'If people are starving they need to eat!'

★

The day after our return to Dili we went to the airport to welcome Bishop Brennan who flew in from Jakarta with the papal nuncio. I had not met Archbishop Sambi before. He was a tall man with white hair who looked every inch the diplomat. Sambi had an impressive record having worked in some of the world's hot spots – Nicaragua, Cuba, Algeria and Burundi prior to his appointment to Jakarta. He would go on to serve in Israel before finishing his career as nuncio to the United States where he died in 2011.

The two of us seemed to hit it off immediately, partly because he had been pro-nuncio in Burundi from 1985 to 1991 and was interested in finding out first-hand about my visit there. He knew many of the people I had met.

Over the next few days we went for long walks where we could talk privately. Sambi was a chain-smoker who would eventually die from related health complications. He smoked as he walked and talked. He had definite views on the East Timorese that seemed more the product of Indonesian propaganda than time spent among them – 'they were lazy, always fighting among themselves. Should Indonesia withdraw civil war would again break out, etc'. All this I had heard a thousand times. He was more interesting when he spoke about the situation in Indonesia. The concern in diplomatic circles there was that Suharto was on the way out. Opposition was developing around the issue of human rights and the excessive wealth being accumulated by Suharto's family. Young Indonesian human rights activists were seeking political asylum in foreign embassies, so copying the strategy employed by the East Timorese. This drew international press attention to the government's poor track record on human rights and highlighted the corruption that led to the abuses. For the first time in nearly thirty years Suharto felt under political pressure.

★

The opening of the seminary was a gala event involving both public and Church dignitaries. We were escorted to the seminary by the military with flashing lights - the full treatment. A very large crowd had assembled and the inauguration proceeded peacefully. However, as the official party made its long slow procession back to the gymnasium that served as the hospitality centre, up went the banners and the shouting began. One banner was a portrait of Xanana and the other read in English 'Freedom'. Chants of 'Viva' began, accompanied by clenched fist salutes and V signs. The reaction of the Indonesian bishops and priests present was almost instantaneous: 'rowdy louts', 'idiots', 'unruly youth', 'never can trust them', 'don't look at them that is exactly what they want' and so on. I stopped, got out my camera, went over to where the disturbance was happening, and took a photo. Only later was I warned by Belo that this was a very dangerous thing to do.

Young people used the cover of the Church to make their voices heard. I had no problem with this, although it was a continuing worry for Belo in his efforts to maintain the peace. He did not want the local Church politicised unnecessarily. However, it required little imagination to guess that the occasion would attract a demonstration of some sort. The police and military were soon into action attacking the demonstrators some of whom were later arrested and tortured.

Following the blessing and opening we returned to the Bishop's residence in Lecidere for lunch. When this was over, Sambi suggested we go for another walk. It soon became clear that he wanted to pump me for information about Jose Ramos Horta and the CNRM. As seemed his custom, the archbishop first told me what he thought: 'Horta represents no one. He is a questionable man and a trouble-maker who has nothing to say about the future, etc.' He went on in this style for some time so I replied in the following vein: 'Look Excellency, I know Jose and have worked with him for some years. For twenty years he has lived in fear of his life, rarely sleeping in the same place two nights in a row. At times he has lived in abject poverty but has kept the promise made to Nicholas Lobato that he be a voice for his people, even when disowned and imprisoned by groups within the resistance movement. When he left East Timor as a twenty-four year-old he knew nothing about international diplomacy or global politics other than what he had picked up during his brief exile in Mozambique. The Foreign Affairs Department in Australia refused to take him seriously when he came seeking their help in 1975. Yet, starting from this position he has educated himself to the point where he is now an internationally recognised expert on human rights. He is seen as a voice of moderation on East Timor and is mounting a complex diplomatic offensive against the Indonesian invasion of his homeland that is proving remarkably effective and gaining momentum all the time. For his efforts he has been nominated for the Nobel Peace Prize three times and was short-listed last year. In international forums he continues to make a telling case for self-determination in East Timor that could, among other options, lead to independence. He does this against the constant background of Indonesia using its extensive diplomatic resources to discredit him and have him banned. The Vatican's assessment of Jose and his influence is simply wrong!'

Sambi then gave me the Vatican's version of history along the following lines: 'In 1975 FRETILIN was riddled with communists, bandits and members of the Internationale. I saw this similar dynamic unfold in Cuba. Many of the 200,000 who have died in East Timor did so at FRETILIN'S hands. East Timor is not viable as a state, since 95% of its economy comes in the form of aid and investment from Indonesia, only 5% is generated locally. The fight for human rights must take into account the fact that Asians do not view the matter in the same way as we in the West do'.

In reply, I pointed out that the economy of East Timor was grossly distorted by Javanese and military monopolies that devalued local agricultural production to maximise profits. The operation of these exploitative monopolies had turned the country into a vast gulag where there was little incentive to work and few opportunities for the young. I also pointed out that people fighting for human rights in Indonesia share common aspirations, not different aspirations, with those in East Timor and other parts of the world. In fact both are currently joining together in common cause. The groups seeking asylum in embassies in Jakarta contain both Indonesians and Timorese. If we need to learn, Rwanda tragically illustrates what happens when the recognition of human rights is abandoned.

As our rather long walk was nearing its end I stopped, turned to the nuncio and asked: 'Excellency, I have listened to you and answered all your questions. Now I would like you to answer one for me. Did Monsignor da Costa Lopes resign or did Rome sack him?'

Without hesitation Sambi replied 'Of course, my brother, he was sacked'. He then went on to explain. Originally, Rome saw da Costa Lopes as an anti-communist, anti-FRETILIN nationalist. In their eyes he was something of a romantic who thought he could bring the different political groups in East Timor together because the leaders were Catholic and he knew them personally, in some cases having taught them in the seminary. However, this project backfired when they began to use him to pursue their own political interests. These leaders had little or no interest in the Church, as such, and would have dropped da Costa Lopes once their political goals were realised. His real problem, in Sambi's account, was that he exposed the local Church, even if unwittingly, to political manipulation and so he had to go. When Nuncio Puente told da Costa Lopes to step down he, as a loyal son of the Church, agreed that his dismissal be treated as a 'resignation' to minimise local resentment.

To my mind there was another side to this story. Da Costa Lopes, by his incessant efforts to moderate the violence visited on his people and to protect their human rights, became a symbol of hope for them. By destroying that symbol the Indonesians hoped to expunge the people's hopes, so better to control them. Da Costa Lopes' removal at Indonesia's insistence meant the Vatican fell victim to the very situation it was trying to avoid – the Church being manipulated for political purposes!

Sambi, seemingly oblivious to this, commented that if Belo were not careful, he too could become a symbol of people's aspirations and so find himself being manipulated by contending political interests. The logic of the situation seemed to be that a bishop *can* take on this symbolic role, but it must be transitional – it has to be limited in scope and it has to be short-term. If not, the Church gets dragged into the political process where it has no place.

In Sambi's view the realpolitik was that the Indonesians would never leave East Timor and, since the resistance could not win militarily, the situation was apparently intractable. The Church in both East Timor and Indonesia had to position itself within this reality. The situation would be resolved by adhering to one guiding principle: Never accept that there is no solution: there is always a solution. History dictates that peace comes eventually. This is the hope the people of East Timor must cling to.

While I appreciated Sambi's candour in responding to my question I was taken aback by the moral ambiguity of his answer. It seemed to me that Church diplomacy shared the pragmatism devoid of principle that characterised Australian diplomacy with respect to East Timor. His comments however did give me some insight into the way in which the Vatican bureaucracy thinks and works.

While Rome is strongly committed to helping the victims of injustice, it seems to draw the line rather selectively at dealing with the structural realities that cause victims in the first place. I had already learned that the political activities of the Archbishop of Kigali, for instance, did not lead to his dismissal! The Church cannot have it both ways: wanting a place in the public square while at the same time eschewing politics. This is an area in Catholic social teaching that needs to be developed and clarified.

★

I travelled home from Dili via Sydney where I met again with Ramos Horta who was recovering from minor surgery. He was very depressed and told me he was pulling out of the struggle. He was sick of the rottenness in FRETILIN and the Church and the infighting among the Timorese. He even attacked Belo as being too timid in his approach to the Indonesians. He had made up his mind to quit and had informed Xanana of his intention.

We spoke at some length and especially about the thousands who had died, including his four brothers and sisters. 'Was this all for nothing, Jose?' I asked. After some time he sparked up and acknowledged 'the Indonesians have not beaten us yet!' then added 'But if we are not careful we will beat one another'.

★

During Belo's rather frosty reception in Rome in 1995 Cardinal Roger Etchegaray the long-serving head of the Pontifical Council for Justice and Peace, had been one of the few senior Vatican officials to make him feel welcome. Belo invited Etchergaray to visit East Timor and he promptly took up the invitation, stopping over in East Timor on his way to the Oceania Synod.

Etchegaray's visit provided a big boost for Belo as he was the most senior cleric to visit Timor since the Pope in 1989. Prior to Etchegaray's visit Pope John Paul II, perhaps stung by President Soares' criticism of him over East Timor, returned fire by telling the new Portuguese ambassador to the Vatican that Portugal should do more to resolve the crisis there. Etchegarary's visit seemed to indicate that the Vatican was lifting its game.

His visit attracted a good deal of international attention and with this came the inevitable risk that young protestors would use the occasion to drive home their message while the press was present. This duly happened with the usual, almost suicidal consequences. While in Dili Etchegaray re-iterated Belo's many calls for 'dialogue' and for 'the recognition of the cultural and social rights of the Timorese'[2]. The Cardinal's unambiguous support for Belo stood in contrast to the latter's treatment at the hands of Vatican officials the previous year and greatly enhanced his standing within the broader Church, but the strain was beginning to take its toll. I had been surprised at how visibly Belo had aged when we had met earlier in the month.

Etchegaray publicly embraced Belo following the Mass celebrated in the cathedral during his visit. This helped assuage the local perception that the Vatican was no friend of East Timor. With Etchegaray's support the tide slowly began to turn for Belo and opened the way for other senior clerics to come out in support of him. In this respect New Zealand's Cardinal Thomas Williams, then president of the Bishops Conference of Oceania was ahead of the game.[3]

★

---

2 UCANews "Papal envoy calls dialogue effective way to East Timor solution" Feb 28th 1996.
3 At the global level the Catholic Church is organised into "cultural regions": Europe, Asia, Africa and Madagascar, Latin America, North America and Oceania. Of these Oceania is the least culturally cohesive including as it does the nations of the Pacific, New Zealand and Australia.

In early 1996 preparations were underway for the first ever Synod of Oceania. Regional synods were part of Rome's strategy to promote serious reflection on the state of the Church as the 20th century ended and a new millennium commenced. When I arrived home from Timor there was a letter waiting for me from Cardinal Williams asking what action the synod's executive could take to support Belo. I replied saying there were three things that might be done: call for a downturn in military activity since the number of killings was again on the rise; request a stop to the transmigration program as this was now fuelling tensions not only along economic lines, but increasingly along religious lines – something new to East Timor; and renew the call for dialogue unfettered by pre-conditions. Williams wrote back in early March saying that the executive would take my advice. I found his words very encouraging - 'Your own resolute support for Bishop Belo and his people is a great inspiration to us. We couldn't not do anything when you are doing so much'.[4] As part of this response Australia's senior cleric, Cardinal Edward Clancy, visited Belo in late July.

★

In Australia a crisis arose for East Timorese refugees seeking asylum here in Australia when in early August they began receiving letters from the Immigration Department saying that their application for refugee status could not be accepted as they were Portuguese citizens. This was despite the fact that they had no family ties with Portugal, had never set foot in the country, and did not speak the language. This development coincided with Cardinal Clancy's visit to East Timor.

On his return Clancy, well aware he had been taken on a 'guided tour', was quite forthright in denouncing the oppressive state of affairs he had encountered in East Timor. The excessive surveillance of his party and the people they met by INTEL agents led him to complain personally to the local military commander. Clancy's visit and his subsequent comments greatly encouraged those in Australia preparing to challenge the new direction of immigration policy now classing many East Timorese refugees living here as illegal migrants.[5]

Cardinal Clancy wrote an article in *The Australian* suggesting that, while the Indonesians were somewhat aggrieved that the Timorese did not appreciate their efforts to develop the province, they were overlooking the fact that 'material improvements are no substitute from freedom, dignity and independence'. He noted that he had experienced the reality that East Timor is an 'occupied country' with all its consequences.[6]

By morning tea time on the day this article was published I had received eight or nine phone calls from Timorese leaders in Australia expressing how encouraged they were by the Cardinal's stand. I immediately wrote to him telling him of the impact his visit had here at home in Australia.

This was a further sign that the tide was turning as, in criticising Australia's stance towards East Timor, the Cardinal was also calling into question the Vatican's stance as well,

---

4   Cardinal Thomas Williams letter to Hilton Deakin 4th March 1996.
5   John Huxley "Cardinal demands action in Timor" *Sydney Morning Herald* 20 August 1996.
6   Cardinal Edward Clancy "No substitute for Freedom in Timor" *The Australian* 27August 1996.

at least by implication. The East Timorese here, aware of what his remarks implied, took great heart from this development at a time when things looked very bleak.

The changing of the tide gathered further momentum on the 16th October when it was announced that Bishop Carlos Belo and Jose Ramos Horta would jointly share the Nobel Peace Prize for 1996. Both Belo and Ramos Horta had each been nominated for the award previously. In presenting the award, the Nobel Committee seemed aware that Belo, living in East Timor, was limited in what he could say, but that Ramos Horta suffered no such limitation. The Committee effectively gave them both an international 'soapbox' from which to speak to the situation in East Timor, and the keys to doors that had previously been locked. The major benefit for Belo was that the award placed him out of range of the 'dark forces' in the Vatican still arguing for his removal. It also protected him from the TNI as no government wants a murdered Nobel Peace laureate on its hands.

In Indonesia news of the joint award was greeted with alarm and an immediate diplomatic offensive was launched to discredit not only the recipients, but the award itself. It is interesting to note that Belo received no message of congratulation from the President of the United States, Bill Clinton. Such still was Indonesia's influence in 1996.

★

In his book *From a Place among the Dead,* Arnold Kohen covers the events associated with the award in some detail so I will not dwell on them here.[7] What is important to say is that Belo received the award for his efforts to bring about peace by setting in place the condition for peace viz respect for human rights. An important part of this task was dissuading his people, particularly young people, from provoking the Indonesians to violence. Few better illustrations of his success here exists than the low key way in which he dealt with the situation after the announcement was made that he was a Nobel laureate. If Belo had allowed public celebrations, the consequent protests would have ended in an Indonesian crackdown in which many people would be beaten and possible killed. Belo celebrated privately, and asked people to respect the fact that this is what he wanted. It is a measure of the standing and the influence that he exercised at the time that people respected his wishes. When the 1996 anniversary of Santa Cruz occurred Belo was in Jakarta for meetings. At one he was jostled and roughed up by protestors. On his return to Dili 200,000 people approximating one third of the population, lined the street on his five kilometre journey from the airport to the bishop's house in Lecidere in silent protest and without incident.

Belo invited both Bishop Bill Brennan and me to attend the presentation ceremony in Oslo on December 10th as his guests. However before that event I ran into trouble in Malaysia in an event that added its own contribution to the tide of international opinion turning in favour of the East Timorese.

★

---

7   See Arnold Kohen *From the Place of the Dead* (New York: St Martin's Press, 1999).

The second Asia Pacific conference on East Timor (APCET II) was scheduled to take place in Kuala Lumpur from the 9th-12th November 1996. The date was chosen to coincide with the anniversary of the Santa Cruz massacre. Some 200 people from 25 countries including 75 representatives of NGOs in Malaysia registered to attend. Under pressure from the Indonesians the government of Malaysia decided to ban the conference four days before it was due to take place.[8] The legal force of the ban was that the meeting could not be held as a public event but could take place as a private, by-invitation-only event if held behind closed doors. Rather than cancel at the last minute, since many delegates were already on their way, the Malaysian organisers opted to hold the conference as a private meeting. As the chair of APCET I flew into Kuala Lumpur on the 7th November when matters were still unresolved.[9] The only change I knew about was that Jose Ramos Horta, who was scheduled to speak, had cancelled when it became clear his participation might embarrass the government.

A sense of apprehension hung over the meeting when we assembled at 9:30am for the opening session. The conference had featured prominently in the local news due to the good work of our public relations people who were not intimidated by a series of bellicose statements from the Malaysian government. Shortly after the introductions were completed, we heard a crowd outside our fourth floor conference room shouting and banging on the locked doors. The agitators seemed unaware that the press representatives and a TV contingent were present inside the room.

When the disruption started the organisers, all of whom worked for local NGOs, asked us to stay calm. We had all had experience of this before at other demonstrations. I suggested that we remove the chairs to the side of the room and then sit together on the ground in the centre of the hall and link arms. This tactic makes it hard for a mob to isolate and attack individuals. One of the TV reporters interviewed our press spokeswoman, Debbie Stothard as the background noise outside grew in intensity. When she said that what we were being subjected to was a small matter compared to what the Indonesians had inflicted on East Timor, we all applauded.

Next, someone set off the hotel's alarm bells and for a short while things were quiet outside. Then suddenly there was a loud bang and the locked doors flew open. A group of about two hundred people calling themselves the 'Malaysian People's Action Front' broke in.[10] They came prepared with banners that said 'Support Indonesia', 'Indonesia and Malaysia are Neighbours', 'Don't Tarnish the Image of Malaysia' etc and yelling 'Get out, get out! We won't leave until you stop the conference'. When the mob broke in I was sitting next to the elderly Bishop Aloisius Soma from Japan, a veteran fighter on justice issues. We decided that whatever happened we were sticking together.

The police arrived about an hour after the disruption began and gained control of the mob. The participants were escorted to another floor and held there. Immigration officials eventually arrived and took our passports. Later still 113 participants were arrested and 46

---

8   Suharto had visited Malaysia in early October 1996 and a return visit by the Malaysian Prime Minister, Mahathir Mohammad, was being negotiated at the time of the conference.
9   On 7 November the deputy Prime Minister, Anwar Ibrahim, who was running the country in Mahathir's absence overseas, threatened to deport people coming to APCET II. Renato Constantine from the Philippines, who was scheduled to speak at the conference, was deported on his arrival.
10 It later emerged that the "Action Front" was formed by the ruling party the day before, specifically to disrupt the conference. *The Age* 10 November 1996.

were subsequently deported. While most were quickly released and then deported, some of us were held in detention for five days before this happened.[11]

These obviously contrived tactics used to break up a peaceful meeting, and the arrest of foreigners, created something of a press frenzy. Diplomats were called in from many countries to sort out the mess which our arrest created. This provided us with opportunity to address an international audience saying why we were meeting and gained much more press coverage for the Timorese cause than would ever have occurred if the meeting had gone ahead. The fact that two visiting Catholic bishops had been arrested in a Muslim country was considered big news there and abroad.[12] An ABC journalist Cathy McGrath was arrested when she followed us to the hotel where we were detained, thus adding to the media frenzy.

In Australia, the incident drew comments from both the Prime Minster and the Foreign Minister, cravenly following the Malaysian line that we were there illegally and so had to live with the consequences.[13] Notwithstanding this, the bullyboy tactics employed backfired significantly with both Malaysia and Indonesia seriously discredited as a result. People from around the international East Timor network subsequently sent me local press cuttings detailing and commenting on the event. The resulting file is quite substantial. APCET II illustrated a simple truth - it is possible to have a very successful conference when no one actually speaks!

★

My unexpected detention in Kuala Lumpur created a problem for me in clearing outstanding Church commitments in Australia before departing on 7th December for the Nobel Peace Prize presentation in Oslo, but with the support of the archbishop and fellow auxiliary bishops, this was managed. When Bishop Soma and I arrived in Oslo, we found that we were in demand by local television stations, and we did a number of interviews about our experiences in Malaysia. We were an unlikely warm-up act for the two major conferences on East Timor leading up to and following the Nobel presentation ceremony itself.

The ceremony provided a chance for people interested in East Timor, whether from a political, academic or ecclesial perspective, to meet, learn and express their support for Belo and/or Ramos Horta. There was a fair spread of representatives from the political parties in East Timor including Florentino Sarmento and Manuel Carrascalao. On the academic side I was interested to hear Professor John Taylor whose work I had studied, and Professor Barbedo Magalhaes who had been my host at Oporto University in Portugal. The latter invited me to join a speaking tour of the U.S. he was organising with Ramos Horta for early 1997. An Indonesian academic, Professor George Aditjondro, presented a scathing account of the way in which the Suharto family's business interests distorted

---

11 Sheila McNulty ' 'The Asian Way' gets a Black Eye' *The Wall Street Journal* 12 November 1996.
12 Darren Gray 'Malaysia arrests Melbourne Bishop' *The Age* 11 Nov 1996. A week later the Malaysian High Court upheld the fact that the meeting was in fact legal and that the government had to release ten locals still held in custody. The Australian line was that the Government could ban the conference even if such a ban were illegal. Geoff Strong 'Canberra upholds Malaysia's "right"' *The Age* 17 November 1996.
13 *The Sydney Morning Herald* 11 November 1996 noted that ten Australians were arrested.

the Indonesian economy. The Indonesian embassy group attending the conferences must have gone home with their ears burning at the erudite way in which speaker after speaker took their efforts in East Timor systematically to pieces, questioning who benefited from the invasion. I learned a number of things from these gatherings. For instance, in 1974 the Governor of East Timor had sent 133 messages to Lisbon seeking to return from Atauro to Dili in order to recommence the decolonisation process without ever receiving a single reply.

★

Politics was never far from the surface in Oslo. In order to win the Indonesian government's agreement for Belo to attend, the Vatican had agreed to a number of conditions: limited media exposure and no visit to Portugal were the two main requirements. Belo himself was keen that neither the Indonesians nor the CRNM could gain any mileage from the event. So he steadfastly refused any joint interviews with his fellow recipient Ramos Horta and would have preferred not to be interviewed at all. The media, particularly the TV journalists, were most unhappy with this and one enterprising group even marched into the sacristy where we were vesting for Mass at 7:00am in St Olav's cathedral, demanding to know why he was avoiding interviews. Eventually he conceded to their request and gave an interview. By then everyone in Oslo, including the Indonesian embassy, knew of Belo's reluctance. Belo invited the Indonesians to the formal ecumenical service and the Mass in the cathedral in what I thought was a wise move. The intelligence service was up to its usual tricks. A group of Indonesian agitators had been imported for the occasion but were obviously out of place in Oslo, and were eventually arrested.

The presentation ceremony itself went off well. Belo was unduly nervous about the event but spoke well. He said he accepted the award not as a politician but as a pastor. He had a biblical warrant to care for the wellbeing of his people. His concern for their human rights was based on the belief that respect for human rights is a condition for peace. This has been constant Catholic teaching reiterated in East Timor's recent history by Pope John Paul II. The most fundamental of human rights for a colonised people is the right to self-determination. This right is recognised by the UN for all colonised peoples. The right had been denied the East Timorese. What the outcome of self-determination would be was a matter for the people themselves, and the Church would respect that outcome. At the end of his speech Belo was given a long, standing ovation.

Ramos Horta was more political in what he had to say, as one would expect. He acknowledged the role the Church played in East Timor and the importance of Xanana Gusmao to any peace process.

★

Belo would have been encouraged by the number of senior clergy, both Catholic and Protestant, who attended the ceremony to express their support for him and for his people. Cardinal Etchegaray was the most senior. Bishop Ferreira from Lisbon attended. There were also bishops from England, Germany, Norway and Sweden. There was a sizable contingent of Belo's Salesian confreres.

I caught up with Jose Ramos Horta just before departing for Australia. He looked absolutely exhausted. His schedule during the week had been punishing. Belo went on to Bergen and then to Sweden after the ceremony, as protocol demanded, and then visited Germany where he met Chancellor Helmut Kohl and spent a good hour speaking with him about the situation in Timor. After that he went on to Rome where his reception by the Pope and Secretary of State was warm, even if that by their officials was at times demeaning.

Belo arrived home to a warm reception and went immediately to the cathedral to celebrate a Christmas Mass of thanksgiving. There an incident occurred that cast a pall over the Christmas festivities. A Timorese member of the Indonesian army brandished a gun and threatened to shoot Belo. Members of the congregation pounced on him and beat him to death. Belo did not consider himself to have ever been in danger. This was one of many unsuccessful attempts made on his life, and to my knowledge the last. The local military used it as a pretext for a crackdown over the Christmas period. While some things had definitely changed in 1996, others remained depressingly the same. The incident dampened rather than doused a burgeoning hope.

In 1996 the international community began to see East Timor in a new light. While this did not change things immediately, we all knew that the game had changed. How decisively, we could neither know nor even imagine.

CHAPTER 23
THE BATTLE FOR MINDS

When East Timor was invaded in 1975, FRETILIN found itself isolated and under resourced in attempting to win over international opinion in the face of the carefully crafted media strategy run by the Indonesians to perpetuate the 'civil war' myth. During the consequent information blackout, imposed by the Indonesian government with support from the Australian government, the media lost interest in East Timor.[1] Their interest was revived for a short time following the Santa Cruz massacre in November 1991, but was then swamped by events in the Balkans. As a consequence, the struggle to have the human rights of the East Timorese recognised, demanded a good deal of consciousness-raising in a world that knew little about Indonesia and less about East Timor. Those advocating for this cause had to win support in the public squares of Asia itself, Europe, and particularly North America, where the real power lay - a formidable task.

The heavy-handed and inept intervention by the Malaysian government in disrupting the APCET II conference in November 1996 publicised the situation in Asia and also in Australia where the press coverage was extensive. In part this was because journalists saw the Howard government playing a double game, promoting democratic reform by criticising government use of gangs in Burma to disrupt Aung San Suu Kyi and her supporters, while condoning their use by Malaysia to break up APCET II. Both sets of events drew attention to the fact that various regimes in Asia were seeking to stifle debate about human rights and democratisation using proxy groups to do their dirty work.[2]

★

The awarding of the Nobel Peace Prize to Belo and Ramos Horta raised awareness of the East Timorese situation in Europe, but did not gain much traction in the United States. Indonesia depended heavily on the United States to supply and train its military and for access to the capital markets needed to support its local development. The structure of the Indonesian economy was such that it had to borrow in order to develop.

---
1   There were exceptions. Freelance journalists, such as Jill Jolliffe and John Martinkus, and ABC journalists, such as Cathy McGrath, assiduously wrote for the print media and TV news in Australia, so keeping the issue alive here.
2   The *Far Eastern Economic Review* addressed the issue in an article entitled 'Devious and Deliberate' charting the rise of 'youth groups' used by incumbent governments to disrupt political opponents and other dissenting groups. What happened at APCET II is quoted as one instance of a much wider practice in the region. See *Far Eastern Economic Review*, November 21, 1996, 16.

Government-sponsored cronyism and monopoly practices rendered Indonesia a risky place for outsiders to do business.

As noted previously with the Cold War long over, major powers were re-aligning their foreign policies, and changing from an anti-communist to a pro-democracy stance. In this new atmosphere, the doctrine of human rights was being widely discussed. The debate was focused by Lee Kuan Yew's assertion that the doctrine of human rights was a Western notion that did not sit easily with 'Asian values'. The idea that 'human rights' might not constitute universal values runs counter to the 1948 UN *Declaration of Human Rights* and so the matter was highly controversial at the time. The 'Asian values' argument was seen in the West as a excuse for the curtailing of individual human rights in the interests of 'harmony' and 'consensus'. When this resulted in the repression of growing democracy movements in South East Asia, the scene was set for confrontation. This created a milieu in which it was possible for human rights advocates to re-argue the case for self-determination in East Timor.[3] A battle, lost in 1975, was being rejoined with some vigour in 1996-97.

★

On my first visit to Dili in 1992 I spent some time at the Salesian College at Comoro, which has since become my home-away-from-home when visiting East Timor. I remember asking Fr Walter Van Wouve, the principal and a serious, no-nonsense Belgian, 'What will bring about change in East Timor?' His succinct response was: 'Change in Jakarta!' At the time this seemed a quite remote possibility. However, five years on, the climate was changing. The growing international critique of Indonesia both in terms of its human rights record and its economic management, particularly the level of corruption, was having an impact. The critique created space for activists and acted as a catalyst for 'change in Jakarta'. While this was at first resisted, it soon swelled and eventually led to the collapse of the Suharto regime in 1998. Jakarta became increasingly sensitive to international criticism, and this opened doors there for renewed advocacy as the local democracy movement grew in strength.

★

This was the context in which I accepted the invitation of Professor Barbedo Magalhaes to join a number of academics taking part in a series of symposia in universities in the United States and Canada early in 1997, organised through the Federation of Portuguese Universities.[4]

The Nobel Peace Prize ceremony in Oslo had provided East Timor advocates from around the world with the chance to meet and map out a course of action to place East Timor back on the international diplomatic agenda. We were encouraged by the new

---

3   Lee Kuan Yew's views, supported by Mahathir bin Mohamad in Malaysia, generated a considerable literature. For a recent treatment see Molly Elgin 'Asian Values: A model for development?' *Stanford Journal of East Asian Affairs* Summer, 2010, 135-45. The notion fell into decline after the Asian financial crisis of 1997-98.

4   The Federation is made up of 24 universities and the conferences were funded by its Foundation. To what extent this was a covert diplomatic initiative of the Portuguese government I was never able to discover. In the course of our travels we were frequently feted by Portuguese consular staff based at the UN or elsewhere in the US and Canada.

UN Secretary General, Kofi Annan, whose willingness to take up the matter at Security Council level followed years of stalling by his predecessor. We also realised that, strategically, effective advocacy needed to influence the foreign policy of the Clinton administration. Our contacts in the East Timor Action Network (ETAN)[5] advised us that the Suharto regime was under some pressure from the administration to 'clean up its act' on human rights. This included its crackdown on democracy advocates and 'the East Timor situation'. The impetus here came from members of the Congress who had recently visited Indonesia and East Timor and reported back to the powerful Committee on Human Rights.

The task of influencing US policy was never going to be easy as people in the United States knew little about Indonesia or East Timor. While Democratic politicians had some interest in the issue, there was little interest on the other side of US politics. Few Indonesians studied in the US and, to our knowledge, almost no East Timorese had sought refuge there. The only realistic option open to us at the time was an indirect one: to influence academic opinion, particularly those academics leading the commentary on international affairs.

Professor Barbedo Magalhaes put together a team made up of Portuguese, Indonesian, and East Timorese academics. ETAN organised for members of the team to meet with US lawmakers and Church leaders. The additional hope was that some of the team, at least, could meet with the new UN secretary General, Kofi Annan, and UN staff whose brief covered East Timor.[6]

I was invited to join the team as someone able to speak authoritatively on human rights in East Timor and *about* the role of the Church in East Timor. I made it very clear that I did not speak *for* the Church there. Belo did that, and he would be visiting the US later in the year.

*

The logistics of the conferences were challenging. Our visit had to occur before Suharto's which was planned for August. Belo was due to visit the United States as guest of the US Bishops' Conference in September. With the willing co-operation of a number of universities, Professor Magalhaes drew up an ambitious program. Our team of twenty-one academics conducted symposia at sixteen universities in three weeks. Some were evening seminars; others were two-day events. The target audience were staff and students dealing with international politics. The visit ran at a helter skelter pace and we had little time for sight-seeing.

Once the Indonesian government got wind of the conferences, it ramped up what leverage it had in the United States, generally through business contacts, so that our host universities were put under pressure to withdraw their invitations. Despite threats to curtail

---

5   ETAN was the most influential of the US-based advocacy groups seeking to overturn US policy that was enabling the Indonesian regime to ignore the human rights of the East Timorese. By 1997 it had a national membership of 8000 and a permanent office in Washington dedicated to changing US foreign policy so that the human rights of the East Timorese under the UN *Declaration of Human Rights* were honored.
6   At the time, long-running, UN-brokered negotiations between Portugal and Indonesia had yet to reach any definitive conclusion.

donations, only one university succumbed to this pressure, claiming that a conference there was simply 'too hot to handle'.[7]

★

Our team assembled in New York in early February. The first of three conferences held in the city was at the New School University. Barbedo, our leader, soon discovered to his dismay that our hosts wanted to play a very active role in the presentations. They were particularly keen to speak on US foreign policy with respect to Asia, and the controversy raging at the time about whether or not human rights was a Western concept that needed to be re-interpreted in terms of 'Asian values'. We had little option but to accommodate our hosts in the matter.

With the stage being shared, we decided that wherever possible our principal speakers would be the Indonesian and East Timorese members of the party. The rest of us would support them in question and answer sessions. I took questions on the roles played by the Catholic Church in East Timor, Indonesia, and Australia, Vatican diplomacy and influence, and the work of the ETHRC in documenting human rights violations in East Timor.

Jose Ramos Horta, as Nobel Laureate, was the drawcard. Americans love a celebrity and Jose, ever articulate, and with dark good looks, was well suited to the role. He was successfully backed up by the equally articulate George Aditjondro, an Indonesian sociologist and journalist whose special field was political corruption in Indonesia.[8] Other members of the group included FRETILIN representative, Mari Alkatari, who flew in from Mozambique where he was living in exile, Joao Carrascalao, UDT leader living in exile in Sydney, and Kastoriius Singa representing Indonesian NGOs working in East Timor. The two most vulnerable members of our group were Armindo Maia, then a senior figure at Dili University, and Arlindo Marcal who had spent 1975-79 in the hills under FALINTIL protection, but was then residing in Dili.

★

While Barbedo was disgusted by the way the US academics were 'hogging the podium', I tried to mollify him by pointing out that what they had to say was quite relevant to the main thrust of our mission. We could not change American policy if we did not know what it was, and more importantly, if we did not know why it was the way it was. We had to listen as well as to speak our own truth.[9] The New School conferences provided me

---

7 My host at the Jesuit University of San Francisco confided that the university lost $500,000 in donations because it hosted the conference.
8 George Aditjondro has built his academic reputation documenting corruption in successive Indonesian administrations. In 1995 he published *In the Shadow of Mount Rameleu* (Lieden: INDOC, 1994), an expose of corruption in East Timor. This so incensed the Suharto regime that he was refused re-entry into Indonesia, and at the time of the conference was in Australia seeking an academic position which he subsequently found at the University of Newcastle as a teacher of sociology.
9 As these early speakers put the situation: from 1965 onwards the US had not developed specific policy with respect to Indonesia as the government there was doing precisely what the Americans were doing in Vietnam, fighting the spread of communism in Asia. However, things now needed to change with the emergence of a democracy movement in the country, and the corrosion of the Suharto regime from within. Nevertheless, US strategic interest still lay in supporting Suharto despite his government's appalling human rights record, because of the access Indonesia gave US nuclear submarines moving between the Pacific and Indian oceans. There was therefore a limit to what delegations such as ours could achieve.

with the chance to meet with Boston-based journalist Arnold ('Arnie') Kohen who was putting the final touches to his biography of Belo.[10] We spent a good two hours discussing our mutual friend.

Our second venue in New York was at Columbia University. The Indonesian Consul General invited Indonesians studying in New York to attend this conference and to question the speakers. The daughter of the Indonesian Ambassador to the UN was, I remember, particularly vocal at these sessions. Around 4:00pm a group of Indonesians arrived whom local ETAN activists identified as INTEL agents. The group was to be our constant companions as we moved around the United States conspicuously taking notes as well as photographing us as we spoke. There was little that we could do to prevent this even though the clear intention was to intimidate.

★

From New York we flew to Washington for hearings of the House of Representatives Committee on Human Rights. Both Armindo Maia and Arlindo Marcal spoke to the situation in East Timor, detailing major human rights violations. George Aditjondro pointed out to the committee members the danger this placed them in. The chair indicated that the US Ambassador to Indonesia would advise the Indonesian authorities that he was monitoring their return and would report back to the Human Rights Committee if needed.[11]

My next conference was as a member of the delegation heading for Johns Hopkins University in Baltimore. Following this I flew with Arlindo Marcal to San Francisco where conferences had been organised at Berkeley and the University of San Francisco (USF). The Jesuits, who run the latter university, acted as my hosts.

When we reached the West coast, the Indonesian agents following us grew in temerity, demanding that they be able to videotape the conference at Berkeley. It was perhaps a measure of how sensitive Jakarta was becoming to the impact of our visit that the government flew in four East Timorese pro-integration agitators for these conferences. Their task seemed to be to disrupt us, if possible. Their tactics, however, were so heavy-handed and obvious that their efforts proved counter-productive. Their presence did have one desired effect; it made the two members of our group who had to return to East Timor increasingly edgy.[12]

To counter Indonesian tactics, the organisers at USF created space in the morning program for the pro-integration group to make their case. This was rather coolly received. Ramos Horta, on the other hand, was feted and awarded the University Medal for his outstanding record in defending human rights.

★

---

10 Kohen's biography was eventually published under the title *From the Place of the Dead* in June 1999.
11 Congressman Patrick Kennedy was as good as his word. When Arlindo and Armindo arrived in Denpasar, they were greeted on arrival by two visiting US politicians signaling to the Indonesians that, as far as the US was concerned, they were 'off limits' in regard to Indonesian harassment.
12 In presenting the case for self-determination in East Timor we chose to speak about the story unfolding there in a non-political way, focusing on the human story and its consequences, thus minimising the risk to our East Timorese participants.

Following the USF conference, the East Timorese and Indonesian members of our group departed for home. The remaining team members flew north to beautiful Vancouver, nestled between the snow-capped mountains and the sea, to speak at conferences organised at Simon Fraser University and the University of British Columbia. This was more difficult territory than the United States had been. Canada had important links with Indonesia through the gold trade, but few, if any, East Timorese were living there. Furthermore, the churches in Canada generally lacked a social justice tradition, so human rights did not seem to figure prominently in either the national or churches' agendas. Our aim was to lift the profile of human rights in academic circles in order to expand debate on the matter. The conferences in Canada focused on human rights. Our Canadian hosts wanted us to explore both the claim that human rights are not universal and the issue of how much credence should be give to the 'Asian values' argument in formulating foreign policy.

We were fortunate that Geoffrey Robinson, a historian from the University of California Los Angeles (UCLA) had been invited to join us to speak to this topic. He was able to demonstrate from a historical perspective that 'Asian values' such as 'consensus' and 'harmony', widely employed by the Suharto and other regimes in South East Asia to justify the abuse of individual human rights, are not prime values in any Asian culture. He made the point that, as a general principle, Asians place greater stress on *collective human rights* rather than on *individual human rights*, as is the case in the West. In this context, the East Timorese people's assertion of their right to self-determination was an affirmation of such a collective right. His was the clearest exposition of the 'Asian values' issue that I had heard. It was a pity this input came at the end of our tour and not at the beginning. Robinson would go on to play an important role as a UN political officer working for the UN in East Timor in 1999. But more of this later.

Ramos Horta flew in for our final seminar at the University of British Columbia. He looked exhausted after three weeks of conferences. He was exasperated at being constantly followed around by Indonesian agents and their paid hecklers. He commented to me that he now knew what if felt like to be stalked. However, he brought good news: members of our team flying back to New York would meet the UN Secretary General, the UN Rapporteur on East Timor, Jamsheed Marker, and members of their respective staffs.

★

On our last night together the Portuguese Consul invited us to be his guests at dinner. This gave me a chance to exchange impressions with Barbedo Magalhaes before we headed home. While we had both been horrified by the lack of morality evident in foreign policy in both the US and Canada, we could see that important policy shifts were underway. Media coverage of our visits had been disappointing, but this was understandable. Academics do not generate media coverage as a rule. They are usually cast in the role of responders.

Barbedo recognised that the battle for ideas was still there to be won and we were bullish about having made an important contribution, at least at the academic level, where the battle had been most keenly joined. The efforts that the Indonesians had made to disrupt and to intimidate members of our party encouraged us greatly.

★

I arrived home just in time for Easter where a letter from Sr Josephine Mitchell, the head of the Mary MacKillop Institute in East Timor, was waiting for me. Josephine wished to know how the conferences had gone. In replying I was able to tell her how fulsomely the Institute's work in developing resources to support teaching in Tetum in East Timor had been acknowledged by speakers at our conferences. I captured my feelings at the time as follows:

> I came home exhausted but I believe the international work was worthwhile as a contribution to sensitising American and Canadian public opinion about East Timor. With virtually no East Timorese living in the United States or Canada, with an economy that is heavily tied into the Indonesian economic scene, and with policy traditions totally lacking in moral principle, we were moving in a scene rather different from the one in Australia. I think we agreed that the United States scene is one of the keys to any East Timorese efforts towards self-determination.[13]

Another letter awaiting me was from Cardinal Tom William's secretary in Wellington asking whether or not it would be politic for him to visit Belo in East Timor. Due to difficulties in marrying the Cardinal's timetable to Belo's the visit did not occur until August 1999.

★

When one is involved in major consciousness-raising efforts, one cannot help but wonder from time to time whether these are having any effect at all. Encouragement to continue sometimes comes from an unexpected source. In my case it was from Bob Santamaria's *News Weekly*.

In early May I had participated in the first of a number of public marches made in support of some 1400 East Timorese refugees whose status as refugees was under legal challenge by the Australian Immigration Department. Prior to leaving for the United States I had been part of a delegation to meet the then Immigration Minster, Phillip Ruddock, in Canberra to discuss their plight. The meeting was very inconclusive. Ruddock came across as a welded-on bureaucrat with little sympathy for the plight of actual people. The marches sought to put pressure on the Federal Government over the issue, complementing the efforts of the sanctuary movement that ensured the East Timorese refugees in question were hard to find while their status was being argued in the courts. More about this important element in Australia's history, in the next chapter.

One of *News Weekly's* subscribers had been offended by my participation in the marches expressing the view that I, as a Catholic bishop, ought to have better things to do with my time. Accompanying his letter was a four-page article from the magazine sent to show me the error of my ways. It was written by Fr Tom Michel, a Jesuit based in Jakarta and was entitled 'East Timor: The Facts, the Fictions.'[14] Fr Michel's piece begins:

---

13 Hilton Deakin, personal diary, 1997.
14 *News Weekly*, May 31, 1997.

> East Timor has been very much in the news in the past year. The vast majority of reports focus on incidents of conflict between the East Timorese people and Indonesian authorities, and most are written from a particular point of view, either that of condemning human rights abuses, of challenging Indonesian sovereignty over the region or both. This overwhelming mass of information, however, is subject to the criticism of being one-sided. When was the last time anyone saw a newspaper or magazine article or a television news report that raised the possibility that integration (ie Indonesian sovereignty over East Timor) of the region with Indonesia has perhaps had some positive effects, much less that culturally-sensitive integration might be viable and could perhaps even offer the best hopes for the future of the region and its inhabitants?[15]

He goes on to make the point that

> ... the politically correct position today advocates the immediate Indonesian withdrawal from the region or, at least, acquiescence in the results of an immediate internationally-supervised referendum, which critics of integration expect to favour East Timorese independence.

The article then provides one of the better presentations of the pro-integration case I have read. At the conclusion Fr Michel identifies four conditions to be met if integration is to be successful: the military presence has to be reduced; the rule of law strengthened; transmigration limited; and training programs must be offered for Indonesians assigned to East Timor to lower the barriers which cultural and religious difference raise – all sensible measures. He concludes:

> The integration of hearts is a process that must take account of the fact of more than three centuries of a different colonisation, which has left East Timorese with their own sensitivities and organisation of social life. A way must be found for East Timorese to make their voices heard, as Indonesians, on matters of importance to them, a way of taking pride in their identity as a people and, as such, becoming by conviction, not only in fact, one of the constitutive peoples of Indonesia.[16]

Like so many interpretations of the situation in East Timor, this intervention was made following a short visit to East Timor, in this case a week's tour facilitated by the Indonesian authorities which, while diligently spent, merely scratched the surface of a much more complex reality. Fr Michel bought uncritically into the 'civil war' fiction, the centrepiece of Indonesian propaganda in 1975, and propaganda holding that FRETILIN killings were on a par with those of the Indonesian military. His further criticism that the East Timorese react strongly to 'trivial incidents', understated the situation by a long shot. I have no doubt about the good faith with which Fr Michel made his intervention. It reflected views I have heard expressed by other Jesuits and even by some diocesan clergy in East Timor. It also reflected Vatican thinking at the time.

---

15 Ibid, 11.
16 Ibid, 15.

The problem with this and similar analyses was that they denied obvious realities. The military's presence in the province was as much driven by the economic interests of its leaders as by any security concerns. Withdrawal would threaten those interests. The rule of law remained non-existent as long as the military could act with impunity and no one held them accountable for their actions. The Indonesians had attempted to 'soften' transmigration by giving preference to Catholics, but this did not lower local resentments in the face of the unequal competition for land and jobs that denied locals opportunity. The underlying problem of cultural and religious differences was perhaps the greatest problem to overcome. The Javanese, whether religious or lay, generally regarded the East Timorese as a race inferior to themselves and it was simply unthinkable to them that the East Timorese could defy their military and achieve independence. No 'course' could address this implicit racism as it was not acknowledged as an issue by the Indonesians even though it was obvious to outside visitors. The prospect of any, let alone all, of these suggestions being implemented was grim. What then were the future prospects of 'successful integration'?

As I read the article, what struck me – the unintended consequence if you like – was how the momentum of public opinion was changing. Those defending integration now felt that it was they who were on the back foot. This was encouraging news indeed in 1997. I set off for my various involvements in solidarity with the East Timorese with a spring in my step!

★

While I was settling back into my usual episcopal routine in Melbourne, others were on the move and their journeys helped build the growing international pressure for the Indonesian Government to honor the East Timorese people's right to self-determination. In May Belo travelled to Portugal for the 80th anniversary of the appearance of Mary at Fatima. Devotion to Our Lady of Fatima is a central part of the Portuguese religious legacy in East Timor. In Lisbon Belo was given a hero's welcome. However, people could not understand why he was disinclined to make public comments on the situation in his home country or why he turned down the Order of Liberty when it was offered to him by the President. As Kohen points out, Belo could not be seen accepting an honour from Portugal, Indonesia's arch-enemy in diplomatic circles, without inviting some form of retaliation against his own people.[17] While Belo was not a politician, he had, and needed to have, acute political instincts.

Following his time in Portugal Belo travelled first to Ireland and then England where debate was raging over the government's supplying arms and aircraft to the Indonesians. Speaking in Liverpool Belo pleaded:

> Please I beg you, restrict still further the conditions under which this trade is permitted. Do not sustain any longer a conflict which, without these sales, could never have been pursued in the first place, nor for so long.[18]

---
17 Kohen, 248.
18 Ibid, 249.

From England Belo moved to Italy and was well received in Salesian strongholds there. He visited Assisi where the rector of the local community wished to make him an honorary Franciscan! His final stop was the United States. There he was given a standing ovation at the Catholic Bishops' Conference in Kansas City. His subsequent meeting with President Clinton at the White House was affable. When Clinton asked him 'Why are the Indonesians still in East Timor?' Belo's reply was simple – 'Oil'!

Belo's meeting with Clinton had an interesting aftermath. On returning to Dili, Belo was summoned to Jakarta to be questioned about the interview. When Washington was alerted to this development, a protest was delivered to the Indonesian government and the matter quietly dropped.[19]

★

Nelson Mandela was another person on the move in 1997. In July he accepted an invitation to visit Indonesia and, in the course of the visit, met with Xanana Gusmao. As the *AustralAsian* reported at the time, Xanana was picked up from jail at 8:00pm and driven to the Presidential palace. He was welcomed to dinner by the South African President and the two leaders talked for two hours.

> What did the dinner mean? Certainly it was an extraordinary publicity coup for East Timor activists. Ever since Xanana's arrest in November 1992 they have likened him to Mandela – leader of a liberation movement, captured and jailed only to emerge (hopefully!) victorious due to world pressure possibly decades later.
>
> Having the two sit down in those august surroundings might suggest Suharto doesn't object to the parallel.
>
> However, did Suharto really 'blink' in the face of world pressure? … Or was he just being polite to his prominent guest, who had asked for the meeting?…[20]

Once it was discovered to have taken place, the meeting in the guesthouse of the Presidential palace was widely covered in the international press.[21] Subsequent events suggest this was Mandela's intention. Nelson Mandela was clearly impressed by the CNRM (National Council of the Maubere Resistance) leader, and when he said so publicly, Xanana's standing in the world rose appreciably.

Mandela travelled to Europe later in the year to attend *Forum 2000*, a gathering in conference of Nobel Peace laureates. Belo also attended. The meeting had two important outcomes for East Timor. The first was a statement of support on self-determination signed by all the laureates present, and the second was Mandela's invitation for Belo to visit South Africa. This he took up later in the year.

★

---

19   Ibid, 251.
20   Gerry van Klinken 'Mandela and Xanana meet face-to-face' *AustralAsian,* August 8, 1997.
21   The meeting was initially kept secret until it was 'scooped' by an Indonesian weekly several days later.

While Jose Ramos Horta is rightly credited for his activism in the East Timorese cause, his actions were driven primarily by a political motivation. Belo took a different tack which he highlighted on many occasions. He participated in the struggle as a pastor concerned for the welfare of his people. His advocacy was based on the moral premise that the human rights of his people, both collective and individual, needed to be respected because this was a condition of peace. There could be no peace without reconciliation, and he worked tirelessly to bring this about in the face of insuperable odds. His message did have political consequences but this was not what drove him to travel around the world speaking, where and when he could, on behalf of his people.

The two men, although joint winners of the Nobel Peace Prize and committed to a common cause, rarely appeared together. Each went about things in his own way and operated within his own ambit of concern. However their efforts did complement each other in building international support for what had been considered for many years a lost cause. The Nobel Peace Prize proved something of a game-changer which both exploited to the full. Belo's award put noses out of joint in the Vatican where acknowledgement of his achievement was largely downplayed. I felt privileged to have known and worked closely with both men and regard them as friends.

Fr Michel's claim that Belo 'personally supported integration' is partly true. Belo's support for integration was always conditional —'if that is what the people choose'. This qualification is important as it implies that the people needed to make an actual choice. This could not happen without an act of self-determination. As 1997 drew to a close, the international community was moving closer to recognizing their right to choose. The huge effort by supporters in many countries to raise awareness about the plight of a small people on the edge of Asia was at last bearing some fruit. While 'change in Jakarta' was the goal of such activism and advocacy, Indonesia had not yet reached the tipping point needed for this to happen. Providentially, this came when the Asian financial crisis hit the country and gave the international community the leverage it needed to effect long overdue 'change in Jakarta'.

East Timor was to be both the beneficiary and victim of this change. The lesson of 1996–7 was that consciousness-raising is a necessary preliminary in bringing about significant change. The battle for minds has to be won before other battles can be engaged.

CHAPTER 24
AN ODD LITTLE CHAPTER

The Australian churches have played an important role in the East Timor story. They can be proud of their support for East Timorese refugees living here in Australia. In future years, however, people writing about Australia's refugee policy will no doubt speak of its inconsistency and its haphazard morality. Certainly, the East Timorese have been victims of its eccentricity, and the churches have done much to redress some of its impacts.

As noted earlier, in 1942 Australian troops effectively invaded East Timor in order to head off the Japanese and succeeded in holding them at bay there for two years. The Australians then withdrew, taking with them some 600 Portuguese nationals and their dependants, including Bishop Goulart, his clergy, and some religious sisters. The East Timorese who supported the Australian commandos were left to their fate as they did not fit the criteria of this country's now notorious 'white Australia policy'.[1] Some 20,000 people died in East Timor as a consequence of Japanese reprisals, setting up hatreds within the country that would last for generations. The Japanese, following the earlier Portuguese example, recruited some tribal groups within East Timor and armed them to wipe out others. This decision of the Australian government to abandon the people, with its terrible consequences, is not something that Australians can easily walk away from or forget. It is a regrettable part of our history.

With the end of World War II, Australia welcomed refugees from southern Europe, and later eastern Europe. These went on to make a significant contribution to national life and the evolution of Australian culture. When Vietnamese boat people began arriving in Australia following the defeat of the American-backed South Vietnamese forces in 1975, the country welcomed them as courageous heroes fleeing communist tyranny. Again, when the Indonesians invaded Dili and boat loads of East Timorese made the comparatively short journey to Darwin, the country welcomed them as we did 20,000 Chinese students in 1989 following the massacre in Tienanmen Square. All of this is a very positive story of a national government capable of compassion towards refugees from the region. However, the story began to turn sour in 1993 when, under the Keating Government, decision-making at the national level began to move from compassion to legal rigidity (and there it seems to have remained since). Since the East Timorese were the first group caught up in this change, events surrounding their situation are part of their story as well as part of

---

1   The White Australia policy was gradually unwound beginning in 1966, as successive Federal Governments became sensitive to its racial overtones. It had effectively lapsed by 1973.

the Australian story. The churches' engagement with East Timor here, while alluded to in previous chapters, is worth drawing out in more detail.

★

Up until 1993, the Australian Government welcomed East Timorese refugees without reservation. The refugees were made up of two distinct communities, indigenous and mestizo Timorese and ethnic Chinese. The East Timorese came in relatively small numbers at first.[2] Some came direct from East Timor and some were resettled in Australia via the family reunion mechanism after originally seeking refuge in Portugal. Following the 1975 invasion of East Timor, some 1600 East Timorese were given permanent residency in Australia. Three hundred of these lived in Melbourne. A decade later the number in Melbourne had increased to nearly 3000. In the period 1990 to 1997, another 4000 East Timorese-born arrived in Australia seeking refuge.[3] Almost half of this community were Catholic.

It may have been this rapid growth in numbers that alarmed the national government as its attitude towards the Timorese hardened appreciably from 1993 onwards when claims for refugee status began to be turned down by the Department of Immigration and Ethnic Affairs and, on appeal, by the Refugee Review Tribunal.[4]

Since a goodly number of the Timorese refugees in Australia were Catholic, the women and children among them received support from the Church, in particular, from religious sisters involved in parish work and schools. The crackdown in 1993 and subsequent years was viewed by these helpers as discriminatory and the Australian Sanctuary Movement[5] was initiated by Sr Kath O'Connor in Sydney in response. Those signing up to the movement were prepared to break the law by hiding any refugees who were refused asylum on the grounds that they were Portuguese citizens – the ruse then being used by the Government to deny their claims. By 1997, when things came to a head, some 10,000 Australians had joined a movement that had become ecumenical and operated nation-wide.

This was a major line of Church support. Another line was that the churches followed closely legal challenges to the rulings of both the Immigration Department and the Refugee Review Tribunal, a process that began in June 1995 after other avenues to influence government policy had been exhausted.

I have previously mentioned our meeting with Minister Ruddock in 1997. While I was in the United States a further delegation of religious leaders met with him. It was suggested that the 1400 or so East Timorese whose cases were under review be treated like the 20,000 Chinese had been in the Hawke era – by way of a 'special program'. While the Minister seemed open to this proposal it was rejected when taken to Cabinet after six months consideration. By this time, thirty cases were on appeal before the Federal

---

2   For instance, the Timorese-born community in Victoria peaked in 2006 at 5014.
3   Origins: Migrant Communities in Victoria at http://museumvictoria.com.au/origins.
4   Some East Timor activists argued that the change of direction was made to appease the Indonesians. If this were the case then it is hard to see why it did not happen much sooner.
5   The original Sanctuary Movement was established by religious congregations in the United States in the 1980s to protect refugees from Central America, most of whom were Catholic, and fleeing from oppressive regimes supported by the US government. A number of US religious were murdered in Central and South America by these regimes in the 1980s without their home government taking any action.

Court. It could take years to resolve them, particularly if any were appealed to the High Court. The government sought to cut off this avenue by changing the Immigration Act to curtail such appeals for those who had not already instigated legal action, and by imposing a $1000 fee on those who did. Removing the Asylum Assistance Allowance was to be a further step down this punitive path. The Howard Government inherited this legal legacy when it came to power in 1996.

*

Government Ministers do not have to wait for directions from the courts to effect their decisions. Much can be achieved by regulation and this was the way in which the Howard Government chose to move. Its tactic was to threaten to withdraw funding for the Asylum Seeker Assistance Scheme which provided an allowance to asylum seekers through the Red Cross. Under the proposed changes, the allowance could not be paid to a refugee once the Department of Immigration had refused his or her application and before any appeal could be made to the Refugee Review Tribunal. The financial hardship this placed on the refugees was unconscionable. It meant, in effect, that the costs of supporting the East Timorese refugees shifted from the government to an already impoverished East Timorese community, or to the Church agencies supporting them.

In October 1997 one appeal that I followed against a decision of the Refugee Review Tribunal came before Justice Finkelstein in the Federal Court in Melbourne.

*

The case says a lot about the way people in the Immigration Department were thinking at the time. The reasoning behind the actions of both the Keating and Howard governments was as follows: Any person born in East Timor before 1975 was in fact a Portuguese national by virtue of his or her birth. As of 1975, and Australia's subsequent recognition of Indonesian sovereignty over East Timor, that person also became an Indonesian national, and so held dual nationality. If a person with dual nationality is oppressed by the government of one of the countries to which he or she is a citizen, then under international law, it is the responsibility of the other country to offer him or her protection.

East Timorese seeking asylum in Australia were seeking protection from a third party when they had not exhausted their claims on Portugal, so Australia had no obligation to provide them protection or assistance. In other words since the East Timorese were under no threat in Portugal, there was no obligation on Australia to offer them protection, and therefore their claim for such protection could be refused. Such was the gist of the government's case.

There were some obvious difficulties with this argument on historical and moral grounds. In 1942 when the Australian government had repatriated its troops from East Timor, it also repatriated 'Portuguese nationals' and their dependants. The East Timorese were not then regarded as 'Portuguese nationals' by the Australian government. The moral argument was that many of those whose cases were being appealed before the courts had been living in Australia for between two and seven years. They had never been to Portugal, had no relatives there, and did not speak the language. Deporting them to Portugal against their will would involve unconscionable personal hardship.

Courts, however, do not work on moral grounds but on legal grounds, and so arguments have to fall within the relevant legal parameters. The test case mounted by Lay Kon Tji, an East Timorese of Chinese descent, turned on the issue of whether or not he could be considered to be a Portuguese national under the terms of international law. The Portuguese government, while not a party to the case, made a number of important contributions to the facts on which the matter was decided.

Prior to the April Revolution in 1974, Portugal was a fascist country. With the overthrow of the regime, Portugal adopted a new democratic constitution and in doing so, reformulated its relationship with its former colonies many of which had since gained their independence. While Portugal's former colonies were now independent, they remained culturally tied to Portugal within the loosely federated Lusophone world. Under the 1975 constitution Portugal granted citizenship to people born in the colonies on the condition that they requested it. In other words, under current Portuguese law a person born in the colonies had to request to become a Portuguese citizen and such requests are considered on a case-by-case basis. So while it was possible for a person from former colonies to have dual citizenship, this did not come as their birthright, but by favour of the state of Portugal. The Portuguese position was that:

> ...(its law) was not designed to assimilate people into the Portuguese nation but rather to avail them of a free choice to live in Portugal until something better comes along for them.
>
> The Portuguese regard this as an option for the East Timorese. Portugal would not want any suggestion or announcement that there has been an agreement forged between Australia and Portugal to force the East Timorese to Portugal.[6]

★

The case was held over from initial hearings in late October 1997 until June 1998 when the judge reserved his decision.

The East Timor refugees heard about the renewed proposal to remove the Asylum Assistance Allowance only after the preliminary hearing in October 1997. So on November 6th acting on their behalf I wrote to the heads of the major religious denominations outlining the situation and pointed out that the Minister was trying to achieve by regulation what he may not be able to achieve legally, that is to reduce people to such a state of penury that they would be forced to agree to move to Portugal. In part, my letter read:

> ...These refugees fled from military oppression in East Timor and have been in Australia between two and seven years struggling to secure refugee status here and to begin rebuilding their lives. For the past two years the Australian Federal Government has been attempting to deport these asylum seekers to Portugal.

---

6   Judgement in the Federal Court of Australia Victoria District Registry, Lay Kon Tji versus Minister for Immigration and Ethnic Affairs, 30th October 1998, 22.

> It has taken a range of steps to hasten and secure deportation including the removal of right of appeal to the Federal and High Court of Australia and also through severely questionable interference with the structure and operation of the Refugee Review Tribunal.

I went on to point out that once the resources of the East Timorese community were exhausted in supporting applicants denied government assistance, then the burden would fall on Church agencies. My belief was that the regulation would not be actioned before Christmas as this would put the government in a very bad light. Rather, it would be actioned in the dead news cycle period after Christmas when Australians were on holiday.

Portugal had made it clear a number of times through its ambassador that it would not accept East Timorese refugees if they did not want to go willingly, so it seemed likely that a stalemate would be the most likely outcome of legal proceedings. This would have a devastating effect on the refugees denied both protection and assistance.

There seemed two practical measures that religious leaders could take. The first was to encourage their people to contribute to the sponsorship appeal about to be launched by the Sanctuary Movement. Such support would give it the financial resources needed to have refugees go to ground in both Melbourne and Sydney. Jose Ramos Horta had volunteered to launch this fund, if it were needed, on 21st December. The second measure was that we hold a joint media conference of religious leaders prior to Christmas in support of the asylum seekers likely to be denied assistance. Concerning this I wrote:

> I believe it is imperative that we speak out strongly in advance of the Government removal of ASAS (Asylum Seekers Assistance Scheme), in order to build pressure and prevent this happening, and to move towards a just settlement of this issue. Details of the media conference will be media-released across Australia and internationally. If you should choose to participate, I will provide further briefings on the issue and will devise a range of angles between participants to avoid duplication in what each says on the day.[7]

The letter was sent to Keith Rayner Anglican Archbishop of Melbourne, Cardinal Edward Clancy Catholic Archbishop of Sydney, Bishop Michael Boyd Challen executive director of the Brotherhood of St Laurence, Rev Pamela Kerr Uniting Church Moderator, Rev Tim Costello Baptist Minister, and Rabbi John Levi. With it I sent a press release from David Scott AO, former President of the Australian Council of Social Services, Director of both the Brotherhood of St Laurence and of Community Aid Abroad, outlining all the steps that the Australian Government had taken since 1993, including the steps discussed above, to strip East Timorese refugees of their rights. Coming from such an authoritative source this made grim reading indeed.[8]

★

---

[7] Bishop Hilton Deakin Auxiliary Bishop, Catholic Archdiocese of Melbourne to Most Rev. Keith Rayner Anglican Archbishop of Melbourne, 6th November, 1977.
[8] David Scott AO 'Ashamed to be Australian' Press Release 16th October 1997.

In writing as I did I was aware that it would be difficult to get all of these people to the one place at the one time pre-Christmas, given their existing commitments. I knew that I would be out of the country from mid-November till early December on Caritas business. However, it was essential that we defeat what I called the Government's strategy of 'deportation by deprivation' which was clearly immoral. Even if the press conference did not go ahead, the fact that it was known to be 'in the pipeline' could, in itself, produce an effect and cause politicians sensitive to public opinion to pause and think.

A decade on, the story of the Sanctuary Movement has largely been lost. But it was an extraordinary development that over 10,000 Australians nationwide, from across denominations and religious faiths, were prepared to break the law to support East Timor refugees by hiding them. While successive Australian governments turned a deaf ear to their plight, this was not the stance of the ordinary people who would eventually come out in their tens of thousands to protest against the government's lack of action. Neither was this the era of armchair advocacy when you protest by clicking buttons on computers in the comfort of your own home, and at no personal risk.

★

Support for self-determination in East Timor was gaining traction internationally in 1997 due to often ham-fisted attempts by the Indonesians to stifle discussion of the matter. The equally ham-fisted attempt by the Australian Government to side step its obligations to refugees galvanised advocates and supporters of East Timor in Australia. The general perception that the Australian Government was engaged in what David Scott called 'a continuing and humiliating deference to Indonesia'[9] was becoming an increasingly heavy burden for the government to carry.

On 30th October 1998 Justice Finkelstein handed down his decision finding for Lay Kon Tji, awarding costs to the government. The judge held that the Portuguese Government did not give the East Timorese Portuguese nationality automatically. So the Australian Government's argument that Tji was in fact Portuguese by birth failed. This being the case, Mr Tji was an Indonesian citizen at law who had applied to Australia for protection, and the Refugee Review Tribunal in arriving at the determination had erred. It would have to reconsider the matter. It was the outcome that we expected, but this did not stop the East Timorese refugees, their supporters and advocates, being relieved when the matter was finally settled.

In 1998 we thought the behaviour of the government with respect to East Timorese refugees to be out of character, legalistic and decidedly odd because of its lack of common humanity. Our history suggested we could do better. However, subsequent events have shown we were witnessing the early onset of a more dangerous sickness, one that would eventually result in people being detained indefinitely without committing any nameable crime, mass detention of women and children in what are in effect concentration camps, and forced repatriations. So perhaps we were not dealing with an 'odd little chapter' in our

---

9   Scott was in the last party of Australians to leave East Timor in 1975 just prior to the Indonesian invasion. He had been involved in the supply of emergency aid. He gives a graphic description of this experience in his book *Last Flight Out of Dili* (Melbourne: Pluto Press, 2005).

story at all, but with the emergence of an odd, indeed a deviant, national conscience in that, as Australians, we are in danger of simply accepting these things. By doing too little, we too easily allow ourselves to be dragged into the moral morass created by governments courting public opinion. In 2003 all cases of refugee status involving the East Timorese were quietly settled. This odd little chapter came to a close for them at least.

CHAPTER 25
PRELUDE TO A NIGHTMARE
1998-EARLY 1999

The real tipping point for 'change in Jakarta', as Fr Walter had earlier put the pre-condition for change in East Timor to me, was the 1997-98 Asian Financial Crisis. It is important to understand how this played out, and its consequences for both Indonesia and East Timor, if one is to make sense of events there in 1998 and 1999.

This financial crisis hit Indonesia harder and lasted longer than in other countries in the region because of the way it was managed both locally and internationally. In 1997 the crisis first engulfed Thailand. At the time Indonesia was viewed in the West as one of Southeast Asia's 'economic tigers'.

Suharto's grip on power had been maintained by granting monopoly rights to companies controlled by his family, the military and his cronies. As a consequence productivity remained low. Many businesses were financed by overseas borrowings, usually in US dollars. The banking sector acted as middleman in these loan transactions. With money easy to come by, property speculation was rife.

When the US Federal Reserve raised interest rates in 1997, there was a flow of investor capital back to the United States. This created a sudden shortage of US dollars for companies and banks in Asia. The consequent demand for US dollars could not be met and competition for those available saw the value of local currencies tumble. As companies defaulted on loans thus creating bad debts for the banks, they in turn failed. The resulting crisis engulfed most Southeast Asian economies.

When the crisis hit Indonesia, the government floated the rupiah which at the time was pegged to the US dollar. Instead of stabilising the situation, this decision saw its value go into free-fall. By the beginning of 1998, the worst year of the crisis, the Indonesian rupiah had lost 70% of its value against the American currency, and inflation was rampant in consequence.

When the price of basic commodities rose alarmingly, what began as a financial crisis quickly evolved into a social and political crisis, as the population protested the cost of basic commodities. To make matters worse, the collapse of some banks caused a run on those remaining solvent, adding to the crisis. People began to hoard food as a hedge against further price rises. A bad situation was made worse when drought hit.[1] The financial crisis

---

1   Some measure of the depth of the crisis can be gauged by comparing Indonesia's GDP and inflation rates in 1996 (prior to the crisis) and 1998. GDP growth in 1996 was 8%, in 1998 it was -13.6%. See Hal Hill *The Indonesian Economy,* second edition (London: Cambridge University Press, 2000), 264.

brought university students, always a potent force in Indonesian politics, out onto the streets in protest and the *reformasi* movement was born.

By early 1998, Indonesia was effectively bankrupt and forced to seek the assistance of the International Monetary Fund (IMF). The country needed a bail out of $43b.[2] In agreeing to this, the IMF imposed severe conditions. These included reform of the financial sector, closure of poorly performing banks, abolition of subsidies on items such as food and energy, and raising interest rates. The IMF was comparatively new to dealing with bankrupted countries and did not give sufficient weight to the likely political and social impacts of its 're-structure' proposals.

Cornered by local political pressure, Suharto reneged on the agreement and the IMF responded by withholding loan payments that were being made in stages. Suharto was forced to negotiate a second agreement. This came with the additional condition that he dismantle the patronage system, seen as an impediment to much-needed foreign investment and improved productivity – necessary conditions for a sustainable recovery.

At the height of this crisis Suharto, whose party had won the 1997 election, was given a seventh term as President by the Indonesian parliament. However, when the new cabinet was seen to include many of his old cronies, the country became a powder keg that exploded when the military shot four university students during a peaceful protest.

Pressed further by the IMF to reduce fuel subsidies, Suharto did so in a single step. This decision added to the growing disaffection with the regime and prompted popular riots in major towns across the archipelago, including Jakarta. Chinese businesses bore the brunt of popular anger. Properties were destroyed and over a thousand people killed before control was re-established.

On May 14th, in a move to placate public anger, Suharto sought to reshuffle his cabinet and, when his new proposals were rejected by the parliament, he stepped down. The recently elected Vice-president, B.J. Habibie, then took control and quickly came to terms with Indonesia's major creditors. His efforts saw the currency stabilise and this won him some much-needed political breathing space.[3] The new president had to juggle not only the financial crisis but also the popular demand for new elections, aware that real power in Indonesia rested not with the people, nor with the political parties, but with the generals.

★

The 1998 Asian crisis had little effect on the bulk of the population in East Timor who were subsistence farmers. The Indonesian authorities had made many attempts to lift agricultural productivity there, particularly coffee and rice, with little success. On my early visits to East Timor in the 1990s, I discovered that the farmers shared a pervasive sense that improving production simply meant creating more money for the military. As one put the matter to me: 'Why should we help the military buy more planes, bombs and bullets to kill us with?' Hard to argue with that!

Coffee is the most lucrative of the cash crops produced in East Timor. At the time of

---

2   With the advantage of hindsight, it is now generally agreed by economists that this early attempt by the IMF to address the situation only made it worse.
3   Habibie had a tenuous grasp on power. He lacked a strong political power base having become President by default. He was viewed by many as a transitional figure.

the invasion some 78,000 hectares were under cultivation. A decade later 27,000 hectares had been destroyed or abandoned. With little incentive for further investment, the west of the country was littered with what had once been small farms. The contribution that coffee production made to the province's economy was modest, of the order $12m.[4] This has to be set against the day-to-day cost of maintaining security which seems to have run at close to $1m per day, not to mention the additional cost of funding the civil service, education, health services and infrastructure.[5] In the face of a national economic crisis, it became increasingly untenable for Indonesia to maintain a military payroll of more than 20,000 men in East Timor, a province that contributed so little to the overall Indonesian economy.[6]

Habibie had limited knowledge of East Timor, and was apparently unaware of the extent of the military's commercial operations there. According to David Scott, he was much more sensitive than his military commanders to the shift in world opinion on Indonesia's human rights record, and in particular the need to 'settle the East Timor issue'. He was being pressed on the matter by the nation's major creditors.

★

The strengthening of the democracy movement and the call for *reformasi* across Indonesia in 1998 also had a significant impact on events in East Timor. Part of the popular demand for change was curtailing the political role of the military as Indonesia charted a path to democracy. Under the *Orde Baru* (Suharto's New Order) the Indonesian Armed Forces (ABRI) was allocated seats in the parliament and a number of generals and ex-generals served as ministers in the government. In addition, policing fell under the ABRI command[7] so that the policing function was compromised if it involved the misdeeds of military personnel. Separating the police from military control was seen as a necessary step in reform.

In preparation for its first democratic election, many of the limitations imposed on political activity during the Suharto years were removed. Early in 1998 Xanana Gusmao, now regarded widely as the 'Mandela of East Timor', seized the opportunity to bring the various political groupings committed to independence in East Timor into a single umbrella organisation, the CNRT (National Council of Timorese Resistance). He was declared the president of the new group and recognised internationally as a key player in all discussions about the future of his country. He was released from prison and put under house arrest and a stream of distinguished visitors met with him at this time including the US Secretary of State, Madeleine Albright.

The new political freedoms prompted a degree of chaos in Indonesia. Popular voices demanded *reformasi* - the removal of the corruption, collusion and nepotism (KKN as it

---

4   CIIR 'Prospects for an independent economy' Special supplement within *Timor Link* No 43, June 1998.
5   John Taylor *The Price of Freedom* (London: Zed Books, 1999), 16.
6   John Martinkus *A Dirty Little War* (Sydney: Random House, 2001), 81. Martinkus acknowledges information from Andrew McNaughtan who was able to access Indonesian pay records.
7   Prior to the Suharto regime coming to power, the military (army, navy and airforce) ran collectively under the acronym TNI. When Suharto came to power this was changed to ABRI. With the fall of the regime the older TNI title was reclaimed. These name changes generate a degree of confusion in reading the literature on East Timor.

was called) that had characterised the *Orde Baru*. There was a strong call for the reining in of the military's political power. Protests became more regular and drew larger crowds as the year progressed. The movement towards democracy divided the generals.

In this heady atmosphere political expression became more open, particularly among students enjoying the hurly-burly of the democratic process. Things came to a head in November 1998 when Habibie requested the armed forces to step in and 'restore' order in the face of escalating demonstrations. In a heavy-handed response, characteristic of the Suharto years, troops opened fire on student protestors using plastic bullets. Twelve were killed and another 200 wounded.[8] This event did little to improve Habibie's standing abroad and only added to his problems at home.

★

The political *aggiornamento* of 1998 had an important impact on East Timor as students studying in Jakarta and elsewhere in Indonesia began to return home. These became the catalyst for a local student-based political movement the long-term hope of which looked beyond democratic reform to independence.[9] It also permitted the formerly clandestine resistance movement to come out into the open.

The CNRT opened offices and set up a political infrastructure across the thirteen administrative regions that make up East Timor. This structure paralleled existing government administrative and military structures with offices or representatives working at the district, sub-district and village levels. Its members set about raising awareness among ordinary people about the options being proposed for the future and CNRT's own plan. They also began building up preliminary voter lists.[10]

In June 1998 President Habibie presented a conditional offer of 'special autonomy' within Indonesia at the Tripartite Talks underway at the UN. He had put this proposal to the Indonesian cabinet in 1997, but it was opposed by the military and so vetoed by Suharto.[11] The conditions attached to his new offer made it unacceptable to Portugal and the CNRT.

Habibie persisted, seeking the support of the Catholic Church and invited bishops Belo and Basilio do Nascimento, recently ordained Bishop of Baucau, to meet him in Jakarta. Anxious not to be caught up in a political contest, the two bishops conferred and released a joint statement setting out the local Church's view. They described Habibie's proposal as a 'transitional solution' to the situation in East Timor. The bishops argued that the 'security approach' to *integrasi* adopted by Indonesia had clearly failed, and that a new mechanism had to be put in place that would 'collect the aspirations of the entire society of East Timor, including guerrillas and people living in the diaspora'. This mechanism should provide a climate 'conducive to sincere and open dialogue between East Timorese

---

8 Matt Frei 'Habibie orders crack down on rioters' *Sunday Telegraph* (London), 15 November 1998.
9 The local student movement drew its membership from the small Dili University, the Polytechnic at Hera, and the Salesian agricultural college at Fatumaca, south of Baucau. These were the three main tertiary training facilities in East Timor.
10 CNRT used the same tactics that FRETILIN had used in 1974 in the lead-up to elections in order to establish a strong grass-roots base outside the major cities.
11 Hugh White 'The Road to INTERFET: Reflections on Australian Strategic Decisions Concerning East Timor, December 1998-September 1999' *Security Challenges* Vol 4, No 1, Autumn 2008, 71.

themselves and the central government'. The letter goes on to advocate the need to establish confidence-building measures such as improving the living conditions of East Timorese, liberation of political prisoners, and the teaching of Tetum in schools.[12]

Only Belo went to Jakarta. While he described his meeting with the new president as 'productive', the goodwill Habibie was trying to create was called into question internationally three days later when a high-level European Union delegation visiting East Timor witnessed a farmer shot dead and five other people wounded when the military opened fire on a crowd during a demonstration.[13] The delegation immediately cancelled the rest of its visit in protest, adding further to Habibie's many worries.[14]

★

Whereas previously the military had simply suppressed any form of dissent in East Timor, the emergence of political parties called for a different response and it took some time to work out what this should be. In the meantime, urban protests by young East Timorese became more common and more provocative, leading to large pro-independence rallies in Dili and elsewhere.[15] When in response Governor Soares threatened to sack any civil servants who showed pro-independence sympathies, a general strike ensued - something unheard of previously.

I arrived in Dili in September 1998 when this 'political spring' was in full blossom. My memories of the visit have faded somewhat except for one event. I travelled with a group of youths to a 'dialogue meeting' held at Ermera, one of the towns in the foothills of Mt. Ramelau, as part of the CNRT's voter education process. Our party travelled in open trucks and the meeting with villagers went well. The sense of excitement that things were changing was palpable, and the young people I travelled with were in great spirits. Returning home, and well out of range of the military, they sang their 'revolutionary' songs and out came the FRETILIN flags which they waved in the breeze as we roared along. The illegality of doing this only added to their sense of excitement. It was hard not to be caught up in the emotion of the moment, that is until you realised that these young men and women were celebrating something that we in Australia just take for granted – the right to political expression. I have often wondered in the years since how many of the young people I travelled with that day lived to see the independence that they so dearly valued.

Shortly after I left Dili, FALINTIL leader David Alex led a retaliatory FALINTIL attack on Indonesian troops stationed at Alas killing three and capturing a cache of weapons. Belo later told me that the Indonesian military responded by killing at least fifty people and possibly as many as one hundred. The number killed could not be confirmed as the area had been sealed while the bodies were disposed of.

As 1998 ended, the atmosphere in East Timor was very tense with repressive patterns of

---

12   CIIR 'Timorese bishops appeal to Habibie' (Translation of the text of their letter of 23 June 1998) *Timor Link* No 44 August, 1998, 8.
13   The group known as the 'EU Troika' consisted of the previous, current and next presidencies of the European Union, with the Netherlands standing in for Luxembourg. *Timor Link*, No 44, August, 1990, 1.
14   CIIR 'EU Troika sees Timorese reality' *Timor Link* No 44, August 1998, 1.
15   Belo deplored this development. In discussion I had with him he described it as 'suicidal'.

behaviour juxtaposed with the new realities of *reformasi*. People wondered what the future held. Hope seemed to be in the balance.

★

East Timor continued to be a political issue in Australia where the government's contradictory policy of appeasing the Indonesian government and its military on the one hand, while holding the position of the need for an act of self-determination at the UN on the other, had relatively little popular support. In 1998 Laurie Brereton, the opposition Foreign Minister and a prominent Catholic, convinced the Labor Party to throw its weight behind independence in East Timor. This stance had formerly been the party's policy. This change in direction had much popular support and enabled Brereton to attack the government over the issue.

With the fall of Suharto in August 1998, the Howard Government conducted a review of its regional foreign policy, a process that went on for some time. It concluded with the Prime Minister writing to the embattled Indonesian President on 19th December setting out what was in fact a coherent policy position – that Indonesia adopt the approach used by France in addressing the aspirations of the people of New Caledonia. There, after a period of local autonomy, the people were asked to vote on whether or not they wanted to stay as part of France. In the interim, the French government had the opportunity to engage with the locals and highlight the value of retaining links with France.

The implication of Howard's proposal was that East Timor remain part of Indonesia for several more years during which time the Indonesians would have the chance to convince the East Timorese of the value of that position. The proposal did not envisage independence. As White points out, the implicit assumption in this proposal was that such a strategy would be successful which was wishful thinking, and should have been recognised as such at the time.[16]

President Habibie initially rejected the new Australian position but, pressed on all sides, seems to have reconsidered it. His concern was that a protracted transition process, such as Howard was suggesting, would lead to sustained violence in East Timor. So if Indonesia was to embark down this path, the timeline needed to be short. On January 27th he announced that if the special autonomy being proposed for East Timor at the Tripartite Talks was not acceptable to the East Timorese, then he would suggest to the Indonesian parliament that East Timor be 'released' from Indonesia.

This move took everyone, the generals, the Indonesian Foreign Affairs Department, the Australian Government and the CNRT, by surprise.[17] In Australia, the decision led to the dusting off and refining of contingency plans already in place to cover what was then seen as the two most likely scenarios for East Timor. The first was that if independence came too quickly, there would be massive internal problems and Australia would be drawn into some form of peacekeeping operation needed to resolve them. The second was that the Indonesian military would subvert the referendum and so make it necessary to evacuate UN staff running the referendum. Both scenarios required that a peacekeeping

---

16 Hugh White, 72-3.
17 Ibid, 74

force be on standby as the international community would expect Australia to play a major role in it.[18]

*

Elements within the Indonesian military did not accept the new position of the central government and decided to subvert it. A number of interpretations of this decision have been made. Was it an attempt to reclaim the power the military enjoyed under Suharto but was now slipping away? Was it due to senior veterans whose careers had been shaped by the East Timor campaign being unwilling to admit that the policy of the Suharto years had been wrong? Did some generals see it as unthinkable to dishonour fallen comrades by walking away from the thousands of Indonesian soldiers buried in East Timor? A more cynical interpretation is that the generals did not want to miss out on the financial benefits to be had from East Timorese oil and gas. What seems sure is that their motives were both mixed and complex.

The available evidence indicates that *Operation Global Clean Sweep* (*Operasi Sapu Jagad*)[19] began to take shape almost as soon as Habibie put the 'special autonomy' option on the table in 1998, and was simply ramped up when this proposal was upgraded to include independence. The strategic aim of the operation was to use all available means to ensure that the UN supervised ballot was won by the pro-integration lobby. In line with this aim and across the rest of 1998 and into early 1999, the Indonesian Government's special forces known as Kopassus re-appeared in East Timor and began to revive and expand the existing militias, as well as create new ones.

*

To understand the subsequent role of the militias it is necessary to understand something of the way the Indonesian military was organised. Two sets of army troops were based in East Timor. The first were the ABRI 'territorials' or regular army that provided the main military structure across Indonesia. The territorials comprised two groups. The first was a permanent force made up mainly of East Timorese operating under Indonesian command. The second was made up of regular troops on rotation to East Timor, but drawn from all parts of Indonesia.

Working outside this structure were the elite troops in counter-insurgency (Kopassus and Kostrad) and military intelligence.[20] The police formed a third force also under military command. The police command had its own elite division known as Brimob (mobile

---

18 Ibid
19 Throughout the lead-up to the ballot Australian intelligence agencies monitored TNI signals and were well aware of what was happening. As the militia violence escalated, this information was leaked to the international press. *Operation Global Clean Sweep* was no secret and was outlined in some detail in the May 1999 edition of the TAPOL Bulletin. 'Tapol' means 'political prisoner' in Indonesian.
20 According to Robinson's report (2003) every major military decision-maker up to the level of government minister associated with the events of 1999, with the exception of General Wiranto, was either a member of Kopassus, or had a background in Kopassus. Geoffrey Robinson *East Timor 1999 Crimes Against Humanity* commissioned by the United Nations Office of the High Commission for Human Rights (OHCHR) http://www.cavr-timorleste.org/chegaFiles/finalReportEng/12-Annexe1-East-Timor-1999-GeoffreyRobinson.pdf

brigade), which functioned as the Indonesian Secret Police for most of the occupation period with all the connotations this name suggests. The unit's special field of endeavour in both Indonesia and East Timor was to eliminate protest movements, and it seems to have acquired a justified reputation for ruthlessness in doing so.

In April 1999 the police were removed from military control and placed under the Minister of Defence and Security. This made little difference to the overall command responsibility since General Wiranto was both commander-in-chief and Minister for Defence and Security.

★

The militias were created as a matter of national policy within Indonesia's counter-insurgency strategy and were not unique to East Timor. Parallel groups existed in all provinces where there was a separatist movement or political groupings that the military saw as a threat.

With 'pacification' in East Timor some of the older militias functioned as a reserve. The return of Kopassus officers in late 1998 and the formation of new militias marked a new phase in the struggle for independence. While the militias were presented to the international media as 'concerned citizens', most had Kopassus members embedded in their units and, when numbers were down, Indonesian troops were added. The new militias also included hundreds of 'volunteers' from West Timor. Some militia leaders were even given the rank of 'honorary members of Kopassus'.

In 1999 control of militias mainly lay with Kopassus or its affiliate, Military Intelligence. The military faction controlling events in East Timor sought to mobilise the full resources of Indonesia's counter-insurgency and military-intelligence capabilities to support the pro-integration cause. In the unlikely event that this cause did not prevail, they sought to so mire the result in controversy that it could credibly be challenged. Either way independence would be frustrated.

Geoffrey Robinson[21] traces the development of the militias in his report to the UN Human Rights Commission, noting particularly how they were funded. In 1999 the central government allocated $5.2m to what it termed a 'socialization' program that aimed at voter education as to the benefits of East Timor remaining part of the Republic.[22] These funds were allocated across the thirteen administrative districts. A good deal of the money was re-directed to funding local militias. Funds for this socialization program had originally been supplied by the World Bank to provide a safety net for those disadvantaged by cuts to subsidies. Also at the direction of the central government, *Bupatis* (district civil administrators) were required to adjust their local budgets to fund local militias. Money originally allocated for basic services was redirected. The military disbursed these funds as wages. Its own contribution was mostly in kind: transport, including the provision

---

21 Geoffrey Robinson was part of our delegation in Canada. He took leave from his position as Professor of History at UCLA to join UNAMET as a political officer. He would write the most definitive account of the violence in 1999 for the United Nations Commission of Human Rights entitled 'East Timor 1999: Crimes against Humanity' published in 2003 and available in pdf form at http://www.cavr-timorleste.org/chegaFiles/finalReportEng/12-Annexe1-East-Timor-1999-GeoffreyRobinson.pdf.
22 This seems a relatively modest investment given the wealth at risk in the Timor Sea.

of motorbikes; ten kilograms of rice per week per man; and automatic weapons and ammunition when these were deemed necessary.[23]

The militias were organised along strict military lines with a central command and district, sub-district and village level cadres. It is difficult to estimate just how many East Timorese were drawn into the new militias in 1999, but the final number was in the several thousands. While some chose to enlist because they were in favour of integration or to support their families, many were coerced into joining as those who failed to accept the 'invitation' to join were considered to be pro-independence supporters, and this could have disastrous consequences. The reason so many men fled their villages at the outset of the violence was to avoid being forced to join militias.

The level of coercion needed to get militia units up to strength created a trust problem when handing out automatic weapons. These were kept under tight control and collected after 'events' as a precautionary measure. Robinson suggests that any event in which automatic weapons were used had the prior sanction of the local territorial command, that provided logistical support, and Kopassus which provided strategic advice and, as needed, operational leadership.[24]

★

By April 1999 at least one militia had been created in all thirteen districts. In some cases the main militia group had subsidiary units operating under a different name at the sub-district or village levels. During the political spring of 1997 military intelligence units and *Brimob* had systematically compiled lists of pro-independence supporters. CNRT members, civil servants and student leaders were identified as targets for intimidation and elimination.

A second tactic was to make voter registration difficult by ensuring that people living in areas favouring independence were forced to flee from their homes and become internally displaced persons. This tactic was being implemented as Indonesian diplomats were negotiating terms for the 'consultation' with Portugal and the UN.

★

While some of the new militias required training to develop discipline and tactics, the older units had the capability to begin the campaign of intimidation early in 1999. The first district to come under attack was Liquica immediately west of Dili. By early April intimidation tactics there had resulted in some six thousand people being displaced due to a combination of violence, arson and rape.[25] Not knowing where to go, the people sought out church properties, police stations, the residences of prominent citizens, or fled to the hills believing that they would be safe there from further attack. Up until early 1999 Church leaders, such as Belo and Nascimento, had been able to negotiate with the district authorities to protect people seeking refuge in this way.

---

23 See Geoffrey Robinson 2003 'The Militias: Funding and material support', 112 ff.
24 Robinson, 7.
25 The intimidation followed a pattern of killings, beatings, burnings and rapes. The East Timorese tradition of mutilating opponents in times of conflict added to the terror. It did not require mass killings to terrorise powerless people. In this sense the violence while appearing random seems calibrated for effect.

Following these attacks on their villages, some two thousand people sought refuge in the parish church compound in the town of Liquica. On April 6th the local militia attacked the compound with the obvious knowledge and support of the local military and police who stood by. At least fifty-seven people were killed, some hacked to death with knives and machetes. Another thirty-five were wounded as people fled the violence.[26] The dead included women and children as well as students.[27] Most of the victims were shot after being driven from the church building by tear gas. Others who had sought shelter in the priest's house found themselves surrounded and trapped. The presbytery then became a killing field reminiscent of events in Rwanda.

When Belo went in a convoy the next day to visit the church to discover what had happened and to comfort his people, the convoy was set upon by the militia as he was leaving, and he was forced to make a quick retreat.[28] It was some months before he could keep his promise to the local people to return.

★

The motivation of the military in initiating the violence at Liquica may have been to derail the Tripartite Talks then underway, but it did not. Rather, it strengthened the Indonesian negotiating position by making the obvious point that if the UN and Portugal did not fall into line with Indonesia's wishes then the cost in human lives could be very high. The upcoming 'consultation' was going to occur on Indonesia's terms, or not at all.

The Agreement of May 5th 1999 set August 6th as the date for a ballot on self-determination. The international press and accredited observers would be present to ensure that the ballot was carried out in a way that was 'free and fair'. Portugal and UN negotiators had little option but to agree to the Indonesian police being in charge of security in the lead up to the referendum. As these were under General Wiranto's control, the TNI would be effectively in charge. The May 5th Agreement left little room to manoeuvre. John Howard found this out when he met with Habibie in Bali a few days later and raised the matter of the security of UNAMET (United Nations Mission in East Timor) personnel.

Australia's concern was that the UN negotiations had left the 'foxes in charge of the chook house'. Pressed on the matter, the Indonesian President did give ground, allowing an unarmed international police force to assist their Indonesian counterparts with security.[29]

★

The Liquica massacre also sent a message to those taking part in the CNRT's Strategic Development Conference at Victoria University in Melbourne called to plan

---

26 The parish priest told me that he and his assistant were detained by the police prior to the militia running amuck.
27 The actual number killed is unknown as it was not known who exactly was there, and the bodies of the dead were carried away in trucks, with some at least disposed of at sea. The numbers here are those of the respected human rights group Yayasan HAK (The Foundation for Law, Human Rights, and Justice), and quoted in Irena Cristalis *East Timor: A Nation's Bitter Dawn* (London: Zed Books, 2009), 130.
28 Journalist Irena Cristalis, who with her interpreter was part of the convoy, describes the event in her book *East Timor: A Nation's Bitter Dawn* in the course of which she acknowledges that people in the convoy really feared for their lives, so tense was the situation. Cristalis, 126-135.
29 Hugh White, 80.

independence.[30] The conference hoped to demonstrate to the world that East Timorese from across the political divide could work together to develop and implement the policies needed in an independent and autonomous state. It also sought to strengthen international perceptions that CNRT was the body best placed to represent the interests of the East Timorese in independence talks, and to confirm Xanana Gusmao's position as its leader.[31] The Australian Department of Foreign Affairs provided the funding necessary to bring forty-five East Timorese to Australia for the occasion. This was a very constructive contribution.

★

In establishing the militias, Indonesian military planners also sought to draw FALINTIL out in reprisals so that the 'civil war' myth used so effectively in 1975 could be revived, and the case for self-determination be undermined. However, this did not occur. In negotiations leading to the May 5th Agreement Xanana Gusmao agreed that FALINTIL would retire to four cantonments until after the ballot and, despite serious provocation, its discipline held.[32] This meant that the militias could act with impunity and FALINTIL was open to the charge that it had not protected the people when they needed it most.[33]

★

Under the terms of the May 5th Agreement, the 'consultation', as the referendum was formally known, offered the East Timorese two options: Option 1 was to enjoy autonomy within Indonesia; Option 2 was to reject autonomy in favor of independence. Responsibility for conducting the referendum was assigned to the UN's Department of Political Affairs. A new body, UNAMET (United Nations Mission in East Timor), led by Englishman Ian Martin, was created to supervise the referendum.[34] UNAMET raised the UN flag at its headquarters in Dili on June 4th and immediately began work as the timeframe for action was very tight.

UNAMET immediately recruited local East Timorese to staff its offices at the district level, so setting the processes of voter education and voter registration in motion. This was no easy task because of language difficulties and the fact that the number of internally displaced persons had risen sharply as the new militias set up early in 1999 became operational and the terror campaign expanded.

From the outset both Kopassus and Brimob identified local UNAMET employees as targets. The assumption was that they were pro-independence and a number were badly

---

30 The conference was the brainchild of Emilia Peres (local CNRT representative and one of the six Timorese who visited me in 1991) and Joao de Freitas, then completing his PhD at Victoria University.
31 David Scott *Last Flight out of Dili* (Melbourne: Pluto Press, 2005), 331.
32 The Indonesian negotiators agreed that their militias would do the same but this was never the case. They held elaborate ceremonies at which weapons were handed in only to be collected later, often to the amusement of the press covering such events.
33 At the height of the militia rampage some 10,000 people trekked to the FALINTIL cantonment at Uai Mori seeking protection.
34 Martin came to the post with impeccable credentials having already served a term as Secretary General of Amnesty International and as a senior UN field leader in trouble spots such as Haiti, Rwanda and Bosnia.

injured and some killed. Despite the threats the process of voter registration continued unabated. In some western regions the act of registering was initially viewed as treacherous. UNAMET staff in Maliana were given such a hard time that Ian Martin flew there and threatened to postpone the referendum indefinitely if the threats of violence continued. This had the desired effect.

*

Early in 1998 I had invited Belo to Australia to launch the Caritas Lenten appeal known as Project Compassion, which he did. I then left for Caritas Internationalis meetings in Rome and was there when UNAMET was established. I had no sooner arrived home in early June than it was necessary to depart almost immediately for PNG on Caritas business. So it was not until early August that I could travel to Dili. Belo met me at the airport and when we were able to talk privately he told me of the 'Garnadi Report,' a translation of which was then in circulation among the press. The report, written by a retired Indonesian General addressed issues associated with the upcoming referendum. The report identified the need for contingency plans to be developed to cover the eventuality that the East Timorese voted for Option 2, that is independence. Ominously, the report suggested that Indonesia destroy 'vital assets' if forced to withdraw. The UN, along with the Australian and Indonesian Governments, all denied the authenticity of this report at the time. Belo was adamant that it was genuine and he was proved correct.[35]

*

The promoters of *Operation Global Clean-Sweep* seemed blind to the fact that their strategy of intimidation and coercion would fail. Their confidence seems based in the fact that they were using tactics that have proved almost failsafe elsewhere in Indonesia. However, the more sanguine among the local Indonesian population could see that Option 1 was a lost cause. The signs were there for all to see: pro-integration leaders had acquired houses in Bali; those who had settled under the *transmigrasi* program were returning to Indonesia; civil servants and teachers were sending their families home; cars were cheap, and even Governor Soares now spent most of his time in Jakarta. According to Belo, the word from senior government officials in Jakarta was that East Timor was lost to the Republic. They saw the task ahead as making a clean break after the referendum and withdrawing with honour. The military faction heading up *Operation Global Clean-Sweep* did not share this view.

With the establishment of UNAMET and the presence of the international press, the violence so rampant up until May subsided a little.[36] Reports of violence still arrived,

---

35 The report made public on the ETAN Website is dated July 3rd 1999. It was written by General (ret) H. R. Garnadi on behalf of the Politics and Security Team in Dili to the Coordinating Minister of Politics and Security in Jakarta.

36 On April 11th people seeking refuge at the compound of Mario Carrascalao, who headed one of East Timor's most prominent families, were threatened by militia. When his son Manuelito courageously went out to speak with the militia leaders on behalf of those seeking refuge, he was killed. This precipitated a wider attack. In May the polytechnic at Hera was attacked and 21 students killed. The college was then looted and closed without comment from the authorities. John Martinkus *A Dirty Little War* (Sydney: Random House, 2001), 200.

but these were from the west and south west where press access was difficult.[37] When I visited the local Caritas office in Dili I began to understand the massive impact that the militias were having. According to Caritas's own figures there were already 13,140 internally displaced persons in Dili and another 44,991 in the west and south-west. The condition of the latter was pitiable as no NGO was allowed into these regions. NGO staff charged with taking food to the displaced persons were threatened by the militias. Caritas personnel helping refugees in Dili were also being threatened. In the strange logic of the militias, helping the refugees was tantamount to supporting independence. Ideology clearly trumped belief for these people, most of whom were Catholic!

★

Also worrying for Belo was another document he had recently been given, more alarming than the *Garnadi Report*. This suggested that in the event of a pro-independence victory, all major infrastructure providing electricity, water and communications be destroyed. Secondly, the homes of pro-independence figures were to be torched. The final page was the most chilling. It contained a list of some 200 people to be killed and Belo was in the number one position. Belo was unsure if it was authentic. I was amazed that he could discuss such things in so matter of fact a manner.

I travelled to Baucau with Belo who was visiting his mother, and met bishop Basilio Nascimento whose eye was very much on the future, and the development projects that would be needed in his diocese post-independence. We discussed how Caritas might help once Indonesia's embargoes on NGO support were removed. Basilio had recently been visited by an advisor to the governor of West Timor who told him that the authorities there were already making arrangements to receive thousands of refugees if, as they suspected, the majority vote was for independence. I found this hard to believe at the time.

On our return journey we could see smoke rising above Dili from quite a distance. 'That will be the militias burning houses' Belo said rather soberly. We stopped at a Carmelite convent to greet the sisters. The major topic of interest to them at the time was that the plumber had not come as promised. The irony in this juxtaposition of tragedy and the mundane seemed exquisite.

My discussions with the two bishops, with Caritas staff, and with a number of others led to the inevitable conclusion that if the East Timorese voted for independence, as seemed most likely, then life would get much worse before it got better.

We were all cheered on by the news from UNAMET that, despite the intimidation of the militias and the displacement of the population, over 390,000 people had already registered to vote. The registration period was being extended by two weeks to enable more people in the west and southwest to register. I was disappointed to learn from Timorese sources in Melbourne that, at that stage, only 600 of the diaspora in Australia had registered to vote.

Life for most Timorese and Indonesians living in the province was now both uncertain

---

37 Australian journalist John Martinkus was particularly active in tracking these down, sometimes at considerable personal risk.

and anxious as the days ticked down to the vote. Ordinary people thought that life was difficult but they were experiencing only the prelude to a nightmare.[38] The real horror was still to come.

---

38 The East Timor International Support Centre, a human rights group based in Darwin compiled a chronology of militia violence in East Timor in the lead up to UNAMET's arrival from November 1998 to May 1999 entitled *Indonesia's Death Squads: Getting Away with Murder*. It is perhaps the most comprehensive account available of events in this period.

CHAPTER 26
HILTON'S ROCK

In the lead-up to the referendum, Abel Guterres, CNRT's representative in Australia (and at the time of writing this account East Timor's ambassador in Canberra), had entered Indonesia under an assumed name. Abel was one of the six who came to my office in 1991 and over the years we had got to know each other well. He wanted to make contact with Taur Matan Ruak the commander of FALINTIL and this meant visiting the cantonment at Uai Mori. I was invited to go with him. I wanted to visit friends and to provide a form of moral affirmation for the stance of CNRT and FALINTIL in seeking peace in East Timor. I also wanted Taur Matan Ruak to know, by conveying it personally, that the stance taken had support within the Church. While the trip involved little personal risk for me, the risk for Abel was significant. If the militia or the TNI found out who he was, then his life would be in danger. For my part, I was concerned not to embarrass Belo who had bent over backwards to ensure that the Church was neutral in the upcoming vote. However, I knew that what Belo could not do personally, he had no objections to my doing.

I was told to be ready at 3:00am and to have a good pair of shoes. At the time I was staying at the Bishop's house and it was thought best that I change base to the Salesian house at Comoro. The militia's main base in Dili was close by and so their movements at that time of the morning could be easily tracked. I bought a pair of sports shoes and gave them a quick wear in. As it happened, our first attempt to travel to Uai Mori was called off when we were advised that the TNI had been tipped off that something was afoot and had set up road blocks.

When 3:00 am became 4:30 am disappointment set in. At 5:30 am, guessing that our visit had again been cancelled, I returned to my room and to bed. I had hardly put my head on the pillow when I heard the crunch of car wheels on the sand in the main courtyard. There was a soft knock on my door and a quiet voice whispered 'Bispo Hilton, we need to be moving'.

The journey took us East along the coast road heading towards Baucau. However at Manatuto we turned south on the road to Laleia where we carefully negotiated our way around the TNI base. We then drove onto the dry riverbed that doubled as our road. We followed this for several kilometres and met up with our FALINTIL guides. The group then headed off on foot along the river bed. By now the sun was up, but fortunately the sky was overcast throwing an eerie light on the gullies and hills as we continued up the riverbed. The countryside was similar to the McDonnell Ranges near Alice Springs with tree-lined gaps, gullies and gorges cut out by the winding river over millennia. In August the river is little more than a stream that can be easily crossed. The steep terrain made it necessary to do this several times.

I found the going very tough. In some parts we made quick time across fairly rocky ground; in other places we found ourselves wading through wet gravel. In places we walked over ground so rough and rocky that the next step could mean a broken ankle or leg. After what seemed like an eternity, but was in fact only a couple of hours, I needed to stop as I was feeling every one of my sixty-six years. I had reached the stage where I could go no further. I sought escape from weariness by sitting on a large flat rock on the river's edge. I was far from encouraged when our guide told us that the cantonment was 'only' five or six kilometres ahead! At this news I collapsed onto what is now called 'Hilton's Rock'. Fortunately, the FALINTIL guides had no objection to stopping although they clearly had no need to do so. For them it was an honour to have the first ever 'Bispo' visit their cantonment and they wanted to make sure he arrived alive![1] So we stopped.

Other groups passed us moving back and forth to the cantonment carrying equipment and supplies. As I struggled to get my breath back and had rested a little, I could not help but think that this journey was symbolic of that made by the East Timorese people themselves. We had covered a good deal of ground where the going was heavy, but we still had a way to go. We were confident we could make it to journey's end, but still had to make the effort to get there.

My early training as an anthropologist has always added a specific character to what I have been able to bring both as an Australian and as a Catholic priest to whatever I do. Doing fieldwork among the Aboriginal groups at Kalumburu Western Australia, I became deeply aware of how place and meaning can coalesce. In Aboriginal cultures, places become the repositories of meaning. We all have places that develop particular significance for us, and sometimes that meaning is shared with others. Hilton's Rock is one such place for me. It remains in my mind clearly even today. It could not be called a tourist attraction, nor would it be considered a natural attraction. It has no such claim to fame, located as it is in the bed of the nondescript Laleia river. In the Australian vernacular it stands 'in the middle of nowhere'. Whenever in future years I found the going hard I picture this rock in my mind and, recalling what it symbolises, I re-engage in the struggle.

★

My reason for visiting Uai Mori was in no small part due to the fact that, for years, I had acted as a conduit for communications between East Timorese families in Australia and their friends and relatives in East Timor, many of whom were part of the growing urban resistance. Some had gone to the hills to join FALINTIL. It was the latter that I was at last going to meet. Indonesian propaganda held that there were fewer than two hundred fighters still in the field. The East Timorese knew this to be nonsense. I wanted to see the strength of FALINTIL for myself as well as meet some of the brave people whom I had helped and who had carried their country's hopes for so long.

---

1   The East Timorese are not good at identifying the age of Westerners and, as I later found out, if my guides had known I was sixty-six they would never have agreed to my making such a long and arduous journey.

During the 1990s I rarely travelled to East Timor or returned to Australia without a list of people to contact by phone or to whom I had to pass on letters. This involved many clandestine meetings usually held as I travelled around the province with Bishop Belo assisting him with his episcopal duties. If Belo was aware of what was happening, he diplomatically said nothing about it. On my part, I was conscious that my activities must not embarrass him. Entries in my travel diaries, often written in Latin, were opaque to the Indonesians, and served as useful *aide memoires* when I reached Melbourne.

★

With so many Catholics in East Timor, Belo's episcopal duties were considerable, not only in managing the diocese and looking after the welfare of his priests, but also being a presence to his people. At the best of times travel around East Timor is difficult because of the mountainous terrain and the poor state of the roads. Visits by Church leaders were therefore rare. Belo used celebrations associated with the sacrament of Confirmation to meet his people. Such pastoral visits took him all over the diocese. It was not uncommon, at least when I travelled with him, to arrive at a village and find that there were five hundred or more people to confirm. The record, as I recall, was eighteen hundred.

The number who could be confirmed at any one ceremony depended on the size of the local church. This often resulted in him saying multiple Masses and, if the number of people to be confirmed was large, the ceremony could go on most of the day. I convinced him to hold the ceremony in the open air rather than in the church and to confirm everyone in one ceremony. We organised the candidates in a big circle and at the appointed time he would start on one side confirming people as he moved clockwise around the group while I started on the other side moving counter clockwise. This streamlined the ceremony to everyone's satisfaction. The arrival of the Bishop was also a gala event and a cause for major celebrations in places that often had very little to celebrate.

These pastoral visits gave me ample opportunity to meet with people in all parts of East Timor in the course of which I was often able to pass on or receive messages. There was nothing sinister in what I was doing. The East Timorese in Australia wanted assurance that their loved ones were still alive. In the awful atmosphere of the times the exchange of messages brought people in Timor hope while in Australia it brought reassurance and in some cases, sadly, grief.

★

When I had recovered, we moved on from Hilton's Rock, and about two hours later reached the cantonment. I was very surprised at how large the camp was. There were at least five or six hundred people living there. The Uai Mori cantonment, the largest of four, was strategically situated in a valley surrounded on three sides by steep hills. This made it easy to defend against ground troops. An air attack would have been another matter!

An armed group met us when we arrived at the outskirts of the camp and conducted us through it. They explained that the camp was divided into four areas with one assigned to each of the independent units living there. They each had their own parade ground. As we walked past the first of these I was surprised to come across a rough chapel dedicated to the *Sagrada Familia* (Holy Family) in the middle of the camp. The chapel consisted of a rough shelter covering an altar where a visiting priest could say Mass. It was a clear statement that many FALINTIL were Catholic and practised their faith as opportunity offered.

The other surprise was that many FALINTIL fighters had their families living on the outskirts of the camp and so the families were protected. Uai Mori was a no-go area for the militias. The swelling numbers in the cantonment were creating considerable logistical problems that were getting worse as the ballot approached and militia intimidation continued.

Our escort had orders to take us immediately to the headquarters of Matan Ruak, the commander.[2] When we arrived we found his 'office' consisted of palm leaves and plastic sheeting. Despite the simplicity of its construction, it lacked little in the way of technology with a generator providing the power for computers and communications systems. Matan Ruak received us most graciously. I had met him on a previous visit to East Timor and had taken film back to Australia for him.

★

Since I was the first Catholic bishop to visit a cantonment, one of the FALINTIL group whom I had met in Sydney some years earlier asked me if I would baptise his son. I was wary of this invitation at first as I was told there were a number of journalists in the camp looking for a story, including Australian John Martinkus. I did not want the ceremony to be turned into a publicity stunt as this would embarrass Belo at a very sensitive time. I agreed to think about the matter over lunch. No sooner had we sat down than the heavens opened. As the rain pelted down I was distracted by the thought of how hard this was going to make the return journey. I could imagine the river rising and turning the gravel we had already waded through into mush.

The baptism of Isaac Freitas did go ahead after lunch while Abel was meeting with the FALINTIL commander. It was agreed that there would be no photos during the ceremony. Once this concluded, things were different. Before we left, Matan Ruak introduced me to 'Anthony', an Australian fighting with FALINTIL. With much fanfare we set out about 2:30pm and slogged our way back to where the car was waiting for us. Our journey home was uneventful as we were told before we left that the road was now clear. I arrived home at about 8:00pm. My Salesian hosts were just finishing their evening meal, so I ate quickly, showered and sank into my bed exhausted at the end of what had been a truly exhilarating day. I was later told we had walked about twenty-six kilometres.

★

There was to be no rest for the weary. I woke next morning very stiff in the joints. However Cardinal Tom Williams from New Zealand was arriving at 11:00 am. Belo picked me up

---

2   Taur Matan Ruak is, at the time of writing, the President of East Timor.

and we went to the airport to meet him. Belo's first comment to me was to ask me how I had enjoyed my walk in the bush. How he found out so soon I never discovered. I had long been aware of the fact that there was little going on in East Timor that he did not know about one way or the other. While we waited Ali Alatas, the Indonesian Foreign Minister, arrived from Jakarta with other government ministers. Belo turned down his invitation to join them for lunch explaining that he had guests.

We took the cardinal back to the bishop's house at Lecidere where over lunch we discussed the upcoming ballot and how things might go once a decision was reached. The mood was sombre.

Cardinal Williams was the third Catholic cardinal to visit East Timor in a relatively short time. Few developing countries around the world have attracted such expressions of solidarity. Belo was very appreciative of the support given by cardinals Clancy, Williams and Etchegaray who had all gone out of their way to express their solidarity with the East Timorese Church at a time when this was not fashionable. Cardinal Williams's arrival, so close to the referendum, was an impressive show of support.

The next day we all set out for Ermera, a mission station in the hills where four priests live and service a number of chapels in the surrounding villages. The cardinal's visit was a gala event with three or four thousand people arriving for an open air Mass. As often happened with visiting Church dignitaries, Belo was concerned that the Cardinal's sermon not be inflammatory, which it was not. In a sign of the times there was a smattering of the local UNAMET contingent organising the ballot among the crowd, as well as local FALINTIL members. There were no members of the TNI or the local civil administration.

From Ermera we drove to Liquica to keep Belo's earlier promise made to the victims of the massacre there on April 6th that he would return again whenever he could. Cardinal Williams was understandably angry at what he saw, as there was still plenty of evidence of what had happened. The visit was sobering. That so many innocent people could be killed for what appeared to be no purpose was disturbing. The visit reminded me of my experiences in Rwanda. I wondered whether or not the Indonesians would try such a radical solution to their problems in East Timor but could not really see this happening. The struggle here was not generated by ethnic loyalties.

The Cardinal's visit to Liquica was a great comfort to the local people because it showed them that senior leaders in the global Church were aware of their plight and thinking about them. That had not always been the message they had received.

★

As I flew out of East Timor a few days later I found it hard to get the visit to Liquica out of my mind, and what it might presage for the time ahead. The journey of the East Timorese people had been one of suffering endured in the hope that they might be free of foreign domination. It seemed obvious that, given any chance to rid their country of oppression, they would take it, whatever the cost. In this sense the result of the referendum seemed a foregone conclusion.

The referendum offered hope, but equally this seemed unlikely to be realised without more suffering. My question as I looked from the plane onto the clouded mountains was:

What further suffering lies ahead for these people?

I could not help thinking back to my experience of exhaustion at Hilton's Rock and ask myself: When you are exhausted what makes you fight on? The answer is hope and solidarity. The referendum offered the first and my hope was that Cardinal Williams' visit to East Timor and my visit to the cantonment might offer the second.

CHAPTER 27
FATEFUL FORTNIGHT IN SEPTEMBER

The three stories that interweave in this book began to converge in dramatic fashion in the first weeks of September 1999. This chapter focuses particularly on how the East Timor story and the Catholic story converged in the immediate wake of the referendum.[1] In particular, it focuses on the military's efforts in implementing its depopulation policy to weaken the influence of the Catholic Church. The attack on convents and the refugees seeking shelter there, the diocesan office, the Bishop's residence, and the International Red Cross compound in Dili, with the associated violence, were part of a carefully calibrated strategy. These attacks were meant to convince the local people that no one could protect them and so when they were ordered to move they should do so. Given the respect accorded women religious and Bishop Belo in East Timor, attacks on their homes had great symbolic value and indicated a major change in stance by the armed forces. The chapter explores how this changed situation came about.

August 31st was set as the date for the referendum. Under the terms of the May 5th Agreement negotiated in New York, the pro- and anti-autonomy groups had three weeks to campaign officially, followed by a further week in which there would be no campaigning. As events unfolded, the ongoing militia intimidation and violence meant that only pro-autonomy groups could operate openly in most parts of the country. This did not particularly concern the CNRT as their network operated largely on a person-to-person basis. This is a very efficient communication system within Timorese culture, one that Belo also used. In his case its efficiency was a matter of life and death. Up until 1999 there had been eleven planned attempts on his life, all of which had been frustrated when people in the military, the police or the militia had sent messages back to him about what was intended and where.[2] I once asked him how he coped with this. He replied 'I say my prayers in the morning because it may be too late in the evening.'

The fact that the pro-autonomy group had the field to themselves seems to have bred a false confidence that Option 1, special autonomy, would prevail, and that their 'carrot and stick' strategy was working. So in the immediate period prior to the vote the intimidation

---

1   While the focus here is on Catholic leaders it must be remembered that Protestant pastors were also caught up in the violence. The ETHRC announced the murder of Rev Francisco Ximenes, pastor of the Hosanna Evangelical Church, on September 10th. He was shot while fleeing with refugees who had sought sanctuary in his church. They had decided that flight was a better option than transportation.
2   Ten of these attempts involved ambushes that Belo avoided by either cancelling a trip or changing his route. The eleventh was an attempt to poison him in his own home.

died down. The presence of the United Nations Mission in East Timor (UNAMET) and of so many foreign journalists in Dili were, no doubt, also factors. While Dili and other towns were awash with red and white flags as the militia led pro-autonomy rallies, out of sight the National Council of Timorese Resistance (CNRT) was confident that it had the numbers.[3]

*

It is hard to make sense of the post-election violence without some understanding of the thinking of the TNI in East Timor at this time as it functioned largely outside the purview of the new central government in Jakarta with whose policies key generals disagreed. Neither the new President, nor the commander-in-chief of the armed forces, General Wiranto, it now seems apparent, had the capacity to control events independently of these senior generals.[4]

When President Habibie agreed to the referendum the UN acted swiftly. UNAMET was created and charged with organising the referendum to a very tight timeline. This caught both the Indonesian Government and the local administration in East Timor off guard and for most of the campaign period they scrambled to fund their 'carrot and stick' strategy. The militias provided the 'stick' forcing pro-independence campaigners underground, while the 'carrot' consisted of money and in-kind benefits disbursed under the 'socialization' program.[5]

Garnadi is explicit in outlining the military's view that autonomy could be bought:

> The task to win Special Autonomy for the people of East Timor is actually not too difficult because what is being fought for is a floating mass whose demand is very simple, that is, for the availability of food and medicine. Whoever can provide food and medical treatment, the people will follow them.[6]

UNAMET sought to offset pro-autonomy tactics by the way in which it ran the voter registration process. Much to the chagrin of the military leaders, UNAMET's efforts were so successful that the pro-autonomy camp demanded extra time for registration when it found itself playing catchup in getting its own members registered, particularly in the western districts.

*

UNAMET's arrival in early June was viewed by ordinary Timorese as a form of liberation. For many years their leaders had argued for some form of UN intervention and now it

---

3 The CNRT replaced the National Council of Maubere Resistance (CNRM) in 1998.
4 In commenting on 'command responsibility' for events in East Timor, Robinson (2003) points out that Wiranto did not have a Kopassus background and so did not belong to the clique of generals and ex-generals giving the orders in Dili or pulling the strings in Jakarta.
5 Militia members were paid around $10 a month and entitled to 10kg of rice per month. This was a considerable benefit to people who would otherwise have been unemployed.
6 Garnadi Report -Translation of full report available at etan.org/news/news99b/secret1.htm

appeared to have come. A number of non-government organizations (NGOs) followed UNAMET bringing with them much needed humanitarian assistance. This only added to UNAMET's aura.[7] The assistance available through the NGOs dwarfed that on offer from the government, making the 'carrot' element of the pro-autonomy strategy problematic, and the 'stick' element all too obvious. This strategic oversight fostered a sense of grievance among the generals who complained repeatedly in the Indonesian press that UNAMET and the NGOs were rendering the election playing field 'uneven'. Distrust of UNAMET was an integral element in the indoctrination of the new militias which were led to believe that UNAMET was rigging the election. In consequence, local UNAMET staff, recruited for roles such as interpreter, computer operator, driver, election official, crowd controller, etc were viewed as 'pro-independence supporters' and subject to harassment by the militia. A small number were killed.

Garnadi outlines the military's thinking about these matters when he writes:

> It's too sceptical if we say that UNAMET takes sides, but the fact is that we are always left behind in responding to the manoeuvres from unfriendly sides, (so that) our initial optimism, which seemed to be convincing, has become less firm.... our space for movement is so restricted (as is) our helplessness in counterbalancing the manoeuvres of UNAMET, inside of which (are) local personnel from the anti-integration group. The UNAMET is dominated by anti-integration groups and there is a tendency that its task is not merely to hold the popular consultation, but is more than that.[8]

With a commendable degree of realism he goes on to discuss the consequences of the pro-autonomy camp failing. While the government in Jakarta might be relieved to wash its hands of East Timor, failure at the ballot box raised important questions: What will happen to the pro-autonomy supporters in East Timor? To Indonesian civil servants? To East Timorese who are serving in the military? To the economic order and the ownership of assets? Reflecting the common Javanese view that the East Timorese were incapable of running their own affairs, Garnadi sees that the real winners, if the vote fails, will be the Catholic Church and the UN. These will be the only viable surviving institutions. Australia, as the power most likely to be asked to intervene in the case of Indonesian withdrawal, will be another winner.

Garnadi decries the lack of a contingency plan in the event of a loss:

> ...(in) responding to the above matters we only have six weeks more to win Special Autonomy, but if this fails a period of six weeks is very short to draft a contingency plan for the pro-integration personnel and other assets. Therefore, the drafting of the contingency plan in response to Option 2 has to be developed as early as possible...[9]

---

7 According to Garnadi 32 NGOs were operating in East Timor at the beginning of July, a month after UNAMET arrived.
8 ibid
9 ibid

He suggests four elements of such a plan: expediting evacuation of Indonesian civil servants, and the TNI and its equipment; setting up of facilities in West Timor to cope with a mass evacuation of pro-autonomy supporters; securing the withdrawal routes; and, if possible, destroying 'vital facilities or objects'[10] (to hinder action by FALINTIL). His report, delivered to senior ministers in Jakarta, challenged the apparent complacency of the military authorities in East Timor and seems to have had the desired effect as, even before the result was declared, the military had begun to implement a province-wide contingency plan the elements of which became clearer to us at the ETHRC as reports came in during the first weeks of September not only from the press, but also from the private networks of the religious congregations with members working in East Timor. Our small team worked frantically to get out press releases based on these sources so that the wider activist community was made aware of what was happening. The East Timor and Indonesia Action Network (ETAN) in the United States then gave these international exposure through its website.

★

In the tense atmosphere on the eve of the vote an incident occurred that could have changed the history of East Timor.[11] Two days before the vote four pro-independence supporters attacked a relative of Eurico Guterres, the leader of the 1500 strong *Aitarak* militia in Dili.[12] The attack was captured by a news crew and shown that night on CNN. The film showed that the assault stopped when a fifth person intervened who later claimed to be the leader of the group. The film footage shows that he put the injured man in a taxi. What happened next remains clouded in mystery. Several hours later, the young man's dead body was discovered at the bottom of a ravine on the outskirts of Dili. Guterres had reported his relative missing, and when he found out that he had been killed came to UNAMET headquarters demanding that the CIVIPOL[13] police track down the offenders otherwise he would unleash his militia in Dili and create such havoc the next day that the vote would have to be cancelled.

Officers attached to UNAMET made enquiries through the CNRT and later in the day a young man named Da Silva came forward identifying himself as the person who had put the injured man in the taxi. When the CNN footage confirmed this, the officers interviewed him and took his statement. The local police were informed and soon arrived at UNAMET headquarters to take Da Silva into custody. This created a moral dilemma for the officers handling the case as they were not convinced of the man's complicity in the murder and had good reason to fear for his safety in local police custody. After

---

10 When the press got hold of this report it was sensationalised out of context with the last recommendation being interpreted as Garnadi recommending a 'scorched earth' policy. This is not what he was proposing.
11 Geoffrey Robinson *We Will Die if You Leave: How Genocide was Stopped in East Timor* (New Jersey: Princeton University Press, 2010), 151ff.
12 Guterres was the face and voice of the militias in the eyes of the international press then based in Dili. As a young man he was recruited into one of the paramilitary gangs set up by Kopassus to infiltrate the urban resistance and act as agent provocateur at demonstrations. Guterres demonstrated considerable organisational skills and his group served as the nucleus of the Aitarak militia when it was formed in early 1999. Guterres was second-in-command in the overall militia structure.
13 CIVIPOL was a civilian police force that was part of the UN mission (UNAMET).

much discussion it was agreed that the accused would stay in UNAMET custody till the next morning. In the meantime, with Guterres' threat to disrupt the referendum still unresolved, the senior UNAMET staff sought the counsel of Taur Matan Ruak who rang Xanana Gusmao in Jakarta. Xanana ordered the young man to give himself up so that the referendum could go ahead. Xanana's decision coincided with the lad's own statement to the police that reads in part: 'What is important is that the popular consultation takes place. It does not matter to me whether I am dead or alive. After the vote I believe I will be free'.[14] The next day Da Silva was handed over as agreed and, while CIVIPOL officers sought a number of guarantees about his safety, they held out little hope that these would be honoured.

The incident had a strange ending. When the violence broke out late on September 4th Da Silva was transferred from the local police station to Becora jail to ensure his safety. Members of *Aitarak* arrived at the jail demanding he be handed over to them. However, they did not know what Da Silva looked like and no one, including the Indonesian guard looking after his section, gave him up. This guard later took him by car from Dili to Atambua in West Timor. There he stayed for two months protected by the guard's family. He returned to Dili only after the INTERFET troops had arrived.[15]

Da Silva typifies the fatalism common among young East Timorese at this time. The attitude underpinned the many courageous, and at times suicidal, risks that young pro-independence activists took. It was an attitude that Belo deplored and discouraged. He had witnessed two generations of young men wiped out and he did not want this to be the fate of a third. In his view the East Timorese could not continue to sacrifice young leaders. The country needed them if it was to have any future. His policy stood in contradistinction to that of the Indonesian military and the militias for whom students constituted a target group to be destroyed. As Martinkus observes:

> The hatred of the militia for the students was almost beyond politics. The militia, recruited from the lowest economic groups, despised the students for their ability and their potential.[16]

Secondly, the actions of the Indonesian guard highlighted the fact that while it is easy to generalise about 'the military', 'the police', or 'the militia', many individuals in these groups did not share the preoccupations of their leaders. As noted previously, Belo and many other East Timorese leaders (and their families) owed their lives to such people.

Finally, the incident indicates the extraordinary hold Xanana had not only over FALINTIL and the CNRT, but also over the urban resistance of which Da Silva was a member.

★

---

14 Robinson, 153.
15 The head of the local human rights group *Yayasan Hak*, Aniceto Guterres, made it safely to Jakarta because Aitarak militia manning the checkpoint did not know what he looked like (Cristalis, 221).
16 Martinkus 2001, 311. The militia also included the unemployed, thugs and criminals, some of whom were psychopaths who had been part of the death squads (Ninjas) used in the 1980s.

By August 31st over 400,000 East Timorese were registered to vote. On polling day 98% of these did so.[17] People living in remote areas trekked through the night to reach voting stations by dawn. They were already gathered in large numbers when UNAMET officials arrived at the polling stations. Most votes had been cast by midday. Voting day was largely free of violence and the overseas observers present declared the vote met the UN's conditions for it to 'free and fair'.[18] However, the day after the ballot, Wednesday September 1st, militia violence resumed and East Timor began what would be a very rapid descent into total chaos. Over the next fortnight the world stood by stunned in shock at what was happening, and then scrambled to respond.

In the face of reports about mounting militia violence across the country, UNAMET staff worked around the clock to get the vote counted. Ian Martin, Head of UNAMET, fearing that the growing chaos might compromise the referendum, called a press conference on Saturday 4th September two days earlier than planned and, speaking on behalf of the UN Secretary General, announced the result: 94,388 votes for autonomy and 344,580 against. In Martin's words 'The people of East Timor have thus rejected the proposed special autonomy and expressed their wish to be in the process of transition towards independence'.[19] The 78.5% vote for independence stunned the pro-integration lobby. Its leaders felt humiliated when they realised how completely they had been duped by the local population. A desire for revenge contributed to the violence.

In retrospect elements in the military leaders' contingency plan can be identified although this was very difficult to do at the time. The plan was predicated on the assumption that the vote would be either a narrow win for the pro-autonomy cause or a loss so close that the result could be contested. In either case, the plan called for the mass transportation of known pro-independence supporters to West Timor from where they could be included in the *transmigrasi* program and dispersed across the archipelago.[20] The public 'narrative' associated with the plan was that these were people 'fleeing persecution' by the pro-independence lobby. The fact that the number transported was nearly three times the number who could have voted for autonomy made a nonsense of the official narrative.

★

To make the transportation of such a large 'floating mass' possible they had to be rendered submissive. This was achieved by moving first against targets with high symbolic value and by the selective use of violence. As the military well knew selective violence is all that is needed to terrorise powerless people and get them on the move. Weakening the position

---

17 Those who did not vote were presumed to be too ill to do so or to have died between the time the registered and voting day.
18 Among these was Laurie Brereton, the Labor spokesperson on Foreign Affairs, who led the delegation to Maliana which had proved a hot spot of resistance to the referendum and the scene of considerable militia violence.
19 Martinkus 2001, 283.
20 According to the Office of US Foreign Disaster Assistance Fact Sheet of 29th September, as of a day earlier the Government of Indonesia had registered 244,310 IDPs in 37 camps at 11 locations in West Timor and nearby islands. 128, 927 were located around Atambua. Another 200,000 were hiding within East Timor out of a population of 890,000.

of the Catholic Church became an important objective in implementing the plan. Its influence had to be neutralised. So too did that of the NGOs.

The first groups to be targeted for 'clearance' were refugees in convents, the bishop's compound, the diocesan centre, and the International Red Cross compound. This happened with a degree of violence. Not only were there large numbers of refugees in these centres, but raiding them first sent out a clear message that the Catholic Church and the NGOs could no longer protect people.

Confidence in the new 'liberator', UNAMET, also had to be destroyed. The day after the vote UNAMET offices across the country came under harassment from the militia. The international and many of the local UN staff had to be evacuated to Dili or Baucau for their own safety. By the time the vote was announced the military and militia had most of the UN staff rounded up in UNAMET headquarters in Dili, so sending out a clear message that UNAMET could not help either.

The final obstacle to implementing the plan was to ensure that it did not occur in full view of the international press. The militia was unleashed again in Dili and had most of the media bottled up in their hotels by late on September 4th. After listening to guns going off outside their windows all night, and seeing a BBC journalist injured with a machete, most needed little convincing to leave the next day. The dozen or so who remained wisely sought refuge in the UNAMET headquarters which by September 5th was itself under siege.

★

Large-scale military operations tend to build a momentum that becomes almost unstoppable. *Operation Clean Sweep* called for a co-ordinated effort by the military, police and militia, which became something of a farce when soldiers began appearing dressed as militia. Far from operating out of sight the violence was filmed extensively by TV journalists being evacuated from Dili. These images flashed around the world and flatly contradicted the official 'narrative' which was robbed of credibility. The Indonesian army had been able to close down information flow in the wake of the invasion in 1975, but advances in technology made this impossible in 1999. The world was awash with reports, photos, TV footage, on-the-spot interviews via satellite phones, uplinks and so on.

★

When Dili's residents found out what was planned, rather than submissively wait to be deported, they did what East Timorese have always done - they fled to the hills and in their thousands. Those in the compounds could not flee, neither could religious sisters looking after orphans and the sick, or those responsible for the refugees. Once the Church compounds had been cleared of people, Dili was then cleared suburb by suburb and the systematic looting and destruction began. The scale of the destruction shocked most observers including a delegation from the UN Security Council. Whether this was the initial intention of the military's plan or an afterthought is still unclear. When its leaders assessed the results of the ballot they must have known Indonesia's time in East Timor was over and that their contingency plan was doomed. To maintain 'plausible deniability' and possible prosecution for 'crimes against humanity', a new narrative had to be created. This was that the destruction was the action of 'rogue elements within the military and the militias running amuck'. The world found this impossible to believe when it discovered that some 500,000 people had been driven from their homes and that the country, from one end to the other, was in flames.

*

In telling the East Timor and Church stories it is important to understand the size and nature of the threat that the militias posed for those supporting independence and for those who came to their aid. Press coverage of this topic was limited at the time by the very real dangers involved in travelling to districts controlled by the militias.[21]

In his 2003 report to the UN Commission of Human Rights, Geoffrey Robinson provides a forensic analysis of the militias and their role in the destruction of East Timor. With access to records recovered by the East Timorese human rights organisation, Yayasan HAK, the International Force for East Timor (INTERFET), various UN investigations and criminal prosecutions, he details what is now known about militia operations on a district-by-district basis. The data presented in his report has been tabulated and collated in the table below.

District	No Militias	Principal	Membership	No Killed*	Formed
Bobonaro	9	Halilintur	120+	229+	1977
Cova Lima	2	Laksaur	600+	190+	N.A.
Liquica	2	Bes Merah Putil	600+	183+	1999
Ainaro	2	Mahadi	1100	34+	1998
Emera	5	Naga Merah	100+	82+	1995
Oecusse	1	Sakunar	N.A	170+	1999
Dili	1	Aitarak	1500	192+	1999
Aileu	1	Ahi	260+	28+	1999
Manufari	1	Albai	100	27+	1999
Manatuto	2	Morok	N.A	32+	N.A
Viqueque	2	Makikit	200	3-30	N.A
Lautem	1	Team Alpha	300	53+	1980s
Bacau	3	Saka	970	43+	1980s

Table: Data on the Militias operating in 1998-99[22]

* The numbers in this column refer to people who have been accounted for. Many killed have never been accounted for as their bodies were disposed of in unmarked graves or at sea.

The column on the left names the thirteen administrative districts in East Timor each of which had its own military command and civil administration. The shaded rows at the

---

21 Martinkus captures this well in describing his visits to Cassa in *A Dirty Little War*.
22 Geoffrey Robinson *East Timor 1999 Crimes against Humanity - A Report Commissioned By The United Nations Office Of The High Commissioner For Human Rights* 'Chapter Nine. District Summaries' (2003), 130ff.

top of the table indicate districts in the west of the country. Those shaded at the bottom indicate regions to the east. While all districts had at least one militia some, like *Aitarak* based in Dili, operated across district boundaries. In some districts the main militia had subsidiary units, sometimes with a different name, operating at the sub-district or village level. The column on the right indicates that while some of the militias existed well before the events of September 1999, most were formed to intimidate and coerce the population in the lead-up to the vote. The longer-standing militias tended to be smaller, better trained and equipped. They were more loyal to the Indonesian cause and more deadly. Most of those listed as 'killed' in the table above died after the referendum. The militias were strongest in the districts bordering Indonesia and it was there that casualties among pro-independence supporters were the highest.

Even after the result of the referendum was known, militia leaders in the west still believed that East Timor would be partitioned with their districts becoming part of Indonesia so the violence continued unabated. They may have been encouraged in their belief by the size of Suharto family holdings there.[23]

*

At least 1200 people lost their lives in the course of Indonesia's 'popular consultation'. The Catholic Church was caught up in this carnage. Prior to 1999 it was respected as a civil institution within the Indonesian state. When the territorial command initiated a public works program in the 1980s the military helped build Catholic churches. Indonesian clergy and religious came to East Timor to provide services to their co-religionists who were in the military, in business, or part of the *transmigrasi*. One of Belo's dilemmas was holding the Indonesian and East Timorese elements in the Church community together, given the imbalance in power between the two groups.

In 1999 Church leaders had to address the plight of the internally displaced persons, who in the main were Catholic, when they began crowding onto Church properties seeking safety. The demand for protection was huge, the size of the task depending on the level of intensity of local militia attacks, for instance between 2000 and 6000 people sought refuge in the Catholic Church complex at Suai. At the time of the vote some 5000 were in the bishop's compound at Lecidere Dili, another 500 were in the grounds of the diocesan office, and 10,000 were camped at the Salesian college in Comoro. As well, groups of refugees were to be found in every convent in Dili. The latter included the eighty-year-old parents of Xanana Gusmao.[24] Most of these refugees had no shelter, little food and no medical help. Many were rightly in fear of their lives.

While Church leaders had a clear responsibility to help the refugees, what help they were able to give was both limited and temporary. A bad situation was made worse by two factors. The military interpreted Church support for the displaced persons in most districts as being 'pro-independence', and so the people seeking refuge on church property

---

23   An article in the *Sydney Morning Herald* on 8th May 1999 headed 'ABRI Inc', sourced to George Aditjondro's research, puts the Suharto family's overall holding at 564,867 hectares.
24   Xanana's parents lived with the Salesian Sisters in Dili. When the militia came searching for pro-independence supporters they hid Xanana's parents in a drying room and were so busy scrubbing the floor in front of it that the militia did not think to look inside. (Cristalis, 239).

across the country became easy targets for selective reprisals once the result was known. Secondly, as the referendum drew near, Indonesian Catholics, particularly those working in the civil service or business, became increasingly nervous and returned home fearing for their own safety. When Indonesian clergy and religious followed suit, an important buffer was removed.

★

The worst of the selective violence against the Catholic Church occurred at Suai, a large village strung out along the main road in the south-west about sixteen kilometres from the Indonesian border. The town is surrounded by sub-tropical 'bush' that threatens to engulf it in the wet season. I visited Suai in my travels with Belo and met the parish priest, Fr Hilario Madeira there and in Dili. My visits to Suai were memorable because a journey there is not for the faint-hearted. Even in good weather the roads are bad.

The Catholic compound in Suai is quite large, two or three hectares. Only two-thirds of the block is cleared, the rest being bush. The compound is bordered on two sides by roads at right angles to each other with the presbytery occupying the corner. Ave Maria church runs parallel to one road with the presbytery behind it and the convent in front facing the Church entrance. The main entrance to the property runs between the convent and the church. There are other buildings on the block, including a shrine being built to honour Our Lady of Fatima, one of the two main expressions of popular religiosity in East Timor.[25] The shrine will eventually become a basilica. In 1999 its concrete façade, boxed in bamboo scaffolding, stood six storeys high. The sidewalls, four storeys high, were then under construction.

The old church was a big open shed with a thatched roof. Its stucco front entrance badly needed painting, and the low sidewalls served to keep stray goats out, while letting the air in. By contrast, the convent was a solid building protected on the street side by a high wrought-iron fence clearly designed to keep intruders out.

★

When the Laksaur militia began its program of intimidation in the surrounding villages in early 1999, the number of displaced persons seeking refuge on the church property was large. People from villages in Cova Lima and adjoining Ainaro districts sought refuge in Suai, much to the annoyance of the militia leaders in these districts. On a number of occasions there were threats to attack the refugees, but these did not materialise. Following the ballot and the military's decision to clear Church compounds, the refugees in Suai became an obvious target.

The day after the result, local Laksaur militia with TNI and police support, began to loot and burn down residences in Suai, including those near the Church. The villagers affected were driven from their homes along the road west to Indonesia. Members of the militia with relatives in the Suai church compound warned them that something 'bad' was planned for the next day. To reduce the risk the young men in the group disappeared into

---

25 The other is devotion to St Anthony of Padua whose shrines dot the countryside.

the bush thinking that the women and children left in the care of the Church would be safe. The sisters moved pregnant women into the convent as a precaution. In all about 1200 refugees remained.

The next morning Fr Hilario was told by the militia leaders that the people in the Church compound were to pack their goods and be ready to move west later in the day. Army and Brimob troops then took up positions around the main buildings to ensure no more people escaped. At noon Fr Hilario told the refugees in the compound to get ready to move and then retired to the presbytery to get ready himself. At 2:30pm the Laksaur militia, now reinforced by members of the Mahadi militia from Ainaro, headed up from the main road towards the old church. Fr Tarcisius Dewanto, a young Indonesian Jesuit recently ordained who had only just arrived in Suai, went out to meet the approaching militia. As an Indonesian he may have thought that he could help organise the safe departure of the refugees. Instead, one of the militia charged at him and hacked him to death in front of the church. When the assistant priest, Fr Francisco Soares, came out of the church to see what the noise was all about he was immediately cut down by automatic gunfire.[26]

This seems to have been the signal for mayhem to begin. In scenes reminiscent of Rwanda, the attackers threw two hand grenades into the church killing many of the people there and then began to shoot over the low wall at those who survived. Some of the women, children and old men attempting to flee the church were hacked to death by the waiting militia and their bodies further mutilated.

Fr Hilario was in his office when the attack began. As he emerged he was fatally shot twice in the stomach.[27] When some refugees were discovered hiding high in the basilica they were driven over the edge of the shelf they were hiding on and fell to their death.

One can only imagine the horror of the sisters and women in the convent as for over two hours they watched events unfold across the road and grimly awaited their own fate. At about 5:00pm with the bloodlust spent and any survivors rounded up, the military approached the convent and ushered those inside away unharmed. They were loaded onto trucks and taken to camps in West Timor. The next day the bodies of the dead were burned or removed. The bodies of the three priests were discovered in a shallow grave in West Timor by Indonesian investigators in 2000. It is not known how many people died at Suai. By 2002 bodies of only 40 victims had been identified.[28] It is thought that as many as 200 people could have been killed during the militia/TNI's two and-a-half-hour rampage with the bodies being disposed of in local crocodile-infested swamps.

On the first anniversary of this event some 10,000 people gathered in the church compound at Suai under INTERFET protection to commemorate the massacre and to pray for the dead.[29] A circle of stones in front of the church marks the place where the bodies of the dead were burned beyond recognition. The basilica remains a work in progress.[30]

---

26 Rajiv Chandrasekaran 'East Timor: A Killing Ground without Corpses' *Washington Post* October 22nd 1999, A01.
27 *Sydney Morning Herald* 13th September 1999 'Nun: Blood of Victims Seeped out of Church'
28 Robinson 2003, 226ff.
29 This event is commemorated in an oil painting hung in the National War Memorial Canberra.
30 The Ave Maria church has been completely restored and now serves as a memorial to those massacred at Suai.

★

Once the referendum result was announced, Belo's position became extremely vulnerable. I have often wondered what he must have been feeling as the various components of the plan he had shown me two weeks earlier began to fall into place one by one.

On Sunday September 5th *Aitarak* militia, led by Guterres, began to clear refugees camped in the Camera Ecclesiastica to the Dili wharf for deportation to West Timor. The Camera was then set on fire destroying 400 years of Church records and East Timorese history. Students, CNRT and local UNAMET staff in this group were singled out for rough treatment. Twenty were tortured and fifteen killed.[31]

About the same time another group of Aitarak militia acting with military and police support surrounded the bishop's compound. When Belo went out to negotiate with the military leaders he was taken into custody and so did not see the 5000 people in the compound marched off to await transportation for West Timor. Nor did he see his house set on fire nor the destruction of the priceless collection of historic artefacts, dating back centuries, that his predecessors had assembled and which constituted a national cultural treasure.[32]

Belo was flown from police headquarters by helicopter to Baucau. There he met briefly with Bishop Nascimento. The military wanted Belo out of the country for his own safety. He was given false identity papers which named him as Louis Rocetta, a UNAMET driver (which fooled no one) and then evacuated with other UNAMET staff to Darwin where he arrived still in a state of shock. So grave was the situation that he had little time to recover.

Two days later Belo flew to Lisbon where he had discussions with the President of Portugal about the deteriorating situation in Timor. He then flew on to Rome to meet Pope John Paul II. Both these leaders added their voice to a growing chorus of international outrage threatening to make Indonesia a pariah state. After his visits to the Vatican Belo had a chance to rest. He promised to return to East Timor as soon as international troops could restore order.

★

Not all groups suffered the vicious treatment meted out to those at the Camera Ecclesiastica or in Belo's compound. The evacuation of the 10,000 at the Salesian centre at Comoro occurred without incident. The Salesian leader, Fr Andrew Wong, together with some of his colleagues and about 500 refugees, were marched to the local airport and flown to Kupang where they were housed in a sports centre. The rest were trucked to the camps in Atambua.

As this was happening Fr Jose, the Director of the Salesian Agriculture College at Fuiloro, arrived with a fellow Salesian who was returning to the Philippines. As they approached Comoro the car was stopped at a checkpoint. He and his companion were

---

31 Robinson 2003, 222ff.
32 The front of the Bishop's residence was completely destroyed but the sleeping quarters at the back remained intact. A group of Canossian Sisters whose convent had been vandalised took up residence there until INTERFET arrived.

ordered out and it was set on fire. They had to complete their journey on foot. At the Salesian house Fr Jose commandeered another car from the rapidly emptying compound and headed back to Fuiloro talking his way past a number of militia checkpoints till he arrived in country where he was known and waved through. Once home, he was able to follow events in Dili on TV. When he realised the systematic nature of the clearances occurring across East Timor he advised the local villagers to flee. Some 4000 headed for the hills around Lospalos where they waited for three weeks for INTERFET to arrive. Many of those who stayed were rounded up and transported to West Timor through the port of Com by the local Team Alpha militia. Fr Jose and his colleagues from Fuiloro joined those in the hills.

In response to the plight of these refugees, a group of religious based in Baucau, where things were relatively quiet thanks to Bishop Nascimento's intervention, set out to deliver food and medicine to those trapped above Lospalos. The group included the sister in charge of the local Canossian community, Celeste De Carvalho, Sr Erminia Cazzaniga, a missionary from Italy, two local deacons, Fernando dos Santos and Jacinto Xavier, a seminarian Valerio Da Conceicao and a representative from Caritas Dili. The leader of the local Team Alpha militia was made aware of their presence and set up a roadblock specifically to stop them. When the SUV stopped three of the militia opened fire, killing the driver and some of the eight passengers. When the survivors got out of the car they were either shot or struck with machetes and then shot. The eight bodies were then thrown into the river. Finally a hand grenade was thrown at the bodies in case anyone was still alive.[33] The SUV was pushed into the river to hide evidence of the crime.[34] The assassination of so many Church workers came as a great blow to the recently established diocese of Baucau.

September 1999 was the Church in East Timor's darkest hour. Belo was gone, Bishop Nascimento was in hiding, and local clergy were either in the hills with their people or in concentration camps in West Timor at the mercy of the militia. The humanitarian situation had become so bad in both East and West Timor that it led the Indonesian Bishop of Atambua Anton Ratu to ask the United Nations to take control of the whole of Timor![35]

It is difficult to understand why the military used the militia in the way they did after the referendum. Many theories have been advanced, some of which seem to go beyond the facts. The simplest explanation may be that having badly misjudged the mood of the people, a similar misjudgement shaped a contingency plan that quickly degenerated into a total disaster for the Indonesian Government which was then left to find the best way to save face. The first two weeks of September were fateful not only for the East Timorese and the Church, but also for Indonesia's standing in the world. Indonesia's action created a huge moral dilemma for the rest of the world, one that it would struggle to address.

---

33 ETHRC Press Release 30th Sept available at ETAN.Org ,Timor Briefings, September 1999.
34 This event occurred after the INTERFET forces had arrived in DILI. When INTERFT arrived in Lospalos an attempt was made to track down the Team Alpha group responsible without success. Taur Matan Ruak offered the help of the local FALINTIL troops who soon rounded them up and handed them over to the UN. The leader of Team Alpha was subsequently sentenced to 33 years in jail.
35 Catholic News Service September 25th 1999 'Bishop in western Timor urges U.N. mandate for all of Timor' available at http://etan.org/et99b/september/19-25/25bish.htm

CHAPTER 28
THE CARITAS STORY

The events that unfolded in graphic detail before the world's eyes in September 1999 bring the three stories central to this book together. When this occurred, Caritas Australia (CA) became lead agency in East Timor for Caritas Internationalis (CI), the Catholic Church's international co-ordinating body in dealing with disaster relief and development. It is this convergence that I want to explore in this chapter.

As I hope is clear by now, the Catholic Church is an extremely complex organisation at both the national and global levels. At both levels it operates a range of agencies that are, at best, loosely federated under the leadership of bishops. As has been mentioned previously, in Australia agencies such as Caritas Australia and the Australian Catholic Social Justice Council (ACSJC) come under the Australian Catholic Bishops' Conference (ACBC).

My role as Chair of Caritas Australia was at the level of policy and governance exercised on behalf of the ACBC. I had some limited involvement with its day-to-day operational activities. The reasons for keeping my role limited were partly geographical and partly intentional. The Caritas main office was based in Sydney and I was based in Melbourne. At the time there were long-standing tensions between Caritas Australia and the ACSJC (also based in Sydney) over the former's advocacy role with respect to human rights issues in East Timor. As chair of the East Timor Human Rights Commission (ETHRC) and a well-known East Timor advocate, my position on human rights was well established. It required some delicacy on my part therefore not to stir up trouble by pushing the issue from inside Caritas, particularly when some in the ACSJC saw Catholic advocacy on social justice issues such as human rights as their 'turf'. The rapidly expanding public profile of Caritas may also have contributed to tensions between these Sydney-based organisations.

The scope of the humanitarian crisis in East Timor tested CA's leaders to the full and the way they coped with it projected the organisation into the public eye in Australia like no other event in its history.[1] It is a tribute to its leadership and staff in this period that Caritas Australia was able to respond as it did. It soon became a welcome Australian presence in East Timor because it was one of the few NGOs that stayed for the long haul. Its presence counteracted the many carpetbaggers arriving in search of quick money.

---

1   As indicated in Chapter 21, the Rwandan crisis certainly had generated an extraordinary outpouring of solidarity from the Australian community in terms of contributions for relief. However, the events in East Timor required a wider, deeper and more sustained organizational response from Caritas Australia, involving it with the broader Australian community at a variety of levels including the political.

I was very proud to have played a small part in this response, but am even prouder of the contributions Caritas Australia and Caritas Internationalis made to East Timor. It was an extraordinary time as I hope the balance of this chapter will make clear.

★

In order to understand the story that follows it will be helpful to first outline how and why the Catholic Church runs disaster relief and development agencies. Catholic organisations committed to international development emerged in force following the challenge offered by Pope Paul VI in his encyclical *Populorum Progressio* (1967). Paul VI was well-travelled as a Vatican diplomat prior to becoming Pope, and so was aware of the dire situation in many developing countries as a matter of first-hand experience.

The Pope's challenge to local churches was that those who have abundance share with those who have not.[2] The encyclical quickly became a foundational document in Catholic social teaching. The Pope demanded more than charity from rich nations. In addressing the needs of poorer nations, he called for *partnership* that would enable them to escape the power imbalances crippling development since colonial times. His successor, Pope John Paul II, developed this theme further in calling for 'solidarity' – a willingness to 'stand with' rather than 'stand over'!

In Paul VI's view there was a pressing need in the 1960s to promote what he called 'integral development' - development that enables people to live with dignity. Since people can live in dignity only when their human rights are respected, 'integral development', including respect for human rights, is a necessary condition for international peace, and fostering it is central to the Catholic Church's mission.[3] Development, justice and peace go together. As Paul VI wrote at the time, 'development is the new name for peace'.[4] Development assistance is a matter of justice, not of any narrowly conceived notion of charity. Paul VI was writing in the context of the 1960s when the empires created by the 19th century expansion of Europe began to collapse, and newly independent nation states emerged. These too inherited a legacy of inequality, great poverty, and a history of violence.

Within the Catholic world some twenty-two national churches had established agencies to promote development in 'Third World countries' prior to the Pope's 1967 encyclical. CAFOD (England), Trocaire (Ireland), Catholic Relief Services (US) are well known examples. The oldest of the agencies set up in Germany in 1897 was called Caritas. As a result of initiatives taken by Monsignor Montini (later Pope Paul VI) in 1954, Caritas Internationalis (CI) was established so that Catholic development agencies would have a

---

2 'The hungry nations of the world cry out to the peoples blessed with abundance. And the Church, cut to the quick by this cry, asks each and every man (sic) to hear his brother's plea and answer it lovingly'. Pope Paul VI *Populorum Progressio* 1967, #3.
3 A direct consequence of the Pope's encyclical was the establishment of the Catholic Commission for Justice and Peace in Rome and corresponding entities in national churches including the forerunners of what was to become the Catholic Commission for Justice and Peace in Australia (CCJP). The ACSJC was the successor to the CCJP.
4 'Nations are the architects of their own development, and they must bear the burden of this work; but they cannot accomplish it if they live in isolation from others. Regional mutual aid agreements among the poorer nations, broader based programs of support for these nations, major alliances between nations to coordinate these activities - these are the road signs that point the way to national development and world peace.' *Populorum Progressio*, #77.

representative voice at the United Nations (UN), and could more easily liaise with UN agencies and so play their role as international citizens when humanitarian crises arose. This development was a practical consequence of the Church seeking to find its place in the modern world after the Second Vatican Council.

As the scale of national emergencies and development needs expanded in the 20th century, these agencies were forced to work together, as no one agency had the skill base or the resources to meet major crises. CI became a co-ordinating agency that liaised with UN agencies to address humanitarian crises. Many national Catholic development agencies subsequently adopted the Caritas name.[5] There are now over one hundred and sixty partner agencies in the Caritas group making it one of the world's largest NGOs.

All Caritas agencies operate within the insights of Catholic social teaching and relationships between them are meant to reflect its core values – dignity of the human person, partnership, subsidiarity, solidarity, and co-responsibility.[6] This is sometimes easier said than done as CI brings together partner organisations with vastly different histories and cultural situations that often give rise to differing interpretations of what these core values mean in practice.

★

Until September 1999 Caritas Australia was a relatively small agency whose work was funded by donations and an annual Lenten appeal called Project Compassion. As a matter of policy, staff numbers were kept small to maximise funds available to partner organisations who were delegated operational responsibility for projects funded by Caritas Australia. A consequence of this policy was that Caritas Australia itself accumulated little expertise in the managing of disaster or development. Its expertise lay in raising finance effectively, developing education programs, advocacy in Australia, and sponsoring a few small-scale development projects overseas, such as the one I had visited in Soweto. Before 1999 Caritas Australia's involvement with East Timor was quite limited. It had helped Caritas East Timor (CET) based in the Dili Diocese to establish a small-scale agricultural program in the Comoro Valley. This was the first real partnership program between the Caritas agencies in Australia and East Timor.[7]

Caritas Australia took its advocacy role very seriously prior to and during the ballot. Its program director, Ann Wigglesworth, met twice with Foreign Minister Downer in 1999 advocating greater Australian engagement. At the second meeting she was accompanied by the CET Director, Fr Francisco Barreto. At his suggestion Caritas Australia helped organise and fund the East Timor Solidarity Program. Under this program fourteen people from Australia[8] went to East Timor in April 1999 to act as 'witnesses' to what was happening there and to provide help and a degree of protection for local CET staff then at risk of

---

5   As Deputy-Chair of Australian Catholic Relief I pushed at ACBC meetings for ACR to be re-named Caritas Australia. This name change was agreed to by the ACBC and effected in 1996.
6   For a discussion of major themes and principles see Pontifical Council for Justice and Peace and United States Conference of Bishops *Compendium of the Social Doctrine of the Church* (Washington: USCCB Publishing, 2005).
7   Caritas East Timor was one of a number of local sources prior to 1999 that the ETHRC could access in documenting local human rights abuses by the Indonesian military and police.
8   The group comprised of 3 laywomen, 8 religious sisters, and 3 priests.

intimidation from the militias. This group became an effective and credible source of information about East Timor, much sought out by the Australian and international media.

Caritas Australia flew six staff members from CET to Melbourne to take part in the National Council of Timorese Resistance (CNRT) Strategic Planning Conference in April 1999. It also invited Bishop Belo to launch Project Compassion nationwide in March 1999, again pointing the media spotlight firmly on East Timor at this crucial time. Finally, Caritas Australia's Program Director volunteered to become a member of ACFOA's team[9] of international observers during the ballot.

Caritas East Timor's local staff played a significant role in assisting displaced persons reaching Dili as the militia violence spread prior to the ballot. This made them a target group sought out by the Aitarak, the Dili-based militia, in the post-ballot period. CET's Director, Fr Barreto, was also targeted because of his work supporting and nurturing young CNRT leaders. When members of the Volunteers Program were repatriated for their own safety on consular advice in September, CET staff had to fend for themselves and this led Caritas people in Australia to fear for their safety.

★

During the Indonesian occupation, CET had served the whole of the country[10] and so made contact with Caritas agencies worldwide. Some, like Caritas Norway, provided funding for special projects operating through Caritas Indonesia.[11] Once the Baucau diocese was created a suspicion grew there that funds allocated to 'East Timor' were being re-directed to projects in the Dili diocese and not equally shared. The lack of transparency in the way CET did business encouraged this view and the perception, which may or may not have been true, became a source of tension between Bishop Belo and the newly appointed Bishop Nascimento. Perhaps in response, the latter established Caritas Baucau[12] whose new director quickly formalised a relationship with Catholic Relief Services (CRS) the major US Catholic development agency.[13] This move fostered the equally dangerous perception among the CET staff that Baucau, with the support of CRS, was 'doing very well' out of CRS. This was far from the actual situation.

In 1999 the Director of Caritas Baucau was one of the few people killed in the post-ballot violence in Baucau which, due to Bishop Nascimento's intervention with the local militia, was quite limited. The Director's death meant that the Baucau agency had to be re-established in a situation of crisis. By the time this occurred, CRS found itself over-extended in East Timor and asked Caritas Australia to take over its responsibilities for food distribution in Baucau. By default, in late 1999 Caritas Australia found itself

---

9   ACFOA is now known as ACFID – Australian Council for International Development.
10 The Baucau diocese did not exist prior to November 1996.
11 Caritas Norway, through the work of Jose Ramos Horta, became a major financial supporter of the ETHRC. In 1996 when visiting Oslo for the Nobel Peace Prize ceremony I was able to thank them personally for their assistance.
12 Caritas Internationalis recognises only national organisations. However, since East Timor was not a 'nation' as in 'nation state', it recognised Caritas Baucau and Caritas East Timor (later renamed Caritas Dili). This produced confusion both in East Timor and outside it.
13 CRS is not only the development agency of the United States Church but also functions as an agent of the US government in implementing its foreign policy. It is well-resourced in terms of finance but, more importantly, also in terms of international expertise in development projects.

supplying food to both Baucau and Dili dioceses.

The lack of trust that characterised relationships between Caritas agencies in East Timor was also operative in the relationship between CET and Caritas Australia. The leaders of these organisations had quite different understandings about the importance of accountability and transparency in dealing with donors' funds. Poor accountability and opaqueness on the part of CET fostered the perception among Church leaders in Australia that funds sent there were not being handled honestly and this was the cause of much frustration. While Caritas Australia and other church agencies here are required to meet external audit standards, no such requirement existed in East Timor. There, bookkeeping seemed regarded as a necessary evil, to be avoided whenever possible! The perception of dishonesty tainted the relationship between churches. While understandable, this perception was not entirely accurate.[14] The dynamic was offset to some extent by the good working relationship between Fr Barreto Director of CET and Caritas Australia's Program Director Ann Wigglesworth, who fortunately spoke Portuguese.[15]

After two decades of oppression in which a corrupt Indonesian administration regularly appropriated goods sent to the country by Caritas agencies and other NGOs and later sold them on the open market, local NGOs, CET included, developed strategies to 'beat the system'. This attitude, informing practice over an extended time, became part of the NGO culture in East Timor – 'how things are done around here'. Under this system CET, for instance, was able to stockpile whatever aid arrived by creating 'phantom' recipients, and later re-distributing food sequestered in this way to needy families on the request of a parish priest. The parish system became the de facto vehicle for emergency relief. The system was opportunistic and operated with little or no planning. While the practice proved beneficial during the Indonesian occupation, it was open to abuse.[16]

In the months prior to the September 1999 crisis, there were emerging tensions building among all three Caritas agencies, and these were bound to boil over once the UN became active in East Timor.

*

On September 9th we received news at Caritas headquarters in Sydney that the militia had killed Fr Barreto and some of the CET staff. This was a cause of great sadness for us as we had met many of these people only a few months previously and even then under very sad conditions.[17] The announcement of their deaths in the local media attracted wide attention. We relayed the news to CI, which at the time was in discussions with the UN about how best to deploy CI's international resources to deal with the humanitarian crisis unfolding in East Timor.

---

14 Church leaders in Australia did not live in a situation where banking services were minimal so that nearly all transactions occurred in cash. In this period the bishops of both Baucau and Dili were forced by circumstances to operate through church bank accounts set up by the Darwin diocese in Australia.
15 Janet Hunt *Evaluation Report: Response to East Timor Crisis* (Sydney: Caritas Australia, 2002), 12.
16 Another example of 'beating the system' involved a local NGO where funds sent to support orphans were redirected to buying a much-needed car. When challenged on this the reply was that the car would be used by NGO members 'to visit the orphans'! Culture is what culture is!
17 The Liquica massacre occurred while the CET group was in Australia and one member of the party lost 20 relatives that day.

With Australian troops on the ground in East Timor, it came as no surprise when Caritas Australia was asked by Caritas Internationalis to act as its lead agency in responding to the crisis. The mandate was to create 'a new organisation in East Timor'.[18] Caritas Australia thus became the Catholic Church's official UN partner in food distribution, reconstruction and emergency relief.

★

In September 1999 Caritas Australia was neither prepared nor equipped for this role. When the crisis hit, the organisation had only 27 staff[19] all of whom were engaged literally around the clock trying to manage the flood of people seeking information about what was happening in East Timor and wanting to help. Its phone system could not cope and soon had to be upgraded. Staff were processing and formally acknowledging donations arriving at 300 or more a day. This was in addition to processing regular donations. These two tasks consumed all the time available and other development work had to be put on hold. Over 9000 donations came in during September and October alone. The donations came from all sections of the community as a result of extensive media coverage. Volunteers had to be brought in to cope with the workload.[20] There was not enough office space to handle the work.

To function as lead agency Caritas Australia had to employ more staff, both short term and long term. The National Director, Tom Story, sought help from sister agencies around the world more experienced in emergency relief and quickly located a project manager, Beatrice Killen, who arrived in Darwin where she joined NGO and UN staff planning to meet the emergency and witnessed Australian troops departing for Dili.

At the meeting UN staff negotiated with the NGOs on how best to allocate responsibilities. Caritas Australia was assigned responsibility for food distribution in Dili and Baucau, food distribution and reconstruction in the remote enclave of Oecusse, and management of the Refugee Transit Centre in Dili. This was a major remit.

The United Nations International Force for East Timor (INTERFET) arrived in Dili on September 20th. Caritas Australia had its personnel on the ground by the 23rd. Within a week an operational base employing local staff had been set up in Dili. Catholic Relief Services (US) provided Caritas Australia with a procurement officer and in a short time 12 five-ton trucks and drivers were acquired. By October 7th Caritas Australia was distributing food provided by the World Food Program (WFP). Even before the INTERFET troops had set foot in Oecusse, Caritas Australia had its representative on the ground there assessing a situation thought to be dire. This was an extraordinary effort![21]

---

18 From the outset CA saw it necessary to have three agencies – Caritas Dili, Caritas Baucau and a national body Caritas East Timor. The former were to have operational and program control in their respective dioceses while the latter was to deal with the international donor community and take on a national advocacy and educational role. My task was to sell this model to the bishops and the directors in East Timor. Suspicion between the bishops however, made my task thankless.

19 According to its records, in 1999 Caritas Australia had 27 staff, which included some part-timers. Two staff were located in Melbourne, one part-time staff member in Perth, and another part-time member in Brisbane. The rest (23) were located in Sydney.

20 Hunt, 30ff

21 Cf. Jamie Isbister et al *Assessment on Caritas: Australia's Shelter Program in Oecusse Draft Report* (Sydney: Caritas Australia, Feb 2002).

Before the 1999 crisis only 23 staff worked in the head office of Caritas in Sydney. As the crisis unfolded in East Timor Caritas Australia added 46 international staff and 11 international volunteers. As well, it also employed 72 Timorese in managing its commitments on the ground in East Timor.[22] The crisis saw major re-assignment of existing staff and significant recruitment to handle the ballooning administrative and financial aspects of the work. Caritas Australia had to expand its Sydney headquarters to cope with the demand for information, particularly from Catholic schools and parishes. Its communications officer was sent to Dili to ensure a steady flow of useful images and stories needed to service this demand.

Caritas Australia's response to the crisis gave it a significant national profile, not only within the Catholic Church, but also in the public square. Its actions on the ground added greatly to the credibility of the Catholic Church. The effort came at considerable personal cost to those who had to steer the agency through this most demanding of times.

Tension between the ACSJC and Caritas Australia erupted and after one fraught meeting between leaders of the two bodies the national director of Caritas Australia, Tom Story, chose to resign believing that the criticism levelled at the organisation he led by the bishop heading the ACSJC lacked foundation. Tom Story had been a very competent leader and his loss at this time seemed an 'own goal' that the Church in Australia did not need to score.[23] His resignation meant that at the height of the crisis the Caritas Australia Board had to find a new director. The organisation certainly needed someone with good management skills but, more importantly, it needed someone with a sound understanding of, and commitment to, social justice. We were fortunate to recruit Jack de Groot who provided Caritas Australia with the leadership it needed at a time of internal and external crisis.

★

In the midst of all this frenetic activity Fr Barreto and his staff, far from dead, re-appeared in Dili. When the militia rampage started in Dili they had hidden in the hills. Fr Barreto was not pleased to discover that Caritas Australia was now in charge. However, Caritas Australia immediately provided him with the funds needed to get the local office, which had been ransacked and looted by the militia, up and running again. To ameliorate any tensions over food distribution Caritas Australia's program leader invited Caritas East Timor to act as its agent in distributing food around Dare, just south of Dili. However, when a snap World Food Program audit discovered that CET was feeding 'phantom' refugees and storing food for distribution according to 'the old pattern' of parish-based distribution, its representatives called a meeting with Belo and Barreto. When the CET Director refused to comply with normal WFP protocols, they closed down any further participation by CET in food distribution. This was an embarrassing development for CA's program leader in Dili.

To help address emerging difficulties between agencies, and to better co-ordinate support arriving from Caritas agencies worldwide, CA's program leader organised a two-day conference in Darwin the following week (October 19-20th). The meeting not

---

22 Hunt, 31-32. The numbers cited cumulated over the time of the crisis and its aftermath.
23 Tom Story was to spend a year in the role of Commissioner of Revenue with the United Nations Transitional Administration for East Timor advising on the new taxation system, dealing with international donors, recruiting staff etc.

only brought Caritas people together but was historic in another regard. At this conference East Timor's four main leaders Bishops Belo, and Nascimento, and CNRT leaders Xanana and Ramos Horta met together for the first time.

After the frantic activity of the previous month, the conference gave the rapidly growing Caritas team a chance to step back and reflect on what had happened and, in the light of comments from the civil and religious leaders, to plan ahead. Belo announced that in future the Caritas agency in his diocese would be called Caritas Dili. This decision, while helpful, did not fully resolve tensions between the local organizations, and these lingered on. Frustrated, the program leader of Caritas Australia in East Timor, Beatrice Killen, decided she would not extend her contract when it expired two months later. Her departure like that of the National Director Tom Story, was a great loss at a critical time.

★

In emergency relief work things have to happen fast or people get sick and die, particularly the most vulnerable, the old and the very young. However, help delivered in this way can be very inefficient and the scale of the task overwhelming. Effective aid delivery requires planning which takes time and time shrinks in an emergency.

In order to meet its assigned responsibilities Caritas Australia needed people with expertise in a range of areas. Recruiting them had to dovetail with the activities of the local Timorese workers needed to construct houses, repair schools etc. At another level this work had to be overseen, so people with project management skills and expertise in personnel recruiting were required. All of this had to happen in a short time and in competition with other NGOs equally committed, but similarly short-staffed.

Recruiting the staff needed to manage the emergency response was, however, only part of the picture. Caritas Australia also had to assess what staff would be required to sustain the development phase once the immediate emergency phase had passed. In 2000 most NGO leaders thought that development aid would be needed for at least five years, two under the United Nations Transitional Administration in East Timor (UNTAET) and at least three under the first national government of Timor Leste. These were matters that in 2000 taxed the Caritas Australia Board whose members like myself were swimming for the most part in uncharted waters.

★

The other challenge facing Caritas Australia was that extreme busyness in meeting primary needs could result in its people losing sight of the organisation's ethos. Additionally, there was a language barrier to be crossed when employing local staff. The fact that the majority of Caritas Australia's international staff were new and had only a rudimentary grasp of the organisation's ethos added to the challenge. In such circumstances it was not surprising that misunderstandings abounded and some relationships broke down.

I flew to Dili three times in 2000 to support leaders in the field. As an outsider with some experience of complex organisations it seemed clear to me that the tensions within Caritas reflected wider East Timorese frustrations with the way the UN operated. From Xanana down, local people felt excluded from real decisions. Having longed to run their own affairs, and having fought for and won that right, when the time came to exercise it they found themselves sidelined. The Director of Caritas Dili, a long-time CNRT advocate, was infected with this sentiment and it, together with his idiosyncratic management style, set a tone that was hard to work around, or overcome. Partnership would come, but it seemed that this would happen only when East Timor moved beyond the emergency phase and had more control of its own fate in the development phase.

My view at the time was that eventually the staffing of the two local Caritas agencies in East Timor would stabilise and relationships be rebuilt. Over time local Caritas agencies would professionalise as a result of their UN exposure and leaders would develop a worldview that was no longer shaped by twenty years of exposure to corruption and oppression.

It is impossible for someone who has not been through that type of experience to understand its impact on the psyche and how it works its way through into relationships. Over my time in East Timor working alongside local Church leaders, I developed some limited insight into how this all happens which made it difficult for me to be critical of them. My working rule was that everyone was doing his or her best no matter how ordinary that 'best' seemed to be.

★

Catholic social teaching places a particular emphasis on exercising a 'preferential option for the poor'. In East Timor no group was poorer or more marginalised by the fight for independence than those living in the enclave of Oecusse. Caritas Australia can look with a certain sense of pride on the way it helped this group.

In 1999, with militia in charge of the area west of the border, it was not possible to make the 60 km trip to Oecusse by road. The only options were to go by sea or by helicopter. Once INTERFET had cleared Oecusse of militia, and Jordanian Peacekeepers patrolled the border, it was possible to begin food distribution and reconstruction. To facilitate this the UN hired a barge that made a daily trip from Dili to the main town Pante Macassar. When I visited Oecusse in 2000 Pante Macassar contained only five intact buildings: three shops, the Catholic church and the priest's house that also served as Caritas Australia's base. I had been fortunate, after several frustrated attempts, to hitch a ride on the daily UN helicopter flight from Dili. Non-UN personnel could fly only if there was an empty seat. A similar rule applied to the barge. NGOs could put their trucks and equipment on the barge only if there was space after the military and UN agencies had loaded up. This could mean off-loading a truck if the military or some other UN agency arrived late. With only twelve trucks at Caritas Australia's disposal, and 50,000 people to feed, having one or two trucks sitting on the wharf idle at either Dili or Pante Macassar hampered food distribution. At the height of the crisis the only time a Caritas Australia truck was off the road was for repairs. They ran 24 hours a day.

The scale of the devastation in Oecusse was almost total. Militias ran riot there for almost a month after INTERFET arrived in Dili. The border between Oecusse and West Timor runs for 60 km through largely inaccessible country which gave militia groups cover. Over 4000 houses had been destroyed in 37 villages. Most of the local people were living in bush huts covered by tarpaulins that lasted for about six months in tropical conditions.

The initial aim of the reconstruction project was to have them all in permanent shelter before the wet season set in in 2001. Fairly basic house kits, made of treated pine imported from Australia, were assembled locally. These were allocated to village-based 'reconstruction committees' for the locals to erect. An immediate difficulty was transport, given the lack of roads. Caritas Australia had to procure trucks and a forklift to get things moving. Some of the villages were so remote that the only way to get the kits on site was by helicopter.

The initial plan was to use traditional roofing materials (palm fronds). It was thought it would be quicker to get the houses completed using local materials. However this plan did not take into account the ecological damage resulting from cutting down enough fronds to roof 4500 houses! The alternative was to use corrugated iron for the task. The difficulty then was how to source the iron, given the demand for corrugated iron in East Timor's twelve other districts. The delay in ordering roofing iron meant that while Caritas Australia had delivered 4500 kits by the target date only about 1000 had been roofed. The day I visited in Oecusse in 2001, after a teeth-shattering ride in one of the UN's huge Russian helicopters, over 1000 of these kits were still stacked up in a great pile outside the priest's office waiting to be delivered.

The second major contribution Caritas Australia made in helping the people of Oecusse was rebuilding the schools. This project was given high priority in order to return some form of normalcy to the lives of children traumatised by recent events. When the militia departed from Oecusse they had looted the schools and stripped the corrugated iron from the roofs. Caritas Australia worked with the United Nations Children's Fund (UNICEF), to clean up and reroof 42 classrooms in Oecusse's nine primary schools. Desks, chairs, blackboards and chalk had to be sourced and delivered so that school could start again by October 2000. The housing and the school repair projects made Caritas Australia the biggest employer in Oecusse in 2000-02. The locals were very sad when we departed mission accomplished!

★

While the main focus of Caritas Australia's work in 1999-2001 was emergency relief, it also had one eye on the future and people's need for some form of closure after the horrific times they had lived through. A number of groups in East Timor realised that the country had to develop its own capability to address matters of justice if peace was to be achieved. On this matter there was disappointing leadership from the CNRT. Both Xanana Gusmao and Jose Ramos Horta were firmly advocating a general amnesty for offenders involved in the 1999 mayhem and murder.

The Catholic Church and the NGOs stood united against this option because it legalised impunity. They argued that the legal impunity enjoyed by the Indonesian military and the militias under Indonesia's rule had caused most of the people's suffering and immunity should not be countenanced by the new state. Belo, as spokesperson for the local Catholic Church, pursued a policy with three elements: a Truth Reception and Reconciliation Commission[24] to deal with 'minor crimes' such as destruction of property and non lethal assaults; a Serious Crimes Unit to address criminal matters such as murder and rape; and the referral of those in

---

24   Belo visited South Africa in 1997 and was acquainted at first hand with the way the Truth and Reconciliation Commission worked there.

the military and the Indonesian government with command responsibility for the violence and destruction to the International Criminal Court.

As I travelled around East Timor in 2000 and 2001 the justice issue was becoming divisive as ordinary people began to think that there would be no justice for the wrongs done to them by the military, that the generals responsible and the leaders of the militia, holed up in West Timor, would not be held accountable. For me the first two elements in the Church's policy were feasible. The third was not. The issue here was not moral, but political.[25]

The *realpolitik* in 2000 was that major states did not want senior Indonesian military put on trial as such a move might threaten a weak democratic regime and return Indonesia to military dictatorship. There was little support for justice in this form from the CNRT leadership who thought it would undermine the prospect of a bi-lateral relationship with Indonesia. The international consensus favoured Indonesia and East Timor each prosecuting its own nationals under existing laws. The Indonesian parliament passed new legislation dealing with the abuse of human rights but the new laws could not be applied retrospectively. So after some token trials the matter was dropped.

In East Timor UN attempts to address justice issues became bogged down by language difficulties, the lack of resources and the lack of expertise. Senior Church leaders criticised the UN for its lack of resolve thinking the UN's mandate would expire before serious crimes ever came to trial. No one was particularly happy with this situation. Despite Belo's many calls for the international community to intervene and bring justice to the people of East Timor it was becoming increasingly clear that this was not going to occur and that East Timor would have to create its own pathway to peace.

Caritas Australia's Human Rights and Justice Program was established in this context. I was unaware of its existence until later after it had concluded, and so can claim no credit for what was a significant development. It is a measure of the new national Director Jack de Groot's political nous in dealing with the Australian episcopacy that he kept me in the dark so avoiding further tension with the bishop who was chair of the ACSJC.[26]

Following Catholic social teaching senior Caritas Australia staff understood that the pursuit of justice is a necessary condition for the pursuit of peace, and without this sustainable development is unlikely. At the time this perspective was unique among the NGOs in East Timor. Most NGOs placed justice matters in the 'too hard' or 'too political' baskets.

Justice in Catholic social teaching seeks the restoration of relationships that have been fractured by intentional human action. To provide justice therefore requires acknowledging what has happened, being willing to restore relationships, and engaging in intentional action to bring this about. Since 'relationship' involves more than one party, reconciliation is an integral element in the pursuit of justice. In this conception, justice involves more

---

25 Prior to 2000 the UN had done the legal ground work and opened negotiations necessary to establish an International Criminal Court, but not enough countries had ratified the UN protocol creating the Court for it to become part of international law. 'Crimes against humanity' in Rwanda and Bosnia were prosecuted in *ad hoc* courts set up by the UN specifically for this purpose. This was not going to happen in East Timor.
26 My Victorian episcopal colleague Bishop Jeremiah Coffey had warned me that the chair of the ACSJC, Bishop Bill Brennan, was privately canvassing some of my fellow bishops to gain support for a complaint to Rome about my advocacy activities. Either Bishop Brennan never received the support he needed or Rome ignored his complaint. His animosity towards CA's leaders was difficult to understand in the circumstances prevailing in 1999-2000.

than legally sanctioned retribution.

The conception of justice promoted by Caritas Australia sought to effect the restoration of relationships between people or between an individual and his or her community. It sought to take both the offender and the victim, not back to where they were, but to a new place. Justice in this restorative form requires acknowledgement by the perpetrator and the victim of what has happened, a willingness to forgive rather than forget, and a mutual commitment to move forward together.

★

As chair of the ETHRC my view was that people be held to account for the abuse of human rights. In also taking this direction, Caritas Australia separated itself out from other NGOs in East Timor. Over time however they too began to see the connections between justice and sustainable development.

Caritas Australia's Human Rights and Justice Program sought to develop local agency by equipping those digging up mass graves with the skills necessary to preserve evidence for criminal prosecution at some point in the future. If this task was approached in a haphazard manner, as was happening, the risk was that valuable evidence would be destroyed. Caritas Australia used contacts in the NSW legal fraternity to bring a number of lawyers to Dili for short periods to run training programs showing local people how to collect evidence, how to analyse it, and how to prepare a brief of evidence that could be used in a court of law. Most of the newly appointed judges and prosecutors appointed by the UN attended the programs. Representatives from twelve different NGOs also took part.

In a second initiative Caritas Australia invited the NSW Senior Deputy Coroner to East Timor to advise on setting up a coronial system. He suggested instead that a better option would be to establish a Missing Persons Unit. Caritas Australia subsequently provided the funds necessary for this to happen.[27]

As life settled down under the United Nations Transitional Administration in East Timor (UNTAET), women became increasingly vocal in expressing their frustration at being shut out of discussions about the future of their country and about justice issues that impacted on them. Many had been raped or otherwise sexually assaulted by militia and wanted redress. Others wanted help in dealing with the psychological effects of their experiences under the military. To address this need, Caritas Australia established a *Sexual Assault Program*. The program sought to train people from a number of NGOs to assist the victims of sexual assault. When response to the program was very positive, Caritas Australia established a Sexual Assault Team to continue the work of 'training the trainers' at village level. The team included both men and women to highlight the reality that sexual assault is something that involves both genders and cannot be addressed without involving both. This initiative contributed to the success of many community reconciliation programs.

Caritas Australia's justice initiatives played out at two important levels. Firstly, they helped clarify the notion of restorative justice. Such clarification was important for those returning home from West Timor and seeking to be accepted back into local communities.

---

27 The Australian Electoral Commission helped by handing over the electoral roll used for the independence ballot. A senior police officer from NSW then volunteered his services to set up the database needed to track missing people given that it was now known who was alive at the time of the vote.

In many places reconciliation failed because the victims were still too traumatised or too angry at the impotence of the authorities in providing retributive justice. East Timor had the facilities and the resources to prosecute and jail only the worst offenders. It took a long time for this realisation to sink in locally.

Caritas Australia's justice initiatives helped pave the way for the Truth and Reconciliation Commission (CAVR) by skilling local people to address complex justice issues. It did this by enhancing the investigative capability of the Commission established by UNTAET with the brief to prepare a comprehensive report based on factual and objective information collected by it or placed at its disposal. This information included material painstakingly collated by the Australian-based ETHRC during the time of the Indonesian occupation.

When the ETHRC ceased operations in 1999 hundreds of files stored for safe-keeping in three four-drawer steel cabinets and kept permanently locked were stored in my house in Blackburn. Some of my friends were nervous about the security risk this entailed. They would not have been surprised if the house went up in smoke! The cabinets were eventually delivered to the UN in Dili in 2003. I have no idea what happened to the contents subsequently. The files constitute a grim record of over twenty years' suffering by men, women and children under Indonesian occupation.

The final report of the Commission for Reception, Truth and Reconciliation (CAVR) entitled *Chega!* (Portuguese for 'Enough', or more colloquially 'no more, stop, enough') is a credible attempt to give those killed as a result of human rights abuses, whether by FRETILIN, UDT or the Indonesians, a 'voice'. By laying blame where it was due the report sought to prevent any 'ideologising' of Timor's recent history. The seven member Commission set up its base in the notorious Becora jail and took four years to complete its assigned task. Members heard thousands of eyewitness accounts at hearings around the country. The Commissioners presented their 2500 page report to the President of East Timor in 2005 and, in accord with CAVR's mandate, he presented the report to the United Nations in 2006 where it was filed along with so many other reports!

The Report's recommendations received a mixed reception both at home and internationally. *Chega!* remains a difficult document to discount.

★

My six-year term as chair of Caritas Australia concluded in 2003. In that period Caritas Australia had contributed significantly to the development of East Timor, but the relationship was reciprocal. Caritas Australia is now a very different organisation from the one I knew in the mid-1990s. Its involvement with East Timor is a chapter in both the 'Australian Catholic story' and the 'East Timor story' that is often overlooked. It is also a rewarding if difficult chapter in my own story. However, to have neglected telling it would have done a disservice to the many dedicated people who helped the East Timorese, especially those who left their families in Australia and in other countries around the world to help their sisters and brothers in East Timor in its time of dire need.[28]

---

28 Caritas Australia completed its mandate on behalf of Caritas Internationalis in East Timor in 2003. Today, Caritas Dili and Caritas Baucau live happily in East Timor with Caritas Australia which still maintains offices in both Dili and Oecusse.

CHAPTER 29
SALVATION, LIBERATION AND OTHER DILEMMAS

Many cultures have a salvation myth at their heart. The need for 'salvation' has a long provenance in Christian experience and still operates at a sub-conscious level in many European cultures and those of the territories colonised by Europe, including East Timor. Over time the meaning attached to this myth has evolved, and now both the secular and the sacred interpretations of it constitute a polar tension within the one culture. Managing this tension creatively is a challenge for both civil and religious leaders.

For African and Pacific peoples colonised in the 19th century, salvation has often meant liberation from the exploitative behavior of European powers. For oppressed peoples in the 20th century in Latin America it meant liberation from US-backed military regimes. Unfortunately in these contexts, Church leaders imbued with the classicist understanding of culture often positioned themselves too close to a secular understanding of salvation in interpreting the institution's 'civilising mission'. This was certainly the case in East Timor under Portuguese rule.

Under Indonesian rule East Timor's Church leaders were forced to take an independent stand as the Indonesian understanding of what 'salvation' meant for their people was anathema to them. In supporting a more religious interpretation of salvation in which God comes to the aid of God's people, they were implicitly supporting the thrust for self-determination and possible independence. Their dilemma was that their pursuit of this interpretation ran counter to what Vatican authorities wanted, putting Belo and later Nascimento, in a 'no-win' situation.[1]

The East Timorese as a predominantly Catholic people living for decades in a culture of violence and impunity, clung to the religious concept of salvation hoping that God would respond to their prayers. Their hope was to be free and they looked to the United Nations as the most likely source of their liberation. What they did not anticipate was what 'salvation' delivered by a secular agency would look like. Nor do they seem to have anticipated the costs associated with healing the wounds created by living for two decades in a culture dominated by corruption, violence and abuse. In many ways the violence in 1999 was the tip of the iceberg.

---

1   When Belo had the temerity to write to the UN Secretary General asking for a supervised act of self-determination without consulting Rome, he drew down upon himself the ire of the Vatican Secretariat of State, whose officials' treatment of him at times bordered on being pathological.

In my visits to East Timor from 2000 to 2003 I frequently asked the people I met: 'How are things different now that you are free?' Their response was almost always the same: 'East Timor is still poor and underdeveloped, but the fear has gone'.

*

Within the Judeo-Christian worldview the first paradigmatic account of salvation is the Exodus event in which God, hearing the cry of oppressed slaves in Egypt, invites Moses to lead them to freedom. While the account in the Bible has been heavily mythologised by Israel's story-tellers, it is clear that Moses had his work cut out leading this band of 'refugees' as they made not only the difficult journey from rabble to a 'people', but also the cultural journey from 'Egypt' to 'the Promised Land' – from oppression to salvation. Traumatised by a form of slavery that had stripped people of their identity, the primordial Israelites struggled to cope with freedom when it was offered. Liberation for them was only a beginning, not an end state. It created an opportunity to be seized. The people had to learn how to cope with the new reality as well as heal scars left by the experience of oppression. There must have been many times during these journeys when Moses, faced with the dilemmas of leadership, asked: 'Why me?' Such is the lot of leaders in liberation movements whether religious or civil, as I am sure Belo and Xanana can testify.

The second paradigmatic account of liberation in the Bible occurs some time later when the Israelites, now a nation, are defeated and enslaved in Babylon for several generations. The agent of their liberation this time is not someone appointed by God, but a foreign King, Cyrus of Persia, who on conquering the Babylonians, decrees that the captives who want to, are free to return to their native land. Amazed by this development, some set out for home to rebuild what is left of the nation. What results is a fundamentalist religious revival led by Ezra, echoes of which still exist within contemporary Judaism and Christianity.

Jesus himself was heir to the tradition of his people. His own salvific mission embraced elements of both spiritual and secular liberation. His religious mission proved a great challenge to the political power-holders in both the Roman empire and the religious community to which he belonged. The powerful witness of his life, death and resurrection would inspire the 'little ones' of this world across the next two thousand years, and very powerfully so in our own time.

Within the Judeo-Christian worldview, salvation involves both providential and human intervention, and the liberation it offers can take different forms and be delivered by different mechanisms. In East Timor's case, salvation delivered by a secular organisation with little time for the people's religious sensibilities, culture and history was always bound to introduce leadership dilemmas additional to those already inherent in the experience of liberation itself. These are the two issues I want to pursue in this chapter.

*

The Catholic Church has always reserved judgment in its support of political liberation. Like most cultures, Church culture is defined by how polar tensions are mediated. Liberation theologian Leonardo Boff gives perhaps the clearest outline I have come across of what is at stake. He contrasts two archetypes of Church that stand in polar tension to each other – the *witness* model and the *dialogue* model. Adherents of the witness model hold that:

> We have the deposit of faith, which contains all the truths necessary for salvation; we have the sacraments, which communicate grace; we have a well-defined morality; we have the certainty that the Catholic Church is the church of Christ; the only true church; we have the pope who enjoys infallibility in questions of faith and morals; we have the promise of permanent help from the Holy Spirit.[2]

The role of the Church in this understanding is to stand as witness in a world incapable of ever achieving its own salvation without the Church's mediation. Salvation in this understanding exists only beyond history.

Standing in tension with this understanding is another sourced in the teachings of the Second Vatican Council whose adherents hold:

> The kingdom is greater than the church and also finds secular fulfilment wherever there is truth, love and justice; the risen Christ has cosmic dimensions and is pushing evolution towards a good end; the Spirit is always present in history and in good people, arriving before the missionary because it was already among peoples in the form of solidarity, love and compassion. God never abandons his (sic) own and offers to all the opportunity of salvation, because he produced them from his heart so that one day they might live happily in the kingdom of the freed.[3]

In this perspective

> …The Church's mission is to be a sign of this history of God within human history and also an instrument for its implementation, together with other spiritual paths. If both religious reality and secular reality are impregnated with God, we must enter into dialogue: exchange, learn from one another, and make the human journey toward the promised happiness easier and safer.[4]

Salvation within history, understood as making the Kingdom of God present in particular contexts, stands as a sign of the salvation beyond history. Since these positions are archetypes, few people stand entirely at the extremes. Real people hold both views to some extent and have to negotiate a balance point between them.

Boff's position is that Popes John Paul II and Benedict XVI, whose approach to leadership was extremely cerebral, moved the balance point too far towards the *witness* understanding as described above, while Pope Francis's holistic approach to leadership is pastoral. By his example Francis has moved it decisively back towards the *dialogue*

---

2 Leonardo Boff *Francis of Rome: Francis of Assisi: A New Springtime for the Church* (Maryknoll N.Y: Orbis, 2014), 26.
3 Ibid, 27.
4 Ibid

understanding. This opens up new possibilities in how the Church understands its mission and how it engages in the public square.

Organisational cultures are determined by how people act which, in turn, is shaped by what they believe and are committed to. Catholics whose outlook is primarily shaped by the witness tradition can easily isolate themselves in a comfortable religious world cut off from the sufferings of ordinary people. Too exclusive an espousal of the dialogue model can lead to religion being co-opted in the service of secular forms of liberation. There is a balance point to be found and where it lies is determined by the context in which people live.

Belo was in constant conflict with Rome on this point. Despite his religious enculturation in Portugal and his love for all things Portuguese which would normally have put him firmly in the witness camp, the suffering of his people led him to act from a more dialogical perspective. While he certainly did not see himself as a liberation theologian, or any form of intellectual for that matter, he had an innate sense of what really mattered, and it was this that enabled him to marshal and apply moral force when the need arose. He had a good grounding in Catholic social teaching and seemed to have an intuitive sense of the direction in which this was developing.

Belo's stance on the need for dialogue often placed him in conflict with the CNRT leadership who thought they knew what was best for the people of East Timor without any great need for consultation.[5] However, he found allies within UNTAET and the NGOs who also, but for somewhat different reasons, saw dialogue as a condition of peace.

★

Belo was also aware that liberation delivered from outside could not by itself end the suffering of the East Timorese unless it was accompanied by healing that comes only through reconciliation. He had travelled to South Africa in 1997 to learn what he could of the approaches to community reconciliation trialled there.

The experience convinced him that reconciliation was vital in addressing the trauma and marginalisation of his people. For him reconciliation was essentially a spiritual challenge and meeting it was essential in rebuilding lives and communities. The faith of ordinary people was a resource to be called on in meeting this challenge. In this his approach was different from the civil approach. In the lead-up to the ballot Belo made a number of attempts to bring the pro- and anti–autonomy parties together, but without success.[6] From this he learned that reconciliation demands a condition of equality between victim and perpetrator and this cannot happen in an atmosphere of fear.

Belo's views on reconciliation owed much to the work of US theologian Robert Schreiter.[7] While I heard him outline his position many times, he did so most clearly in launching Caritas Australia's project Compassion Appeal in Melbourne early in 1999. He

---

5   Belo had a good ally in Bishop Nascimento in this regard and when ill health and mental exhaustion got the better of him, he was quite prepared to hand leadership over to him.
6   These meetings were formal meetings known as Dare I and Dare II held at the Catholic Seminary at Dare in the hills behind Dili.
7   In the 1990s Schreiter acted as consultant to a number of Truth and Reconciliation commissions attempting to bring peace to violence-ridden countries in Africa and Latin America. See Robert Schreiter *The Ministry of Reconciliation: Spirituality and Strategies* (Maryknoll N.Y: Orbis Books, 1998).

began his presentation by quoting Nelson Mandela, 'to make peace with your enemy, one must work with that enemy, and that enemy becomes your partner' and continued:

> What does he mean by that? Simply that in order to make a new start to lives fractured by violence and fear, we must talk with our persecutor. Recognition must be made by the perpetrators of crimes as to the facts of what happened and the victims need to be prepared for the recognition that crimes in which they suffered need to be put to rest and the burden of shame, fear and anger can be relieved. This needs to happen in a mutual process based on equality and dignity for all concerned.[8]

This understanding, as noted in the last chapter, stood behind the Community Reconciliation Process adopted by CAVR and influenced the flawed Commission for Truth and Friendship adopted as the vehicle for effecting reconciliation between Indonesia and East Timor.[9]

The moral force of Belo's leadership in East Timor owed much to his consistent appeal to the principles and insights of Catholic social teaching, and the points of contact these made with the secular aspirations of people working for NGOs and the UN. His words above invoke the considerable moral authority of Pope John Paul II but transpose the latter's understanding of 'dialogue' into a new sphere, that of social justice and reconciliation.[10] In doing this I believe he made his own contribution to the development of this teaching.

★

In 1999 the UN was itself looking for salvation after peacekeeping debacles in Rwanda (1994) and Srebrenica (1995) where people under the protection of a UN peacekeeping mission were abandoned and later slaughtered.

UNAMET was sent to East Timor on a political mission rather than a peacekeeping mission. In negotiations leading to the May 5th Agreement the UN took a gamble that Indonesia would maintain security in the land up to and during the ballot. The international NGOs (INGOs) protested that this was an untenable position. However the UN was faced with Hobson's choice. Indonesia would not agree to the ballot being run as part of a peacekeeping mission as this called their sovereignty of East Timor into question. The choice facing the UN was simple: political mission or no mission! When UNAMET arrived in Dili in 1999 to stage the August referendum, the ordinary people thought that salvation had arrived principally because the level of militia intimidation eased off. For them, UNAMET was the United Nations.

When the post-ballot violence broke out, much as the INGOs had warned it would,

---

8   Text of speech given at Camberwell Feb 18th 1999. Hilton Deakin personal papers.
9   The Deputy Chair of CAVR was a Catholic priest, Jovito Araujo, appointed to the role by Belo. He served as one of the seven CAVR Commissioners from 2001 to 2004.
10 In *Redemptoris Missio* (1990) #57 John Paul II speaks of the need for a 'dialogue of life' in relation to ecumenical and interreligious dialogue. 'Dialogue of life' in this context means 'forming a relationship with' and 'working together with'. Belo extends this notion to include dialogue between perpetrators and victims and between people pursuing human rights whether motivated by religious or secular interests. Downloadable from the Vatican website.

the UN was looking at another epic disaster. With no nation willing to accept the 1500 refugees in the UNAMET compound, it looked like they would have to be abandoned to their fate.

Faced with another public relations catastrophe, the UN Security Council jumped at John Howard's offer to have Australia's *ad hoc* peacekeeping force, then assembled in Darwin, land in Dili and put an end to the militia violence. Despite protestations to the contrary, the transitional government in Indonesia must also have privately welcomed a development that strengthened its relatively weak hand in dealing with a fractious military. The speed with which the UN acted to approve the *ad hoc* INTERFET force is unprecedented in modern times. The quick response also seems to have taken TNI leaders directing *Operation Clean Sweep* completely by surprise and frustrated their plans. The genocide then underway was halted.[11]

Australians watching events unfold in East Timor, with little understanding of how the UN operates, interpreted the evacuation of UNAMET staff as the UN abandoning East Timor. Certainly this was the way East Timorese in Australia viewed the matter. My friends here in Australia were in despair thinking that September 1999 marked the end of hope.

The INTERFET intervention in East Timor was made possible by a combination of what I term 'moral force', the Indonesian government's powerlessness and the UN's need to save face. In international affairs, moral force, understood as the collective exercise of conscience, stands as a polar opposite to national self-interest.[12] There seems little doubt that international opinion mobilised by the churches, the NGOs and the civic groups, shocked by pictures of the devastation in Dili and attacks on the UN's international personnel, forced the pendulum to swing so that decisions normally made on the basis of national self-interest responded instead to 'moral force', prompting the UN to act on principle rather than pragmatism. The amazing thing is that it did so, and decisively. For those who interpret salvation in a religious sense this development seemed providential.

★

A single incident illustrates how moral force can replace self-interest in resolving leadership dilemmas. As the second tense week in September 1999 unfolded, a drama was being played out at UNAMET headquarters in Dili. UNAMET was housed in a compound that previously served as a teachers' college with a training school next door. With the collapse of the education system in 1999 the school ground had become UNAMET's car park. The walls of the UNAMET compound were topped by razor wire to ensure security. The car park was not secured.

Following the violence at Belo's compound a short distance away, refugees fled to the UN car park hoping for UN protection. These included families driven from their homes, Catholic sisters and children in their care, relatives of CNRT leaders, and student leaders unable to flee to the hills. The number camped in the car park soon swelled to well over

---

11 'Genocide' under international law includes not only selectively killing off an ethnic group but also displacing them from their homeland against their will.
12 At their best, churches and NGOs are agents of 'moral force', while governments often act as agents of self-interest.

a thousand. In clearing this group, *Aitarak* and the TNI may have been initially deterred by the presence of a dozen or so international journalists known to be in the UNAMET compound. These were working literally around the clock to get the story of what was happening in Dili out to international media outlets.[13]

When the militia began to threaten this group of refugees, Robinson recounts what happened next:

> ...At about 8:00pm ... a barrage of automatic and homemade weapons fire erupted nearby. Terrified, and not realizing that the side entrance to the compound had been opened to let them in, the refugees began to throw their children over the high fence topped with razor wire. In less than an hour roughly one thousand people had joined the five hundred already inside the compound. Remarkably, the only injuries suffered that evening were to the refugees and UNAMET staff who had held back the razor wire with their hands to let people over the fence.[14]

This development created two crises for UN senior staff. The first was logistical. The UN did not have sufficient supplies to support the number in the compound. The second was moral. Orders had come through from New York to evacuate all international UNAMET staff to Darwin till things settled down. This meant leaving the local UNAMET staff and the refugees to their fate, despite earlier assurances that this would not happen. When the refugees found out what was being planned, the news created panic and was met with disbelief by some of the UN staff. They did not want to be party to the UN repeating the mistakes it had made in Rwanda and Bosnia. The announcement had a devastating impact on morale within the UNAMET compound.

The Head of Mission, Ian Martin, aware that morale was low, conducted a straw poll to find out who would be willing to stay, if the worst came to the worst. Some ninety UN staff offered to stay. Angry journalists in the compound added to the pressure on Martin by threatening to reveal what the UN had in mind. Local Australian diplomats compounded the UN's problems by refusing to provide travel documents to local UN staff so they could be evacuated to Darwin. When this objection was resolved by Canberra, the bulk of the UN staff and some 'extras' were flown to Darwin. The latter included Jose Ramos Horta's sister and her children. Another group of local UNAMET staff were flown out of Baucau including Belo who had been provided with travel documents nominating him as a UNAMET driver. The irony here was that he was never known to drive a car!

As the week progressed, the situation in Dili deteriorated for the refugees and remaining UN staff. Food and water were in short supply. New orders came through from New York that all remaining UN staff were to be evacuated. It was left to Robinson to break this news to the refugees which he did with great sadness. After he had spoken, a young Canossian nun, Sr Esmeralda, responded for the refugees. Her words made an indelible impression on Robinson:

---

13 As Irena Cristalis, who was one of the journalists recalls, the demand was never ending because when Europe went to sleep, the United States woke up, and when the United States was going to sleep Australia and Indonesia were waking up. Irena Cristalis *East Timor: A nation's bitter dawn*. Revised edition. (London: Zed Books, 2009), 225.
14 Robinson, 164.

'Whatever else may happen… this referendum has removed any doubt that East Timorese wish to be free. For conducting it, we will always be grateful to UNAMET'. Wiping tears from her eyes, she went on: 'We knew there would be violence after the vote and we hoped that you would stay. And yet, we are not surprised that you plan to leave us now. We are used to being abandoned in our times of greatest need… Before you leave, please consider whether in years to come you will be able to sleep soundly knowing what you have done'.[15]

Shamed by the force of this response the UN staff made further representations to Martin arguing that the decision to evacuate and leave the refugees behind was unconscionable. Sr Esmeralda's words had galvanised opposition. Twelve UN staff, including two Australian CIVIPOL (civilian police) officers, indicated they were prepared to disobey orders and remain behind when the others left to offer what protection they could to the refugees. Their decision forced Martin to postpone the evacuation for twenty-four hours. This proved fortuitous.

The next day a delegation from the UN Security Council that had been negotiating with the government in Jakarta on the need for UN peacekeepers arrived unexpectedly. They made a last minute decision to accompany General Wiranto to Dili to see the devastation for themselves as they did not believe what he had told them. The violence ceased during this visit making a point then widely recognised – that the Indonesian military controlled the militia and the violence.[16] Wiranto was shocked by what he saw.

Members of the delegation met the surviving UNAMET staff and the refugees now including Pedro Unamet Rodriguez, three days old, who had been born in the compound. Before departing, the head of the UN delegation gave the refugees the news they most wanted to hear: 'We will not leave you. I give you my word'.[17]

The next day, acting on Wiranto's advice, President Habibie capitulated allowing peacekeepers into East Timor. The remaining UN staff, along with all the refugees, were airlifted to Darwin. The UN's reputation was enhanced once news of this drama got out. Moral force had triumphed over self-interest.

★

Salvation has many forms. Salvation from oppression can come as a result of either revolution or through external intervention. The CNRT interpreted the arrival of INTERFET and the United Nations Transitional Administration in East Timor (UNTAET) as indicating that they had triumphed in a 'revolution'.[18] They therefore expected to form the transitional government working in partnership with the UN. At conferences in Portugal and Australia held in 1998 and 1999, CNRT representatives from across the political divide had thrashed out both a national constitution and a development plan.

Coming directly from Kosovo, UNTAET leaders had a totally different understanding

---

15 Robinson, 177-8.
16 As the British member of the delegation, Sir Jeremy Greenstock, later commented 'the TNI could turn the violence on and off like a tap' (quoted in Robinson, 197)
17 Robinson, 198.
18 CNRT rhetoric at the time.

of the political situation in Timor. For them the CNRT represented the interests of the pro-independence lobby only, while the refugees in West Timor represented the interests of the pro-autonomy lobby. Both the country's political system and its national constitution had to emerge from *dialogue* between these two groups. This position was supported by Belo and other Church leaders.[19] The consequence of the clash of interpretations was that in the period before the UN's head of mission, Sergio de Mello, arrived in East Timor, CNRT leaders found themselves sidelined. Xanana Gusmao, the CNRT Chair, was so disgusted that he did not even meet de Mello at the airport. The situation was similar for FALINTIL leaders. The twelve hundred FALINTIL fighters living in cantonments expected that they would become the nucleus of a national security force or at least its police force. INTERFET, and later the UNTAET administration, however, regarded them as pro-independence militias comparable to the pro-autonomy militias both of which had to be disarmed. This added to the East Timorese's disenchantment with 'the new invaders'.

Initially lower echelons of the UNTAET mission misread the political and military situation in East Timor badly, and this poisoned relationships with the CNRT. Subsequently, a *rapprochement* between De Mello and Xanana saw them flying around the country together explaining to local communities the nature of the UN presence and the tasks set for it by the Security Council.

★

The United Nations is one of the world's largest bureaucracies made up of a multitude of agencies. Comparison with Caritas is helpful. Caritas is made up of over one hundred and sixty-five *national agencies* whose support in dealing with an emergency situation is co-ordinated through Caritas Internationalis (CI). CI appoints a lead agency that is given a formal mandate. Other agencies support the lead agency through CI so that the mandate can be fulfilled within an agreed timeframe.[20]

The UN works to a similar paradigm except that it is made up of *functional* agencies co-ordinated through the office of the Secretary General. In supervising the ballot in 1999 the lead agency was the UN's Department of Political Affairs. When militia violence erupted, the Secretary General's Department made the judgement that, with TNI backing, militia activity could continue at high intensity for some time. East Timor was deemed to be a peacekeeping operation rather than a political operation. The Department of Peacekeeping Operations was appointed the lead agency. Most of the senior UNTAET staff were drawn from this department. It is worth remembering that the UN had no prior experience to call on in establishing an independent state. East Timor was going to be a 'first' and mistakes were bound to be made.

When UN staff met with NGO leaders in Darwin in September 1999 prior to the UNTAET mandate being issued, they faced three immediate tasks. The first was to mobilise UN agencies and the INGOs to address a major humanitarian crisis. The World

---

19 CIIR 'The constitution-making Process in Timor Lorosa'e: The Church's Position' *Timor Link* (No 53 August 2001), 5.
20 The lead agency may be the Caritas agency of the particular country in which the emergency occurs as has been the case with the Nepal emergency in 2015, or it might be from another country as was the case with CA in East Timor.

Food Program estimated that 80% of the East Timorese population of 890,000 would need food aid for an indeterminate period. Most of this would have to be imported. Crops could not be planted in the window of time available due to the displacement of the population. A bad situation was made worse as thousands of traumatised people headed to Dili in search of humanitarian assistance and reports began to filter through about living conditions over the border in West Timor. The logistics of dealing with the unfolding food and health crises on both sides of the border were overwhelming.

The second task was to halt the violence so that humanitarian assistance could be delivered safely. The third was to assess the situation on the ground and determine the extent of support needed to re-establish essential infrastructure. Once these tasks were addressed, the UN, the CNRT, the churches and the NGOs could begin to address the challenges of nation-building.

Initial planning took place in Darwin in September 1999 as INTERFET prepared to decamp to Dili. At that point the United Nations Transitional Authority, UNTAET, did not exist. It was another month before UNTAET was given a mandate, the Special Representative of the Secretary General appointed, and responsibility for East Timor transferred from Indonesia to UNTAET. Operations on the ground were well underway before people knew what the UNTAET mandate was and what the UN's timeframe for involvement would be.

★

The UN Secretary General, Kofi Annan, played a lead role in the liberation and subsequent developments in East Timor. His reading of the international mood in 1999 determined the UN's timetable. He estimated that there was a three-year 'window' in which to establish the necessary conditions for independence in East Timor. The constitution and government had to be in place within this time as international attention would then move to other matters.[21] Such a short timeline ran contrary to CNRT plans which envisaged independence occurring within a much longer timeline, possibly up to ten years. The national infrastructure had to be re-established and the skill-base required to run an independent nation developed. However the poor working relationship between CNRT and UNTAET ensured that both agreed to the shorter timeline.

When the Secretary General's Special Representative Sergio de Mello arrived in Dili, the chaos he encountered bordered on total. The UN compounded the problem by employing a fleet of 'experts' who knew little or nothing about East Timor, its history or its culture. Business people flooded in from Darwin seeking to profit from the UN's emergency and reconstruction efforts. Dili became a carpetbaggers' paradise awash with development money, most of which went to ex-pats much to the chagrin of the locals. One of the few visible benefits came in the form of a new industry – eateries for ex-pats!

★

---

21 He was correct. After the September 11th 2001 attacks in New York, international interest in East Timor faded rapidly.

In any objective assessment of the situation in East Timor, two groups were fundamental in re-establishing a civil society. In September 1999, the Catholic Church's basic organisation remained intact. The militia members most of whom were Catholic seemed to have drawn the line at totally destroying churches, presbyteries and convents. The CNRT with some help from the Church and NGOs quickly re-established its degraded organisation. UNTAET leaders initially decided to keep the Catholic Church at arm's length in re-building the civil society in East Timor. They may have considered that they had enough problems without adding church-state relations to the mix.

Bishops Belo and Nascimento recognised that the advent of democracy meant the role of the Church in East Timor would change. How it would, or should change were the issues, as was the nature of the Church's role in the formation of a new state. Some clergy were of the view that Church leaders should remain 'neutral'; others sought to become 'players'.[22]

Faced with this dilemma Belo set his views out very clearly in a Pastoral Letter published early in 2001. He did this in six propositions:

1. By its very nature and mission as proclaimer of the Gospel of Jesus the Church has to play a major role in the political sphere.
2. This role is in the moral and religious area of political life and activity.
3. The Church calling on Catholic social teaching provides guiding moral principles for the proper governance of the community and acts as a complement to the government in this role. The Church acts as the moral conscience of the government; it stands in critical solidarity: critical when required, solidarity when necessary.
4. Lay people play a role in partisan politics.
5. It is a wise and prudent policy for priests and religious to refrain from partisan involvement in politics so as not to divide the community. No political program can be seen as the only option compatible with the Gospel.
6. In the process of nation-building the Church and the government find common ground in promoting the common good. The good of our new country is a moral value that everyone has to defend and promote.
7. In light of the above the Church will conduct its own moral and religious program regarding politics. The purpose of the program will be civic education.[23]

In Belo's view the Church's role was to counter the government's natural tendency to act from self-interest. Its mission was to be an agent of moral force. In a country in which 90% of the people are Catholic, this role inevitably gives it a political profile, and with this comes responsibility. Belo in his pastoral letter spells out clearly how this responsibility will be met.

During the occupation, despite its protestations of remaining 'neutral', the Church had, in fact, helped sustain the hope of a better life through its consistent defence of human rights and Timorese culture. While this was a moral position, it had political overtones when those in political power denied these basic rights. It also had political overtones

---

22 For instance, Fr Domingo Soares ('Fr Maubere') played a pivotal role in the re-emergence of the CNRT. Fr Filomena Jacob Abel SJ became Minster for Education in the transitional administration.
23 Summarised from Carlos Belo 'Pastoral exhortation on politics in East Timor' *Timor Link* (No 53, Jan 2001), 4-5.

when, partly in consequence, the Church's membership rose from 30% of the population to over 90% during the occupation. 'Catholic' became synonymous with East Timorese identity.

Liberation raised a new question: How should this cultural reality be acknowledged and incorporated into the new state arrangements, and what degree of activism would be required to ensure that the cultural connection between Church and people remained strong? The place of the Catholic Church within the emerging society was as much a cultural question as a religious question. This became clear in my three visits during 2000 when the future of Timorese culture was very much on people's minds, no more so than around the vexed question of language.

★

Language is important as both a cultural resource and a cultural identifier. In 1999 the CNRT decided to adopt Portuguese as the official language of an independent East Timor. This was done for convenience as well as for cultural reasons. As a new country East Timor needed a cultural narrative. The country's connection with Portugal, somewhat romanticised, provided this connection. It provided the East Timorese with access to a literary, art and architectural heritage that leaders were familiar with and at home in, since most of the senior CNRT leaders and Church leaders were fluent in Portuguese.[24]

The choice did not suit a younger generation of Bahasa speakers educated in Indonesia or in East Timor where the language of instruction for a generation had been Bahasa. Bahasa was rejected as the national language because it had been the language of the oppressors. This did not prevent it being the language of the courts.[25]

A third alternative for the national language was Tetum. Most East Timorese were familiar with some form of Tetum. The Church had supported its development by mandating that its liturgy be in Tetum. Tetum has very little to offer in way of a literary heritage and only became the language of instruction in schools as the result of sustained student unrest in the late 1990s.[26] As an oral tradition, Tetum had no sponsoring body and no official dictionary. This made it impractical as the language of law.[27]

When schools began to be repaired and re-opened in 2000-2001, Portuguese was mandated as the language of instruction. Many educators working in East Timor expressed to me that they saw this decision to be ideological and a nonsense. There were simply not enough competent Portuguese-speaking teachers to implement this decision. Teachers were imported from Portugal in an attempt to keep East Timor within the Lusophone world. School education became the victim of a culture war and a new generation of students its casualties. Both CNRT and Church leaders were complicit in this bizarre development.

---

24 Some, like Mari Alkatiri, had lived in Portugal or Mozambique for most of their lives.
25 The UN transitional authority continued to use Indonesian law as the basis of the legal system in 1999-2002.
26 Student disruption of Indonesian teachers in particular became an element in the overall strategy of the urban resistance, leading many to request a transfer to other parts of the archipelago.
27 The National Language Institute was established on January 1st 2000 to codify Tetum and top priority was given to producing an authoritative dictionary. This opened up the possibility of developing normative teaching materials. The Mary MacKillop Institute that produced teaching materials for Catholic schools pre-2000 had used Australian linguist Geoffrey Hull's dictionary but this was thought to be dated and inaccurate.

Many of East Timor's most influential supporters speak English, and the majority of international communication is in that language, so a case can also made for English as the national language. The result of the 'culture war' fought over a national language has meant that East Timor is poly-lingual. Portuguese and Tetum are the 'official languages' and Bahasa and English the 'working languages'. The constitution is written in Portuguese and the language dilemma remains largely unresolved.

★

In moving from oppression to independence, the people of East Timor faced a number of unique challenges as did the NGOs, the churches and the United Nations. These raised dilemmas for leaders. What was their proper role in the creation of the new nation once sovereignty passed from the UN to an elected parliament? There were questions associated with healing and reconciliation, an area in which the Church felt its moral and religious remit was evident. The Church had been the principal agent in defending the right of East Timorese to an indigenous culture, and in preserving their culture. What would be the Church's proper role now in shaping the culture of the people and the basic institutions of the new state? What role would it play in education?

It was clear to Belo and Nascimento as it was to Xanana and other secular leaders that changes were afoot and had to be negotiated. What was missing in 2000-2002 was any framework within which this could happen. Lacking this, the political power of a relatively weak government was going to run up against the moral force of a credible Church. What Belo had signaled in his Pastoral letter, and what I believe Xanana understood more clearly than most, was that the Church was serious in its offer to stand in 'critical solidarity' with the new government. This offer provided a key in resolving the leadership dilemmas that civic and religious leaders faced.

CHAPTER 30
END OF THE BEGINNING

The UN's nation-building program went into overdrive in mid-2001. The program operated at two related levels: effecting reconciliation and political development.

In order to advance the cause of reconciliation, the UNTAET established the National Commission for Reception, Truth and Reconciliation (CAVR). This was the outcome of multi-party discussions involving the National Council of Timorese Resistance (CNRT), the Church, the NGOs and the United Nations Transition Administration in East Timor (UNTAET) that had gone on for some time. The timing of the inauguration of this independent commission corresponded with Indonesia's attempts to resolve the refugee situation in West Timor.[1] With better knowledge of the numbers likely to return to East Timor it was possible to more accurately develop CAVR's terms of reference. As part of this development I received a letter from UNTAET in April requesting the files held by the ETHRC on human rights violations. I indicated that these could be shipped to Dili once CAVR was formally in operation.

The election of the Constituent Assembly to act as the government-in-waiting under UN authority, and to formally adopt the nation's constitution, was the next major step in political development. Political parties began to register in May 2001. The CNRT, which had acted as a united political front, was dissolved in June and elections held in August. The formal announcement of the results occurred on September 10th the day before the destruction of the Twin Towers in New York.

I was in East Timor at this time and discussed the likely outcome of the election with Belo among many others. His view was that FRETILIN would win only about 40% of the vote and would need to go into coalition with other parties to form a government. Others thought FRETILIN would win outright with between 60-70% of the vote. As it turned out FRETILIN won 55% of the vote, and so formed government. This result was accepted by the priests with little enthusiasm. A number had campaigned against FRETILIN. They found it difficult to accept that a 'Catholic country' should be led by a Muslim Prime Minister with a communist past. For them, this was a recipe for disaster. Mari Alkatiri, unwisely, did little to assuage the clergy's concerns. This set the scene for later antagonisms and public protests over religious instruction in schools and about legalising abortion that would contribute to the fall of his government. It would have been politically wise for him to build a relationship

---

1   June 7th 2001 was set as the date by which all refugees had to declare their intentions to either settle in Indonesia or return to East Timor. Many could not return immediately as they had crops still to harvest.

with Church leaders based around Belo's notion of 'critical solidarity'.

The Constituent Assembly was sworn in on September 15th a few days before the first anniversary of the INTERFET intervention. Its first act was to establish a final timetable for independence. May 20th 2002 was set as the date for independence to take effect. The handover ceremony was planned for Sunday May 19th. UNTAET's mandate was extended to correspond with this date.

In February 2002 the draft constitution was approved and became the subject of a largely symbolic consultation process. A month later, almost unchanged, it was adopted by the Constituent Assembly. East Timor now had a parliament and a constitution. All that remained was to elect the President.

★

Across 2000 and 2001 rumours were rife among my contacts in East Timor that various political parties, including FRETILIN, were out to 'bring down' both Xanana and Ramos Horta. Xanana opted to run for President with the support of minor parties and without the support of FRETILIN. The tensions between the former FRETILIN allies were such that Alkatiri let it be known that he would not be voting in the presidential election. There was sufficient concern among Xanana's supporters about the outcome of the presidential election to raise campaign funds among the diaspora and East Timor activists in Australia. I was happy to contribute when asked.

As things turned out, this concern was misplaced. While Xanana's support among the new 'political elite' made up largely of returned exiles was not strong, his support among ordinary people was such that he scored 83% of the primary vote.

If the UN's transitional administrator Sergio de Mello thought that with a parliament, a constitution and a president in place the UN could say 'mission accomplished', he soon had to think again. UNTAET found itself dealing with a Prime Minister with executive power and a President with huge popular following who were not talking to one another.

Xanana thought that the office of President was being demeaned when he was assigned quarters so cramped that they could not accommodate his staff. He also objected to the office of the President being sited in the same building as the ruling party as this created the impression that the President was not independent. In a public relations masterstroke, Xanana moved his office to a secured section of the otherwise burnt out Motor Registry Building that he dubbed his 'palace of ashes'. This was a carefully calibrated symbolic act that sought to convey a message about the need for austerity at a time when the new government was spending lavishly. The action gave him considerable moral authority and credibility. Government ministers, often lacking both, were left to grind their teeth as Xanana's popularity both at home and abroad soared.[2]

★

Aware that independence celebrations would draw international attention on East Timor and provide it with the chance to present itself to the world, the country embarked on a

---

2   Jill Jolliffe 'Gusmao sets the Tone with his Palace of Ashes' *The Age*, 29th October 2002.

unique experiment – to develop a national development plan by consulting the people both widely and systematically to identify their hopes for the future. Xanana Gusmao headed the Commission that guided this consultative process. Emilia Pires, who some years later would become Finance Minister in the Gusmao government, acted as its executive head.[3] In the course of January and February 2002 over 38,000 people took part in 980 discussion groups covering every *suco* in the country. The consultation process aimed to give men, women and secondary school students a voice. The process stood in marked contrast to the one used to develop the national constitution.

The aim of the discussions was to identify national priorities and what to do about them. Priorities were identified and a 'vision' developed for each. In order of importance these were: education, health, agriculture, economy and employment, infrastructure, helping the poor, empowering women and helping young people, peace and reconciliation, co-operation between peoples and democracy and good governance. For each of the priorities the following were set out: the 'vision'; the goals; the challenges to be faced implementing these; what the people say they can do; what the people say the civil society can do; and what the people say the government should do. This is followed in each case by government plans for the next five years and a set of measures by which progress can be assessed.

The plan was endorsed by East Timor's five key leaders at the time: Xanana Gusmao, Sergio Vieira de Mello, Mari Alkatiri, and Bishops Belo and Nascimento, all of whom commented on the aspirations that the plan embodied. Xanana noted that for twenty-five years independence has been the dream and reminded people that dreams of themselves do not change present realities. What is different now, he reminded them, is that the people have the chance to bring change about. De Mello saw the consultative process as a sign of great hope for the ability of the East Timorese to work together in bringing about change. Alkatiri viewed the plan in moral terms. Its implementation would repay the debt owed to all those who had lost their lives in striving to create a better future for coming generations. Belo viewed the plan as an important step in reconstructing a fractured society; Nascimento saw it as the first step in building the strong institutions that the country was going to need.[4]

It was hard at the time not to agree with Emilia Pires's comment in introducing the plan:

> ...It represents a significant world achievement. This is something unique of which we, the people of East Timor, should be proud... For the first time in our history we have been given the opportunity to voice our vision and our priorities, contributing to policy making on the future development of our country. The outcome is both moving and powerful.[5]

The release of the development plan on the eve of independence added to the buoyant mood I discovered when I arrived back in Dili on May 16th as Belo's guest for the

---

3   Emilia had been one of the six Timorese to visit my office in 1992.
4   Planning Commission *East Timor 2020: Our Nation Our Future* Dili, April 2002, 3.
5   Ibid, 2.

Independence Day celebrations. Waiting for me on the docks was a container holding the ETHRC records on human rights violations due to be handed over to UNTAET for the Truth Reception and Reconciliation Commission to consider.

★

Belo sought to capitalise on the media attention which the independence celebrations attracted by writing a leader in the *Washington Post* under the heading 'Freedom is not enough'. He aimed to have the US increase the level of its development aid so that more young people could get job-training and so be employable. Belo might have been a Catholic bishop, but he was a Salesian also, and was imbued with his order's sensitivity towards young people and their needs. With an eye to the future he wrote to an American audience:

> ...Subsidising on-the-job training for companies willing to invest in East Timor would foster a good atmosphere for business. This is important not only because of the dignity of work but because unemployment, especially among youth, breeds instability. Many areas in our small but beautiful island nation are rich in species of wildlife and plants. Jobs for youth to protect the environment in these sensitive rural areas and to beautify the devastated towns, would make a wonderful contribution to the development of our new nation.[6]

Further on he continued:

> ... an independent body should be set up to co-ordinate employment-related efforts in East Timor on the basis of merit and common sense. By now many developing nations have learned hard lessons about the costs of corruption. I am determined to fight these maladies before they arise. If we are asking for support from the international community, we must be prepared to meet high standards of performance and transparency in all areas. Nothing less will suffice.

As I read this I could not help but think that all of Caritas's battles with the local Church in East Timor over accountability and transparency had not been in vain. The piece indicates that Belo took his notion of 'critical solidarity' very seriously. It not only covered relationships with government but also with NGOs and other partners as well.

★

The politics playing out in the background as Independence Day approached were fascinating. Mari Alkatiri had fallen from grace with the army and was seen by some as 'corrupt'. A more measured view seemed to be that he was not a listener, and was increasingly operating in government as a one-man-band. Xanana wanted him out of office and did not hide his view.

---

6   Carlos Belo 'Freedom is not enough' *The Washington Post,* May 18th 2002.

Independence Day celebrations were slated for Sunday 19th March. The Friday night before the celebrations a number of us gathered at Belo's house for the first formal dinner there since it had been restored. The guests included the Cardinals from Lisbon and Jakarta as well as the Papal Nuncio. We toasted Belo and East Timor, still amazed that independence had really come.

The independence celebrations were held over a long weekend as Monday, the first day of independence, had been declared a public holiday. My task on the Saturday was to collect the Vatican's official representative Archbishop Martino from the airport and bring him to Belo's house in Lecidere for a reception. There I met Sergio de Mello for the first time. He was impressive, tight, alert and oozing authority and command. It was easy to see why he had been the Secretary General's choice for head of mission. The big talking point at the reception was three uninvited Indonesian navy ships and some 2000 troops sitting in Dili harbour. They were ostensibly there to provide security for the Indonesian President, Megawati Soekarnoputri, during her three-hour visit to take part in the celebrations later in the evening. There were quite a few undiplomatic comments made about the Indonesian military over this show of force.

★

The Independence Day celebrations provided a classic example of a clash of cultures. There were two parts to the ceremony. The first was the religious celebration run by Church representatives. Independence was occurring on Pentecost Sunday and it would have been foreign to Timorese culture to omit a religious dimension to the celebrations. People had prayed for decades that this day would come so it would make no sense to them not to thank God that it had arrived at last. The occasion, given the presence of so many senior clergy, called for an impressive liturgy.

The Mass was to be followed by the formal celebrations organised by the UN and governed by protocols covering the presence of the Secretary General, the President of the US, the Prime Minister of Australia, etc. Both ceremonies were to be held at Tasi Tolu the site used for Pope John Paul II's visit in 1989 which could hold the more than 100,000.

When people from Belo's office arrived at the venue at 11:00am to set up there was no altar, as agreed, on the main dais and they were told somewhat bluntly that they would have to make other arrangements. When this was reported back to Belo he took off for Tasi Tolu and according to accounts feathers really flew. It took a lot to get Carlos mad but if you did manage to do so, then look out!

In part the real problem was that the UN people saw religion as intruding on 'their' celebration and the diocesan people thought the whole ceremony should have been carried out within a religious context. After all it was a sacred event!

When the official Church party arrived at Tasi Tolu from Belo's house at 6:00pm there was an altar on the main dais and about 60,000 people had already assembled. I felt sorry for Bishop Anton Ratu who had bravely made the journey from Atambua. As a proud Indonesian, this day must have been something of a humiliation for him. The Mass began at 6:30pm. The choir sang four-part harmony in Portuguese and was excellent. Xanana carried the Timor Leste flag to the altar where Belo blessed it. The nuncio read out a good-will message from the Pope announcing that Our Lady of Fatima was the official patroness of the new country.

The High Mass proceeded more or less to time. In big Masses it is hard to know how long it will take to give out communion, particularly when you have to estimate the crowd, so some time was lost there. The UN crew made their displeasure known at this by creating a racket behind the dais as the religious ceremony was concluding.

The first part of the ceremony over, the cardinals, bishops and priests headed off to unvest. When we returned to the official dais we found that the UN people had taken their revenge. There were only four seats allocated to the whole of the Catholic Church party. Bishop Nascimento had to give his seat to the nuncio and stand with the rest of us off stage.

Kofi Annan began the formal ceremonies and spoke in his measured way encouraging people to deal with the inevitable trials that would come in the days ahead once the euphoria of independence had faded. He spoke of the virtues and responsibilities of living in a free secular state. He then formally handed all authority to Xanana Gusmao who took the oath of office as President. The UN flag was lowered and the East Timorese flag earlier blessed by Belo was raised. Xanana then spoke to the crowd in four languages - English, Portuguese, Tetum and Bahasa. It was well past midnight when he finished speaking, and the crowd stopped cheering. We were all caught up in the moment.

I met up with a number of Australia's East Timor activists after the ceremony including Shirley Shackleton, wife of Greg Shackleton, one of the five Australian journalists killed at Balibo. We had all been somewhat sobered by the same thought expressed in different ways, but carrying a common meaning - 'our work, our passion and all that this has entailed over the years is now history'.

It was nearly 3:00am by the time we made our way back to the Salesians' House in Comoro where I was staying. We had all shared that rare sense that comes with being part of history.

The next morning everyone was a bit subdued as we relived the ceremony at breakfast. While the general reaction was positive, the Salesian priests were disappointed that at no time in the ceremony was the contribution that the Church had made in the struggle for independence mentioned. It seemed to them that the process of forgetting was already underway, and that the Church would need to ensure that it was stopped.

That night we joined 100,000 young people at Tasi Tolu for a youth concert which marked the end of the official celebrations. It was a wonderful experience to observe their energy and share their hopes.

★

The day following Independence Day was a time for announcements. The Papal Nuncio announced that the Vatican was establishing diplomatic relations with Timor Leste. While the two dioceses would still come under Rome's direct authority, the bishops would report to the nuncio in Australia not Jakarta. The UN announced that UNTAET had fulfilled its mandate and that UN involvement would be scaled back. The UN personnel remaining would be given a new mandate as the United Nations Mission of Support in East Timor

(UNMISET). By the end of the week a large number of UN personnel had departed and with them a major slice of the local economy.

I stayed on for a further week and took part in Timor Leste's first priestly ordination, that of Fr Julio Xavier SDB at Fatumaca College. For me this was a good way to bring an end to the beginning of Timor Leste.

★

In the years that followed independence I have visited Timor Leste regularly, always at least once a year in my role as the Chair of the Oan Kiak Scholarship Trust Fund. At the time of independence, management of this Fund was transferred from Victoria Australia where it was established to Dili. There the day-to-day management is handled by the East Timor Development Association. The Trust was established initially to provide an education for the children of FALINTIL veterans killed in the fighting after 1975. Its present aim is to get students from remote and marginalised backgrounds into schools. Some 200 students are currently being supported and over 600 recipients have completed their secondary education. The capital base for the fund came from a bequest made by one of the soldiers who served in East Timor during World War II, augmented by the efforts of a number of rock bands in Australia in the 1970s and 1980s who made and sold CDs specifically to support the fund.

In October 2003 I travelled to Timor Leste as guest of the Victorian Government to take part in the opening of Balibo House. This was an initiative taken by Steve Bracks, the Premier at the time, to honour the Australian journalists killed at Balibo in 1975. Belo was recovering from a prostate operation and, as Bishop Nascimento was unavailable, I was co-opted as an advisor to the planning committee who knew very little about how such ceremonies were handled in East Timor, but were willing to learn. The official party was based at the Hotel Turismo which had enjoyed quite an exotic history since my first stay in 1992. While having breakfast there I met Jim Dunn then working with the CAVR Commission. At that time CAVR had some 250 workers in the field running community reconciliation processes and collecting evidence.

The dedication ceremony was attended by Xanana who arrived in a well-guarded convoy. He then changed into full traditional ceremonial dress. Bracks and his wife arrived directly from Dili by helicopter. The ceremony was a very emotional occasion for some of the relatives of those killed. Others seemed totally indifferent to the occasion. It seemed a strange reaction. After the blessing, prayers and speeches, we adjourned for refreshments to the old Portuguese fort with its grand view over the forest and out to the sea.

Once the formalities were concluded, I headed off with Frs Domingo Soares and Jacob Abel to Maliana and then on to Atsabe. That night and the next day between us we baptised four hundred people and married ten couples. About 2000 people attended the ceremonies and the celebrations that followed. This was Catholicism on an industrial scale!

On our way out of Atsabe we stopped and prayed at the graves of two priests who died during the occupation. Frs Renato Stefani and Hilario Madeira are buried at Atsabe. Renato was the priest responsible for getting Max Stahl's film of the Santa Cruz massacre out of the cemetery so that it could be spirited to Darwin and shown to the world. He died in a car accident. Hilario was shot by the militia at Suai. The visit was a sad reminder of times past. As well, it was a reminder that those times had passed and that we should be grateful for that.

When I arrived back in Dili I had time to catch up with people and to look around. What surprised me most was that almost all trace of the damage done in 1999 had been erased.

★

The worst kept secret among the Salesians in Dili was that Belo was leaving at the end of the month. The rumour was that he was retiring. I did not meet him during this visit as he was staying with his mother and sister Juliette in Baucau. However, when I asked people about how he was the news was not encouraging. The general impression was that he had reached the end of the road. He was in poor health and his prostate problem would need further treatment. Psychologically he was worn out. There were some problems with Rome over the division of the diocese and how the costs associated with setting up a new diocese would be met. There were problems with the major seminary that was now too small for the number of seminarians, forcing Nascimento to send his students to Portugal. And so the list went on.

While Belo had been ill, Bishop Nascimento was running both dioceses. The two of them went to Rome later in the month on their *ad limina* visits and while there the Pope accepted Belo's resignation and confirmed Nascimento as administrator of Dili and Baucau dioceses pending a new appointment.

Belo was fifty-five and had been bishop through the most trying of times for almost twenty years. I think he found the prospect of another twenty years as bishop simply overwhelming. For me, his departure marked the end of an era and a new beginning for the Church in East Timor. After his departure it was announced that, as of 2006, the Dili diocese would be divided to create the diocese of Maliana. The import of this decision was that, with three dioceses, East Timor could create its own Episcopal Conference, have its own Nuncio, and so escape from Rome's direct control which had blighted its development in so many ways.

Jill Jolliffe contended that Belo's retirement was partly the result of a disagreement with Rome over the division of the diocese.[7] While there may have been some argument over the timing, there would have been none over the principle. Belo's resignation quickly became international news, and just as quickly he faded from sight. My reading of the situation was that he was a Salesian and must have missed the community life that goes with that - something I have shared for many years in my adopted home at Comoro. The life of a Catholic bishop can be a lonely one and is not for the faint-hearted, or for people who are mentally and psychologically drained. Today we would probably account for Belo's psychological collapse in terms of post-traumatic stress disorder. This was recognised then, certainly in his case. We understand the condition better these days and can do something about it. Belo returned to Portugal for treatment and then spent a short time in Maputo in Mozambique before returning to Portugal with more health issues, where he remains.

---

7   'Bishop quits amid talk of Vatican rift' *The Age* 28th November, 2002.

★

East Timor's introduction to democracy has not been without its teething problems that are now well documented. Its biggest problem was always going to be developing the political skill-base necessary to thrive. Many of the early government ministers did not bring the necessary background to their jobs and this held back development and has resulted in the courts being used for political ends in prosecuting them for their perceived incompetence.

A number of Timor's problems are a legacy of decisions made in the UNAMET era, particularly in dealing with FALINTIL veterans. A group of these almost assassinated Xanana and Ramos Horta in 2006. But through this and other trials East Timor has survived.

The country's problematic relationship with Australia continues, particularly over oil and gas, and seems unlikely to be resolved soon. There is great hope that oil and gas revenues will eventually fund development along the south coast. However, at this point of time, this remains only a hope.

The East Timor story seems currently to be at the end of an important chapter. This year (2015) Xanana stepped down as Prime Minister. For many people in East Timor this development really does mark the end of the beginning as Xanana, more than any other politician, has the standing to keep the international community sympathetic to the country's development needs. However, there is a recognition in and beyond East Timor that there must be generational change. The new Prime Minister Dr Rui Araujo seems to be well respected in the international community, so that at this stage there is much for which to be thankful.

★

The Church story seems no less complex. While many see in Pope Francis's pontificate the end of the *imperium,* the one thing we have learned from the *Star Wars Trilogy* is that 'The Empire Fights Back'! I feel much more at home in Francis's Catholicism than I ever did in that of John Paul II or Benedict XVI. As my good friend Bishop Jeremiah Coffey told me at the end of his long career: 'I have lived through the reign of seven popes, Hilton. I have supported and obeyed them all, but at last we have one who agrees with me'.

The sex abuse scandal, while it has rocked the Church and destroyed the faith of many, has had one good effect. It has undermined much of the hubris associated with clerical life in general, and episcopal life in particular. This humbling experience makes it possible for bishops and priests to heed Francis's message to become more pastorally sensitive and engaged with people, their cares and their concerns. The present Pope's capacity to model this message in a consistent way is a great force for change and a good illustration of how to mobilise moral force effectively. He is bringing change by the force of his example rather than by executive decree.

His big test is still to come, however, and that is whether or not he can effectively decentralise the Church so that we do not have the accumulation of power at the centre where a bevy of ecclesiastical limpets clings to the trappings of papal authority, making their own lives significant and everyone else's a misery.

The growing realisation among Catholics that the Kingdom of God is broader than the Church is a tremendously freeing one in that it opens up a new imaginal horizon in regard to how we think about the Church's mission in the world, and how people of faith relate to one another. The Pope's emphasis on pastors 'smelling like their sheep' is another of these notions that frees up the imagination.

Leonardo Boff makes an interesting observation in outlining developments in Catholicism at the present time. He holds that in the first millennium the Church functioned as a set of communities with the Bishop of Rome recognised as a centre of unity. In the second millennium a much more legal interpretation emerged that has resulted in a distorted notion of papal (and Roman) authority, one which borders on 'popolatry'. The pope has taken God's place. The chance is there at the beginning of the third millennium for Catholicism to address this distortion.[8] The re-orientation process began at Vatican II but has since been moth-balled. However the loss of moral credibility that Church leaders have experienced in the past decade as a result of scandals creates a condition in which this project can again be taken up. Indeed, doing so might be the necessary condition for re-establishing the credibility of Church leaders in the eyes of ordinary Catholics. This is the hope of many. We need to move beyond 'the end of the beginning' and just keep going!

*

As I hope this story illustrates, I have lived an interesting life. As a young priest I could never have imagined it would turn out as it has. In all our lives there are turning points - what I called earlier 'moments of destiny'. As I look back over the events covered here four seem to stand out, and they do so as images. The first is the image of myself standing on the Catholic Truth Society box at Yarra Bend feeling personally nervous but quite confident in what I had to say. This was the beginning of a mission, at that time narrowly conceived, but subsequently blossoming in marvellous ways, that would consume most of my life. The second is standing in front of a mirror with blood on my face saying 'bugger' and then realising that I had a voice. While this was a trivial incident, it had life-changing symbolic value for me. The third is sitting in the dust in Kalumburu listening to the stories and myths of the indigenous people and learning to see the world through their eyes. From then on I have always cast an anthropological eye over theological propositions for their, usually implied, cultural content and this has shaped the way I see the Gospel and try to communicate it to others. The final image is of myself sitting in my office in the Cathedral when my secretary comes in and says: 'There are people out here who want to see you. I am not sure of their nationality.' Perhaps that was the most significant moment of all. Little did I know how our lives would become intertwined across the next two decades.

Apart from moments of destiny, I count being made an auxiliary bishop as a great blessing. It opened so many doors for me even if I sometimes had to knock quite loudly to let people know I was there. As an auxiliary bishop I was fortunate to work with 'bosses' who may not always have agreed with what I did, or the stance I took, but still supported

---

8   Leonardo Boff *Francis of Rome & Francis of Assisi* (Maryknoll N.Y: Orbis, 2014), 14-16.

me (or at the least refrained from putting obstacles in my path). They did this because they knew deep down that Belo needed support, that his position in Timor was diabolical given Roman policy, and although they followed the party line, they were sufficiently generous not to mind that I did not.

Trying to balance my episcopal roles in Melbourne with my commitments to Caritas and East Timor and other social justice causes was never easy and from time to time I had to rely on colleagues to step into the breach. They did this generously and for this I remain thankful.

★

My experiences in East Timor taught me a lot about how 'big organisations' work and the amazing people who work in NGOs. It also taught me that even the biggest organisations, such as the UN, are relatively small compared with the Catholic Church. This is something that I had never realised before.

My training as an anthropologist was most useful in dealing with issues in East Timor. At the very practical level anthropology invites a person to experience the world as other people do. This is quite different from the theological tradition in which I was trained, a tradition that analyses individual experiences in terms of universal principles, and often strips individual experience of its context. One comes to deal with abstractions rather than with real people.

I discovered there is a real 'conversion process', to use a religious term, in making the translation from one perspective to the other, but once it is made there is little inclination to go back. As I listen to the interminable debates that engage some of my colleagues, I wonder how their abstract moral theories would stand up to three years' living as an anthropologist in Kalumburu! I remain grateful to Archbishop Knox for having the foresight to send me to study anthropology. In the context of the times it was a brave move on both our parts.

The immediate result of his initiative was the Aboriginal Mass. This landmark celebration was to become an early victim of Rome's cultural police who still seem to reign supreme. I was delighted to find recently that the Aboriginal people themselves hold the 1975 Mass in memory. A group of them badgered ABC TV to track down the original tape in their archives so that it could be digitally recorded and burnt onto CDs. From there it is a short journey onto the internet and posterity. This grassroots development stands in contrast to attempts to homogenise and Latinise liturgy by the culture police who think that saying the Mass in understandable English somehow makes it plebeian and lacking in reverence. The last thing the Church's elitist culture police want is for liturgy to be 'relevant'.

Liturgy is an aspect of Boff's *witness* model that I really value and have done since I was a child. I like to pray for all the people who are cut off or alienated from this aspect of our religious tradition by the snobbery of certain elements in the Church. I also pray for the day when the liturgical tradition can be properly inculturated in local cultures by local churches.

Social justice remains one of my passions and as an 'elder statesman' in this field now, I am surprised at how many people seek my advice. It is a humbling experience. While one can study the principles of Catholic social teaching, my own introduction to them really came early in my life and in a most practical way. The Mercy sisters in Finley lived them out in their service of the poor and marginalised and their loving attitude was caught more than taught. Later this early introduction was depthed in working with Belo in East Timor. There these great principles were tested in fire and stood the test. I have always been attracted by Belo's concept of 'critical solidarity' in working with others. It presents a way forward in working with a whole range of very different yet committed colleagues.

I was perhaps fortunate to know and make friends with many of East Timor's immediate past and present leaders before they became famous. Some now regard me as a kind of unofficial family chaplain. This can make standing in 'critical solidarity' with them a challenge. In some instances it means listening to the politicians criticising the bishops and offering 'a word to the wise', then soon after finding myself repeating the exercise but now from the other side of the fence. Critical solidarity is built on trust and depends on credibility.

★

It would be fitting to conclude this portrayal of the role of the Catholic Church in East Timor's struggle for independence in the words of its chief proponent Carlos Belo. In the aftermath of the 9/11 attacks in 2001, Belo was invited to address the Nobel Centennial Symposium in Oslo about the Church's role in East Timor. He was too ill to attend at the time so he prepared the paper and it was read on his behalf. In what follows, I have selected themes that I know are dear to his heart:

> …In a world where the personal and social consequences of sin are evident, peace must be built on the basis of justice. Christians are called on to live out a tension between their vision of the reign of God and its concrete realisation in history. In East Timor we live in the tension between the 'already but not yet'. We already live in the grace of the kingdom but it is not yet the completed kingdom. We are a pilgrim people in a world marked by conflict, trauma and injustice….
>
> The justice that people demand is the quest for truth: 'You shall know the truth and the truth shall see you free'. Mothers, widows and orphans in every village I visit want to know what actually happened. If the truth is established, then we can replace a society that was based on lies and violence…
>
> Truth and justice are two things required to bring about forgiveness and reconciliation…
>
> True reconciliation will not be possible until justice is done. It will be incomplete. The establishment of a justice system is a high priority for peace building…
>
> The Timorese people will need to learn how to function in a democratic context and how to manage differences within a democratic framework. During the election the Church conducted civic education on citizens' rights and obligations, about political parties, election processes and how to discuss political issues in an appropriate manner. During this time we also clarified the respective role of church and the state.

> Without the establishment of democracy – and especially processes and forums to discuss different ideologies – peace and reconciliation will not be possible.
>
> Education for peace is essential. Peace building activities should be included as part of the new school curriculum. I would add too, that part of this curriculum should include a realistic representation of Timorese history. We need to retain in our collective memory the history of the struggle for human rights, justice and peace. The very development of this history could be a helpful process not only in developing our national identity but also in our collective healing.
>
> Finally, the Church in East Timor is also renewing itself… We have recently launched an intensive pastoral planning exercise to define our vision of the church in the new society. I am committed to make it a church of the people, a participatory church…[9]

The whole speech is comprehensive and moving. It stands as testament to a man dragged from obscurity and thrust into a role he did not seek but which, in faith, he accepted. Like most of us Belo lived his life in the struggle between his blessings and his demons. The experience shaped his thinking even as it took a heavy personal toll. Belo's insights into the core values in Catholic social teaching grew out of grim pastoral experience in an environment where he had little or no official support. He was not a theoretician about human rights, reconciliation, justice and peace. He was a practitioner from whom we can all learn. He earned his Nobel Peace Prize in the school of very hard knocks.

East Timor stands as testimony to the fact that religion is not simply 'a private matter', the mistaken myth of secular Western culture. How religion finds its place within a culture is a matter of great importance. In this context Belo's concept of 'critical solidarity' has much to offer a world whose problems cannot be solved by ignoring the role religion plays in how most people on the planet make sense of their lives. It remains the elephant in the room.

---

[9] Carlos Belo 'Peacebuilding in East Timor: The Role and Contribution of the Church'. Paper delivered to the Nobel Centennial symposium in Oslo December 2001. CIIR: *Timor Link* No 55, 2002, 5-8.

BIBLIOGRAPHY

Boff, Leonardo *Francis of Rome: Francis of Assisi: A New Springtime for the Church* (Maryknoll N.Y: Orbis, 2014)

CCJDP *The Church and East Timor* (Melbourne: Catholic Commission for Justice, Peace and Development, 1993)

Cleary, Paul *The Men Who Came Out of the Ground: Timor 1942 – Australia's First Commandoes* (Sydney: Hachette, 2010)

Costigan, Michael (ed) *Congress of the People* (Melbourne: Advocate Press, 1973)

Cristalis, Irena *Bitter Dawn: East Timor - a People's Story* (London: Zed Books, 2002)

Curran, Charles *Catholic Social Teaching 1891-present: A historical, theological and ethical analysis* (Washington: Georgetown University Press, 2002)

Deakin, Hilton *The Unan Cycle: A Study of Social Change in an Aboriginal Community* Doctoral Dissertation, Department of Anthropology and Sociology, Monash University, 1978

Duncan, Bruce *Crusade or Conspiracy? Catholics and the Anti-communist Struggle in Australia* (Sydney: UNSW Press, 2001)

Dunn, James *Timor: A People Betrayed* (Sydney: ABC Books, 1996)

Godin, Henri and Daniel, Yves *La France: Pays de Mission?* (Paris: Editions de Cerf, 1943)

Griffin, James *Daniel Mannix: Beyond the Myths* (Mulgrave: Garratt Publishing, 2012)

Hall, Edward *The Silent Language* (New York: Anchor Press, 1973)

Hill, Hal *The Indonesian Economy*, second edition (London: Cambridge University Press, 2000)

Hogan, Michael (ed) *Option for the Poor: Annual Social Justice Statements of the Australian Catholic Commission of Justice and Peace 1973-1987* (University of Sydney: Department of Government and Public Administration, 1992)

Luzbetak, Louis *The Church and Cultures* (Techny Illinois: Divine Word Publications, 1963)

Henderson, Gerard *Mr Santamaria and the Bishops* (Sydney: Studies in the Christian Movement, 1982)

Jolliffe, Jill *East Timor: Nationalism and Colonialism* (Brisbane: University of Queensland Press, 1978)

Jolliffe, Jill *Cover-Up: The Inside Story of the Balibo Five* (Melbourne: Scribe, 2001)

Kohen, Arnold *From the Place of the Dead* (New York: St. Martin's Press, 1999)

Lennox, Rowena *Fighting Spirit of East Timor: The Life of Martinho da Costa Lopes* (London: Zed Books, 2000)

Longman, Timothy *Christianity and the Genocide in Rwanda* (New York: Cambridge University Press, 2010)

Lucas Brian, Slack Peter, d'Apice William *Church Administration Handbook* (Sydney:

St Paul's Publications, 2009)

Malinowski, Bronislaw *Argonauts of the Western Pacific* (London: Dutton, 1961)

Martinkus, John *A Dirty Little War* (Sydney: Random House, 2001)

Masure, Eugene *The Parish Priest* (Notre Dame: Fides Publishers, 1955)

O'Malley, John *What Happened at Vatican II* (Cambridge: Harvard University Press, 2008)

Mount, Frank *Wrestling with Asia: a Memoir* (Ballan: Connor Court Publishing, 2012)

Potok, Chaim *In the Beginning* (Harmondsworth: Penguin, 1976)

Pour, Julius *Benny Moerdani: Profile of a Soldier Statesman* (Jakarta: Yayasan Kejuangan Panglima Besar Sudirman, 1993)

Press, Margaret & Connelly, Susan *Mary MacKillop East Timor 1994-2006* (St. Mary's: Sisters of St. Joseph, 2007)

Pro Mundi Vita Dossier *East Timor* (Brussels: 1984)

Robinson, Geoffrey *We Will Die if You Leave: How Genocide was Stopped in East Timor* (New Jersey: Princeton University Press, 2010)

Robinson, Geoffrey *East Timor 1999 Crimes against Humanity - A Report Commissioned by the United Nations Office of the High Commissioner for Human Rights,* 2003

Schreiter, Robert *The Ministry of Reconciliation: Spirituality and Strategies* (Maryknoll N.Y: Orbis Books, 1998)

Scott, David *Last Flight Out of Dili* (Melbourne: Pluto Press, 2005)

Sheehan, Michael (Archbishop) *Apologetics and Catholic Doctrine* (Dublin: M.H. Gill & Son, 1918)

Jean-Francois Six *Church and Human Rights* (Slough: St Paul's Publications, 1991)

Sibomana, Andre *Hope for Rwanda: Conversations with Laure Guilbert and Herve Deguine* (London: Pluto Press, 1999)

Smythe, Patrick *'The Heaviest Blow' - The Catholic Church and the East Timor Issue* (Munster: Lit Verlag, 2004)

Taudevin, Lansell *East Timor: Too Little Too Late* (Sydney: Duffy and Snellgrove, 1999)

Taylor, John *Indonesia's Forgotten War: The Hidden History of East Timor* (London: Zed Books, 1992)

Taylor, John *The Price of Freedom* (London: Zed Books, 1999)

Vatican Sources *Statistical Yearbook of the Church* (Libreria Editrice Vaticana: 1975, 1985, 1995, 2005 and 2009)

Waters, Ian 'Knox, James Robert (1914-1983)' *Australian Dictionary of Biography,* Volume 17, http://adb.anu.edu.au/biography/knox-james-robert-12752

White, Hugh 'The Road to INTERFET: Reflections on Australian Strategic Decisions Concerning East Timor, December 1998-September 1999' *Security Challenges* Vol 4, No 1, Autumn 2008

Wilcken, Patrick *Claude Levi-Strauss: The Poet in the Laboratory* (London: Bloomsbury, 2010)

Wanandi, Jusuf *Shades of Grey: A Political Memoir of Modern Indonesia 1965-1998* (Singapore: Equinox Press, 2012)

Papal Documents (All papal documents cited in this work are downloadable from the Vatican website)

INDEX

Numbers in *italics* refer to the *pages of photographs*, in sequence.
ET = East Timor or East Timorese
HD = Hilton Deakin
Other abbreviations are spelled out on pp. ix–xi.

2/2 Independent Company (Australia) 129, 165

Abel, Fr Jacob 303
Aboriginal cultures 63–7
    dialects 64
    exchange systems 64
    governance 66
    Mass and 60–2
    property 66
    social control 66
'Aboriginal Mass' 60–1, 63
Aborigines 30, 38, 47, 54
ABRI 240, 244
    see also TNI
abuse of children 71–2
abuse of power 62, 71–2
ACBC 21–3, 188, 190–1
ACFID 274n9
ACFOA 19, 142, 274
ACM 188, 190
Aco, Fr Julio 91
ACR 107, 140, 188
    Santamaria and 143
    see also Caritas Australia
ACSJC 146, 187, 190–1
    Caritas Australia and 271, 277
Aditjondro, Prof. George 217, 223–4
administration, church 51, 53
Advocate, The 54
AEC 137
    see also ACBC
Age, The 36
aggiornamento 58
Aileu, ET 94–5, 101, 165–6
Aitarak militia, ET ix, 261–2
Albin, Hugh 70
Alex, David 242
Alkatiri, Mari (former PM of ET) 223, 297, 299–300
All Party Timor Talks 177
Amaral, Xavier 104
Ambon Is., Indonesia 129
Amnesty International 175
animism 82–3, 113
Annan, Kofi (former Sec.-Gen. of UN) 222, 293, 302
Antara newsagency 92
anthropology 54, 56–62, 192
    church's models of 123
    see also culture/s
APCET 208
APCET II 216–17
APEC 1995 Conference 178
APODETI 88, 92–3, 100, 104
apostolic administrators 84n10
April Revolution (Portugal, 1974) 82, 154
Araujo, Dr Rui (PM of ET) 305
Araujo, Fr Jovito 288n9
ASDT
    origin, priorities 87–9
    part of 'Popular Assembly' 104
Asian financial crisis 230, 238–40
'Asian values' 221, 225
Atambua, West Timor 95
Atauro Is., ET 95, 152
Augustine, St 50
AustralAsian 229
Australia
    ET and 8, 88–9, 96, 98–100, 128–35, 137–40, 143, 173n5, 179–80. *see also* Australian Governments and ET
    Japan and 131
    Rwanda and 194, 203–4
Australian, The 214
Australian Catholic Church
    ET and 12, 107
    ET refugees and 232, 234–5
Australian East Timor Association 141
Australian Governments and ET 18
    CCJP and 146
    Fraser Government 146
    Howard Government 206, 233–7, 243, 247, 273, 289

Keating Government 231–3
Whitlam Government 89, 98n6, 143
during WWII 231, 233

Balibo, ET 96
'Balibo Five' 96, 157n10
Balibo House, Balibo, ET 303
Barreto, Fr Francisco 273–5, 277
Barros, Fr Norberto 133
Bathurst Is., NT 47
Batugade, ET 95
Baucau, ET 181
Beek, Joop 142
Belgium and Rwanda 196–7
Belo, Bp Carlos Filipe Ximenes
   ad limina visits 180, 304
   attempted assassination of 258
   in Australia 7, 186, 278
   Brennan and 147
   Caritas and 278
   character of 11, 154–6
   Church divisions and 108
   civil authorities and 111
   CNRT and 287
   da Costa Lopes replacement 103, 121
   on ET conversions to Catholicism 13
   on ET development plan 299
   in Europe and US (1997) 228–9
   Gusmao and 174, 278
   Habibie and 241–2
   Horta and 230, 278
   human rights and 123–4, 206
   Indonesia and 155–6, 180
   on integration 230
   on job training 300
   justice after 1999 referendum 280–1
   life story 154–5
   on M. Wanandi 172–3
   media and 208, 218
   Nascimento and 274, 278
   on nation-building 294
   Nobel Peace Prize nominee 181
   Nobel Peace Prize recipient 207, 215, 218
   on peacebuilding 308–9
   photos with HD *10, 14*
   post-referendum movements 269
   priorities 12
   protest movement and 160
   on reconciliation 287–8
   resignation 304
   as seminarian 101
   Vatican and 144, 180–1, 213, 215, 284n1, 287
   voice in wilderness 171–82
Benedict XVI, Pope 184, 286
Benedictines 63–4
Bertone, Card. Tarcisio 192
bishops 23, 187–8
Boas, Franz 57

Boff, Leonardo 285, 306
Bonner, Neville (former senator for Qld) 47
Box Hill, Melbourne 52
Bracks, Steve (former Premier of Vic) 303
Brazil 189
Brennan, Bp William
   on ACSJC and Caritas Australia 190–1
   civil authorities and 182
   complaint about HD 281n26
   development of ET and 187
   opening of new ET seminary 208
   photo with HD *8*
   support for Belo and 147
Brereton, Laurie 243, 263n18
Brimob 244–5, 248–9
Britt, Maria 177
Buddhism 112
Burundi 196–7, 199–200
Butare, Rwanda 201
Byrne, Louise 16

CAFOD 272
Callinan, Capt. Bernard *11*, 129, 131–3
Canadian and US symposia on ET 221–5
Canalini, Abp Francesco 144
Canning, Sr Agnes 34
Canossian Sisters 78, 269n32
CARE Australia ix, 199
Caritas 271–83
   in Rwanda 9
   in Zaire 204
   see also Caritas Internationalis; *specific Caritas agencies, e.g. Caritas East Timor*
Caritas Australia
   ACR's new name 107n26, 188–9
   ACSJC and 271, 277
   aid and development 278
   Caritas Baucau and 274–5
   Caritas ET and 273–5, 277–8
   Caritas Internationalis and 271, 275–6
   in ET 271–83
   ET crises of Sep 1999 and 276–7
   expertise 273
   funding 273
   Human Rights and Justice Program 281–2
   internal challenges 278
   international involvement 190
   justice after 1999 referendum 280–3
   Oecusse, ET and 279–80
   Rwanda and 7
   Sexual Assault Program 282
   see also ACR
Caritas Baucau
   Caritas Australia and 274–5
   Caritas Dili and 279, 283n28
   CET and 274
Caritas Dili 274n12, 278
   Caritas Baucau and 279, 283n28

Caritas East Timor 273–4
  Caritas Australia and 273–5, 277–8
  Caritas Baucau and 274–5
Caritas Internationalis 4, 6, 192, 199–200
  Caritas Australia and 271, 275–6
  structure 292
  UN and 272–3
Caritas Rwanda 201
Carnation Revolution, Portugal 82, 154
Carrascalao, Joao 223
Carrascalao, Manuel 217
Carrascalao, Mario (former Gov. of ET) 160, 168
Carrascalao brothers 86n1
Casaroli, Card. Agostino 21
catechists 11
Catholic Action 36–7, 142
Catholic Church
  cultural regions 213n3
  culture and 123–4
  culture of 183–4
  governance 136, 184–5
  Kingdom of God and 306
  local churches 23n7
  mediator role 181
  mission 124, 138, 286–7
  models of 286–7
  organisation of 22–3
  'pilgrim people of God' 58
  politics and 285–7
  see also Catholic Church in specific countries; politics and religion; specific Church agencies; specific episcopal conferences; specific members of Catholic Church
Catholic Church in Australia
  communism and 138–9
  ET and 21, 107, 137–47, 187, 190–1
  Melbourne archdiocese 53
  missions 63–7
  in society 30–1
Catholic Church in ET
  Catholic Church in Australia and 135
  civil society in ET and 294
  clergy attitudes 169–70
  clergy resources 165
  conversions to 13–14
  divisions within 107–8
  FRETILIN and 93
  human rights and 120–7, 178–9
  IDPs and 266–8
  independence of ET and 302
  Indonesian Bishops' Conference and 116–18
  Indonesian clergy and religious in 172–3
  information source 102
  leadership of 111, 113
  literacy and 79
  mediation by 171–2
  ministry and education 115–16
  peacebuilding and 308–9
  politics and 211–12
  post-referendum violence against 264–70
  protection of population 102–3
  seminary 208, 210
  size 11, 114
  UNTAET and 294
Catholic Church in Indonesia
  civil authorities and 181
  Islam and 116
  ministry and education 115–16
  size 114
  spread 112
  see also Indonesian Bishops' Conference
Catholic Church in Rwanda 195–7, 200
Catholic Education Office, Melbourne 52
Catholic Evidence Guild 40
Catholic identity 58
Catholic social teaching
  application 3, 139, 192
  core values 272–3, 281–2
  freedom of conscience and 126
  human rights and 122–4
Catholic Worker, The 36–7
catholicity 192
CAVR 283, 297, 303
Cazzaniga, Sr Erminia 270
CCJP
  East Timor: A Forgotten People 146
  Fraser Government and 146
  information sources 144
  origin 272n3
  report on ET to AEC (1974) 137–8
  social analysis teaching in Australia 145–6
Centre for Strategic and International Studies 94
Cervantes, Fr (Andres?) 166
Chamberlain, Fr Fred 16
Chamberlin, Michael 55
chefes de sucos 80
Chega! 283
childhood abuse 71–2
Chinese in ET 99–100
Christian Brothers 34–6
Christians and Muslims 119
church see Catholic Church
Church and Human Rights (Six) 124–6
church and state 9–11, 37, 40, 59, 126, 294–5
'Church in the Modern World, The' (Vatican II) 10, 52–3, 58
CIIR 144
CISET 21n5, 144
civilisation 123
CIVIPOL 261
Clancy, Card. Edward 8, 187, 214–15, 256
clericalism 50–1, 97n1, 187–8, 192, 305
Clinton, Bill (former Pres. of USA) 173n5, 215, 229

CNN 261
CNRM 173, 177, 208
CNRT
   civil society in ET and 294
   dissolution 297
   independence for ET and 247–8, 287
   origin 240
   structure 241
Coffey, Bp Jeremiah 305
collegiality 136–7
colonisation 123
communications from ET 78, 102, 106, 143–4, 178–80
communications within ET 130
communism 29, 37, 97, 138–9
Confoy, Sr Maryanne 205–6
Connelly, Sr Susan 187
Connors, Bp Peter 8, 71, 183
Conquest, Fr Dan 3, 52
conscience 125–6
Constituent Assembly of ET 297–8
Constitution of ET/Timor Leste 298
Cooktown, Qld 47–8
Coolgardie safes 28
criados ix, 132
critical solidarity 300, 309
CRS 167, 272, 274, 276
CSIS 92, 142–3, 169, 173
cultural change and power 66–7
'cultural evolution' 57, 196
cultural relativism 57
culture/s 56–62
   Catholic Church and 123–4
   indigenous 9
   Indonesian 113
   liturgy and 61
   power of 206
   religion and 29–30, 60–2, 309
   rights and 123
   sensitivity to 174
Curia, Roman 185
   see also Vatican
Curic, Fr Vjeko 202
Curran, Fr Charles 125

Da Conceicao, Valerio 270
da Costa Lopes, Msgr Martinho
   apostolic administrator of ET 102–3
   CCJP meeting (1983) 146
   character of 11, 90, 172
   civil authorities and 111
   editor of *Seara* 87
   famine in ET and 143
   Indonesian atrocities and 101, 153
   Indonesian Bishops' Conference and 114
   local Timorese priest 135
   mediator 84, 171
   photo *11*
   priorities 12, 90, 124
   seminary studies 83
   teacher at minor seminary 90
   Vatican and 121, 155, 211–12
   on Vatican and Indonesia 21
'Da Silva incident' 261–2
Dare I, Dare II 287n6
De Carvalho, Sr Celeste 270
de Groot, Jack 277, 281
de Magalhaes, Prof. Barbedo 176
de Mello, Sergio 292–3, 299, 301
Deakin, Alfred (uncle of HD) 33
Deakin, Bp Hilton Forrest
   anthropology lecturer 68, 70–1
   assistant priest 49–55
   auxiliary bishop 8, 183–93, 306–7
   'Bispo Maubere' 3
   Caritas Australia leader 7
   childhood (Finley) *1*, 27–33
   da Costa Lopes Medal recipient (2012) 2
   destiny 306
   with East Timorese for first time 15–24
   Eastern Churches involvement 52
   Essendon, Melbourne 49
   ET fundraiser, Melbourne *11*
   with ET leaders *14*
   in ET photos *10*, *12–13*, *15*
   ET refugee advocacy letter (1997) 234–5
   ET visit (1992) 151–60
   ET visit (incl. Uai Mori cantonment) 252–5
   ET visit (Jan 1996) 208–12
   ET visit (Sep 1998) 242
   ETHRC co-founder 17n2
   Eucharistic Congress 1973 5
   Fatumaca, ET *13*
   Glen Iris, Melbourne 54
   Jerilderie parish, NSW 31
   Kailaco, ET *15*
   Kalumburu, WA 4, 56, 63–7
   Kenya visit (1994) 205–6
   local church and 12
   Medal of East Timor recipient 2012 2
   to Melbourne at wartime 33
   ministry, early 3, 49–55
   ministry, episcopal 190
   ministry, parish 69–70
   ministry as priest and anthropologist 56–68
   ministry to homeless 52
   My Fellow Australians 53
   ordination as bishop 186
   ordination as priest 49
   Our Lady of Lourdes School, Thornbury, Melbourne 34
   Parade College, Melbourne 36
   parish priest 69–70
   Pell and 185–6
   pianist 52
   Portugal visit 176

respite 1986 at Finley 73
Rwanda visit (1994) 6, *9*, 198–204
sabbatical year (1978) 67–8
at Santa Cruz cemetery, ET *12*
school years *1–2*, 34–41
seminary years *2*, 42–8
siblings *16*, 31
St Augustine's Church, Melbourne 8
St Francis Xavier's parish, Box Hill 52
St Joseph's School, Finley 30
St Monica's parish, Moonee Ponds 49–50
St Patrick's Cathedral choir, Melbourne 34–6
St Patrick's School, North Fitzroy 35
St Raphael's Church, West Preston 39
St Thomas More's Church/parish, Mt Eliza *6*, 69–70
surgery 72–3
TV work 50
Uai Mori cantonment (ET) visit 252–5
university study 54, 56, 59, 63–7
US and Canadian symposia on ET 221–5
vicar general 7, 8–9, 23–4, 71–4
Zaire visit (1994) 204–5
Deakin, Frederick (grandfather of HD) 28
Deakin, John Francis (great grandfather of HD) *1*, 27–8, 30
Deakin, Nanette (sister of HD) *1*, *16*, 31
Deakin, Robin (brother of HD) *16*, 31
Deakin, Ruby (mother of HD) *2*, *16*, 28, 31–2, 35
  ancestors 31–2
Deakin, Sarah (nee Godier, great grandmother of HD) 27–8
Deakin, Stan (father of HD) *1–2*, 28, 31–3, 39–40
Deakin, Valerie (sister of HD) *16*, 31
Deakins' Corner, NSW 28
Declaration of Human Rights (UN) 123n6, 125–6, 221
Declaration of the Rights of Man and of the Citizen (1789) 124
Declaration on Religious Liberty (Vatican II) 59, 125–6
democracy 113, 221
Democratic Republic of the Congo 199, 204–5
deportados 78, 81, 131
Depression, the 27–31
Derby, WA 66
Descombes, Fr Michel 200–1, 203
development, integral 272
development plan for ET 298–9
Dewanto, Fr Tarcisius 268
dialects 64
dialogue 91, 122, 191
Dignitatis Humanae (Vatican II) 59, 125–6
Dili, ET
  HD's first visit 152–3
  Japanese invasion of ET 131–2
  post-referendum destruction 264–5
  UNAMET drama, Sep 1999 289–91
Dili Cathedral *11*, 128, 134–5, 157
Dili jetty 100–1
Dili massacre 9–10, 16–18, 107, 158–60, 164, 176–7
Dili seminary 172–3
Diocesan Priest, The (Masure) 46
discrimination 10–11
do Amaral, Xavier 90
Dominicans 82
'domino theory' 89
Duncan, Jessica (Jessie) 31–2
Dunn, James 92, 98, 100, 128, 173n3, 303
Dutch
  in ET 128–9, 132
  in Indonesia 112

Ear and Eye Hospital, Melbourne 38–9
East, Roger 101
East Timor *10–13*, *15*
  administration 79–81, 130
  Asian financial crisis and 239–40
  attempted ceasefire, 1983 105
  Australia and 8, 88–9, 96, 98–100, 128–35, 137–40, 143, 173n5, 179–80
  'civil war' 95–6, 98, 248
  communications from 78, 102, 106, 143–4, 178–80
  communications within 130
  concentration camps 105
  culture/s 186–7
  Decolonisation Commission 93–4
  demographics 77–8, 104, 106
  development 81, 104
  development plan 298–9
  economy 164
  education 82, 115, 123, 163, 174, 241n9
  election (2001) 297
  food supply 105
  human rights and 106, 120–7, 177
  IDPs 250
  independence of 87–96, 164, 179, 298, 301–2
  indigenous religion 82–3
  Indonesia and 11–15, 88–9, 92–108, 113, 144, 161–70, 191, 209
  Indonesian Bishops' Conference and 116–18
  Japan and 84, 131–4, 231
  languages and literacy 78–9, 104, 186–7
  law and order 171
  Malaysia and 216–17
  media and 207, 220–30
  migrants in Australia 187n7
  military 82
  political groups 87–90
  political options 208, 227–8, 241–2
  'Popular Assembly' 104

Portugal and 11, 77–87, 94–7, 104, 123, 128–30, 133–4, 138, 164, 176–7, 234–6
post-independence politics 305
post-referendum justice 280–3
post-referendum violence against 265–70
protests 210
re-colonisation 97–108
reconciliation 177
resistance 106–7, 158. *see also* CNRT, FRETILIN
social control 67
social organisation 79–81
sterilisation program 106
tertiary training 241n9
tourism 171
UDT coup (1975) 94
UN and 302–3
US and Canadian symposia on 221–5
Vatican and 3–4, 88, 102–3, 113–14, 119, 145, 156, 222, 302, 304
Vatican II and 84
World War II and 11, 20
see also Australian Governments and ET; Catholic Church in Australia, ET and; Catholic Church in ET
East Timor: A Forgotten People (CCJP) 146
East Timor Solidarity Program 273
East Timorese in Australia 179, 207–8, 214–15, 226, 231–7
Ecclesiam Suam (Paul VI) 91
Ephrem, Br *10*
Epilogue (TV segment) 50
episcopal conferences 136–7
Esmeralda, Sr 290–1
Essendon, Melbourne 49
Estado Novo x, 86
ETADEP 167
ETAN 1, 21, 222
Etchegaray, Card. Roger 155, 186, 218, 256
  in ET 213
ethnography 62
  see also anthropology
ETHRC 17n2, 177–8, 271, 283
ETRA 208
Eucharistic Congress 1973 *5*, 53–4, 60–1
European Union 242
Evangelii Gaudium (Francis) 184–5
Evangelii Nuntiandi (Paul VI) 90–1
evangelisation 90–1, 124, 185
exchange systems 64, 78, 102n17

FALINTIL 242
  Catholic Church and 163, 209
  Gusmao and 173
  origin 106
  protection of civilians 161, 248
  UN and 292
famine in ET 143, 153n2

Farano, Abp Vincenzo 94, 101–2
Fatumaca, ET *13*
  Salesian College 154
Ferreira, Bp Januario 208–9, 218
Finkelstein, Justice Raymond 233, 236
Finley, NSW *1*, 28–33, 73
First Peoples of Australia 30, 42
  see also Aborigines
'Five Principles' 13, 111–13, 120
Forrest, Emily 31
Forrest, John 31
Forum 2000 229
France: A Mission Country (Suhard) 45
Francis, Pope 286–7, 305–6
  Evangelii Gaudium 184–5
Francis Xavier, St 112
freedom of religion 59
Freire, Paulo
  Pedagogy of the Oppressed 79n1
Freitas, Joao de 247–8
Freitas, Salustiano 16
FRELIMO 89
FRETILIN 89–96
  Catholic Church in ET and 93
  communism and 97
  de facto government of ET 98–100
  election victory 297–8
  Indonesia and 97–8, 103–6, 117
  literacy and 78–9
  Portugal and 99–100
  Ribeiro and 90–1
  UDT and 89–90, 92–6, 99
  Van Wouwe and 163–4
From a Place among the Dead (Kohen) 215
Fuiloro, ET 209, 269–70

Gahamanyi, Bp Jean-Baptiste *9*, 201
'Garnardi Report' 249, 259–61
Gaudium et Spes (Vatican II) 10, 52–3, 58
genocide 289
German East Africa 195–6
Gerry, Bp John 143
Glen Iris, Melbourne 54
Goma refugee camp, Rwanda *9*, 199, 204–5
Gomes, Sebastiao (Sebastian Gomez) 16, 158
  grave *12*
Good Samaritan Sisters 34
Goulart, Bp Jaime *11*, 83–4, 90, 129–30, 133–5
governance, church 51
Great Depression, the 27–31
Griffin, Fr Leo *2*
Gruber, Georg 34
Gusmao, Xanana (former Pres. of ET)
  on Alkatiri 300
  CNRM leader 173
  CNRT leader 240, 248
  on conversions to Catholicism 13
  on development plan for ET 299

FRETILIN leader 105
with HD *14*
with Horta, Belo and Nascimento 278
with Mandela 229
post-referendum amnesty 280
as Pres. of ET 298, 302
resignation as PM of ET 305
on resistance and religious celebrations 174
resistance leadership 262
resistance restructure 106
Salesian school student 166
suspicion about 164
on UN administration of ET 292
Guterres, Abel 252
Guterres, Eurico 261
Guterres, Justino 15–16

Habibie, B. J. (former Pres. of Indonesia) 239–44, 259, 291
Habyarimana, Juvénal (former Pres. of Rwanda) 197–8
Hart, Abp Denis *8*
Heath, Damien 44
Hilton's Rock, ET 253
Hinduism 112
historical consciousness 57, 183–4
Holland 144
 see also Netherlands
Holy See *see* Vatican
homeless, ministry to 52
Hornay, Br Crispim Nicolas 162–3
Horta, Jose Ramos (former Pres. of ET)
 deportado 81n5
 ETHRC co-founder 17n2, 177
 father's exile to ET 86n1
 with Gusmao, Belo and Nascimento 278
 with HD *14*
 maubere article 87
 Nobel Peace Prize recipient 207, 215, 218
 personal cost of struggle for ET 213
 on political options for ET 208
 post-referendum amnesty 280
 priorities 230
 reception internationally 98, 219, 225
 Sanctuary Movement appeal launch 235
 University of San Francisco University Medal recipient 224
 Vatican and 211
Hotel Turismo, Dili, ET 152–3, 157
Howard, John (former PM of Australia) 206
Hull, Geoffrey 187
human rights
 Catholic Church on 10–11, 59, 90–1, 120–7, 272
 culture and 221
 ET and 106, 117, 120–7, 177
 Indonesia and 112–13, 175
Human Rights and Justice Program (Caritas Australia) 281–2
Humanae Salutis (John XXIII) 125
Hunt, Mick 38

identity 121–2
IDPs 263n20, 266–8
IMF 239
imperium model of church governance 184–5
inculturation 61–2, 65–6
indigenous cultures 9
Indonesia
 Asian financial crisis and 238–9
 Belo and 178, 180
 culture 113
 democracy 113
 demographics 112
 education 115
 ET and 11–15, 88–9, 92–108, 113, 144, 161–70, 191, 209
 FRETILIN and 97–8, 103–6, 117
 government 181, 210
 human rights 112–13, 175
 Japan and 131
 Javanese 101, 174
 law and order 176
 military 104–5, 173–4, 209, 240–1, 244–5, 263–70
 militias 245–6, 248
 Netherlands and 112
 Portugal and 92–3, 99, 112
 religions 113
 secret police 245
 UDT and 95
 Vatican and 121, 180–1
 West Papua and 98n5
Indonesian Bishops' Conference 107, 121
 ET and 116–18
'Indonesianisation' 104, 122
INGOs 288, 292
integral development 272
integrasi x, 12–14, 104, 177, 227–8, 241
INTEL 152, 157, 161, 173, 224
Interahamwe 198, 201
INTERFET 270, 276, 279, 289
intimidation 246–51
Islam 112

Jansenism 50–1
Japan
 Australia and 131
 ET and 84, 131–4, 231
 Indonesia and 131
Javanese/Indonesians 101, 174
Jerilderie parish, NSW 31
Jesuits 42–3, 53–4, 78, 115, 142, 172
John Paul II, Pope
 Belo and 155–6, 180
 with Clancy and HD *8*

ET visit 155–6
Indonesia and 121
key social values 123, 272
Sollicitudo Rei Socialis 118
John XXIII, Pope
Humanae Salutis 125
Pacem in Terris 10, 123n6, 125
Jolliffe, Jill 96n9, 102, 220n1
Jones, Dr Percy 34–5
Josephite Sisters 79n2, 186–7

Kabgayi, Rwanda 201–2
Kagame, Paul 198
Kailaco, ET *15*
Kalumburu mission, WA *4*, 63–7
    Aboriginal peoples and cultures 63–5
    development 65–6
    founding myth 65
    governance 66
    property 66
    social control 66–7
    World War II and 33
Karen, Nairobi, Kenya 205
Kenya 205–6
Kigali, Rwanda 203
Killen, Beatrice 276, 278
Kingdom of God 306
Kivumu, Rwanda 202–3
KKN 240
Knight, Lesley-Anne 192
Knox, Card. James *5*, 53, 59–61
Kohen, Arnold 121, 224
    From a Place among the Dead 215
Kohl, Helmut (former Chancellor of Germany) 219
Kopassus 244, 248–9
Kostrad 244
Kuan Yew, Lee (former PM of Singapore) 221
Kulari and Kwini peoples, WA 63

La Repubblica 185
Lang, Jack 28
languages and literacy 78–9, 295–6
lay catechists 11
Lay Kon Tji 236
Lebanon 119
leprosy 66
Levi-Strauss, Claude 57–8, 68
liberation 284–7
Liquica massacre, ET 101, 246–7, 256, 275n17
literature 43
Little, Abp Sir Frank *6*, *8*, 16, 21, 50, 67, 71–3, 151, 183
Little, Dr Gerry 72
Little Sisters Nursing Home, Northcote, Melbourne 39
liturgy 60–1
liurai x, 79, 83

Lobato, Nicolau 104–5
Lobato, Rogerio 94
local churches 23n7
Locatelli, Fr Eligio *13*
Lonergan, Bernard 57, 183–4
lulik houses x, 83
Lusitania 158
Luzbetak, Louis 123

Macarthur, Gen. Douglas 133
MacKillop Centre 79n2
Madeira, Fr Hilario 267–8, 303–4
Magalhaes, Prof. Barbedo 217, 221–2
Maia, Armindo 223–4
Malaysia and ET 216–17
Malaysian People's Action Front 216
Maliana diocese, ET 304
Malik, Adam 15n1
Malinowski, Bronislaw 56
Mandela, Nelson (former Pres. of South Africa) 229
Manning, Bp Kevin 145, 208
Mannix, Abp Daniel 16, 34–5, 37, 51–3
Manshon, Joan 15
Marcal, Arlindo 223–4
Marist Brothers 115
Maritain, Jacques 44, 125
Marker, Jamsheed 225
Martin, Ian 248–9, 263, 290
Martinkus, John 220n1, 255, 262
Martino, Abp Renato 301
Maryknoll Sisters 166
Mass and Australian Aboriginal cultures 60–2
Masses in solidarity with ET 15–16, 18–21
    homilies 19–21
Masure, Fr Eugene
    Diocesan Priest, The 46
Mattiussi, Odoric 112
Maubara, ET 101
maubere, the x, 14, 79, 83, 87, 90
Mayne, Charles 44
McGrath, Cathy 217, 220n1
McInerny, Fr James 48
Medeiros, Bp Jose 157–8
media, the 50, 92
    ET and 207, 220–30
    see also Radio Kupang, West Timor
Melbourne cathedral choir 34–6
Melbourne University 70–1
Mercy Sisters 30
MFA 86–7
Michel, Fr Tom 226–7, 230
militias 245–6, 248, 261–2, 265–70
Miller, John 1
minor seminaries 90n5
misinformation 11–12, 93, 97–8, 144–5, 191, 227, 253
Missionaries of the Sacred Heart 47

mission/s of Catholic Church 63–7, 124, 138, 286–7
Mitchell, Edward (uncle of HD) 31–2
Mitchell, Elizabeth (grandmother of HD) 31–2
Mitchell, John (2nd husband of grandmother of HD) 31–2
Mitchell, Sr Josephine 79n2, 187
MMET 187, 226
MMI 187
Moertopo, Gen. Ali 142
Moonee Ponds, Melbourne 49–50
Motael, Dili, ET 16–17
Motael Church 12, 157
Mount, Frank 142–3
Movement, the 40, 139
Mt Eliza, Vic 6, 69–70
Mugunga, Rwanda 204
Mulwala Channel, NSW 28
Murdani, Gen. 'Benny' 92, 102, 105, 117, 119, 173n3, 175–6
Murtagh, Fr Jim 54
Murtopo, Gen. Ali 92, 173n3
Muslims 82, 88, 119
My Fellow Australians (H. Deakin) 53
mythology 57–8

Nagambie, Vic 31–2
Nagambie Tragedy 32
Nairobi, Kenya 205–6
Nascimento, Bp Basilio do
    administrator of Dili diocese 304
    Caritas Baucau and 274
    on ET development plan 299
    with Gusmao, Horta and Belo 278
    Habibie and 241–2
    post-referendum violence and 270
National East Timor Consultations 141–2
nation-building in ET 293–4, 296–300
NATSICC 190
NCC 139
NCJP 140
    see also CCJP
NCRM 142
Nelson, Br Leo 36
Netherlands
    ET and 128–9, 132
    Indonesia and 112
networking 191
new theology movement 44
News Weekly 93, 139, 142–3, 226
Ngabu, Bp Faustin 204
NGOs 102
Nguyen Van Thuan, Card. Francis Xavier 186
'ninjas' 162, 208
Noronha, Cancio 16
Noronha, Maria 16
Nsengiyumva, Abp Vincent 197
Nsengiyumva, Bp Thaddée 200

Ntamwana, Bp Simon 200
Nunamogue, ET 133–4
Nyundo, Rwanda 203–4

Oan Kiak Scholarship Trust Fund x, 303
O'Connell, Bp Joe 183, 187–8
O'Connor, Sr Kath 232
Octogesima Adveniens (Paul VI) 10–11, 139
Oecusse, ET 80, 82, 279–80
O'Kelly, Bp Greg 53
O'Loughlin, Bp John 47
O'Malley, John 136
Operasi Komodo x, 92, 95
Operation Global Clean Sweep 244, 249, 264–5, 289
Orde Baru x, 111–12, 175, 240
O'Rourke, Fr Leo 39
Our Lady of Lourdes School, Thornbury, Melbourne 34

Pacem in Terris (John XXIII) 10, 123n6, 125
Packer, Kerry 139
Pallotine Fathers 201
Pancasila x, 13, 111–13, 120, 155, 163, 168, 180
papal nuncios 23, 172, 206
Parade College, Melbourne 36
pastoral care 12
Paul VI, Pope
    on culture 124
    Ecclesiam Suam 91
    episcopal conferences 136
    Evangelii Nuntiandi 90–1
    Octogesima Adveniens 10–11, 139
    Populorum Progressio 272
Pedagogy of the Oppressed (Freire) 79n1
pela dialect 64
Pell, Card. George 8, 151n1, 183, 188
    HD and 185–6
Peres, Emilia 247–8
Perkins, Bp Eric 188
personal development and stories 6–14
piano 35, 52
PIDE 86–7
'pilgrim people of God' 58
Pires, Emilia 15–16, 299
Pires, Fr Antonio 133
Pires, Mario (former Gov. of ET) 94
Pires, Palmyra 15–16
Pius XII, Pope 36, 44–5, 184
Point of View (TV segment) 139
political development 297–9
politics and religion 9–11, 37, 40, 59, 126, 294–5
Pomerleau, Fr Yvon 199
Pontifical Council for Justice and Peace 155
Populorum Progressio (Paul VI) 272
Portugal
    1974 coup 86–7

bishops 120
  Concordat with Vatican 83–4
  economy 81
  Estado Novo 86
  ET and 11, 77–87, 94–7, 104, 123, 128–30, 133–4, 138, 164, 176–7, 234–6
  FRETILIN and 99–100
  Indonesia and 92–3, 99, 112
  political parties 86
  Santa Cruz massacre and 176–7
  secret police (PIDE) 86–7
postos xi, 80, 130
power, abuse of 62
power and cultural change 66–7
Prasko, Bp Ivan 52
prayer 43
preferential option for the poor 279
priesthood 39, 45–7, 138
Pro Mundi Vita 144
pro-independence activism, ET 242–3, 262
Project Compassion 273
propaganda 11–12, 93, 97–8, 144–5, 191, 227, 253
property and Aboriginal cultures 66
prophetic voices 8
protestors in ET 160, 213, 245
Publico 180–1
Puente Buces, Abp Pablo 102, 119, 121, 144, 155

racism 47–8
Radio Kupang, West Timor 92–3, 96, 100
Ratu, Bp Anton 209, 270, 301
reading 38, 43
reconciliation 287–8, 297
  in ET 177
reconstruction in ET 280, 293
Red Cross 207
referendum (ET, 1999) 13
  campaigning 258–9
  death toll 266
  polling day 258, 263
  post-referendum violence 263–70
  prelude to 247–62
  vote count 263
reformasi movement in Indonesia 239–41
religion and culture 309
religion and politics 9–11, 37, 40, 59, 126, 294–5
religious tolerance 113
Renato, Fr Stephano 17
resistance 174
  see also CNRT; FRETILIN
ressourcement 58–9
restorationism 59
revolutionary brigades 89–90
Ribeiro, Bp Jose
  character 101, 172
  on culture 124
  on Declaration on Religious Liberty (Vatican II) 59
  FRETILIN and 90–1
  Indonesian propaganda and 11, 93–4, 97
  manner 84
  Seara closure 87
Ricardo, David 31
rights, human 10–11, 272
Robinson, Geoffrey 225, 245, 265, 290
Rock, The 37–8
Romero, Abp Oscar 189
Ross, David 132–3
Royal Commission into Institutional Responses to Child Sexual Abuse 72
RPF 194, 197–9
Ruak, Taur Matan (Pres. of ET) *14*, 255
Ruddock, Phillip 226, 232
Rwanda 6–7, *9*, 194–204
  Australia and 194, 203–4
  Belgium and 196–7
  Catholic Church and 195–7, 200
  reconciliation 202
  Uganda and 197–8

sacred, the
  cultures and 60–2
Salazar regime, Portugal 11, 81, 86
Salesian Sisters 78
Salesians 78, 115, 154, 208–9, 269
salvation 284–5, 288–9, 291–2
Sambi, Abp Pietro 121n3, 144, 208–9, 211–12
Sanctuary Movement 232, 235–6
Santa Cruz cemetery *12*
Santa Cruz massacre, ET 9–10, 16–18, 107, 158–60, 164, 176–7
Santamaria, B. A.
  ACR and 143
  CSIS and 92
  influence of 36–7, 44, 138–43
  religion and politics 40–1
Santos, Fernando dos 270
Sarmento, Florentino *10*, 167–8, 217
Scott, David 235–6, 240
scripture study 44
Seamen's Mission 8
Seara 87
Second Vatican Council
  'Church in the Modern World, The' 10, 52–3, 58
  Declaration on Religious Liberty 59
  ET and 84
  liturgy and 35n2, 60–1
  models of church and 286
secret police 86–7, 245
self-determination for ET 229, 236
self-image 66
seminaries, minor 90n5

September 11 attacks, USA 293n21
sexual abuse scandal 184, 305–6
Sexual Assault Program (Caritas Australia) 282
Shackleton, Greg 302
Shackleton, Shirley 302
Sheehan's Apologetics 40
Shreiter, Robert 287
Sibomana, Fr Andre 201–2
Sidoti, Chris 141
signs of the times 125–6
Simonds, Abp Justin *3*, 49, 51, 53
Singa, Kastoriius 223
Singapore 131
Sisters of St Joseph 79n2, 186–7
Six, Jean-Francois
   Church and Human Rights 124–6
Smythe, Fr Patrick 3, 10n6, 141
Soares, Abilio (former Gov. of ET) 242
Soares, Fr Domingo 303
Soares, Fr Francisco 268
Soares, Mario (former Pres. of Portugal) 176, 181
social analysis 145
social anthropology 56–62
social justice 29, 37, 44, 113, 139–40, 189, 192
   see also Catholic social teaching; human rights
Sodano, Card. Angelo 180
Soeharto *see* Suharto, Muhammad (former Pres. of Indonesia)
Soekarno *see* Sukarno (former Pres. of Indonesia)
Soekarnoputri, Megawati (former Pres. of Indonesia) 301
Soerabaja 128
solidarity 117–19, 272, 300, 309
Sollicitudo Rei Socialis (John Paul II) 118
Soma, Bp Aloisius 208, 216
South Africa 189
Sparrow Force (Australia) 131
Spence, Maj. Allan 129–35
spirituality 43, 46–7
St Augustine 50
St Augustine's Church, Melbourne 8, 50, 52
St Dunstan's Church, Canterbury, England 70
St Francis Xavier 112
St Francis Xavier's parish, Box Hill, Melbourne 52
St Joseph's School, Finley, NSW 30
St Monica's parish, Moonee Ponds, Melbourne 49–50
St Patrick's Cathedral and choir, Melbourne 34–6
St Patrick's School, North Fitzroy, Melbourne 35
St Raphael's Church, West Preston, Melbourne 39
St Thomas More 69–70

St Thomas More's Church/parish, Mt Eliza, Vic *6*, 69–70
St Thomas More's Church/School, Tequimata, ET *15*, 70
St Vincent de Paul Society 38–9, 137
Stahl, Max 17, 159, 303
Stefani, Fr Renato 303–4
Stewart, Paul *11*
stories and personal development 6–14
Story, Tom 276–7
Stothard, Debbie 216
'strategic hamlets' 105
student-based political movement 241
Suai massacre, ET 267–8
Suarez, Fr Demetrio 165–6
sucos xi, 80
Suhard, Card. Emmanuel 44–5
   France: A Mission Country 45
Suharto, Muhammad (former Pres. of Indonesia)
   Asian financial crisis and 238–9
   on CSIS 173n3
   Dili massacre 174
   fall 243
   family's businesses 210, 217–18, 266n23
   incorporation of ET in Indonesia and 104
   on invasion of ET 98
   Orde Baru 111–12
Sukarno (former Pres. of Indonesia) 13n12, 112
Sword, Kirsty 207–8
symposia in USA and Canada on ET 221–5

Tasi Tolu, ET 301–2
Taylor, Charles 183–4
Taylor, Prof. John G. 77, 106, 217
tebe tebe xi, 165
Tequimata, ET 70
Tetum 186–7
Thomas More, St 69
Thornbury, Melbourne 33–5
Thrower, Terri 199
Tjan Silalahi, Harry 142–3
TNI 95–6, 162, 240n7, 259, 267–8
   see also ABRI
Tocumwal, NSW 27–8
Toer, Pramoedya Ananta 175
tolerance, religious 113
Topasses 82
transmigration 12, 104, 214
transport 49
Trocaire xi, 272
trust 172–3
truth and certitude 183–4
TV work (HD) 50

Uai Mori cantonment, ET 252–5
UDT

coup (1975) in ET 94
  FRETILIN and 89–90, 92–6, 99
  Indonesia and 95
  origin, priorities 87
  part of 'Popular Assembly' 104
Uganda and Rwanda 197–8
Ukrainian Catholics 52
UNAMET 247–9, 259–60, 263–4, 288–9
  Dili HQ drama Sep 1999 289–91
UNAMIR 203
Unan / exchange system 64
UNICEF 280
United Nations
  Belo and 156
  Caritas Internationalis and 272–3
  Declaration of Human Rights 123n6
  independence of ET and 302–3
  'Popular Assembly' in ET and 104
  post-ballot crisis and reconstruction in ET 292–3
  structure 292
  see also INTERFET; UNAMET; UNAMIR; UNICEF; UNMISET; UNTAET
United States 103, 175, 189
UNMISET 302–3
UNTAET 278, 282, 287, 291–2, 298
  Catholic Church and 294

Van Thuan, Card. Francis Xavier Nguyen 186
Van Wouwe, Fr Walter 17, 163–5, 221
Vatican
  Belo and 180–1, 213, 215, 230, 284n1, 287
  clericalism in 192
  Concordat with Salazar regime 83–4
  ET and 3–4, 88, 102–3, 113–14, 119, 145, 156, 222, 302, 304
  Indonesia and 121, 180–1
  see also specific papal nuncios
Vatican Council, Second *see* Second Vatican Council

Vattaparambil, Fr Jose 166, 209, 269–70
vicars apostolic 84n10
vicars general 8n2
Victorian State Library, Melbourne 38
Vietnam war 89

Walesa, Lech 118
Wanandi, Markus 169, 172–3
Wanandi, Yusuf 92, 94, 142–3, 169, 173, 175–6
  Santamaria and 143
Werribee seminary, Melbourne 42–8
West Papua and Indonesia 98n5
WFP 276–7, 292–3
white Australia policy 231
White Fathers 195
Whiteley, Michael 107, 143
Whitlam, Edward Gough (former PM of Australia) 89, 98n6, 143
Wigglesworth, Ann 273–5
Williams, Card. Thomas 213–14, 255–6
Willis, Msgr Vin 3, 49
Wiradjuri people, Finley, NSW 30
Wiranto, Gen. 244n20, 245, 259, 291
Wong, Fr Andrew 269
worker priest movement 45
World War II 11, 20, 32–3, 36
  ET and 128–35

Xavier, Fr Julio 303
Xavier, Jacinto 270
Xavier, St Francis 112

Yarra Bend, Melbourne 40
Yarrabah, Qld 47
YCS 142
YCW 37, 142

Zaire 199, 204–5

RECOMMENDATIONS

When Hilton Deakin was Vicar General of Melbourne in 1991, a group of East Timorese refugees asked him to say Mass for those who had been killed since the 1975 Indonesian invasion of their country.

This simple request changed the course of the rest of his life.

Bonded through Tragedy, United in Hope tells the story of how a Catholic bishop committed to Catholic social justice came to be a witness to, and a significant actor, in global events.

Bishop Deakin weaves into the story his childhood in rural NSW, his early contact with Catholic social teaching; his very early involvement with indigenous people, his commitment to the intellectual life of the Church; his struggles against a rigid church hierarchy (especially in the seminary) and his PhD on indigenous communities in Western Australia.

This is a tale, not just for those interested in East Timor, but also those looking to learn more about how one person, committed to a cause, often in defiance of an indifferent or even hostile hierarchy, can make a difference. It is a rare person, especially a Catholic bishop, who combines both studies for the priesthood with an anthropological degree, and a life living the gospels as they are meant to be lived.

The journey on which Hilton Deakin takes us demonstrates both a profound understanding of other cultures and their power structures, as well as a deep personal commitment to people. While the focus is on the long struggle of the people of East Timor for independence, it also ranges across Vatican politics, the Rwanda massacre in which many of the elements of the later massacres in East Timor have resonance, the deficiencies of the United Nations, and the inaction by many countries, Australia included, while the East Timor struggle went on over decades.

While the book largely ends about 2003, Hilton Deakin briefly refers to two issues which are of great concern to many people today: the treatment of refugees held on Nauru and Manus Island (with a long troubled history back to the treatment of East Timorese refugees by the Keating and Howard governments), and the sexual abuse of children by clergy.

For many Catholics though, the most troubling theme will likely be the indifference of the Australian (and other) bishops to the events occurring in East Timor. Hilton Deakin ends with a positive message, hoping that the present Pope will use failures such as these to decentralise the church so that power is not held centrally "where a bevy of ecclesiastical limpets cling to the trappings of papal authority, making their own lives significant and everyone else's a misery".

Elizabeth Proust A.O.
Company Director

RECOMMENDATIONS

Hilton Deakin is the one Australian Catholic Bishop who has stood by the people of Timor Leste through thick and thin. Having been the parish priest of a very comfortable Catholic parish at Mt Eliza outside Melbourne, having written a doctoral thesis while living with the Aboriginal people of remote Kalumburu in the Kimberley, and having been the vicar general of the vast Archdiocese of Melbourne, he encountered Timorese refugees who were seeking spiritual sustenance in Melbourne. They wanted mass offered for their murdered relatives who were victims of the Indonesian takeover. From these personal contacts, he developed a lifetime commitment to the cause of justice and independence for the Timorese. He went out of his way to befriend Bishop Carlos Belo, the bishop of Dili. Through these Timorese friendships, he was able to build an international network of support. This is a ripping yarn of how one solitary Australian bishop was able to traverse the ecclesiastical and political worlds to stand in solidarity, against the odds, through oppression and liberation, with downtrodden people who rose up and established the newest nation in our region. He found a whole new life in the politics and advocacy of human rights, mixing with all sorts of people he would never have met in the Church. He loved joining arms and voice with those who were "an irritant to the ordered world of bureaucrats, ecclesiastics and politicians, a challenge to the 'wise' men and women of academia, and the beloved (or the belittled) of the media." Together they mobilised Australians in support of the Timorese, despite the power and received wisdom of the politicians and Vatican officials. Prior to the 1999 popular consultation, Bishop Deakin was bonded through tragedy with the Timorese people. He has been blessed to live and be united in hope with them as a self-determining nation though still seeking justice in its dealings with its large neighbours. Jim and Therese D'Orsa have succeeded admirably in transcribing the bishop's larger-than-life voice which has witnessed so much human misery and triumph.

Fr Frank Brennan SJ
Professor of Law
Australian Catholic University

Bonded through Tragedy, United in Hope is a very engaging account of East Timor moving toward independence through the detailed memoirs of Australian Bishop Hilton Deakin, a key participant observer. The reader is invited to immerse oneself in this complex and painful history by moving smoothly through this very well-written, flowing narrative told in the first person by Bishop Hilton and in collaboration with Jim and Therese D'Orsa. The particular stories of Bishop Hilton, East Timor, and the competing interests of the Church are intriguing in themselves, but even more so as they intersect tightly throughout the book. Furthermore, insightful references by the authors to the broader political, economic, social, ecclesial, and theological contexts provide deeper layers of understanding. Truly, a story of tragedy and hope worth reading!

Fr Roger Schroeder SVD
Louis J. Luzbetak Professor of Mission and Culture, Catholic Theological Union, Chicago

From 2003 for over a decade, Australian Catholic University worked with the Marist Brothers' Instituto Católico para Formação de Professores (ICFP) in Baucau, in support of teacher education for East Timor. What a godsend it would have been to those of us involved in this collaboration had Bishop Hilton Deakin's memoir been available at that time, informing our visits to East Timor and efforts for ICFP. However, in 2003 later elements of his very significant contributions to the then newest nation, captured in this book, were still in the making.

Bonded through Tragedy, United in Hope – The Catholic Church and East Timor's Struggle for Independence: A Memoir by Bishop Hilton Deakin with Jim and Therese D'Orsa is a major work which is a chronicle of 'an interesting life' and, at the same time, a detailed and captivating account of East Timor coming to nationhood, and of the impact of the pre- and the post-Vatican II Church on both the personal and national narratives. The volume encompasses three stories – Hilton's story, the East Timor story and the Church story and their convergence.

Hilton's story identifies 'moments of destiny' which afforded him the life experiences and provided the circumstances to play a pivotal role in the evolution of East Timor and also to influence wider Australian and Church agendas. This is the story of the 'boy from the bush' born during the Great Depression, whose parents of English Catholic background 'did it tough' but, through a loving home environment, fostered in their son an innate sense of social justice, of giving people a fair go. In Finley, Hilton's boyhood friendships with Indigenous youth also shaped his sense of justice.

Perfect pitch enabled Hilton become a choirboy at St Patrick's Cathedral in Melbourne and gain a scholarship to attend Parade College. This educational opportunity was pivotal as was his thirst for knowledge which saw Hilton in his teens drawn to the State Library of Victoria and, in particular, its collection on Indigenous Australians. A commitment to oratory and taking the Church to the public square began at seventeen years of age with speaking at Yarra Bend on behalf of the Catholic Truth Society and selling the *Catholic Worker*. He credits his former parish priest, Fr Leo O'Rourke, with giving him an understanding of the 'service dimension of priesthood' as distinct from the 'cultic dimension' which he knew from experiences in his cathedral choir.

Hilton's 'hard' decision to go to the seminary curtailed such activities but fortunately their 'roots' were only dormant and would bear fruit later as 'moments of destiny' prepared him for his life work. While critical of the 'clerical socialisation process' of the 1950s seminary, Hilton acknowledges that his seminary years 'taught you how to pray' and developed the 'deep love of the Mass and the liturgy' acquired in his childhood.

Following ordination, Hilton was appointed Assistant Priest. During this period and also as a seminarian he made visits to Indigenous communities. As Assistant priest he also gained an appreciation of working with the media as presenter on Channel 9's *Epilogue*. When newly-arrived Cardinal James Knox discovered Hilton's interest in Australia's Indigenous peoples, he sought his input into planning Indigenous involvement in the 1973 Eucharist Congress. In preparation for this 'assignment', Knox took the unconventional step of sending Hilton to Monash University to study anthropology, firstly through a Bachelor of Arts and later doctoral studies, including fieldwork in the Kimberley Ranges. In this way Knox was the leader who 'had the greatest impact' on Hilton's life. The initial outcome was the Aboriginal Mass conceived for the Eucharistic Congress which broke 'new ground in front of an international audience'.

Next as Parish Priest, Hilton sought 'to assist the community *look beyond itself and its own needs* to those who are more needy'. His subsequent appointments as Vicar General in 1986 and Auxiliary Bishop in 1992 were 'life-changing' and opened many doors. In particular, as Vicar General, Hilton had visit from representatives of the Melbourne East Timorese community seeking a Mass in the Cathedral to mark 16 years since the Indonesia invasion of East Timor. During the planning period for the occasion, it evolved into a funeral following the Santa Cruz massacre. Hilton was subsequently invited to be a spokesman for the East Timorese community. As he had earlier sat with and learned from Australian Indigenous peoples, similarly he now immersed himself in the East Timorese community, both in Australia and through countless visits to their homeland.

In parallel with his episcopal duties in the Archdiocese of Melbourne, Hilton took up the fight for justice of East Timor, often 'swimming against the tide' of official Church and Government approaches. He was involved in demonstrations but also networks fostering dialogue and seeking to build ways forward through consensus. He writes that his 'reputed left-wing orientation has its source in a concern for people'. That concern saw Hilton achieve a rare depth of understanding of the East Timorese and their resilient culture, and also of the complexity of the Church's situation in East Timor. He brings to the book an insider's perspective on the East Timorese Church and the role that is played, as a Church of the people, in East Timorese culture and politics and achieving independence. The book's foreword by Xanana Gusmão, First President of the Republic of East Timor, reinforces how well Hilton knows the key Church and political leaders of East Timor and the East Timorese people.

As Auxiliary Bishop, Hilton was elected President of Australian Catholic Relief which, under his leadership, becomes Caritas Australia, and then a Vice-President of Caritas Internationalis. Caritas provided 'an international platform' for him to speak on behalf of the East Timorese but also saw Hilton visit Rwanda in 1994 shortly after the genocide halted to see how Caritas Internationalis could assist. He writes that this was one of his 'most formative experiences'. Hilton underpins this development ministry with his quest for knowledge, reading extensively to understand the situation in developing countries, as a new expansion of the 'service dimension of priesthood'.

The three stories in the book – of Hilton, East Timor and the Church – converge with the outbreak of post-ballot violence in September 1999, when Caritas Australia became the lead agency for Caritas Internationalis and the Church's official United Nations partner in coordinating relief and development in East Timor. This role led, in turn, to significant development of Caritas Australia and this volume also tells that story. The detail of Hilton's memoir makes it clear that his 'commitments to Caritas and East Timor and other social justice causes was never easy'.

Hilton, now an elder statesman of social justice, writes of how much more at home he feels in the Church of Pope Francis who is bringing about change by 'the force of his example'. Reading this powerful memoir it is clear why Hilton is so comfortable with Pope Francis' approach of moving from certitude to searching, from a Roman model of Church to decentralisation, to re-emphasising the Church as a pilgrim people, to putting advocacy for human rights and social justice centre stage.

A key element throughout the evolving stories in the book is Hilton's deepening understanding of Catholic Social Teaching and its applications. Hope-filled by Vatican II, he recounts how his anthropological background gave him leading insights into how 'to be in history and in culture, and to have a mission of service to people without reservation or exclusion'. Informed by theology, anthropology also provided him with a means to improve pastoral practice.

During his time as Vicar General, Hilton lost his voice for an extended period when his vocal chords were damaged during surgery. His subsequent recovery provided a life-changing second chance when he lost that 'sense of fear' and resolved to speak out. The metaphor of finding his voice, 'both literally and figuratively', is woven through the memoir in each of the stories and their convergence.

Bishop Hilton Deakin and Jim and Therese D'Orsa are to be congratulated on this fine volume. In an effective collaboration underpinned by extensive background research and access to original records, they have captured the distinctive and often challenging voice of Hilton and opened up to a wider audience both his unique story and new insights into the struggles for East Timorese independence. I commend wholeheartedly *Bonded through Tragedy, United in Hope* – The Catholic Church and East Timor's Struggle for Independence: A Personal Memoir by Bishop Hilton Deakin with Jim and Therese D'Orsa – its exceptional stories were waiting to be told.

Professor Gabrielle McMullen AM
Trustee, Mary Aikenhead Ministries

www.ingramcontent.com/pod-product-compliance
Lightning Source LLC
Chambersburg PA
CBHW040741300426
44111CB00027B/2995